THE JEWS OF ST. PETERSBURG

THE JEWS OF ST. PETERSBURG

EXCURSIONS THROUGH A NOBLE PAST

MIKHAIL BEIZER
translated by Michael Sherbourne

edited, with an introduction and maps by
MARTIN GILBERT

AN EDWARD E. ELSON BOOK
THE JEWISH PUBLICATION SOCIETY
Philadelphia · New York ·   5749 / 1989

The publication of this book was made possible by a gift in honor of
Charles Myer Elson, Louis Goodman Elson, and Harry Elson II,
who have shown an appreciation and understanding of,
and a respect for their heritage.

Copyright © 1989 by Mikhail Beizer
First edition   All rights reserved
Manufactured in the United States of America
Library of Congress Cataloging in Publication Data

Beizer, Mikhail.
    The Jews of St. Petersburg / Mikhail Beizer; translated by
Michael Sherbourne; edited and introduced by Martin Gilbert.
        p.   cm.
    Translation from Russian.
    Bibliography: p.
    Includes index.
    ISBN 0-8276-0321-5
    1. Jews—Russian S.F.S.R.—Leningrad.   2. Leningrad (R.S.F.S.R.)—
Description.   3. Leningrad (R.S.F.S.R.)—Ethnic relations.
    I. Gilbert, Martin, 1936–   II. Title.
DS135.R93L463   1989
947′.453004924—dc19   88-8285
                                                                CIP

Designed by Adrianne Onderdonk Dudden

To those who remain

CONTENTS

LIST OF MAPS

LIST OF ILLUSTRATIONS

INTRODUCTION

Martin Gilbert

In the late summer of 1982, news began to reach the West of a young Jew in Leningrad who was taking fellow Leningrad Jews on tours of the city, to show them sites connected with Leningrad's Jewish inhabitants of past decades. He was not, apparently, an historian, but a mathematician who had been refused an exit visa for Israel two years earlier, at the age of thirty, and was part of a small group of similar "refuseniks," as they were called, who were determined to find out as much as possible about their Jewish heritage.

The young man's name was Mikhail Beizer. In January 1983 the information about his tours was confirmed by two visitors from London, Eileen and Stan Freedman, to whom Beizer had shown part of the Leningrad Jewish Cemetery. He had walked with them for three hours in the snow along the rows of tombstones, describing the history of many buried there and telling of the events of which these Jews had been a part. The Freedmans' story of this cemetery tour reached me while I was writing a book about the Jewish presence in nineteenth-century Jerusalem. Here it seemed was a kindred spirit, seeking, under infinitely more difficult circumstances, to discover as much as possible about the Jewish past of a center of Jewish life and culture of which far less was known.

In March 1983 I visited Leningrad, hoping to meet Mikhail Beizer and to join his tours. We met at the Alexander Column — Beizer, myself, and a friend of mine — and spent several hours together, on a bitterly cold morning, as he showed us houses and corners in that particular part of the city that he had identified with particular Jews or with episodes in Jewish history.

Returning to London, I began to correspond with Beizer about his tours and to learn from him of his efforts to extend them. While we were together, he told me of how his work had been influenced by the Jewish historian Simon Dubnow, who, eighty years earlier, had similarly sought to give the Jews of what was then St. Petersburg an understanding of their historic, cultural, and national identity.

In May 1983, in one of his first letters to me after my return to London, Beizer wrote: "I am now engaged in studying Dubnow's life in order to make a tour around Vassilevsky Island." This letter reminded me of my own visit, as a result of Beizer having given me the address, to see a house on Vassilevsky Island (Vassilevsky Ostrov) in which Dubnow had lived and taught. In looking up at its ordinary, somewhat stark facade, I had been struck by the extent to which a young man's enthusiasm had animated this, and many other facades, with the people and ideas of a distant past.

Nor was it a distant past of mere curiosity; the example of Simon Dubnow, to whose life in St. Petersburg Beizer was eventually to devote a whole chapter — a veritable city-wide excursion — showed that the Jews then were much more than a disparate, scattered group: they were a nation. The very Jewish national self-consciousness that Dubnow had sought to stimulate at the turn of the century and earlier was being aroused again by Beizer from the outset of his tours. Indeed, even as Beizer's tours were in their early stages, Igor Krupnik, a Soviet ethnographer, published in Moscow his own questions, reiterating Dubnow, on the need to rediscover the Jewish past. As Beizer explained in one of the last essays in this volume: "Dubnow considered the Jews to be the only example of the preservation of nationhood with the loss of state independence and the loss of their own common territory." Beizer believed, with a fervor that I experienced when seeing Leningrad through his eyes in the cold days of March 1983 and again in the intense heat of August 1985, that by rediscovering the recent Jewish past of the streets, homes, schools, journals, and institutions of his city, he could lead at least some of his fellow Jews back to their national origins.

Mikhail Beizer did not work alone. His tours, and the notes that he wrote about them, became, as he later recalled, "a part of the hope of many people and helped them to change, to return to their sources." A group of young Jews, hitherto cut off from any knowledge of their heritage, were now caught up in a voyage of discovery, often harassed by the authorities, constantly afraid that the tours would be forbidden altogether, aware that Beizer himself could even be arrested. Yet they were determined to work together as a group in order to become Jews once more.

What had begun in the summer of 1982 as a sort of sightseeing quickly extended its scope, giving Beizer and those around him a purpose and a goal. "As for my life," he wrote to me in June 1983, in sending me details of locations he had just added to his tours, "I go on studying the same subject, read what I can find out, and try to think it over. By and by history is becoming my second specialty, not just tour guiding."

With each letter, it became clear that Beizer was not going to relax his efforts. "My research work has improved a little," he wrote with understandable pride that September. "For example, now I could show you at least five places where Dubnow lived." Each fact was acquired with difficulty. "We haven't any knowledge," he explained a month later, "of what books are being published on Jewish history."

The young Jews of Leningrad with whom Beizer worked had already begun to publish on their own a clandestinely circulated typescript, which they called the *Leningrad Jewish Almanac*. Its first issue, prepared in September 1982, contained articles on Jewish religion, culture, and history. This first issue explained:

> During the past few decades we have been witnessing the process of national awakening throughout the world and this process has affected the Jews as well, especially us, the Jews of Leningrad. Hundreds of thousands of us have been looking at ourselves with new eyes, and have been asking ourselves once again — what does it mean to be a Jew?

Beizer's Excursion One appeared in this issue.

The desire to be a Jew and the desire to live in Jerusalem animated Beizer and his friends in equal measure. One could feel in each of his letters the pain of being refused an exit visa. "My patience to wait and hope is almost ended," he wrote to me in February 1984. But in this same letter, as in all his letters, he did not indulge in self-pity, nor even ask for help in getting out. Instead, he searched for more and more material to add to his knowledge and his folders. "Maybe," he wrote in this February letter, "you could look through some biographies or memoirs of famous people about their former life in St. Petersburg–Leningrad. Maybe you know some living descendants from here, who remember former Jewish life in Leningrad. For example" Beizer added, "(1) The family of Leningrad rabbi Lubanov now live in Israel. Where? (2) Hebrew poet Saul Chernyakovsky was in Petrograd in 1917 and took part in the revolution. But where, and what, and when? (3) Herzl visited Petersburg in 1902 and met with Pleve (Minister of Interior). Where did he stay? And so on."

By correspondence and through visitors, Beizer gained further details for his work. But his main achievement was to delve into such books, pamphlets, and old brochures as he could find in Leningrad itself and to talk to eyewitnesses of the far-off days, of the vibrant life that he was seeking to reconstruct and convey. "Every week I am finding more and more new facts, names, addresses," he wrote to me in April 1984 and then set out several pages of his most recent discoveries. "And one last fact for today," this letter ended. "Dubnow's address from 1913 to 1922 was in former Bolshaya Monetnaya Street 21, now Skorokhodova Street 29." Even an ordinary picture postcard as bought by hundreds of tourists could stir Beizer to historical comment. That month he sent me a postcard of the St. Peter and St. Paul Fortress, which on our tour he had pointed out to me across the Neva. "Among its prisoners," he wrote on the card, "B. L. Edelman (1898) — one of the founders of the Russian Social-Democratic Workers' Party."

Not everything could be ascertained; when I asked Beizer to tell me what had been carved on an inscription that he had earlier written was now destroyed, he explained: "I don't know yet what the inscription was on the memorial to M. Hertzenstein. I only saw a cartoon about this in an anti-Semitic paper. There was a pig on it."

Beizer's second excursion appeared in the third issue of the *Leningrad Jewish Almanac,* several copies of which reached the West in the summer of 1984. It was suggested to him that he might consider publishing his work in the West in book form. To this end, I began to prepare a short introduction and, in preparing it, asked him to tell me about his own family. I asked whether they had suffered in the war. He replied:

> There is not a Jewish family here which passed the war without losses. In my own family my little brother (also Misha) died in 1943 at the age of one, and my father lost his right hand being a sapper on the Leningrad front. All my father's and mother's relatives who didn't succeed to evacuate from the Ukraine and White Russia perished in ditches and ravines. There were dozens.

As Beizer worked toward the goal of publication in the West, he photographed, and then smuggled out, the text of successive excursions. Sometimes the film was too poorly prepared to be readable. At other times pages were missing. Using whatever material reached us, Michael Sherbourne translated the hundreds of barely legible prints, each of them diligently blown up as large as possible by Studio Edmark in Oxford. Month after month the process continued, each arrival of a visitor with another roll of film being a cause for excitement and concern. Would this film fill a gap, or would it be a duplicate? Would it be legible? Would it be a completely new excursion or extra material to add to an existing one?

Even as Studio Edmark and Michael Sherbourne worked on the films and the translations, Mikhail Beizer was adding and seeking yet more material. A letter that he wrote to me in August 1984 showed the extent to which he was still assembling material, or seeking to do so:

> "My queries:
> I need P. Rutenberg's biography.
> Did Lord Sieff come from Petersburg?
> Was Isaak Yulyevitch Markon (left Leningrad 1925) a librarian in Jewish communal library in London in the 1930s? Or is anything known about him in England?"

The reference to Lord Sieff, who volunteered that he was not descended from the Sieffs of St. Petersburg, led Beizer and me to exchange letters about the business world of the Russian capital. "I pay less attention," he explained, "to Jewish commercial and financial life in Petersburg than to cultural activity." Nevertheless, he subsequently gave a number of important details about Jewish business involvement. At the same time, he became aware of just how wide he could spread his net, if he wished. In September 1984 he wrote:

"Now I am toying with the idea to do special work on Dubnow's places in Petersburg—where he lived, worked, rested, visited meetings and friends. Some of these places—dozens—can be found accurately. What do you think? Is it worth doing?"

As more and more pages reached us, it seemed that it was indeed "worth doing"; Beizer was now assembling material that had never before been published in the West and that was building a previously unknown picture of the extent and variety of Jewish communal and individual achievement in a city not widely associated with such things. In reply, for example, to a letter from me about Grigory Benenson, whose daughter Manya Harari had included a brief account of her childhood in her memoirs, Beizer replied:

Grigory Osipovitch Benenson. In 1917 he lived on Moika Canal, No. 16. He was a merchant of the first guild. He was a director-manager (and partly an owner) of a trading-industrial association "Grigory Benenson," and a chairman of the society for the achievement of elementary education for Jewish children living in the Peski district. He was also a member of the management of two mining companies, and a leading figure in the Anglo-Russian Bank. He owned a house at the corner of Nevsky Prospekt and Sadovaya ulitsa (Nevsky No. 52). Both his Moika and Nevsky houses are still extant.

The problems Beizer faced in finding material were considerable. As befitted someone who was following both literally and professionally in the footsteps of Simon Dubnow, he realized the difficulties and dangers of research without access to archives. Of a certain address that he had been seeking for some time, he wrote to me in October 1984: "I cannot and probably won't be able to find it." He added: "It is difficult for me. I have not every historical document at my disposal."

Even as we received, developed, and translated Beizer's work, he was correcting it. In this same letter of October 1984 he wrote: "Unfortunately, when I look at my work I find more mistakes. For example, the address of the Jewish University in 1919 I thought was Angliskaya embankment 4 (formerly S. Polyakov's palace). Now I see it was, most probably, the house of another Polyakov—Yakov, Angleeskaya Naberezhnaya 62."

This letter also contained a single sentence that stressed the extent to which Beizer was working under abnormal circumstances and that his main struggle was not to continue his work in Leningrad but to live in Israel. "Our life here goes without much change, as usual from hope to depression and back, but never to Silence." A month later he wrote again, after setting out an account of the descendants of Horace Guenzburg: "Our life here, as I see it, became more tense and nervous. On the one hand a little more hope, on the other—much more troubles. But still we live."

As well as his excursions, all of which had been transmitted to the West and translated by the end of 1985, Beizer now worked on several extra sections, dealing with individuals who had lived in St. Petersburg, such as Dubnow, or had made important visits to the city, such as Sir Moses Montefiore. One of these individuals was Marc Chagall. Once more Beizer delved into the family aspect. "Chagall had two sisters in Leningrad," he wrote in February 1985. "One of them, Manya Perelstein, lived in Sadovaya str 75 in 1922–23. Now she is dead, but there is a daughter whom Chagall visited when he was in Leningrad in about 1974. Another sister still lives in Leningrad." Two months later Beizer wrote again: "It is a great pity that Chagall died right at the moment we began to study his life in Petersburg. Nevertheless we should even more continue with it. His father had seven sisters and a brother. All his descendants, except Chagall's own, live now in Leningrad — all of them, including little children." Beizer then set out the details of these descendants, and he added: "Of course, I don't pretend that anything is unknown about Chagall. As a matter of fact his Gentile son-in-law wrote a great volume about Chagall's life. But still . . ."

Beizer's work was now almost done. A completely revised text of all the excursions and extra chapters reached the West in the summer of 1985 and was translated by Michael Sherbourne. In August 1985 I returned to Leningrad and discussed various points with Beizer; Sherbourne, visiting him in February 1987, was able to check many details. Then a month later, when the book was ready for publication, a final chapter arrived on film, was developed, translated, and incorporated in the text: it was Beizer's detailed study of the Jewish institutions and individuals connected with a single house on Vassilevsky Ostrov, the house on 5th Liniya.

"The task of the historian," Beizer had written in an introduction to his first excursion, "is to prevent the knowledge of the past of a people from disappearing, to prevent the nation from being ignorant of its own self and its own origins, to preserve the memory."

Beizer's work does this and more: it enables the memory to serve a new generation of Jews, who, cut off from access to so much of their heritage and denied free movement to the places where such access is possible, struggle nevertheless to remain Jews and to absorb as much as possible of a national and cultural heritage that, however much it is under attack or pressure, cannot be easily extinguished. Beizer's contribution to that struggle is evident in every page of this, his achievement in exile.

In May 1987, within a few days of the arrival in the West of his chapter on the house on 5th Liniya, Mikhail Beizer received permission to leave the Soviet Union. He now lives in Israel, where he is continuing his studies of Jewish history at the Hebrew University of Jerusalem.

Martin Gilbert
Merton College, Oxford
September 15, 1987

PREFACE

The Rabbi of Keonigsberg, Lev Epstein, in his book Hapardess, *written in the 1750s, during the reign of the Empress Elizabeth Petrovna (1741–1762), said that it was ordained by Providence that Jews should not live in St. Petersburg as in the summer months there is no night (the "White Nights") and consequently it is not possible to define the times for morning and evening prayers.*

From the article "St. Petersburg" in the *Yevreiskaya Entsiklopedia*

The history of the Jews and St. Petersburg: What do they have in common? It is known that at the beginning of this century there were five and a half million Jews living on the territory of the Russian Empire, but they lived mostly in the Pale of Settlement. And even in the most favorable times up to the end of the nineteenth century the number of Jews in St. Petersburg never reached 20,000, compared, for example, with Odessa, which had about 150,000. And to what extent were these Jews typical? The majority were to a significant extent assimilated. Education, clothing, speech — everything about them followed the Russian style. Only in Moscow could it be said that the Jewish population was more Russified.

The fact is, however, that these few thousands of our fellow Jews living in the capital made up by far the most educated, cultured, and often the wealthiest and most influential of Russian Jews. They were the leaders along those paths that *nolens volens* — willy-nilly — our people followed. Their activities were well recorded, as much among Russians as among Jews. The newspapers and magazines that they published, as well as their personal example, greatly influenced every succeeding generation, especially from the last third of the nineteenth century. These were the people who to a significant extent were responsible for the successes and the failures of the Jews in Russia in the twentieth century. In fact, it was not only in Russia, since the most important

Outside the Leningrad Choral Synagogue: one of Mikhail Beizer's tours (Beizer in center, wearing light raincoat), Spring 1983

positions in contemporary Jewish life, both in numbers and in significance, are occupied by emigrants from the then Russian Empire and their nearest descendants.

You are reading this guided tour, which means that the subject under discussion is of some interest to you. We need only to go out onto the street and have a look at Jewish places in old St. Petersburg. But where are they, these places? Even native-born residents of Leningrad can only rarely remember something specifically Jewish in the town, apart from perhaps the Choral Synagogue and the Preobrazhensky Cemetery. (One or two can still recall that until 1948 there was a Jewish restaurant on Nevsky Prospekt.) And it seems very sad that today's Leningrad Jewish population of some 140,000 souls knows so very little of the history of the people of whom it is a part — a history that occurred in the town where they now live. Seventy to a hundred years ago the picture was completely different. If we carry out a few excursions round the town, we shall see that this was so.

It is said that Hasidic Jews have their own map of the world, a map that is completely different from the normally accepted one, on which their spiritual center, Lubavitch and Medzhibozh, occupy more central and much more important positions than London, Paris, or Rome. We too, on our guided walks, will not turn our eyes toward the palaces and buildings that are most significant in the ordinary understanding of these things, but we shall stop principally at ordinary houses of so-called capitalist construction, because it is not architecture that is important for us, but history — our own history. First and foremost we are interested in people — how they earned their livings, what they thought. Who can tell us what processes, what events affecting the fate of our people, went on behind the monotonous facades of these substantial houses? This is what we want to know.

Today it is already very difficult to search for the traces of our recent past. Tomorrow it will be impossible. Knowledge is gathering dust in forgotten old books, is locked away in the dark corners of shelves, is dispersed throughout the world, or lies in graves together with those who possess it. The task of the historian is to prevent the knowledge of the past of a people from disappearing, to prevent the nation from being ignorant of its own self and its own origins, to preserve the memory.

We approach what looks like an ordinary house. A house like any other house. The architecture is nothing special. The walls tell us nothing about anything — there is no memorial plaque. Yet, if we know something about who lived here, what was here, we shall know that someone did exist, someone wrote something down, possessed a memory, published a book, however small the number of copies, told his children and his friends . . . and we shall be grateful to these people.

Mikhail Sulyevitch Beizer
Hebrew University, Jerusalem
September 15, 1987

ACKNOWLEDGMENTS

To Grigory Kanovitch and Lev Utevski (formerly of Leningrad, now living in Israel), who seven years ago awoke in me a real interest in Jewish history.

To Boris Kelman and Simeon Frumkin (both refuseniks since 1980), who did a great deal to help me — gathering material and taking photographs — and whose shoulders I could lean on at every difficult moment.

To Isaak Furshtein (now in the United States), who was among the first to give me advice and who was the first to show me the graves in the Leningrad Jewish cemetery.

To Alexander Sheinin and Michail Ezer (Makushkin) (both now in Jerusalem), who invited people to my first tours.

To Yuri Kolker (now in Jerusalem), who wrote an excellent poem specially for the book.

To Dorrit Hoffer (Jerusalem), who during these years sent me many letters of encouragement, often containing historical information that was otherwise inaccessible to me.

To Rita Gimmelshtein (now in Jerusalem), who edited and typed the first version of the book in Russian.

To Boris and Anna Dubrow (now in Israel), who produced two slide shows on the Jewish history of Leningrad based on the contents of the book and adding much to its popularity in Leningrad.

To Aba Taratuta (fourteen years in refusal, now in Israel), for his special encouragement and help in enabling many of the chapters of this book to be made available inside the Soviet Union to those interested in Jewish culture.

To all my friends — elderly residents of the city — who shared their own recollections with me, and to the most important among them — Bertha Davidovna Joffe (now 86 years old and in Israel), a daughter of the Petersburg Rabbi David-Tevel Katzenellenbogen. Thanks to her clear memory, and her deep understanding of life, my book took a few steps closer to the truth.

To Donna Lynn Wosk (United States), whose enormous help gave me the opportunity to see my book in print as a free person in Israel.

To all those who I cannot mention yet, but who did help me; those who gave me books from their private libraries and showed me their archives, as well as those who read the manuscript and corrected errors in it or introduced me to others who could give me information. Thanks also to those who helped me in my everyday life, who often fed me or gave me medical care, and in every way enabled me to complete the project.

Finally, I am grateful to everyone who listened to my lectures in Leningrad, attended my tours, and showed genuine interest in the topic and sympathy to my work, proving thereby that the Jewish people in Russia still live, still want to know their history, and are still capable of being active in the making of it.

FINLAND

Usikirki
Vyborg
Tereoki
(Zelenogorsk)
Schlüsselburg (Petrokrepost)
St. Petersburg

ESTONIA
Luga
Malaya
Vishera

Rybinsk

Baltic Sea

LATVIA
Riga
Libava

COURLAND

LITHUANIA

Moscow

Königsberg

EAST
PRUSSIA

Vitebsk
Vilna
Smolensk

BIELORUSSIA
Minsk

T S A R I S T

R U S S I A

Malkin
Bialystok
Tschanovets

Kozlovo
Yelts

Warsaw
Brest-Litovsk
Pinsk

POLAND

Radom

Kursk
Voronezh

Lublin

Pieny
Ostrogoshsk

Zamosc

VOLHYNIA

GALICIA
Lemberg
(Lvov)

Kiev

Kharkov

UKRAINE

AUSTRIA-
HUNGARY

PODOLIA

Yelizavetgrad
Yekaterinoslav

BESSARABIA

Kishinev

Odessa
Kherson
Mikhailovka

Sofievka
Sea of
Azov

Kerch

Western border of
Imperial Russia
1815-1917

The Jewish
'Pale of Settlement'
1835-1917

Yevpatoria
CRIMEA

Simferopol
Alushta
Yalta

© Martin Gilbert 1988

Black Sea

0   miles   200
0   kilometres   300

Lake Ladoga

Western Russia

The Jewish Pale of Settlement in Tsarist Russia

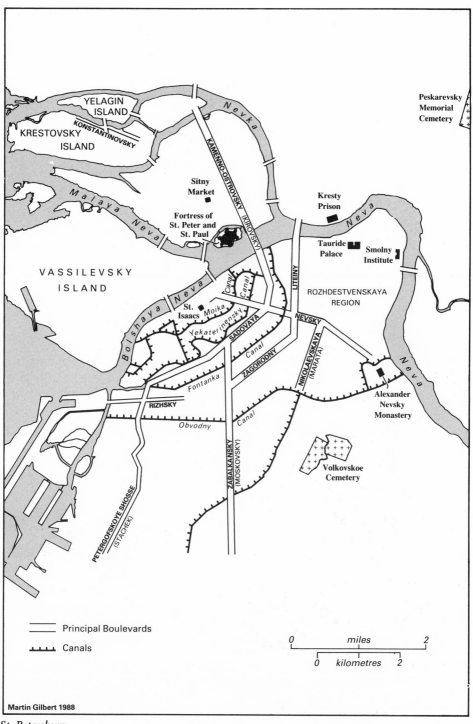

YELAGIN ISLAND

KONSTANTINOVSKY

KRESTOVSKY ISLAND

Peskarevsky Memorial Cemetery

Nevka

KAMENNO-OSTROVSKY (KIROVSKY)

Sitny Market

Kresty Prison

Neva

Fortress of St. Peter and St. Paul

Malaya Neva

Tauride Palace

Smolny Institute

VASSILEVSKY ISLAND

Bolshaya Neva

ROZHDESTVENSKAYA REGION

Canal

Canal

LITEINY

St. Isaacs

Moika

Yekaterinensky

SADOVAYA

NEVSKY

Neva

Fontanka

Canal

ZAGORODNY

NIKOLAEVSKAYA (MARATA)

Alexander Nevsky Monastery

RIZHSKY

Obvodny

Canal

ZABALKANSKY (MOSKOVSKY)

Volkovskoe Cemetery

PETERGOFSKOVE SHOSSE

(STACHEK)

———— Principal Boulevards

⊥⊥⊥⊥ Canals

0   miles   2

0   kilometres   2

Martin Gilbert 1988

St. Petersburg

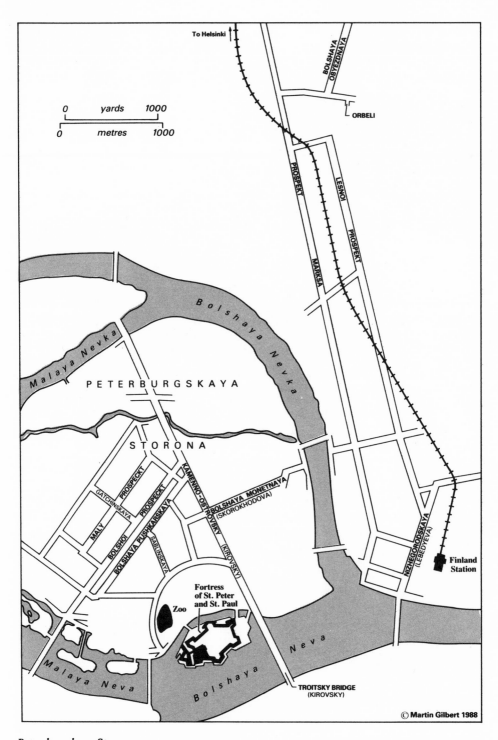

Petersburgskaya Storona

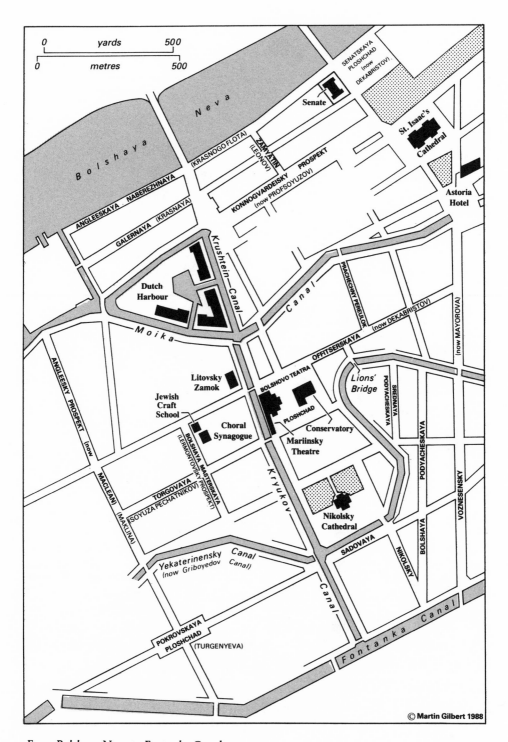

From Bolshaya Neva to Fontanka Canal

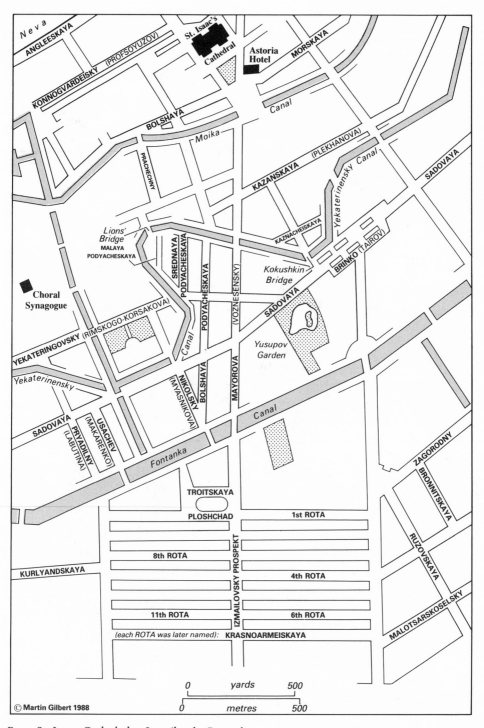

From St. Issacs Cathedral to Izmailovsky Prospekt

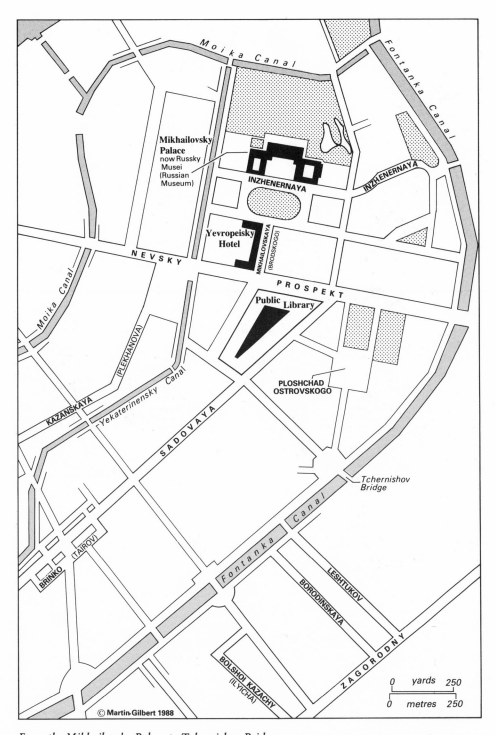

From the Mikhailovsky Palace to Tchernishov Bridge

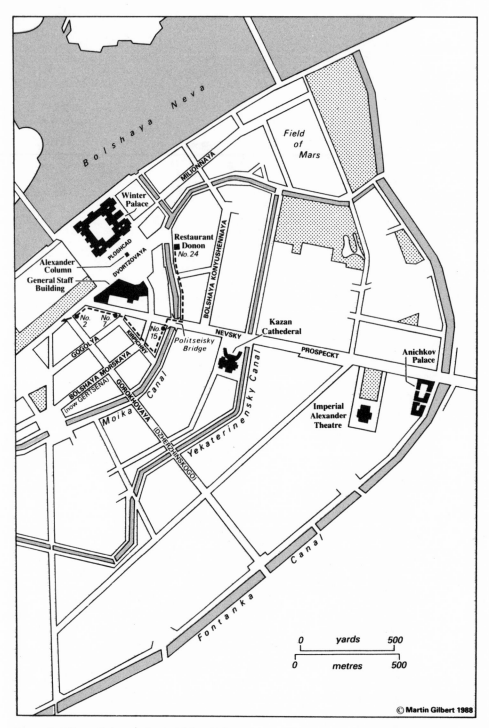

From the Winter Palace to the Anichkov Palace

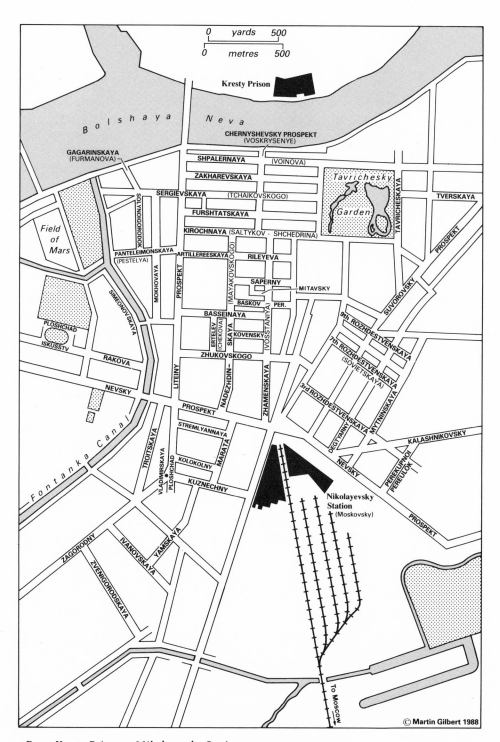

From Kresty Prison to Nikolayevsky Station

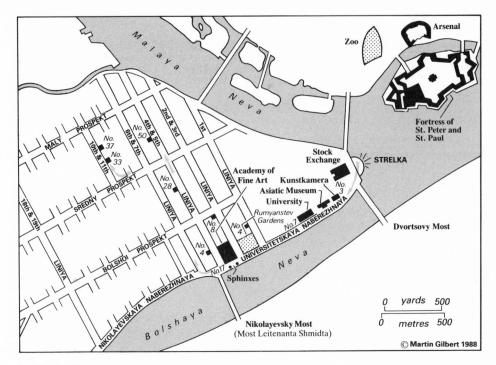

Vassilevsky Ostrov

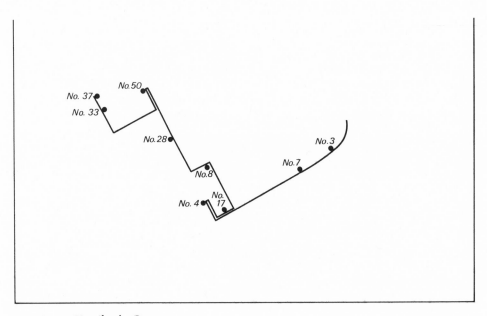

Excursion on Vassilevsky Ostrov

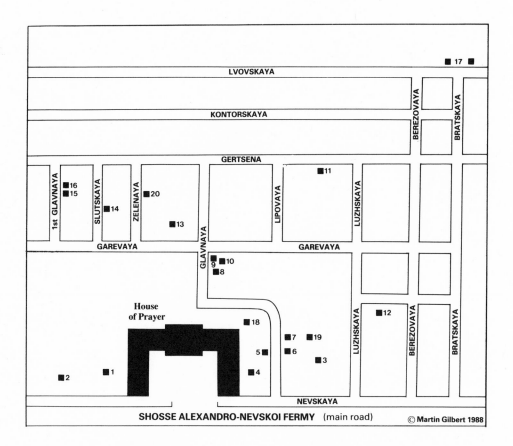

1. Rabbi Katznellenbogen
2. Professor Harkavy
3. M. L. Maimon
4. L. I. Katznelson
5. L. Y. Sternberg
6. M. M. Antokolski
7. Warshawski family vault
8. Councillor of State Friedland
9. Kaplun family vault
10. Berka Burak and Moshka Frisno
11. Sergeant-Major Ashanski
12. Polyakov family vault
13. The Guenzburg stone
14. Vera Slutzkaya
15. Five second world war victims
16. Holocaust memorial meeting place
17. Communal war graves
18. Rabbi Lubanov
19. The Dembo tombstone
20. M. I. Kulisher

The Jewish Cemetery

PART ONE

EXCURSIONS THROUGH THE PAST

EXCURSION ONE
THE INNER CANALS

At that moment when Russia asks us:
— Where are ye, O Sons of mine? —
We shall answer her in harmony:
— We are here, mother dear!

Lev Levanda (from a letter to M. F. de Poulet)

WE SHALL START our tour at an ordinary four-storied terrace house on Prachechny Pere'ulok No. 6. Today there is still a printing press here, but in the early years of the twentieth century here was located the famous publishing house of Brockhaus and Yefron, which left an indelible mark on the cultural life of Russia. The personality of one of the publishers, Ilya Abramovitch Yefron, is of particular interest. Son of a merchant and learned Talmudist, the future great publisher I. A. Yefron was born in Vilna in 1847. He was named after his maternal great-grandfather the Vilna Gaon (Eliahu ben Shlomo Zalman, 1720–1797). After a solid Hebrew education guided by his father, Yefron passed the entrance examination for the Gymnasium (high school) and attended lectures at the Warsaw High School. His publishing activity dates from 1880. From 1890 to 1907 the publishing house of Brockhaus and Yefron published the *Russian Encyclopedic Dictionary,* which was the first of its kind both in size and scope as well as in importance; it consisted of eighty-six volumes. For Jews the most important event in publishing history was the advent of the sixteen-volume *Yevreiskaya Entsiklopedia* in the Russian language, published in conjunction with the Society for Learned Jewish Publications in 1908–1913. The subtitle of this Jewish encyclopedia — *A Collection of Information about Judaism and Its Culture in the Past and the Present* — gives a true characterization of the contents of this learned work. Everything connected in any way with Judaism and the Jews, starting from the Bible (Tanakh) and the Talmud and ending with the Right Social Democrat Bernstein or the composer Georges Bizet, is conscientiously and precisely detailed in the encyclopedia. Do you want to know the origin of the surname *Ginzburg* or *Lifshitz* and which famous persons bore the name? Just take a peek into the *Yevreiskaya Entsiklopedia*. Are you interested in the members of the Beni-Israel Jewish community in Bombay, how they dress, and what they eat? There is an article about them too. And in the article on St. Petersburg you will find much of what has come into this present guidebook.

The *Entsiklopedia* was produced under the general editorship of three prominent activists in the field of Jewish culture at that time: Lev Izrailyevitch Katzenelson (who was a doctor of medicine, a historian, and a public benefactor), Baron David Goratzievitch Guenzburg (a well-known orientalist who possessed a valuable library of Hebrew books and manuscripts; he was son of the famous St. Petersburg banker and philanthropist Baron Horace Yevselevitch Guenzburg), and the orientalist Albert Abram Yakovlevitch Harkavy. The editors performed an enormous amount of work in a short time, arranging for the translation of many articles in the American *Jewish Encyclopedia,* which had been published only a short time previously; they brought in the finest scholars to write original articles on the history of the Jews of Lithuania, Poland, and Russia and themselves wrote a great deal. The present-day reader who knows only Russian can quite simply not find anywhere else another work so exhaustive on the subject as this one.

The very fact of the publication of such a work clearly indicated the deep changes that had taken place by this time in Russian Jewry. In fact, less than a hundred years earlier the Jews in Russia lived a secluded life; their world was narrow but harmonious. They drew upon the Torah and the Talmud for every answer to every problem that confronted them. They all knew Hebrew, and hardly any one of them knew any Russian. The Jews of that time could not see much point in the publication of a Jewish encyclopedia, especially if it was in Russian. The language was not intelligible to them. They did not study their religion from articles that gave a general survey, and secular studies held little interest for and even somewhat frightened them.

The first Jewish enlighteners — the Maskilim — of the 1840s and 1850s made great efforts to break through the self-imposed isolation of the Jews and bring the education, language, and style of living of the (Jewish) people closer to the accepted norm of the country; by the start of the twentieth century nobody needed to be convinced of the need for secular education. Quite the reverse in fact, for there was a clear-cut breakaway on the part of the Jewish intelligentsia from its people, a departure from its language and culture, a rapid assimilation and even sometimes a change of religion. As a result of the pogroms, revolution, and mass flight of Russian Jewry to the West, there arose a real danger of a loss of many cultural and historical monuments. These tendencies as well as the countertendencies of a rapid development of Jewish historiography and litera-

The entrance to the Brockhaus and Yefron publishing house, where the Yevreiskaya Entsiklopedia *was published*

ture by a small group of intellectuals who remained loyal to their national ideas—these became the reason for the publication of the *Yevreiskaya Entsiklopedia*.

NOW WE SHALL take a few short steps in order to reach the second object on our tour. We proceed along Prachechny Pere'ulok, turn to the right along Dekabristov ulitsa (formerly Offitserskaya ulitsa) and into Teatralnaya Ploshchad (Square). We shall now recall in general terms the origins of Jewish history in St. Petersburg.

It is not surprising that Jews arrived in St. Petersburg together with the birth of the town itself. At first they were only converts: Maria Yan d'Acosta,*

* Also spelled Dacosta, Lacosta, and Acosta in other contemporary sources.

Tsar Peter's favorite court jester; Abram Ence, staff surgeon of the Semyonovsky Regiment of Life Guards; Commissioner General of Police of St. Petersburg, Count Anton Manuilovich Devier (also spelled Divier), the son of a Portuguese Jew who was brought to Tsar Peter from Holland and baptized in Russia; and, finally, Tsar Peter's Vice-Chancellor, Piotr Pavlovitch Shafirov (1669–1727), the equivalent in our time of minister of foreign affairs. He was of Jewish descent, a fact, of course, that shocked the members of the Imperial Court.

Then some individual "real Jews" began to appear on the scene, although as yet only as individuals, for Jews were still forbidden by law to reside in Russia. But, as often occurs in cases of extreme need, the laws were bypassed and Jews did live in the capital. One example is Zundel Hirsh, who had contracted to supply silver for the Royal Mint during the short reign of Catherine I, from 1725 to 1727 (she was the widow of Peter the Great). In accordance with the Ukase (Decree) of 1727, under which all Jews were formally banished from Russia, Hirsh and others should have been deported. It would, however, have meant a considerable loss of revenue for the Royal Treasury, so Hirsh was allowed to remain "until the rest of the silver can be brought from across the sea" (as quoted in the decision of the Privy Council).

At about the same time, Levi Lipman, a Jewish immigrant from Courland, with the titles of Oberhofcommissar and commercial agent, was the financial representative at the court. Lipman was particularly close to Biren (one of Empress Anne's favorites), which gave one foreigner an excuse to write that it was Lipman who was ruling Russia. After Biren was exiled, the foreign press stated that the Oberhofcommissar had also been dismissed, but this rumor was officially denied in the *Saint-Petersburg Gazette*.

Catherine II, taking into consideration public opinion, and at the same time bearing in mind the interests of state, officially forbade, but secretly encouraged, the presence of individual Jews in St. Petersburg. It was in fact during her reign (1762–1796) as a result of the three partitions of Poland (1773, 1792, and 1795) that Russia suddenly found that she had become ruler over the world's largest Jewish community. In a letter to Diderot in 1773, in reply to his question about the Jews, the empress wrote: "The whole of Bielorussia is swarming with them, and three or four of them have been living for some time in St. Petersburg. I had a church confessor in whose house they were living. We tolerate them in spite of the law, pretending we don't know they are in the capital."

Through her decrees of 1791 and 1794, Catherine was responsible for that shameful invention of the Russian autocracy — the Pale of Settlement. Nevertheless, in spite of this innovation, by 1826 there were already 159 Jewish families living in the capital — in all 248 souls, mainly merchants and artisans.

There were some anecdotal cases. There was the well-known complaint submitted, during the reign of Nicholas I (1825–1855), by the chief procurator of the Holy Synod to the minister of the interior. It referred to the arrival in St.

Petersburg from Mogilev of a certain Meyersohn, a grinding and polishing craftsman, "in order to study the dogmas of the (Russian) Orthodox Church and to undertake baptism" (because he was afraid to do so in his own country). "As the situation regarding the Jews" the complaint went on, did not have a specific clause permitting entry into the capital for the purpose of baptism, the police sent him back. To prevent such occurrences in the future, the senior procurator approached the tsar with a humble petition that the law should be eased on this point. Nicholas I handed it to the state council for consideration, which threw it out, maintaining that the study of the dogmas of the Orthodox Church was only an excuse invented by the Jews so that they would be able to live in the capital for quite different purposes.

The Jewish population of St. Petersburg grew significantly with the reforms of Alexander II (1855–1881) in the 1850s and 1860s, when permission was granted for residence outside the Pale of Settlement to Merchants of the First Guild, persons with higher education, craftsmen, and retired officials. The most well-to-do lived in the Kazanskaya area (the district of Plekhanov Street, between Griboyedov Canal and the Moika River), in the Spasskaya area (along ulitsa Sadovaya between Griboyedov Canal and the Fontanka), and in the Moskovskaya area (Zagorodny Prospekt), which was where craftsmen and intellectuals lived. In 1868 the Jewish population in these sections was: 635 in the Spasskaya area; 423 in the Moskovskaya area; and 324 in the Kazanskaya area.

The total number of Jews in all quarters of St. Petersburg was 2,612 — no more than 1 percent of the population. In reality, however, these official figures were very much underestimated. Many Jews were living illegally in the town, as confirmed by the more exact figures in Table 1, showing the number for 1869 as 6,654.

TABLE 1-1. POPULATION OF JEWS IN ST. PETERSBURG

Year	Men	Women	Total	Jewish Percentage of Total Population of St. Petersburg (%)
1826	—	—	248	—
1869	3,751	2,903	6,654	1.00
1881	8,839	7,987	16,826	1.95
1890	8,079	7,252	15,331	1.61
1897	8,942	8,002	16,944	1.34
1900	10,714	9,671	20,385	1.41
1910	17,766	17,229	34,995	1.84
1917	—	—	about 50,000	—
1920	11,700	13,753	25,453	3.52
1923	25,739	26,635	52,374	4.89
1926	—	—	84,480	—

When studying this table of Jews in St. Petersburg, one must bear in mind that before the 1917 Revolution the figures did not include converts to Christianity or those living illegally in the capital. After the Revolution, at the census-taking, individuals decided their own nationality, so the figures after 1917 do not include those Jews who denied being Jewish (about 20 percent).

In comparison with the non-Jewish population of the capital, the Jews of St. Petersburg were conspicuous by their high standard of literacy, but the difference was not as marked as that in the provinces. Thus, in 1868, literacy among Jews was 72 percent for men and 47 percent for women*; among the Russian Orthodox the figures were correspondingly 54 percent and 41 percent. These people were, in the main, craftsmen, physicians, journalists, and merchants. In 1881, of a total population of 800,000 in St. Petersburg, there were already 17,000 Jews. Of these, on average, about 2,000 considered their mother tongue to be Russian, 500 German; 90 Polish; 50 Tatar; 37 Turkish; and 14,000 Yiddish. By 1910, no more than 55 percent of the Jews of St. Petersburg considered Yiddish to be their mother tongue. In this respect St. Petersburg was strikingly different from the western provinces of Russia, where almost everyone spoke Yiddish. By the turn of the century the center of Jewish life in the capital had shifted to Kolomna, the area along the Kryukov Canal. Here is where we shall find the majority of the sites in our excursion.

□ ON TEATRALNAYA SQUARE (formerly Bolshoi Theater Square) the most important place is house No. 2, where the most popular Russian Jewish journal *Voskhod* (Daybreak) was published and printed. Its publisher, Adolf Yefimovitch Landau (1842–1902), has gone down in history under the nickname of the "Jewish Sytin."† This uncensored monthly educational, literary, and political magazine was founded in 1881 and continued until April 1906. In order to appreciate the role played by *Voskhod* in the communal life of Russian Jewry of that period, we must pause, if only briefly, to examine two very important features closely connected with the journal: the Haskala and Russo-Jewish literature.

The Haskala (Enlightenment) was a social and cultural stream in Jewish life, not only in Russia, that arose in the middle of the nineteenth century to overcome the national and religious seclusion of the Jews. The Maskilim (Enlighteners) fought with the orthodox rabbinate for a reform of Judaism and advocated a popularization of secular education and European (for the most part Russian) culture in Jewish circles. They believed that equality before the law and recognition by Russian society would come to the Jews if their culture and way of life would become the same as those of their Christian neighbors.

---

* This refers to literacy in Russian; every boy, from his earliest days, could read Hebrew.
† Ivan Sytin (1854–1934) was the owner of I. D. Sytin & Co, a well-known publishing house in St. Petersburg, and owner of many bookshops in St. Petersburg and elsewhere.

"Be a citizen on the streets and a Jew in your own home" was one of the chief slogans of the Haskala.

The Haskala movement was brought into existence by internal and external pressures, among which we may note:

1 The influence of the ideas of the German-Jewish enlightener Moses Mendelssohn
2 The destruction by Nicholas I of Jewish communal autonomy
3 The crisis in traditional Judaism
4 The rapid development of capitalism in Russia and the reforms of Alexander II
5 The influence of the rapid development of Russian culture, particularly literature
6 The growing interest throughout the world in national history and national culture (national awareness was everywhere gradually squeezing out religious consciousness)

The first activists of the Haskala came from wealthy families of border towns: Solomon Rapoport, Nachman Krochmal, then Joseph Perl, Lev Man-

The editorial offices of Voskhod. *Rabbi Katzenellenbogen also lived in this house in the 1920s.*

delstam, Osip Rabinovitch, Lev Levanda, Yehuda-Leib Gordon, Moses Lilienblum, and others.* The Haskala was not a uniform current — just as Jewish society was no longer a single or monolithic entity. There soon branched out from it various nationalistic, assimilatory, and, later, revolutionary tendencies. Nevertheless, three quotations that follow are characteristic of the attitude of the majority of the Maskilim of the 1860s.

Sarin, a Maskil in the novel by Lev Levanda entitled *The Burning Time* says:

My heart tells me that in the course of time the Russian people will love us. We can make them love us. How? With our own love.

Leib Gordon:

We were slaves in Egypt, and what are we today? Are we not sinking lower with each year that passes? Are we not tied up in the ropes of the absurd, in the bonds of Sophism, with every sort of superstitious prejudice? It is no longer those of another religion who oppress us, our tyrants are inside us ourselves, our hands are no longer fettered, but our souls are in chains.

Lilienblum (who was from Odessa):

At a time when all thinking people in Russia are seized with the new ideas of Chernishevsky and Pisariev who are putting forward solutions for the great problem of universal happiness, our great Jewish writers are making a to-do over some obscure commentary to a Biblical phrase and are making a deep study of ancient tomes whose ideas are as dry and as withered as leaves that have fallen from a tree.

The Haskala, being a complex and contradictory stream, contributed equally contradictory and far-reaching results to Jewish communal life: the development of Jewish language and literature (at first in Hebrew and then in Yiddish) and, at the same time, the destruction of the Jewish community, its way of life, and even its morals; the development of the science of Jewish historical research and romanticism of the national past, together with assimilation and even conversion to Christianity among Jewish intellectuals; the appearance in Jewish circles of socialist and Palestinophile ideas. All of this was one way or another tied up with the Haskala. We are also indebted to it for the growth and development of Russo-Jewish literature, that is, literature in Russian language on Jewish themes.

At first the aim of such literature was to reach and influence the Russian

* Their dates were: Rapoport (known as "Shir"), 1790–1867; Krochmal (known as "Ranak"), 1785–1840; Perl, 1773–1839; Mandelstam, 1819–1889; Rabinovitch, 1817–1869; Levanda, 1835–1880; Gordon (known as "Yalag"), 1830–1892; and Lilienblum, 1843–1910.

public and in that way to improve its attitude toward the Jews. (See, for example, *The Wailing of the Daughter of Judaea* by Leib Nevakhovitch.)* This objective was also partially pursued by the first Russian Jewish journal, *Rassvet* (Dawn), which appeared in Odessa in 1860, published by Osip Rabinovitch. It soon became apparent, however, that this objective was going to be difficult to attain, and all Russian Jewish publications began to be orientated toward those Jewish readers for whom the Russian language had become more natural than Yiddish. Everything that was of interest in those years to the Jew who was educated, in the secular sense of that word, could be found in those journals: national history, culture, communal life, even the struggle for equality before the law—it was all there.

Now it is clear how important a place was occupied by the chief Russian Jewish periodical published in St. Petersburg, the typical product of the Haskala—the magazine *Voskhod*. This journal was preceded, however, by the ten-volume historico-literary collection of Adolf Landau (the editor of *Voskhod*) under the general title *Yevreiskaya Biblioteka* (The Jewish Library). The collection started to appear in 1871 and contained critical articles and literary compositions of known Haskala activists. Included, for example, was the novel of Lev Levanda, *The Burning Time* (quoted previously), and also his article "Fear of School," directed against those orthodox parents who did not want to send their children to government-funded schools.

In view of the fact that the Maskilim waged implacable war against the Hasidim, it is worth mentioning the article by the Jewish jurist and historian, Ilya Orshansky (1846–1875), entitled "Thoughts on Hasidism," which appeared in volume one of the *Yevreiskaya Biblioteka*. (This article incidentally was reprinted in the 1960s in a Soviet publication, *A Critique of the Jewish Religion*.) The great Hebrew poet L. Gordon wrote two reviews of Jewish literature for it. These collections also included many translations from Western European Jewish literature. The *Yevreiskaya Biblioteka* was printed and published at the same address as *Voskhod* was later, Teatralnaya Ploshchad, house No. 2.

Voskhod began to appear at a difficult and critical time for the idealists of enlightenment, brought about by the first pogroms and the severity of the anti-Jewish legislation in the so-called May Laws of 1882. Many did not believe in the possibility of Jewish equality before the law in Russia and called for emigration. In the journal, discussion raged over where to emigrate to— America or Palestine. Those who remained behind were compelled to think of

---

* Lev Nikolayevitch (Yehuda-Leib Ben Noach) Nevakhovitch 1776–1831, one of the earliest of the Maskilim. His conversion to Lutheranism in 1809 turned many people away from Haskala. His grandson, Ilya Mechnikov (1845–1916), was the first Russian Nobel Prize winner (1908), in biology and pathology. He had earlier emigrated to Paris in protest against the anti-Semitism of the tsarist regime.

ГОДЪ СЕМНАДЦАТЫЙ.

ВОСХОДЪ

ЖУРНАЛЪ

УЧЕНО-ЛИТЕРАТУРНЫЙ И ПОЛИТИЧЕСКІЙ

Издаваемый А. Е. ЛАНДАУ.

Апрѣль.

С.-ПЕТЕРБУРГЪ.
Типо-Литографія А. Е. Ландау. Площадь Большого Театра, 1.
1897.

*The front page of
the journal* Voskhod

what to do — what to propose to the five-million-strong Jewish population of the Pale of Settlement as an alternative to emigration. This is how the activity of *Voskhod* was described by the greatest Jewish historian of that time, Semyon Markovitch Dubnow:

> There were still the believers who hoped for a quick change in the internal policies of Russia and who considered it their duty to continue with the fight for civic emancipation and for a cultural revival of Jewry. The most independent of them were grouped round *Voskhod* . . . . After the demise of the two Russian journals for Jews *Rassvet* (Dawn) and *Russky Yevrei* (The Russian Jew), which were published between 1879 and 1884, *Voskhod* was for many years the only expression of opinion of the progressive intelligentsia, standing between assimilation and nationalism and gradually inclining towards the latter. . . . It served for a long time as a citadel where, after the former fighters for emancipation had suffered defeat, the last zealots of progress and equal rights had built their stronghold. The monthly issues of *Voskhod* published all the best of what the then contemporary Jewish thought could donate in the

field of literature in the Russian language. Here could be seen nearly all of the best verses of Frug . . . the latest novels of Levanda and Bogrov . . . the researches into Jewish history, especially in Poland and Russia, of Harkavy, Bershadsky, and others. The dissertations of *Voskhod* stood on the ground of the old positions of the seventies for a long time without giving way to the new nationalistic movement, but it conscientiously fulfilled its duty in the struggle for equality and rights.

Of those mentioned here by Dubnow, one, Sergei Bershadsky (1850–1896), one of the first historians of Lithuanian Jewry, was not himself a Jew. Another, Grigory Bogrov (1825–1885) was baptized shortly before he died. A third, the scholar Albert (Abram) Harkavy (1835–1919), was perhaps best known for his exposure of the fabrications of the Karaite scholar Abraham Firkovitch.

The variety of articles in *Voskhod* was remarkable. What, for example, did it publish in 1894? Take the article "The Present and the Future of Jewish Colonization in Argentina." The subject matter was the community founded by Baron de Hirsch, the German financier (1831–1896) whose object was to settle a part of Russian Jewry in Argentina, where they would undertake agricultural labor on settlements purchased specially for this purpose. The author of the article, Lapin, went to Argentina on behalf of the community and drew up a detailed report on the progress of the colonization. The article gives a geographical and economic survey of life in Argentina and evaluates the possibility of the resettlement there of a large number of Jews from Russia.

This report is followed by an article written by the French philosopher and historian, Ernest Renan (1823–1892), "Jews under the Domination of the Roman Empire: Herod the Great." In the same issue is a sentimental-moralistic novella, *The Shoemaker's Daughter,* which tells the tragic story of an educated Jewish girl from a poor family who commits suicide because of the gulf between her idealistic representation of what life should be like and the living reality. We also have here translations from the Bible; an economic account of the Jewish (agricultural) settlements in Kherson province; an essay by Baron David Guenzburg on exegesis (Bible study), with quotations in Latin, Hebrew, German, and French; and a review of recently published literature on Jewish themes — in Hebrew, Yiddish, Russian, and German. There are also reports on the history of the Jews in contemporary England and Italy; notes by a traveller on the difficulties of settlement in Palestine; and articles on the one thousandth anniversary of the birth of the Jewish philosopher Saadya Gaon, the greatest of the scholars of Babylonian Jewry.

Of special interest is a review by the famous lawyer Oscar (Israil) Osipovitch Grusenberg (1866–1940) of a novel by Pyotr Dmitriyevitch Boborykin (1836–1921), *The Crossing.* The review is included in the journal under the rubric "Literature and Life." The hero of the novel considers that enmity toward the Jews is not so much of a racial or of a competitive nature as it is related to the influence of the Jews on European and Russian culture, philosophy, and religion:

They, their prophets and their teachers, shook the age-old and healthy understanding of Good and Evil. According to their teachings everything that from the beginning of time was good, everything strong, brilliant, rich, gifted, generous, brave — all that is considered by them to be evil. Jewish morality with its preaching of altruistic love of one's neighbor represents a danger for humanity. Judophobia is a rebellion, not against the Jews as such, but against their "wretched, sickly morality." The conclusion to be drawn is that of a sympathy for any kind of anti-Semitism on any pretext whatsoever.

In his review, Grusenberg identifies the philosophy of the hero of the story with the author's own attitude and finds in it an exact reflection of the philosophy of Nietzsche. It was Nietzsche who wrote that the Jews were an amalgam of the wealthy, the godless, the bad, those inclined to violence, the poverty-stricken, the holy, the friend. According to Nietzsche, the Jews were exacting vengeance for their own enslavement by inculcating into Europe their own slave morality.

Many items of interest are to be found in *Voskhod*. It is sufficient to say that the Russian translation of "The Antiquities of the Jews" by Josephus Flavius was printed in a supplement to the periodical — and since that time has never been republished. Dubnow called *Voskhod* a fighter in the struggle for Jewish emancipation.

IMMEDIATELY OPPOSITE THE editorial offices of *Voskhod* is the large building of the Leningrad Conservatoire — the first conservatoire in Russia. It was founded in 1862 by Anton Rubinstein, the famous musician and composer, who was director of the conservatoire from 1862 to 1867, in 1882, and from 1887 to 1891. Rubinstein was baptized as a child, as was his brother Nicholas, who was born after him. It was Anton Rubinstein's conversion that enabled the brothers to receive their education and, later, to take their renowned place in the history of Russian music and Russian culture. For a long time baptism was a panacea for any Jew against acts of lawlessness. Even during the reign of Tsar Nicholas I, zealous persecutor of Judaism that he was, there was the well-known case of the convert to Christianity, Mikhail Pavlovitch Pozen (1798–1871), who was appointed to the position of administrator of the chancellery of the Department of War and was a wealthy landowner in the Poltava region. (Incidentally, on the commission dealing with the liberation of the serfs, Pozen was the leader of the right wing and proposed that the serfs be freed without granting them any land.)

Until the 1880s, however, there were only a few rare individuals among the Jews who were prepared to pay such a price to buy their emancipation. Only in the last two decades of the nineteenth century was there any significant increase in the number of conversions, mainly among the intelligentsia, who were indifferent to religion.

By now, however, even conversion to Christianity was no guarantee that the Jew could escape from his past. During the reign of Alexander III there were the first instances of converted Jews not being appointed to responsible government posts on account of their Jewish origins. Anti-Semitism based on religious affiliation began to be replaced in Russia by anti-Semitism based on blood. Even in the case of the altogether successful Anton Rubinstein, we shall see that his fellow citizens did not repay him in the best fashion for his services in the development of Russian music. The conservatoire that he founded does not bear his name, nor are the monuments erected next to it in his honor. It is interesting to note that the great musician, unlike many other converts, did not make a complete break from his people. He was, for example, often to be found in the home of Baron Horace Guenzburg. Over a long period of time Jewish students who received grants from Guenzburg studied in the conservatoire.

The outstanding violinist Henryk Wieniawski (1835–1880) was professor at the conservatoire and taught there from 1862 to 1872. An even more noticeable mark on the history of the conservatoire was left by another famous violinist and teacher, Leopold Auer, who taught there for almost half a century, from 1868 to 1917. Auer's school acquired considerable fame. Among his pupils were such famous musicians as Jascha Heifets, Efrem Zimbalist, Victor Walter, Mikhail Wolf-Israel, Joseph Ahron, Sibor (Lifshits) Ellman, and Fiddleman.

A Jewish community meeting, held in the small hall of the St. Petersburg Conservatory, January 7, 1914

Leading Jewish musicians who taught the piano at the conservatoire in Soviet times were S. Savshinsky, N. Perelman, and Chalfin; such composers as M. Kreinin, M. Gnessin, and A. Veprik also have a close connection with the St. Petersburg Conservatoire.

The St. Petersburg Jewish community hired the small hall of the conservatoire on a number of occasions for its meetings, such as the meeting of January 7, 1914, of which a photograph survives. A major event, the seventh all-Russian congress of the Zionist Organization was held here in 1917.

ANOTHER MOST INTERESTING object to look at is No. 18 Teatralnaya Ploshchad, which housed the former Jewish high school (Gymnasium).

The question of secular education for Jews in Russia at the beginning of the century was a very difficult one. The quota system was in operation not only in higher educational establishments but also in the secondary schools. Among Jewish youth there was the widespread tradition of taking the examina-

The Eisenbet Jewish Gymnasium at Teatralnaya 18 (from 1910 to 1917)

tion for the school-leaving certificate as external students. This was no easy task, but it did give some hope for the future to those who were deprived of schooling by the quota system. Then the government extended the quota system to include external students, and the straw they had been able to clutch at slipped from the grasp of Jewish young men and women.

Some of the wealthier parents started to place their children in the small number of private educational establishments that had liberal regulations in regard to the "Jewish question." But even the wealthy now found another problem: education in general Russian schools speeded up the assimilatory process.

The founder and director of the first Jewish private secondary high school in St. Petersburg, Ilya Hilarovitch Eisenbet, a candidate of philosophy, was faced with the problem of giving young Jewish people the opportunity to acquire sufficient knowledge (as well as the right) to enter the university while not omitting elementary education on Jewish culture and history. His high school opened in 1906 at No. 7 Nikolsky Pere'ulok (now ulitsa Myasnikova). Later it transferred to the much older building on Teatralnaya Ploshchad.

Eisenbet succeeded in establishing a very high standard of tuition. For every subject he selected only the best teachers, among whom were Zinovy Kisselgoff and A. E. Markov. If the memory of one of the former pupils is correct, other teachers included A. S. Dolinin (a specialist on Dostoyevsky and Russian literature); the future professor of Leningrad University S. N. Valk (history); Desnitsky, the friend and researcher of the works of Maxim Gorky; A. I. Pinsker, who was friendly with Maeterlinck (French language); N. I. Soloveitchik (German language); the traveller M. M. Shnitzler (geography); and M. M. Tchernin (modern Hebrew).

Many graduates of the Secondary High School (the Jewish Gymnasium) became famous. It is regrettable that we do not, as yet, have access to more detailed and fully reliable information on the history of this important beginning.

IF NOW WE leave Teatralnaya Ploshchad, and go behind the Conservatoire, we shall come out onto Canal Griboyedova (formerly Yekaterinensky Canal) and see on our right an ordinary five-storied house with a courtyard, surrounded by a stone wall. The address is No. 113 Canal Griboyedova. In this house lived Yosif Notovitch, the publisher of the only Russian liberal newspaper of the 1880s and the 1890s—*Novosti*. Its editorial offices were here.

The story of Notovitch was typical of a certain section of the Jewish intelligentsia. Son of the rabbi of Kerch, he was born in 1849, converted to Christianity in his youth, graduated from the faculty of law of St. Petersburg University, was awarded the degree of doctor of philosophy, and became a journalist. After the Revolution of 1905 he left Russia. The author G. Rosenzweig recalls that *Novosti* was very popular with the Jews in the Pale of Settlement and was produced in editions of tens of thousands of copies. The Jews thought that Notovitch had some influence in "higher spheres" and "was on chatting terms with the Minister." Many of them appealed to the newspaper for help in the sincere belief that the editor really could help. The author tells the following anecdote.

> A Jew came into the editorial office. An employee of the newspaper asked him:
> "I suppose you've come about a residence permit?"
> The Jew, shaken by such perspicacity, replied:
> "How did you guess? Can Notovitch help me?"
> The clerk decided to joke with the simple provincial:
> "Sure, take out a subscription for the first edition of *Novosti*. As soon as you show your receipt at the police station, they'll frank it with a red stamp." (This, in fact, was for *exit* permits.)
> "And how much is a subscription?"
> "Seventeen rubles."
> The supplicant tried bargaining.
> "I'm a poor man. Can I have it a little cheaper?"
> "All right. Eight rubles for the second edition."
> A short while later the Jew was expelled from the capital, and then a letter from him arrived at the editorial office:
> "Dear Mr. Notovitch, I was expelled from the capital some while ago. You can at least send me your newspaper."
> The victim's request was granted.

Journalism was the most favored occupation of the Jewish intellectuals who turned away from religion. Because it was out of the question to make a career in governmental service, Jews turned to the liberal professions: medicine, law, and, for the most part, journalism. Great Russian literature was, as yet, out of the question as well for those whose parents did not even know the Russian language. One more generation, and among those of Jewish extraction would appear the first great Russian poets, writers, and belletrists who had come from a Jewish milieu: Osip Mandelstam, Boris Pasternak, Sasha Tcherny, Edward Bagritsky, and Isaak Babel.

Jews quickly mastered the art of working for newspapers and magazines. Anti-Semites wrote that the Jews had taken over the newspapers and referred to the press itself as "an invention of the Yids," but the Jewish writers working on Russian newspapers hardly ever openly defended the rights of their co-religionists.

Even in *Voskhod* there once appeared a verse in which the poisonous tongue of the press was likened to vodka and its publisher to a Jewish bootlegger:

Stop! Paper-man, you're a louse!
You and the Jew, you're the same.
The Yid opens up his drink-house,
You open a journal in your name.

Apart from Notovitch we must also mention among the Jewish publishers the great banker Maxim Propper and his son Stanislav, who published for business circles the paper *Stock Exchange News (Birzheviye Vyedomosti)*. People of Propper's type, although they did not actually convert to the Russian Orthodox Church, were almost completely assimilated and quite indifferent to Jewish life. There is nothing surprising in that. Language dictates literary themes. Whoever wants to write well must take an interest in the culture of the people in whose language he or she writes. An intermediate position cannot be a firm one. This is why there are so few literary creations of significance in the Russian language, written by Jews for Jews.

THE NEXT STOP on our excursion is No. 24 Bolshaya Podyacheskaya, the residence of the painter-academician Moisei Maimon. Painting, like sculpture, was a forbidden activity in orthodox Judaism. Let us recall the second of the Ten Commandments: "Thou shalt not make unto thee any graven image or any likeness of anything." This is why Jewish students began to appear in the Academy of Fine Arts later than in other educational institutes. The first Jew to graduate from the academy was Leon Bakhman, who graduated in the 1850s. By the start of the twentieth century there were a number of Jewish artists and sculptors who brought fame to the Russian school of fine arts: Mark Antokolski, Ilya Guenzburg, Isaac Levitan, Leon Bakst, Marc Chagall, and Natan Altman.*

The new generation tried to interpret the (second) commandment in the spirit of the time — only as a prohibition against creating new idols; but as a rule, their aspiration to devote themselves to painting or to sculpture was very much frowned upon by their parents. The example of Maimon is of special interest to us because, although he transgressed the traditional prohibition, in his creative artistry he always remained faithful to national tradition. With some justification he can perhaps be called a Jewish artist.

Moisei Lvovitch Maimon was born in 1860 in one of the "shtetls" of the Pale of Settlement. In 1880 he moved to St. Petersburg and entered the Academy of Fine Arts. In his memoirs he tells us that there were only three Jews in the course. At first nobody in the academy persecuted them. Some of the more liberal teachers even took them under their wings. Yet, in general, the atmosphere of liberalism was rapidly changing at that time with the tyrannical policies of Alexander III, and the young men began to encounter harassment, both from their fellow students and from the administrators. The poverty-stricken young student from the provinces had to live on his own in St. Petersburg, without money, family, or the intense Jewish life and mutual aid that was characteristic of the shtetl. So he looked for and became friendly with a family

* Their dates were Antokolski, 1843–1902; Guenzburg, 1859–1939; Levitan, 1860–1900; Bakst, 1866–1924; Chagall, 1887–1985; and Altman, 1889–1970. Bakst's name was Lev Samoilovitch.

Moisei Maimon's painting, The Marranos

of similar provincial, poor Jews and went to them for warmth, for conversation, and for spending the Sabbath with: in fact, to find company to rub shoulders with.

Once, while he was celebrating the Passover seder with this family, Maimon was witness to a dreadful, but alas typical, scene of that time. The doors of the flat were burst open and in charged police, demanding to see the permits allowing them to live in St. Petersburg. Not satisfied that the papers were completely in order, the police took the old man away there and then and ordered the rest of the family to get out of town immediately. The young man walked away from the broken up festival in a state of shock. On his way back through the deserted streets to his own quarters, he made a resolution that he would not rest until he had painted a picture on the subject of the scene he had just witnessed. Some time would elapse before he achieved his objective.

Maimon graduated from the academy in 1887 with a gold medal and the academic rank of "Classic Artist First Grade," for his picture *The Death of Ivan the Terrible,* and he soon acquired fame as an outstanding portrait painter. His craftsmanship grew, and with it the number of commissions—and his income.

The year 1893 was designated for a painting competition at the academy, and 1892 marked the four hundredth anniversary of that tragic event in Jewish history—the expulsion of the Jews from Spain. Maimon made up his mind to submit to the competition a picture that would portray the tragedy of the Jewish situation to his contemporaries.

The theme of his proposed subject, "The Marranos and the Inquisition in Spain," did not arouse any suspicion. Maimon was even given his own large studio workshop in the academy. But before getting down to work he toured Spain, Portugal, Holland, and England to gather material. In those times pictures were not created in one day. The conscientious artist was determined to get to know the country, clothing, furniture, tableware, and elements of the interior of medieval Spain; to make a large number of sketches; and to read historical works on the period. The authenticity of the representation, the true portrayal of details, were valued highly at that time by the classical school. By the time he returned, the artist could already visualize the composition of his picture and the first draft sketches were prepared.

A reproduction of this picture in the *Yevreiskaya Entsiklopedia* shows the interior of a wealthy home of Marranos of late fifteenth century Spain. The family, whose members are dressed as Spanish grandees, has gathered at the table to celebrate the Passover. At the head of the table is a gray-haired old man, with a strong-willed face, dressed all in white. Police officers and members of the Inquisition have just burst into the room. On their faces, all the unfortunate secret Jews clearly show they know the fate awaiting them: burning at the stake.

The picture was only half finished and the time for acceptance of entries was drawing near, but the artist had not yet found a model for the most important figure—the old Marrano. Then, at a society reception, he saw the face he had been looking for. A well-known artillery general, Arnoldi, had just come into the room; he was adorned with medals, orders, decorations, and badges of distinction, a hero of several wars. There was a considerable distance between the artist and this senior army officer, but Maimon did manage to introduce himself and even to persuade the general to sit as a model for the picture. The old man came frequently to the studio and became very interested in the subject of the painting.

On the day of his last visit, Maimon finally learned why General Arnoldi had agreed to sit for him. It seems that the old artillery officer had been born a Jew, but as a young boy he had been pressed into the army in the reign of Nicholas I as a cantonist and baptized; he knew almost nothing about his people or their culture. He remembered only that there was a Pesach and a Yom Kippur. He told Maimon: "I agreed to help you because you had seen in me the Jewish soul that I have been bearing for nigh on eighty years, although I carry a cross round my neck."*

---

* The system of "rekruchina" introduced in 1827: At the age of eighteen, a specified number of Jews were to be drafted for twenty-five years' army service, but they could be and often were taken at the age of twelve (or even less) for several years of preparatory training, during which every means (including flogging and torture) was used to make them convert to Christianity. Many did so convert, and many committed suicide.

НОВЫЯ ЕВРЕЙСКІЯ КНИГИ:

Х.-Н. БЯЛИКЪ
Пѣсни и Поэмы.

ТЕОДОРЪ ГЕРЦЛЬ
фельетоны.

Вл. ЖАБОТИНСКІЙ
фельетоны.

С.-ПЕТЕРБУРГЪ   1913 годъ.

Leaflet printed by the Vostok publishing house, 1913

Х.Н. БЯЛИКЪ
Пѣсни и Поэмы
авторизованный пер.
съ еврейскаго языка и введеніе
Вл. Жаботинскаго

ПЕТРОГРАДЪ
1917

Cover of Songs and Poems by Chaim Nachman Bialik, translated by Vladimir Jabotinsky

The Marranos was a resounding success at the academy exhibition, and for this work Maimon, at the young age of thirty-three was elected to the academy. The academy decided to purchase the canvas for the Alexander III Museum, but this was not ratified because the Church protested against its alleged "anti-Christian content." The picture then went on tour in Vilna, Warsaw, and other towns in Russia and Europe. People flocked to see it. Everyone saw in it just what the artist wanted to portray: his own fate.

Maimon did several other works on Jewish themes. One well-known picture is his *Return to the Motherland,* in which he shows a wounded Jewish soldier of the Russian Army returning in 1905 from the war with Japan to find his home burned to the ground.

☐ BEHIND TEATRALNAYA PLOSHCHAD and Kryukov Canal at the corner of ulitsa Soyuza Petchatnichov (formerly Torgovaya) and Lermontovsky Prospekt (formerly Bolshaya Masterskaya) in the early 1910s was the book publisher and bookstore Vostok (The East), located at No. 11 Torgovaya. Here one could also buy the new *Voskhod.* There were, of course, other Jewish book publishers and booksellers in St. Petersburg, such as the bookstore Ezro at No. 52 Sadovaya Street. However, Vostok is of special interest to us because its activity reflects the birth of a new direction in Jewish public life, namely Palestinophilia and then Zionism.

In 1882 a booklet was published in Berlin, in German, by a well-known physician and public figure from Odessa, Lev Semyonovitch Pinsker. It was called "Auto-emancipation" and was the rallying call of a Russian Jew to his fellow Jews. It was very soon translated into Russian. In this work Pinsker declared that the Jews could not attain real equality of rights among other peoples simply by the gaining of civil rights. Pinsker maintained that the only way to a solution of the "Jewish Problem" was the creation of their own Jewish state, and he called upon Jews to take an active part in building their own future.

"'Now or never!'—that must be our slogan!" he wrote. "Woe to our descendants, woe to the memory of the Jews of today if we do not utilize the present time! . . . Help yourselves and God will help you!" Pinsker's ideas, reinforced by the new pogroms and the rise of political Zionism in the West (Herzl's book *The Jewish State* was published in 1895, and the first Zionist Congress took place in Basel in 1897) found a powerful response among Jewish intellectuals in Russia.

I have before me a leaflet of the book publisher Vostok for 1913. It is advertising three books. First, a collection of verses by Chaim Nachman Bialik, *Songs and Poems* translated by Vladimir Jabotinsky; then, *Pamphlets* by Theodor Herzl with an introduction by Jabotinsky; and finally a book of essays by

Jabotinsky himself, containing all his important articles and speeches for the previous eight years. All three books were published in hardcover editions on quality paper. The first two have photographs of the author: the distinguished-looking, bearded man with a strong face and folded arms is Herzl; the restless intellectual in a somewhat strained pose, with a powerful forehead and round, but lined, features is Bialik.

The magazine *Sovremennik* (The Contemporary) wrote about Bialik:

Great joy has fallen to the lot of the Muse of Poetry such as she has not known for a long time. We refer to that poetry that is common to all in no matter what tongue or what dialect it is first pronounced. Now its songs have been sung in the ancient, but vibrantly live tongue of the Hebrew people and their singer is Ch. N. Bialik; that name is worth noting for it belongs to a true poet.

Bialik is a prophetic singer for his people, and for us, people of another race, of other customs, he is first and foremost a remarkable artist with words.

In the Year Book of the newspaper *Ryetch* (Speech), Kornei Tchukovsky wrote:

How can one not call to mind for example that outstanding book of Jabotinsky's *The Songs and Poems of Chaim Bialik,* in which, with obvious tension, under strain, almost beyond his strength, the gifted publicist-journalist tries to hand on with the vigour of his verses, the passionate Biblical poetry of the new prophet of Israel.

In fact, the burning love of Bialik for his people transformed him into a poet-prophet, into a poet-warrior, fighting not only the outward slavery of the Jews but also their inner spiritual enslavement, striving to bring them closer to spiritual Zionism. With his denunciatory verses he hoped for the spiritual renaissance of his people.

Like withered grass, like a great fallen oak,
A decaying corpse, thus perished my folk.
The voice of th'Almighty cried out from on high —
But the people heard not, paid no heed to the cry. . . .

The slave sleeps. He's forgot how to rouse at the call,
Only the cane or the whip can stir him at all,
To the fanfare of trumpets of the battle at dawn,
The dead body wakes not, the corpse's slumber's not torn.

Let us examine one more review, this time of Theodor Herzl's *Pamphlets* in the literary supplement to *Niva* (Cornfield) of 1913:

The famous motivator and leader of the contemporary Jewish national movement has shown in this book another side of himself, for which his name is less well known. If the name of Herzl was not so closely connected with Zionism, his pamphlets alone would save him from oblivion. This is no brazen-faced gossip, ignorant of everything, to which the journalistic trivialities of our day have accustomed us, and which has compromised the very literary genre of pamphlets. . . . Herzl's pamphlets are the quiet, intimate, conversation of a man of the world, who is also a wise man. On them all there lies the imprint of a deep, sincere, cultured mind, of an excellent, but not overly-heavy education, and a kindly, clear soul. . . . It would be difficult to find such an affectionate friend, such an understanding, witty conversationalist.

You will already have noticed that a link for the three booklets advertised is the name of Vladimir Jabotinsky; first as translator, then as the writer of the introduction, and finally as author of the book himself. This is the man who later became one of the leaders of the Jewish national movement.

Vladimir (Zeev) Yevgeniyevitch Jabotinsky (1880–1940) was born in Odessa, where he went to secular high school (Gymnasium), before studying law at the universities of Rome and Berne. He began his literary career at the age of nineteen and was first published in the Russian liberal press *Rus* (the ancient name for Russia), in *Nasha Zhizn* (Our Life), and then, becoming attached to Zionism, in Jewish periodicals. In 1902 two of his plays were presented at the Odessa Theater. The *Yevreiskaya Entsiklopedia* writes of him as an energetic party activist and an excellent orator and journalist. One does not have to share the views of Jabotinsky in order to recognize the scale of his personality and his energy from political activity to the most difficult of poetic translations.

THERE WERE THREE Russian Jewish magazines called *Rassvet* (Dawn). The first was published in Odessa in 1860, another in St. Petersburg from 1879. The third *Rassvet* was a weekly that came out on January 1, 1907, in St. Petersburg, and was inclined toward support for Zionism.

To see where the editorial offices were we need only to go a little way along Torgovaya ulitsa to No. 17, although in 1913 the offices moved to No. 11. *Rassvet* replaced several magazines published one after the other from 1904, as each one was suppressed by the tsarist censor: first *Yevreiskaya Zhizn* (Jewish Life), then *Khronika Yevreiskoi Zhizni* (Chronicles of Jewish Life), then *Yevreisky Narod* (The Jewish People). The editors were, in succession, M. Rivkin, I. V. Sorin, A. D. Idelson, and others who devoted themselves to the development of questions related to Zionist theory and practice. In this weekly magazine, the editors and their authors fought assimilation, discussed the practical problems of colonization in Palestine, carried on disputes with the Jewish socialist party — the Bund — and debated internal Zionist matters. They also sometimes published authors who held other opinions, such as Simon Dubnow. Among the frequent contributors to *Rassvet* were D. Pasmanik and Jabotinsky. The latter wrote an article in 1909, "New Turkey and Our Perspectives," devoted to a clarification of the national movement in Turkey in relation to Zionist aspirations.

In one of its 1912 issues, *Rassvet* published the financial accounts of the Palestine Committee based in Odessa. The figures showed that for the three previous years the committee had collected 231,000 rubles, of which, for 1910, Odessa had provided 16,000; Moscow, 13,000; Warsaw, 9,000; Lodz, 10,000; and St. Petersburg, 8,700. The money thus collected was used for the purchase of land in Palestine, for building work there, and for the needs of emigration.

No. 17 Torgovaya was known before *Rassvet* came there; it had in fact been the editorial office of the first Hebrew journal in Russia, *Ha-Melitz* (The Advocate), founded in 1860 by the well-known Jewish journalist and public figure, Alexander Zederbaum. *Ha-Melitz* was close to the original popular intelligentsia and later tended toward Palestinophilia, but it also included literary writings by Yeduha-Leib Gordon, who was its editor from 1886 to 1889. At the beginning of the twentieth century the editor was L. A. Rabinovitch. It became a daily in the European pattern from the early 1890s. Previously, it had been a weekly.

The house itself belonged to Alexander Guenzburg, banker and industrialist and one of the sons of Baron Horace Guenzburg.

☐ **FROM THE OFFICES** of *Rassvet* we shall walk back a little way along Torgovaya ulitsa. Turning left at Lermontovsky Prospekt, we come to the Leningrad Choral Synagogue at No. 2.

Several Jews, or even several thousand, living in one town do not make a community. A Jewish community implies a number of communal institutions and some form of communal life. This would include a *cheder* (Hebrew and religion classes for children), a burial society, a *pinkas* (community minutes book, or chronicle), a cemetery, a *mikve* (ritual bath), a *shokhet* (ritual slaughterer), and of course a rabbi and a synagogue (or at least a prayer house).

The formal history of the Jewish community in St. Petersburg begins in 1802. A note in the first community chronicle, referred to in the *Yevreiskaya Entsiklopedia,* records the purchase from the Lutherans of a plot of ground in the Volkov cemetery for Jewish burials. The community paid ten rubles for each funeral. The formation of the Jewish community is linked with the name of Nota Notkin, a well-known merchant from Shklov and purveyor to the Russian Army. However, the first chronicle soon comes to a halt as the community itself fell into decline.

When an appreciable group of wealthy and educated Jews arrived in St. Petersburg during the reign of Alexander II (1855–1881), they did not want to mix with those low-ranking officials who were already living in the town and whose rabbi was an ordinary policeman. The merchants founded their own prayer group by the Lions' Bridge and started looking for an educated man to appoint as rabbi. In 1868, on the initiative of David Feinberg, they took steps toward the construction of the Choral Synagogue, and in 1869 permission to proceed was granted.

Lermontovsky Prospekt No. 2, the Leningrad Choral Synagogue

Choosing a site was not easy, as they had to ensure that it was not in close proximity to a local church. The Board of Management was formed on April 1, 1870. Yevsel Guenzburg was elected chairman, and as rabbi they appointed Abram Drabkin, doctor of philosophy, a graduate of the Volozhin Yeshiva, and a pupil of the historian Heinrich Graetz. Among other community leaders, we should remember Horace Guenzburg, David Guenzburg, Mark Warshawski (chairmen of the board before 1917); Rabbis M. G. Olswanger, Z. Lande, David-Tevell Katzenellenbogen, and Moisei Eisenstadt; the poet Yehuda-Leib Gordon; the physician Isaak Dembo; and academics Abram Harkavy, Isaak

TOP LEFT: *Gate decoration at the entrance to the courtyard, Leningrad Choral Synagogue*

BOTTOM LEFT: *The Leningrad Choral Synagogue (an old postcard)*

BELOW: *A corridor inside the Leningrad Choral Synagogue*

Markon, and B. M. Sapotnitsky. After 1917 the chairmen of the Board of Management were Y. B. Eiger, S. M. Lessman, and Gillel Pechersky; the rabbis were M. Gluskin and, up to 1973, A. R. Lubanov.

The authorities did not give permission to build a synagogue until 1874 because the owners of the surrounding rented buildings objected, fearing that the neighborhood would be filled with Jews and the values of their property would drop!

The art critic Vladimir Stassov took part in the discussion on the design of the synagogue. In his article in the *Yevreiskaya Biblioteka,* he suggested that it be built in the Moorish style. Since the Jews had played a considerable part in the upsurge of Arab culture, he thought that North African architecture would be closest to Jewish national aesthetic representation. His advice was accepted, and the project was developed in this style by Professor Shaposhnikov of the Academy of Fine Arts. The interior decoration was the work of Leon Bakhman, the first Jew to enter the Academy of Fine Arts.

The first amendment to the project was rather expensive; it was a reduction of the scale of the facade, done on the order of the government, which feared that the exterior of the synagogue would compete with the Nikolsky Cathedral nearby. Two of the three proposed entrances were turned into windows, to leave only a single entrance; fountains planned for the front courtyard were abandoned. One way and another, the building work dragged on. It was not until 1886 that the smaller prayer house in the courtyard was consecrated, and the main synagogue was not opened till 1893. The total cost of the building came to 500,000 golden rubles. Baron Horace Guenzburg donated a large part of this sum.

The synagogue has a traditional structure. Oriented to the east, it has a ladies' gallery and the *Aron Kodesh* (Holy Ark) with the *Sifrei Torah* (Scrolls of the Law) at the eastern wall. In front of the Ark is the *Ner Tamid* (Eternal Light), a symbolic reminder of the seven-branched candelabrum that was lit by the High Priest in the Temple. The synagogue was built with seating for 1,200. There is a special hall for weddings. The wrought-iron grill in front of the synagogue is the work of Y. G. Gewirtz, the architect responsible for the prayer house at the Preobrazhensky Cemetery.

It was settled that the annual dues payable to the synagogue should be twenty-five rubles per member. Those who paid this sum had the right to vote at the election for the Board of Management and the Auditing Committee, but their number rarely exceeded 300 to 350 by 1910. In 1916 it reached 500. The low membership numbers are principally explained not by the high subscription fee but by the general indifference to religion among many of the wealthier St. Petersburg Jews. In fact, in 1881 the community included 197 Merchants of the First Guild alone, 82 with academic degrees, and 115 with higher education. None of these people could in any way be considered hard up. About one thousand members of the community paid less than the annual subscription; for them, the membership dues were an obstacle.

The Ark in the small prayerhouse at the Leningrad Choral Synagogue

The small prayerhouse, Leningrad Choral Synagogue

The Jewish Communal House, next to the Leningrad Choral Synagogue

⌐ TO CONTINUE WITH our first excursion, the next building in ulitsa Dekabristov, No. 42, a corner house, also belonged to the Jewish community. From 1893 this building housed the public library, which had a large assortment of books on Hebraica and Judaica, the collection of which was made possible with the help of the historian Abram Harkavy. He was a member of the Society for the Spread of Enlightenment among the Jews of Russia (OPE), founded in 1863, and an elder of the synagogue. In this building, there were also vocational schools for Jewish boys and girls (OPE schools).

By January 1, 1902, there were 221 pupils in the boys' school and 208 in the girls' school. Most of the children, because of the poverty of their parents, had free education. The remainder paid between seven and eighteen rubles per annum. The boys' school had nine classes: two preparatory, three elementary, four craft and trade; the girls' school had eight classes: one preparatory, three elementary, and four trade.

In the elementary classes the boys studied divinity (which included prayers and ritual, Pentateuch *(Humash),* and the Prophets), Biblical Hebrew, history of the Jews, Russian language, arithmetic, geography, Russian history, science (physics and nature study), drawing, singing, handwriting (calligraphy), and handicraft. In the craft classes they were taught Scripture *(Pirkei Avot),* Jewish history, Bible study, Russian language, arithmetic, accounting, geometry, physics, elementary technology, sketching and technical drawing, metalwork, and woodwork.

The courses for the girls included divinity (a short course on the most important rituals, the festivals, and basic dogma), biblical Hebrew (mainly reading), translation of the Bible and some prayers, Jewish history, Russian language, arithmetic, geography, Russian history, and specialized subjects such as drawing, reading, handwriting, and needlecraft. Together with preparation for a trade (ladies' tailoring, dressmaking, flower arranging), the girls continued to study Scripture, Jewish history, Russian language, arithmetic, and drawing, and they had talks on nature study.

During out-of-school hours the teachers took the children on trips around the town, visiting museums and factories. They also celebrated the festivals with them. The children took books from the school library, and some of them sang in the synagogue choir. In the summer, sickly children were taken into the country to specially organized camps, where food and medical help were supplied free of charge. The school had professional-style workshops with all the necessary equipment, and its basement contained a working steam engine, specially obtained for educational purposes. Some of those who passed through the school later became craft teachers themselves, either in this school or in the provinces.

At the beginning of 1902 the headmaster of the boys' school was A. M. Konshtam, and the girls' headmistress was P. P. Antokolskaya. Among the teachers of those days were some of the most well-known cultural and educational activists in St. Petersburg: Zinovy Kisselgoff, A. E. Markov, the Yiddish writer M. S. Rivesman, the journalist M. D. Rivkin, A. I. Kongisser, and I. Y. Krasny. The Hebrew teachers included M. M. Tchernin and the future author of the famous Hebrew-Russian dictionary Felix L. Shapiro.

Later, until 1917, the headmaster of the school was Moisei Solomonovitch Yugenburg, formerly head of the model Jewish primary school in Vitebsk. The financial affairs of the school were handled by a board of guardians elected from the members of OPE.

The school's chief advantage was that the examination in craft taken by all pupils on completion of the course gave them the right to live outside the Pale of Settlement. However, although the right to receive education at the school was guaranteed by law, here too the children encountered difficulty. In practice, for each child brought from the western provinces to study, the management of the society had to apply for a residence permit, submitting individual tearful requests to the Ministry of the Interior. It seemed as if there did not exist any law permitting the learning of a trade outside the Pale of Settlement. This situation was zealously maintained by the government — especially by the minister of the interior, Vyacheslav von Plehve — as it was afraid of a flood of revolutionaries arriving in the capital in the guise of guardians of the Jewish children.

After 1917 this building housed No. 5 Jewish National School (directed by T. Y. Zeitlin), which in 1931 was moved to No. 1-a Matveyeva Pere'ulok. Its name was then changed to No. 34 Fully Jewish National School. It existed until 1933.

LEAVING THE SYNAGOGUE, we go back along ulitsa Dekabristov as far as Kryukov Canal. Let us look at a group of houses along the canal between the Moika River and ulitsa Dekabristov. All of them were obviously built in the last sixty years, although most of the buildings in this district are much older. In fact, from a historical point of view we are looking at an empty site, as at one time the only thing here was an investigation prison — the Litovsky Zamok, or Lithuanian Castle.

Imagine the two-story prison complex that was built according to a project of I. Starov and had its main gate facing the ulitsa Dekabristov. Built as a military barracks in 1787, during the reign of Catherine II, at the end of the eighteenth century and during the first decades of the nineteenth century, a Lithuanian regiment was stationed here; hence its name. It became a prison from the 1820s, holding mostly common criminals, and from shortly before 1917 it was a military prison.

Following the example of the Bastille, the Litovsky Zamok was set on fire during the February 1917 Revolution, together with the building of the Circuit Court (now the KGB Leningrad office) on Liteiny Prospekt, and remained in ruins until 1927. In the Litovsky Zamok, Yehuda-Leib (Lev Osipovitch) Gordon, the well-known Hebrew poet and Maskil, was imprisoned for six months. An elder of the St. Petersburg community and secretary of the OPE, Gordon had been arrested following a false denunciation to the authorities, written by his opponents in connection with the election of a new rabbi in 1879. Gordon got off comparatively light — a year in exile in the Olonyetsk Guberniya. Thanks to the efforts of friends and relatives, he was then able to return to St. Petersburg.

The poet's recollections of this period of detention are of some interest. He and his son were placed in a cell with another prisoner, a student. It was a relatively liberal time, and this was reflected in the prison conditions. During the day, while the cells were being tidied up, the prisoners were allowed out into the corridor and could talk with each other. Once a day they exercised in the prison yard. After morning tea the overseer visited the cells and wrote down what each one wanted to buy from the nearby shop, and before supper the food that had been purchased was brought to the prisoners. Gordon writes that on the third day of his imprisonment his brother was able to bring him some oranges. His dinner was always brought from a nearby kosher restaurant, as he refused to eat the cutlets prepared by the prison cook. Of course, such concessions were available only to those who possessed the necessary financial means, which fortunately Gordon did have. The whole family had been arrested at the time, and Gordon had taken with him all the ready cash and valuables in the house. As a result, not only was nothing stolen, but his life in prison and on the journey into exile was thereby considerably eased.

☐ ALONG THE ODD-NUMBERED side of ulitsa Dekabristov we now reach the square where today stands the sports complex of the Lesgaft Institute. Near it in a house, No. 39 (now rebuilt), there was a theater of the famous Russian actress Vera Kommissarzhevskaya. In this theater from March 30 to April 30, 1908, the popular Jewish troupe of Abraham Isaac Kaminsky from Warsaw held its performances on tour.

In tsarist Russia the Jewish theater had hardly developed, mainly because from 1883 it was forbidden by law to put on shows in Yiddish. But as soon as the prohibition was lifted or relaxed, as in 1905, talented theatrical troupes appeared. Kaminsky's theater was very popular in Warsaw and has deservedly taken its place in the history of the Jewish theater. His wife Esther Rochil and their daughter Ida Kaminskaya were recognized as top-grade actresses. The arrival of the Kaminsky Theater in St. Petersburg coincided with the tour of the famous Moscow Arts Theater. Stanislavsky, Kachalov, Moskvin, and other actors from this troupe attended one of the Yiddish performances and after the show went backstage to praise the performers.

☐ OUR NEXT STOP is No. 50 ulitsa Dekabristov, former home of two Jewish organizations: the quarterly *Ha-Kedem* (The East) and the Society of Lovers of Ancient Hebrew Language (Hovevei Sfat Ever). We have already seen how great a contribution the Haskala made in the development of the study of Jewish history and the Hebrew language. Hebrew became, to the exclusion of all else, the conversational and literary language of the Maskilim. Up to now it had been used almost entirely only as the language of prayer. In half a century, secular literature in Hebrew had progressed from the imitative romanticism of Avraham Mapu* to the brilliant versification of Chaim Nahman Bialik. Not only were magazines and newspapers appearing in Hebrew, but also — and most important — people were speaking it in their everyday lives. The Society

---

* Abraham Mapu (born in Kovno in 1808, died in 1867) was the creator of the modern Hebrew novel. On a short visit to St. Petersburg in 1861, he made his first acquaintance with opera, which much appealed to his romantic imagination.

of the Lovers of the Ancient Hebrew Language had as its aim the dissemination among Jews of a deep knowledge of the language and the broad development of Hebrew literature.

The chairman of the society was David Guenzburg, his deputy was Lev Katzenelson, and among its active supporters were Isaak Markon, Abram Idelson, and I. I. Margolin. At first the society existed as a subcommittee of OPE, and only in 1907 did it become an independent organization. The society's concern was to provide the appropriate standard of tuition in the cheders, the yeshivas, the Talmud Torahs, and the private schools. It published Gordon's writings, as well as those of P. Smolenskin, I. Erter, and other writers; it subsidized a pedagogic journal in Palestine; and it arranged for the creation of model cheders, schools, and Jewish libraries. The members of the society undertook to speak to each other only in Hebrew.

By 1910 the society had about sixty branches in a number of towns, including Warsaw, Lodz, Yekaterinoslav (now called Dniepropetrovsk), and Bialystok. The quarterly *Ha-Kedem,* under its editors I. Markon and A. Zarzovsky, began to appear in 1907 and published articles on Jewish lore and semitology, not only in Hebrew but also in European languages. The journal published the results of research into ancient Hebrew texts, as well as articles on ancient Jewish history and so on. In general *Ha-Kedem* and the Society of Lovers of Ancient Hebrew Language acted in mutual cooperation with each other, and it is not surprising that often the same people worked in both.

Here it would seem appropriate to mention one of the main activists of the society and of *Ha-Kedem*—Counsellor at Court I. Yu. Markon, who lived with his family in house No. 50 in a large five-room apartment with a balcony on the first floor.

Isaak Yulyevitch Markon was born in Rybinsk (now renamed Andropov) in 1875. He graduated from the faculty of Oriental studies of St. Petersburg University, where he also defended his predoctoral thesis. After marrying a daughter of Vydrin, the well-known Talmudist and relative of the banker Polyakov, Markon established both his financial position and his personal standing in the St. Petersburg community, becoming an elder of the synagogue and participating in banking transactions.

Markon always remained attached, however, to his vocation of Oriental studies and Jewish history. Many communal projects in this direction found him taking the main initiative, such as *Ha-Kedem,* the Society of Lovers of Ancient Hebrew Language, teaching the courses of Oriental studies organized by David Guenzburg, and working with Hebrew manuscripts in the Imperial Public Library. Markon was phenomenally erudite in Hebrew studies. This may be why his own scientific attainments were so modest. It used to be said that his knowledge and memory were so great that if he started to write he wrote in quotations.

In the 1920s Markon became professor of Jewish history in Minsk, then emigrated to Germany in 1926. Toward the end of his life he worked at the Montefiore College in Ramsgate in England.

AS WE CONTINUE further along ulitsa Dekabristov to where it crosses Macleana Prospekt, we see that No. 60, which is of interest to us, is no longer extant and that in its place is a new building. But because the organization that was housed in the former building was of great significance for the Jews at the turn of the century, we must stop here for a moment. The organisation was the Jewish Colonization Association (ICA).

We already know that in the 1880s Russian Jewry once again (for the nth time) had to decide, where do we go from here? The situation in the country was steadily getting worse. Many could see no prospects of a normal human life in the foreseeable future in the country of their birth. The only alternative was to emigrate.

But where should they go, and how could they do it?

A steady but small stream of young people, inspired with the ideals of Zionism, were making their way to Palestine. A much larger portion of those who left went where they thought it would be easier to settle and to obtain the means of subsistence: to America. In 1892 alone, seventy-six thousand Jewish emigrants went from European Russia to the United States of America.

Overwhelmed by the pogroms as well as by the new anti-Jewish laws and regulations that began to pour out in a flood after 1882, and following the horrors of the mass expulsions from Moscow and other towns in 1891, the Jews of Russia filled the border towns of the country and made their way in massive streams to the capitals of Western Europe. Believing in the Talmudic precept "A change of place brings a change of luck" *(meshanne makom, meshanne mazal)*, people hoped that elsewhere — anywhere — they would be allowed to earn their daily crust of bread without the constant fear of what the morrow might bring.

It must be pointed out that, for a very large number, emigration at that time was no easy matter. For the Jew in the shtetl to get to America seemed as hard as getting to the moon, with his extreme poverty, very large family, lack of any professional training or education, and the traditional age-old fear of everything on earth. Moreover, nobody in the West was waiting for him with open arms.

Government policies openly encouraged emigration, however, as a means of solving the Jewish problem. To the annual report for 1888 of the governor of Podolsk, in which it stated that "the eviction from the Empire of the Jewish proletariat would be extremely desirable," Alexander III had added the comment "And even very beneficial."

In this situation the establishment in London in 1891 of the Jewish Colonization Association (ICA) was more timely than ever before. ICA was the brainchild and the creation of the German Jewish philanthropist and multimillionaire Baron de Hirsch, who had made his wealth from the construction of railways in Ottoman, Turkey. The Baron had never been deaf when approached for charity, and he became even more generous after the death of his only son. When he attempted to alleviate the situation of the Jews of Eastern Europe, he quickly realized that in Russia this was impossible.

On Hirsch's instructions, his experts looked for a country where large groups of Jews might be able to live secure lives, with no restrictions on their rights, working in industry, or preferably in agriculture. They unanimously chose Argentina. ICA issued 20,000 shares for a total of two million sterling. Baron de Hirsch himself purchased 19,990 of these shares.

The St. Petersburg branch of ICA was opened in 1893. At the request of Hirsch himself, it was headed by Horace Guenzburg. Although Guenzberg himself did not sympathize with emigration, he did not feel it was possible to remain indifferent to this mass movement.

The Council of Ministers supported the initiative of ICA, which proposed to take out 3,250,000 Jewish emigrants of Russia during the next twenty-five years. It was agreed to give the emigrants exit documents without any charge and to release them from obligatory military service on condition that they did not return. Later, the council established favorable rates of railway travel for emigrants, and the minister for maritime affairs even proposed to pay several rubles for each emigrant in order to speed up the departure of the Jews.

The news of the philanthropy of Baron de Hirsch caused tens of thousands of people to get on the move. Nevertheless, although considerable sums of money were expended on resettlement, the effect of the association's activity was significantly less than had been anticipated. In the first three years only six thousand Jews arrived in Argentina, half of whom settled in Buenos Aires. As regards the agricultural settlements, the following is the impression they made on the correspondent of *Voskhod,* who wrote in 1894:

> There are many difficulties such as locusts, drought etc. The administrators of the Association know nothing whatsoever about agriculture and the colonists themselves are just as ignorant. The settlers declare that they are ready to do any work and do not consider it necessary to have any training, and they have no interest in financial matters as they do not fully appreciate their economic-legal position vis-à-vis the ICA. The worst workers of all are the Hasidim, the best are the emigrants from Lithuania. It is most difficult for former "intellectuals" (merchants, businessmen, commission agents). The father—a former merchant—ploughs the soil, his son—a former student—tends the sheep, the daughter, who had been a pianist, milks the cow, the mother, a middle-class lady, works in the kitchen: they have all been torn away from their accustomed habitat, and live in a rancho, a hut with walls made of beaten clay and gravel, with a thatched roof and no ceiling or floor.

Just the same, in spite of the difficulties, ICA managed to relieve the sufferings of emigration for some tens of thousands of people. In 1906 alone, about nineteen thousand emigrants took advantage of its services; in 1909, thirty-three thousand. Later ICA broadened the horizon of its activity and began to help emigration to all countries, including America and Palestine, provided professional training and education for Jews, and undertook very many other charitable activities.

WE SHALL VISIT two more places of interest to us on this excursion. House No. 140 on Griboyedova Canal Embankment (Naberezhnaya), a two-storied red-brick building, was the home of the Society for the Provision of Assistance to Poor Jews (OPB), a cheap Jewish restaurant, and a *mikva* (ritual bath) for the poor.

Since earliest times, charity *(gemilut hasadim)* has been one of the most important elements of Jewish life. Charity is considered to assume the following forms:

Providing hospitality for and feeding of the hungry
Providing clothing and footwear for the poor
Visiting and taking care of the sick
Burying the dead and attending funerals
Consoling the mourners
Redeeming prisoners of war
Arranging marriages for poor girls

The Society for the Relief of Poor Jews, situated on the Griboyedov Canal, No. 140 (from 1910 to 1917)

Charity has been looked upon by Jewish law not as an act of good-will but as an act of religious duty for everyone. We know that according to Mosaic Law, charity was compulsory: the edge of a field was to be unreaped and left for the poor to harvest; fallen ears of corn were not to be gathered but similarly left for the poor; once in seven years the land was to be left uncultivated and anything that grew on it in the fallow year by itself was to be left for common use.

The prophets pronounced the theme of charity even more clearly: "This fast that I have chosen (saith the Lord), is it not to share thy bread with the hungry, to bring into thy house the poor that have no shelter? When thou seest the naked is it not that thou shouldst clothe him . . . ?" (Isaiah 58:7)

In the Bible and the Talmud there is frequent reference to the importance of the inner feeling of a person at the moment of his act of charity. The needy should be helped with a willing heart, so as not to offend his personal dignity. In general, an act of charity is considered to be just as important for he who gives as it is necessary for he who takes. A Roman nobleman once asked Rabbi Akiva, "If your God so loves the poor, why does he not take care of them himself?" To which Rabbi Akiva replied: "In order to grant grace to the giver of charity."

Today it is somewhat difficult for us — here in Leningrad — to imagine the inner lives of our forebears, related to the feeling of the daily duty to come to the aid of one's neighbor.

The OPB society was formed in April 1907. Previously, the granting of help to poor Jews in the capital was in the hands of various boards of trustees, such as the Committee of Bikur Holim* (annual expenditure 3,500 rubles) and the Committee of Tsedoko-G'deilo† (2,500 rubles). Both these committees were accountable to the financial management of the St. Petersburg Synagogue. In addition, a special committee provided help for the Pesah festival, and there was also the Jewish People's Dining Room, which existed as an independent establishment.

Internal disagreements often made the work of the charities difficult to carry out and led to complaints of cheating, extortion, embezzlement, and professional beggars. The OPB was created to combat these evils and to bring some measure of control and planned economy over the charity that was donated. This act brought all the Jewish charitable institutions of the capital into one single body.

Baron Horace Guenzburg was elected chairman of the Board of Management of the society, and his son David was elected deputy chairman. The sixteen members of the board, the chairman among them, included B. A.

* *Bikur Holim,* a Hebrew phrase meaning "Visiting the Sick," is used for institutions such as hospitals and clinics.
  † *Tsedoko Gdoilo* is a Yiddish form of Hebrew words meaning "Charity is great"; that is, it is a great thing to perform charity.

Kamenka (finance), I. S. Soloveitchik, V. Z. Friedlyansky, and A. M. Lessman. The society was granted premises in the communal building at No. 140 Yeka-terinensky Canal, which also housed a cheap restaurant, a ritual bath *(mikva),* and a few apartments, the rent from which brought the society a small income. Later, the society opened an almshouse on Vassilevsky Ostrov.

The scale of activity of the society during the first year of its existence was very impressive. By the end of 1917, OPB was paying 213 pensions to old, sick, and crippled Jews. These payments averaged 916 rubles per month, in addition to individual single grants of payment to 981 persons, a total of 5,309 rubles for the year. For needy Jews in the hospital (especially new arrivals), the society provided an improved quality of kosher food, including tea, sugar, wine, white bread, eggs, milk, chicken, and soup. About twenty Jewish pharmacies in the town provided medicines to the poor free of charge or at half-price against prescriptions from the society. Moreover, sick people were given monetary help, either in the form of one-time payments or on a regular basis. OPB also helped Jews from other towns who were in St. Petersburg without any means, to enable them to return home, and it also sent aid to Jews detained in prisons. Each person in this last category was accorded three rubles for each Jewish festival.

The representatives of the society took every possible step to ensure that the help they provided really went directly to those in need and was not subject to cheating or fraud. If, for example, a person asked for help to pay for winter fuel, or for rent, the society preferred to pay the bill and not to hand cash over to the individual himself. And for provincial Jews leaving St. Petersburg, the society bought the train tickets and only handed them over at the railway station immediately prior to the departure of the train.

The cheap Jewish People's Restaurant had been in existence since 1879. At the time of its transfer to the control of the OPB, it had already for some time been run properly by the lady trustees: Baroness Matilda Guenzburg, V. A. Guryan, A. A. Soloveitchik, and A. R. Nisselovitch. Lunches were available daily from 12 noon to 3 P.M. and twice on Fridays—ordinary lunch in the morning and a special Sabbath dinner in the evening. The meals were of three grades: a ten-kopeck meal (soup with meat, buckwheat, or kasha, and a pound of bread) was sold for six kopecks; a twenty-kopeck meal (soup, roast beef, bread) went for fifteen kopecks; a thirty-kopeck meal (a twenty-kopeck meal plus fish or stewed fruit) cost twenty-five kopecks.

On Fridays and Saturdays Jewish soldiers were given free meals, and on festival days all comers received free meals. In all, during 1907, the restaurant supplied 33,000 subsidized and 23,000 free meals for 8,768 rubles. In that same year there were 630 names on the society's list of donors.

At the beginning of the twentieth century the number of Jewish charitable organizations in Russia was several thousand, several in each one of the 1,300 to 1,400 towns, villages, and shtetls of the Pale of Settlement. The importance of philanthropy increased during times of war, revolution, emigration, and pogroms. A small instance is that during the Russo-Japanese War of 1904, Jewish soldiers in Manchuria were sent kosher food and matzot from St. Petersburg.

The entire Jewish population of Russia could, in essence, be categorized as belonging to one of two groups: givers of charity and recipients of charity. According to data in the *Yevreiskaya Entsiklopedia,* in 1909, of 150,000 Jews in Odessa, there were 60,000 in the latter group. Of 11,000 Jews in Kharkov, 4,000 were receiving charity, and in Mogilev, 43 percent were. In Minsk, the percentage was even higher.

☐ THE FINAL STOP on this excursion is No. 123 Sadovaya ulitsa. Here, at the end of the last century, lived an outstanding lawyer, communal leader, public benefactor, and publicist who at that time was an assistant barrister. His name was Oscar Osipovitch (Israel Yosifovitch) Grusenberg.

Oscar Grusenberg was born in 1866 in Yekaterinoslav (now Dnieprope-trovsk). On graduating in 1889 from the faculty of juridical sciences at the University of Kiev, he was offered the opportunity to qualify for the professorial examination for the chair of criminal law. However, the young man declined the offer because he would have had to change his religion, and he did not want to start his career with a step that he considered to be, at the very least, unethical.

Grusenberg moved to St. Petersburg and very quickly became distinguished as a talented defense counsel, with a deep knowledge of criminal law. However, because of the quota system limiting the number of Jews on the legal list of advocates, the Ministry of Justice would not confirm him as a barrister until 1905, when he was already thirty-nine years old.

Apart from his appearances in purely criminal cases, the young Grusenberg gained considerable fame for himself by acting as the defense counsel for a number of prominent writers and public figures, such as Gorky, Korolenko, Anensky, Poshekhonov, Milyukov, Petrozhitsky, and Tchukovsky. The times were such that there were many trials, and for good advocates work in Russia in those days provided a comfortable living.

Starting from the 1890s, Grusenberg acted in many trials for industrial and agrarian lawsuits. He headed the team of defense lawyers in the case *The Soviet of Workers and Deputies of St. Petersburg* and was defense counsel in the *Vyborg Appeal* in the Senate.* The Armenian intellectuals approached him over the most acute nationalist cases. In spite of the generally accepted public opinion that it was inadvisable to use Jewish lawyers to defend Jewish cases, Oscar Grusenberg did participate in all the major Jewish trials, starting from *The Case of the Minsk Pogrom* on to *The Case of the Kishinev Pogrom,* The

* After the First Duma had been dissolved, the majority of the deputies, meeting in Vyborg, issued an appeal to the public not to pay taxes and not to go into the army.

Присяжный Повѣренный
О. О. ГРУЗЕНБЕРГЪ.

Oscar (Izrail) Grusenberg
(from an old postcard)

Dashevsky case, the David Blondes case, and others. But Grusenberg achieved his greatest fame in the celebrated trial for the Beilis case, in which he was leading defense counsel. This case, with its traditional accusation against the Jews of ritual murder "blood-libel," is worth examining a little more closely.

So much has been written in anti-Semitic literature about Jewish ritual murders that one is almost compelled to ask oneself whether it is not perhaps true that somewhere within the hidden depths of the Talmud, or perhaps in the Apocrypha, it is stated that Jews must bake in the matza the blood of Christian children, and if we ourselves have never come across it, perhaps nevertheless there is some secret sect among the Jews.

The blood-libel was believed to be true by Martin Luther, Nicholas I, the famous Russian poet Gavril Derzhavin, and other famous personalities. The first accusation of ritual murder was in England in the Middle Ages (William of Norwich in 1144), and since then this dreadful fabrication has constantly pursued the Jewish communities of Europe, giving rise to real legal trials against real living people. In Russia alone, without having to think deeply, one can immediately call to mind the trials at Velizh, Saratov, and Kutaisi, as well as other instances. And, of course, the notorious Beilis case.

On March 20, 1911, the body of a Christian boy, Andrei Yushchinsky, was discovered in a suburb of Kiev. All the evidence indicated that the child had been killed by a gang of thieves led by a woman, Vera Tcheberyak, because he had threatened to tell on them. Almost at once the Kiev branch of the Union of the Russian People organized a mass demonstration against Jewish ritual murder. The situation was exploited by the government as an opportunity to distract public attention from revolutionary agitation and use the Jews as scapegoats, not for the first time. The public prosecutor of Kiev was instructed to gather as much evidence as he could of the guilt of the Jews. At the same time, there was a secret instruction to find the real murderers, which was done, but the result of this second (secret) investigation was kept under lock and key by the police until 1917.

The official case revolved around the scenario of a medieval nightmare. Two medical professors were bribed to give evidence that the blood had been drained from the body of the child while he was still alive. The Jewish manager of a brick factory, Mendel Beilis, was arrested and charged with ritual murder. Every available means of interrogation and duress was employed to persuade him to confess his guilt. When, in spite of this, he refused to admit his guilt, his cellmates gave evidence to the investigator that Beilis had supposedly confessed to them. They even stooped to use evidence given by Vera Tcheberyak herself, a woman with a long list of crimes to her record.

By the middle of 1912 the obvious absurdity of the investigation and the accusation had become clear to every normal and thinking person. The case aroused a powerful wave of protest in the West and then inside the country. Even the Dreyfus case had relied on more probable-seeming evidence.

Toward the end of 1912, a liberal journalist, Brazul-Brushkovsky, began a private investigation. He found the real killers; that is, he revealed what for some time had already been known perfectly well by the authorities and the Ministry of the Interior. When he published the results of his private investigation, some of the leading advocates in Kiev and in St. Petersburg publicly declared that they did not believe in the guilt of Mendel Beilis. Some of them, including Oscar Grusenberg, volunteered their services to defend him. In 1913 Mendel Beilis was finally acquitted.

It was quite obvious that the government had been behaving as if Beilis's guilt had already been proved. After the trial Nicholas II himself bestowed orders and titles, awards, and promotions on those who had taken part in the investigation against Beilis, the indictment, and the trial.

Thus, at the beginning of this century the blood-libel had become one of the keystones of the Russian government's policies.

As for Grusenberg, his popularity grew even more after the trial. After the February Revolution, as a member of the Cadet (Constitutional Democrats) Party, he was appointed speaker of one of the two departments of the Senate (one of the most distinguished posts in the juridical system). Then, as he did not support the October Revolution, he emigrated. He lived at first in Berlin, then in Riga, and finally in Paris. He died in France in 1940. In 1950 his remains were transferred to Israel, according to his will.

With this tale of the blood-libel, a classic tale in Jewish history, we conclude our first excursion.

EXCURSION TWO

THE CENTRAL SQUARES

Rabbi Bar Zemina said: "If our people of old were like the angels, we are like simple mortals; and if they were simple mortals, then we have not developed much beyond the asses, and not asses like those of Rabbi Hanina ben Dosa or Rabbi Pinhas ben Yair, but the most ordinary."

*Aggadah,** Translated from the Russian version of S. Frug

Our second excursion will be mainly around the admiralty quarter in the center of town; we shall now be dealing with the wealthier segment of Jewish St. Petersburg. It has always been expensive to live in the center, and by the 1890s, apartment rents already exceeded a hundred rubles a year. Another point about our excursion is that since the admiralty quarter is one of the oldest areas of the city, the time scale of the events we shall be covering is much longer than in our other excursions — nearly two centuries in fact.

☐ WE SHALL BEGIN the excursion at No. 24 on the Moika River Embankment (Naberezhnaya). The building has been rebuilt several times, giving the facade a very ordinary appearance. Only the original features of the courtyard entrance reveal that there was once something interesting here.

From the 1820s to the end of the New Economic Period (NEP) in the 1920s, one of the most fashionable of St. Petersburg's restaurants, the Donon, was situated here. The story by Lev Klyatchko (also known as Lvov), the renowned early twentieth-century journalist of the paper *Ryetch,* tells of the

---

* Homiletic passages in rabbinic literature, as gathered by Bialik and Ravnitsky before World War I.

connection between this completely un-Jewish place and events important for Russian Jews. We shall base our excursion on his story called "The Secret Room" as we describe the events.

Aristocratic types were the main clientele of the Donon Restaurant. Ministers, generals, and grand dukes could be seen on the restaurant's luxurious premises. Only the finest and rarest wines and cognacs were served. The cuisine was exemplary, and the waiters were trained to the standards of Maxim's. All customers were known and addressed by their first names and patronymics.

The first floor of the restaurant was divided into private rooms, one of which was particularly isolated and reserved for special patrons. It was not available to everyone, and it witnessed many historical meetings. In its time, the room hosted Rasputin, the informer Azef, and Father Gapon. When it seemed, in 1906, that the Cadets (Constitutional Democrats) would come to power, General Trepov met its leaders here in secret.

In the early 1880s, the waiters, who were surprised at nothing, occasionally witnessed intriguing scenes such as the following: a full general, his tunic loosened, would be dozing alone in an armchair at a table covered with the remains of a sumptuous meal. Three men sauntered along the corridor past the door that was slightly ajar. Two of them were obviously Jews. One of them was tall, burly, portly, with an aquiline nose; the other was short, with a small gray beard, an unusually mobile face, and intelligent eyes unusually bright for his age. The third was a tall, thin, colorless man with the pronounced appearance of a bureaucrat.

Suddenly the small man split away from the group and cautiously tiptoed into the room. Approaching the general, he gently raised the sleeper's tunic with one hand and reached into his pocket with the other. The other two "conspirators" watched through the crack of the door. It looked as if they would now quietly stab His Excellency, pour poison into his wine, or at the very least steal something.

None of these took place. On the contrary, the small gray-bearded Jew took an envelope out of his pocket and put it in the inside pocket of the general's tunic. Then, just as quietly, he left the room and joined his companions.

A few minutes later all three looked into the room. The general was still sleeping. The routine was repeated, and another envelope disappeared into the capacious pocket of the sleeping fat man. This was repeated several times until finally the distinguished person woke up and rang the bell.

At that moment the conspiratorial trio entered the room, deliberately making a lot of noise and greeting the general. He smiled at them and said, "Yes, I've had forty winks. Time for us all to go home. I'm pleased to be of service. All that can be done will be done."

He then withdrew, together with the thin servile bureaucrat. Everyone seemed to be pleased with what had taken place.

But what was going on? Was it an antigovernment plot, the sale of military secrets to a foreign power, or an unsuccessful attempt at an assassination? Who were these people involved in this secret affair?

The sleeping general was Alexander III's Minister of Internal Affairs, Count N. N. Ignatiev. The bureaucrat was his secretary. The tall, burly man was the famous philanthropist, chairman of the board of the Jewish community of St. Petersburg, the only Russian Jewish baron, Horace Yevselevitch Guenzburg. The small gray-bearded man was the well-known Jewish public figure, one of the promoters of the construction of the St. Petersburg Synagogue, and Guenzburg's private secretary, David Faddeyevitch Fainberg. The whole rigmarole was a means devised by Ignatiev himself to receive bribes from the Jews.

The envelopes that Fainberg put into the minister's pocket contained ordinary credit notes. After each envelope had been placed, the count woke up and counted the contents. If he found that there was not enough, he continued to doze. The minister woke up only when he was completely satisfied with the amount. And he had to be satisfied since it was he who decided whether further repressive measures would be taken against the Jews.

The point is that Ignatiev was the instigator of the new anti-Jewish legislation, adopted on May 3, 1882, that has gone down in history as the May Laws.

The Moika River Embankment, No. 24. The Donon Restaurant was located in the courtyard of this building.

These notorious laws had the following background. In 1881, following the assassination of Emperor Alexander II, a wave of pogroms spread over the Pale of Settlement. There was a strong belief that pogroms had been instigated by the government to divert the population from the revolutionary movement. There were so many pogroms that the new tsar, Alexander III, suggested that Ignatiev look into their causes and make proposals to avoid their recurrence.

The count drew up a report from which it was clear that responsibility for the Jewish pogroms lay with "the Jews themselves," who, he declared, "mercilessly exploited the Russian Orthodox rural population." It was therefore proposed that Jews should be evicted from the villages (a very traditional idea).

Ignatiev did not like Jews, but he was very fond of money and never had enough. Therefore, before presenting the tsar with his proposals, he showed them to Horace Guenzburg and hinted that for two million rubles (another source says one million), the proposals could be redrafted. The baron could not lay his hands on such an unheard of sum, but in return for partial bribes (in all around a hundred thousand rubles), the proposals were somewhat moderated.

By the terms of the May Laws, Jews were forbidden to settle anew in the villages of the Pale of Settlement and to acquire any real estate there. They were prohibited from dealing in alcohol. Parish councils were given the right to evict a Jew from a village by a simple majority vote. The May Laws were so scandalous and would have been so calamitous for the majority of Russian Jews that the tsar decided not to place the draft for ratification, as was the usual practice, before the State Council. Instead, these new repressive measures were adopted as "temporary laws" to avoid the usual debate in the State Council, which, incidentally, was by no means composed of liberals.

As we all know, however, there is nothing more permanent than temporary measures. The May Laws survived right up to the fall of the autocracy in 1917.

       LET US NOW move along the Moika Embankment up to where it crosses Nevsky Prospekt. Here on the Narodny (formerly Politseisky) Bridge, on June 4, 1903, an event took place that became the talk of all St. Petersburg. The event has entered history as "The Dashevsky Affair." But first a few words about the Kishinev pogrom.

Everyone knows at least something about this terrible event. One of the main instigators of the pogrom was P.A. Krushevan, the publisher of the only Bessarabian paper at that time, called *Bessarabets* (The Bessarabian). The paper supported the violently anti-Semitic organization known — and hated — as the Black Hundreds. As a result, it consisted almost entirely of anti-Semitic propaganda. One of Sholem Aleikhem's stories tells how Jews always bought *Bessarabets* to find out what new misfortunes awaited them. Plehve, who was then minister of internal affairs, not only refused to license any other paper in the province, but also actively subsidized this particular publication. So, when in

The Nevsky Prospekt crossing the Moika Canal, at Politseisky Bridge, the site of the attempted murder of P. A. Krushevan

early 1903, some peasants found the mutilated corpse of a Russian child on the outskirts of Kishinev, the local population was already mentally prepared to act "as required." Even though the child's uncle publicly confessed to the crime, *Bessarabets* accused the Jews of ritual murder.

At Easter a group of government emissaries arrived in Kishinev to conduct secret discussions with Krushevan and the local authorities. Leaflets, printed in Krushevan's printing press, soon appeared, calling "for the Jews to pay with their blood." People gathered in public places and openly talked of a pogrom.

On Sunday, April 6, 1903, a crowd of young hooligans, clearly acting on a signal, began to attack Jewish houses and shops. The police made no attempt to interfere. By evening looting had turned to murder. For twenty-four hours, while the police remained in their barracks, Jews were being beaten and killed all around. Finally, after a telegram from Plehve at five o'clock on the evening of April 7, soldiers came out onto the streets and dispersed the crowds. By that time fifteen hundred shops and houses had been looted and destroyed, forty-five people had been killed, and eighty-six wounded and maimed. Russian eyewitnesses described people being torn in half, eyes gouged out, children with smashed skulls and stomachs ripped open, tongues cut out, breasts cut off women, men castrated, hanged, killed, and so on. These horrors are described in Chaim Nahman Bialik's angry poem "In the City of Slaughter."

The news of the bloody pogrom quickly spread throughout Russia. Many of the Russian intelligentsia reacted to it with indignation. News of it even spread to the West. Mass protest meetings were held in all the main capitals of Europe and in America. The protest was so powerful that the Russian government was forced to take a few modest steps to calm public opinion. The governor-general of Bessarabia was replaced, and several of the mobsters who had participated in the pogrom were brought to trial, though they received very lenient sentences.

Therefore, it was not surprising that a young student of the Kiev Polytechnical Institute, Pinchas Dashevsky (born in 1879), decided to stand up for the honor of his people and punish the person whom he justly considered reponsible for the bloody crime — Krushevan.

By that time Krushevan had already moved to St. Petersburg and lived on Bolshaya Morskaya Street. He dined at the Medved (Bear) Restaurant on Bolshaya Konyushennaya Street, where the Estrada (Variety) Theater is now. It was at this spot on the Politseisky Bridge that the young man attacked the publisher of *Bessarabets* and stabbed him in the neck. (Dashevsky did not choose a pistol as his weapon, as he did not wish to harm any casual passersby.) As he lacked experience in killing, the assassination attempt failed. The knife struck the starched collar and lost much of its force, only scratching the neck. The wound was so insignificant that when Krushevan was taken to the nearest pharmacy he refused first-aid, when he discovered that the chemist was a Jew. No doubt he feared that he would be finished off there.

Dashevsky was arrested and put on trial. The circuit court sat behind closed doors. Krushevan's lawyer, Alexei Shmakov, delivered an anti-Jewish tirade in which he accused the Jews of ritual murder. The court found Dashevsky guilty of premeditated assault but recommended mercy. He was sentenced to five years in a penal battalion, as well as deprived of all rights and property. An appeal to the Senate by the lawyers Oscar Grusenberg (mentioned in Excursion Number One) and Mironov was rejected. Only in 1906 did an imperial edict release Pinchas Dashevsky as a result of a petition brought by Grusenberg. However, there was no restoration of rights.

Thus was justice done for Jews and for anti-Semites. (Later, Shmakov was to serve as one of those who defended the accusers of Mendel Beilis in the Kiev blood-libel.)

Krushevan escaped retribution, but the man who had sanctioned the Kishinev pogrom, von Plehve, did not. He died at the hands of a young Socialist Revolutionary (SR) terrorist named Sazonov in 1904. As for Dashevsky, he was again arrested, in the Stalin era, as a "Zionist," and he died in a labor camp in 1934.

NO. 15 NEVSKY PROSPEKT now houses the cinema Barricade. The present building was erected in the early classical style between 1768 and 1771 for the chief of police, General N. I. Checherin, by the architect J. B. Ballen-Delamotte. Pushkin dined here (in the Talon Restaurant), and the place was frequented by N. G. Chernyshevsky, N. A. Nekrassov, D. I. Pissariev, and N. G. Pomyalovsky. In the late nineteenth century a "noble gathering" met here for literary evenings at which Turgeniev and Dostoyevsky spoke.

Before any of these events and buildings, in the first half of the eighteenth century, the site was occupied by the Noviy Gostiny Dvor (New Shopping Arcade). (The old arcade, built way back in the first years of the city's existence, was on Troitsky Square on the Petrograd side.) The Noviy Gostiny Dvor stood here from 1719 to 1735, when it was burned down. However, all this early history is of interest to us from a different point of view. It was on this very spot on Admiralteisky Ostrov (Admiralty Island), near the new Gostiny Dvor, that on May 15, 1738, the citizens of St. Petersburg were gathered to witness a terrible medieval-type scene — the burning at the stake of two people: Borukh Leibov, a tax farmer from the Smolensk Guberniya, and Alexander Voznitsyn, a retired naval lieutenant-commander. Let us go back 150 years to the time of Anna Ioannovna,* before Poland was partitioned and when very few Jews lived in Russia.

Borukh Leibov, the tax farmer from Smolensk Guberniya, in Bielorussia, went to Moscow on business from time to time. There he met and became close friends with Alexander Voznitsyn. They frequently traveled together, and then the lieutenant-commander suddenly went with Leibov to Poland, where he was circumsized and secretly converted to Judaism. Voznitsyn was denounced by his wife, who had noticed (it was impossible not to) that her husband began to pray with his face to the wall and not toward the icons, had become choosy over his food, and on one occasion suddenly went to the house chapel (Voznitsyn was a member of the nobility and a landowner) and began to throw the icons into the river.

The denunciation was treated very seriously. The Russian authorities had very vivid recollections of the grandeur of the Novgorod Jewish heresy of the sixteenth century, when even members of the family of Tsar Vassily III yielded to Judaism, and members of the various sects close to Judaism. Leibov and Voznitsyn were arrested and brought to St. Petersburg. On Anna Ioannovna's personal instructions, the investigation was conducted with extreme severity. Voznitsyn was tortured. The house serfs on his estate were interrogated, as were the owners of the coaching inns at which the "miscreants" had lodged and the coachmen who had driven them. Naturally, they were found guilty. Voznitsyn was sentenced to the stake for "conversion to the Yiddish faith" and Leibov for perverting him.

---

* The Tsarina, or Empress, Anne, known as Anna of Courland, reigned from 1730 to 1740.

The people were gathered to watch the execution. Voznitsyn tried to cheer up his comrade in misfortune. This was in the European capital of St. Petersburg in the enlightened eighteenth century.

Voznitsyn's estate was not confiscated but transferred to his wife as a reward for the denunciation.

Now, relatively new houses stand in the block formed by Nevsky Prospekt, Kirpichny Pere'ulok, and Hertzen and Gogol Streets. Previously, in the eighteenth century, the area had been occupied by the wooden palace of the Tsesarevna (heir to the throne) Elizabeth, and before that by the palace of Peter I's vice-chancellor, Peter Pavlovitch Shafirov. He was, in effect, the minister of foreign affairs. It is here that, strictly speaking, the history of a Jewish presence in St. Petersburg begins. This is what the Brockhaus and Yefron *Encyclopedic Dictionary* says about this family:

> The Shafirovs are an extinguished baronial family, descended from the Jew Shafir, who was baptized in 1654 with the name Pavel. His son Pavel Pavlovitch was an interpreter in the ambassadorial service, and his grandson Pyotr Pavlovitch was a well-known government figure of the eighteenth century who, in 1710, was awarded the rank of Baron by Peter the Great. He was stripped of this in 1723, and once again re-instated by Catherine I in 1726. Pyotr Pavlovitch's grandsons died without leaving any heirs. No heirs to his barony, that is; but he did have four daughters, each of whom married into the highest aristocracy. Among their descendants were Pushkin's friend Count Vyaziemsky (1792–1878); the Prime Minister and Minister of Finance, Sergei Witte; the writer Count Aleksei Tolstoy.

In his *Course of Russian History* (Vol. IV, Moscow, 1958) V. O. Klyuchevsky writes that Baron Shafirov was the son of a captured baptized Jew who served at the court of the Boyar Khitrov and who then worked in the shop of a Moscow merchant. This contradicts the Brockhaus and Yefron version. Klyuchevsky is probably confusing the son with the grandson. It is most curious that such a "detail" as the Jewishness of a third-generation baron was known to all at court, and it certainly irritated them. The ignorant gentry of Peter's time were no less angered by the erudition of the vice-chancellor. Klyuchevsky also makes the following comment: "Educated and honored people like Bryus, Shafirov and Osterman were not inclined to break the ties of their new fatherland with the western European world, and their scholarship and abilities aroused the intense anger of the ignorant and idle majority of the Russian aristocracy."

☐ LET US NOW move on to a large gray impressive building of Finnish granite, somewhat reminiscent of a Florentine or Venetian palazzo. It stands on the corner of Nevsky Prospekt and ulitsa Gogolya (formerly Malaya Morskaya) at 7/9 Nevsky Prospekt. Now occupied by Aeroflot, it was built from 1911 to

The Wawelberg banking house, now the offices of the Soviet State Airline, Aeroflot, at the corner of Nevsky and Gogol

1912 by the architect M. M. Peretyatkovitch for the bankers Gunne-Nussen Wawelberg. Previously the bank had occupied premises at No. 25 Nevsky Prospekt near the Kazan Cathedral, now the site of the restaurant Kavkazsky. The firm had been founded by Hippolity Andreyevitch (Gunne-Nussen) Wawelberg (1843–1901), one of the wealthiest bankers of the Kingdom of Poland. Wawelberg's story, like that of so many other Jewish bankers, was closely linked to the liberalization in domestic policy under Alexander II and the involvement of Jewish capital in Russia's economic development. Wawelberg grew up in Warsaw and there attended the Gymnasium (secondary high school); he studied at the Novo-Alexandreesky Polytechnical Institute and then at the Academy of Commerce. In 1869 he moved to St. Petersburg and founded his own banking house. His financial operations were successful, and he soon possessed a large fortune.

Wawelberg lived at a time when the majority of the Jewish intelligentsia and influential circles thought that the only way to achieve Jewish equality was to give up Jewish separateness and even the consciousness of Jews as a separate nation. They considered that being a Jew was only a religious phenomenon and that one could not be simply a Jew, but could be, say, a German Jew, a Polish

Jew, and so on, just as there are German Catholics or German Protestants. This view derived from the exaggerated significance that historians gave to governmental and material attributes in the formation of nations. They considered that the state was composed of "scraps" of various national groups and that sooner or later they would all inevitably mix to form one nation. Moreover, they insisted that this process was progressive and that it should be, therefore, assisted in every possible way. They considered the spiritual factor as being of secondary importance in the formation of national self-consciousness. In this they ignored the elementary fact that the Jewish people had contrived to retain their national consciousness for over two thousand years without having such "fundamental" national attributes as a cohesive territory, state independence, or internal commercial and economic links.

Brought up in the educational tradition of Mendelssohn,* Wawelberg desired to merge Polish Jews with Poles, and he personally donated a large part of his fortune to Polish philanthropic purposes. There was no field of charity in Poland from which he was absent. Cheap editions of Mickiewicz, Sienkiewicz, and Oszezko and other Polish writers were published with his money. At the same time he established a prize at Lvov University, then in Austria-Hungary, for essays on the history of Jews in Poland. Times changed, however, not only in Russia but also in Poland. Anti-Semitic outbursts increased, it seemed, faster than the number of Jewish assimilationists. For this reason, by the end of his life Wawelberg gave up the path he had chosen earlier and began to show a greater interest in the national affairs of his own people. In St. Petersburg he became a member of the board of the Society for the Spread of Education among Russian Jews (OPE) and then the treasurer of and an active participant in the Jewish Colonization Association (ICA).

The building of Wawelberg's bank was erected by his heirs a decade after his death.

☐ LET US MOVE away from Nevsky Prospekt along Admiralteisky Prospekt up to ulitsa Dzerzhinskogo (formerly Gorokhovaya ulitsa). The corner house (ulitsa Dzerzhinskogo No. 2) was designed by G. Quarenghi and built at the end of the eighteenth century. Before the Revolution, the office of the town governor of St. Petersburg was located here. As a memorial plaque indicates, the All-Russian Extraordinary Commission, CHEKA,† occupied the building between December 1917 and March 1918.

On our excursion we say little about the participation of Jews in the

---

* Moses Mendelssohn (1729–1786), philosopher of German Enlightenment, spiritual leader of German Jewry.

† Cheka (Extraordinary Commission) set up in 1917 to combat counterrevolution. It was renamed GPU (State Political Administration) in 1922; OGPU (Unified GPU) in 1924; NKVD (Peoples Commissariat of Home Affairs) from 1934 to 1946; MVD (Ministry of Internal Affairs) from 1946 to 1953; and then, after Stalin's death, the KGB (Committee of State Security).

revolutionary movement. This is for two reasons. First, in St. Petersburg there was hardly any Jewish proletarian working class at all; the Bund was active mostly in the Pale of Settlement. Second, the majority of the revolutionaries, from extreme right to extreme left, had gone so far away from Jewish national and cultural traditions in their ideas and in their lives that the single fact that they were Jewish by birth hardly seems a valid reason to devote much space to them in an excursion that is devoted to Jewish history. Their own blood membership of Jewry hardly meant anything to them at all.

However, it is well known that many of the most active Jews in Russia took part in revolutionary activity and that Jewish participation in the political struggle and in both revolutions was disproportionately high. In all the revolutionary parties, Jews were prominent among the leaders. We shall name only a few of them. In the Cadet (Constitutional Democrats) Party: Maxim Vinaver, Isidore Gessen, Y. Yollos, and M. Ostrogorsky; in the Menshevik Party: F. I. Dan (Gurvitch), A. Axelrod, L. Martov (Y. Zederbaum), Mark Lieber (Goldman), and Nikolai Sukhanov (Gimmer); among the SRs (Socialist Revolutionaries): Grigori Gershuni, the brothers Mikhail and Abram Gotz, M. A. Bobrov (Natanson), and I. N. Steinberg; the Trudovik* L. M. Bramson; and, of course, the entire Bund with their leaders: Abramovitch, M. Raffess, and Henryk Erlich.

Lieber, of the Menshevik leadership, was also a leader of the Bund. In November 1937, at the height of the purges, he was executed; Sukhanov, imprisoned in 1939, died two years later. According to Pokrovsky, as quoted in the article on the Jews in the first *Soviet Encyclopedia,* Vol. 24, 1932, "According to the data of different Congresses, Jews constituted from one quarter to one third of the active participants of all revolutionary parties" — from, in fact, the far Left to the Cadets. Among the Bolsheviks, the best known Jews are Zinoviev, Kamenev, Trotsky, Radek, and Litvinoff (Soviet foreign minister in the 1930s).

It is of interest to note the blood relationship of many of the revolutionaries with activists in the field of Jewish culture. For example, L. Martov (Yuly Tsederbaum) was a grandson of the Jewish publisher A. Y. Tsederbaum, who published moderate Jewish newspapers in Yiddish, Hebrew, and Russian. Henryk Erlich was the son-in-law of the Jewish historian S. M. Dubnow; Isaac Nahman Steinberg was the brother of Aaron Steinberg, the learned specialist on Jewish philosophy who taught at the Jewish University.

Since no history of a people can exist without the history of its social movements, we will take advantage of the fact that we find ourselves by the building where the Cheka, an organization born of the October Revolution, was located and will talk about one of its leaders, Moisei Solomonovitch

* The Trudovik (Trudovaya Gruppa) were members of the first state Duma, 1906, consisting of well-to-do peasants and some intellectuals. From 1912 to 1917 there were ten Trudoviki in the Duma, led by Kerensky, who left them to join the Social Revolutionaries. The party disappeared in 1917.

Uritsky. His biography can be found in the *Bolshaya Sovietskaya Entsiklopedia* (Great Soviet Encyclopedia) (first and third editions). Moisei Solomonovitch was born in 1873 in the town of Cherkassy into a merchant family. In 1897 he graduated from the law faculty of Kiev University. Uritsky joined the revolutionary movement in the early 1890s. He was first arrested in 1897 for organizing a secret Social Democratic press in Berdichev, and he was exiled to Yakutsk (in the very remote far northeast of Siberia) for five years.

After the founding of the Russian Social Democratic Workers' Party (RSDRP) in 1898, Uritsky became one of its first members. When the party split at its second congress in 1903, he tended toward the Mensheviks. He was exiled to the North and to Siberia several times for his revolutionary activities and participation in the 1905 Revolution. After the February 1917 Revolution, Uritsky returned from abroad to Petrograd and joined the Bolshevik Party together with the inter-Rayon* group at the sixth congress of the RSDRP (Bolshevik). There, he was elected a member of the party's Central Committee. During and after the events of October 1917, Uritsky was a member of the Petrograd Military Revolutionary Committee and then a commissar in the Cheka responsible for the constituent assembly. He also held other important posts. He opposed the peace of Brest-Litovsk and together with other "Left" Communists wrote for the journal *Communist*. From March 1918 he was chairman of the Petrograd Cheka.

It was here in the Cheka building that the historic encounter between Uritsky and the famous Russian Jewish writer Isaak Babel took place. The writer described the meeting in his autobiographical story *Doroga* (The Way). In this story, Babel describes the Petrograd of December 1917, where he had arrived from the army, frozen and hungry, not having eaten for two days. Outside it was twenty-four degrees below zero Celsius. Two machine-guns had now been placed in the foyer of the former town governor's building, and here Babel presented letters from his friend Kalugin, a Cheka investigator. He was sent to the Anichkov Palace. The writer walked along the dead and hoarfrost-covered Nevsky Prospekt with no hope of reaching his destination. "There is no longer any need to conquer Petrograd," he mused, and he tried to recall the name of the Jewish poet and thinker crushed by the hooves of galloping Arab horses at the beginning of his journey during the Crusades. It was Yehuda Halevi. At the Anichkov Palace, Babel fainted—literally into Kalugin's arms. When he came to, he washed and was given a dressing gown with buckles, a shirt, underwear, and socks made out of woven silk, all of which had once belonged to Alexander III. Then he and Kalugin smoked cigarettes and cigars, a present from Sultan Abdul Hamid to the Russian tsar. They spent the rest of the

* In Russian Mezh-Raiontsy, an organization set up in 1913 with the aim of bringing together Bolsheviks and Mensheviks. Its most prominent members were Uritsky, Trotsky, Lunacharsky, Yosse, and Volodarsky. On failing to reunite the two branches of the former Social Democrat Party, most of them joined the Bolsheviks in July 1917; their action in doing so played an important role in the Bolsheviks' subsequent success.

night sorting out the toys that had belonged to Nicholas II—his drums and trains, his notebooks, and his baptismal shirts. Babel read the diary of the Danish Princess Dagmar (the Dowager Empress Maria Fyodorovna); he looked through the photographs of the grand princes who had died in childhood and fingered locks of their hair.

In the morning, Kalugin took the writer to Uritsky at the Cheka. Let Babel speak for himself:

> The Commissar for Internal Affairs of the Commune of the Northern Region came out of his office on unsteady feet. His sore eyelids, swollen from lack of sleep, bulged out over the lenses of his pince-nez. I was appointed a translator in the foreign department, and I was provided with a military uniform and luncheon vouchers. I was assigned a corner in the hall of the office of the former City Governor of St. Petersburg and I set about translating depositions handed in by diplomats, agents-provocateurs and spies.
>
> No more than a day had passed and I had everything—clothes, food, work and comrades, loyal in friendship and death, comrades the like of whom are not to be found anywhere in the world other than in our country.
>
> So began thirteen years ago my marvellous life so full of meaning and gaiety.

The life "full of meaning and gaiety" ended for Isaak Babel in 1939, when he once again fell into the hands of that organization, now no longer as a colleague, but as a victim of the terror of the 1930s.

As for "the Commissar for Internal Affairs of the Commune of the Northern Region," at the time of his meeting with Babel he had no more than six months to live. In August 1918, Uritsky was assassinated in his room in the general staff building by another Jew—Leonid Kanegisser—as a result of a plot "inspired and organized," according to the official *Bolshaya Sovietskaya Entsiklopedia* (first edition), by two members of the Central Committee of the Right SRs, Abram Gotz and D. Donski. Uritsky was buried in the Field of Mars (Marsovoye Polye). Dvortsovaya Ploshchad (Square) in Leningrad was renamed in his honor. According to other sources, Kanegisser, a poet, was not part of any plot and was not involved with the SRs in any way, but was motivated by a desire to prove that Jews—as Jews—were not responsible for the Terror, despite the many Jews actively involved in it, especially in Petrograd.

☐ NOW, ALONGSIDE THE building of the Senate and the Synod, we shall come out to the River Neva, on Naberezhnaya Krasnogo Flota (Red Fleet Embankment)—formerly Angleeskaya Naberezhnaya—at No. 4. Everyone who is interested in the history of the architecture of Leningrad knows this building. Here, at one time, was one of the palaces of Count Stroganov, constructed with the participation of the architect Voronikhin. It was then rebuilt by Thomas de Thomon, to the order of Countess Laval. It was referred to by the name Dom Laval in all the guidebooks of St. Petersburg.

The Laval House (Dom Lavala), home of the Jewish railway builder, Samuil Polyakov

A great deal could be told about this building, such as, for example, how it was furnished. Madame Laval had considerable taste and money. On her honeymoon throughout Europe she acquired and brought back a great number of famous paintings, Greek statues, and other articles of value, including the Mosaic floor of Nero's villa on the Isle of Capri. All these valuables were assembled here. The story of her marriage is an interesting one. Laval himself was an unimportant French courtier who fled from the French Revolution of 1789 and came to Russia. Paul I himself personally arranged the marriage. The parents of the bride were opposed to the match, declaring that "he is not of our faith [he was of course a Catholic], he is not of high rank, and in general nobody knows him," to which the Tsar Paul replied: "He is of our faith, he is a Christian, I know him, and he will soon be of high rank." Thus the marriage was agreed upon.

In the early years of the nineteenth century Countess Laval's salon was very popular. Every foreign envoy considered it to be an honor to be accorded an invitation there. This salon was frequented by Pushkin, Zhukovsky, Lermontov, Krylov, and many other poets, writers, artists, and musicians. Here, on May 19, 1828, Pushkin read *Boris Godunov* to Adam Mickiewicz and Alexander Griboyedov. Laval's daughter was married to Prince S. P. Trubetskoi, but on the day of the revolt of the Decembrists, he deliberately stayed at home to avoid trouble for his family. However, it was from here that his wife set out a little later to join her husband in Siberian exile.

Toward the middle of the nineteenth century the Laval family fell on hard times. A large part of the valuable works of art were sold, and the house came into the hands of Samuil Solomonovitch Polyakov and belonged to him and his family from 1870 to 1911. S. S. Polyakov, son of a small Jewish merchant, was born in 1836 in the village of Dubrovno. He died in 1888 in St. Petersburg with the rank of privy councillor. He started his career by working as a foreman on the building of railways somewhere in Bielorussia, and thanks entirely to his personal qualities, in a short time he became the most powerful contractor in railway construction in the whole of Russia, a banker, and a millionaire.

Polyakov built the Kozlovo-Voronezh-Rostov railway, as well as the Orel-Gryazy line, the Kursk-Kharkov-Azov line, and many others. He wrote a great deal on the policies of railway construction, built the first railway school in Russia, which he set up in Yelts, and founded a number of banks: the Moscow Land Bank, the Don Land Bank, the Azov-Don Commercial Bank, and so on. In the last years of his life, Polyakov began to take part in the life of the Jewish community of St. Petersburg. The St. Petersburg Synagogue was built with his cooperation. In recognition of his magnificent contributions to Russian charitable institutions, Samuil Polyakov was elevated to the nobility and appointed privy councillor, a rank equivalent to that of minister. He had two brothers, Lazar in Moscow and Yakov in St. Petersburg. Both became privy councillors and nobles.

To the credit of this nouveau riche banker, we must remark that when he took possession of the Laval palace he decided not to change or rebuild anything, relying on the taste of the hereditary Russian aristocracy. After S. Polyakov's death, the house was inherited by his son Daniel, a court councillor, owner of the Commercial Bank of St. Petersburg, and chairman of the Society for Craft and Agricultural Labor among the Jews of Russia (ORT). Later, the mansion was bought by the state and transferred to the expanding State Senate.

In spite of the fact that the mass of Russian Jews were extremely poor, individuals such as Polyakov represented rare but very typical exceptions. The liberalization of Alexander II's reign led to the rapid emergence of several very rich Jews, industrialists, and bankers in the central towns of Russia. Their initial capital was usually accumulated in the wine trade or from commerce with the West. Some of the more successful Jews launched themselves into the business life of the country by taking advantage of the economic upturn in Russia at that time, the availability of the redemption money released by the emancipation of the serfs, the permission granted to merchants of the first guild to live outside the Pale of Settlement, and the financial links with the Jewish banks of Europe. Many acquired a considerable fortune. The majority of Russia's railways were built by Jewish contractors and major railway magnates such as Polyakov, Kronenberg, Rafailovitch, Natanson, and Efrussi. Wawelberg owned banks in Warsaw and St. Petersburg. The Efrussi bank specialized in the export of grain from Odessa. At one time the Meier and Company Bank in St. Petersburg was second in size only to the I. E. Ginzburg Bank. The Wissotzky firm of tea merchants is now known throughout the world. One third of the sugar industry was controlled by Jews before the Revolution, the leading sugar magnates being Brodsky, Zaitsev, and Etinger.

And yet, however distant at first glance may have been their lifestyle, with its plenty and elegant luxury, from the extreme poverty of their fellow Jews in Russia, over it there fell the giant shadow of the dreadful, calamitous situation of the Jewish people: the blood-libels, the humiliating lack of any protection by law, and the horror of the pogroms.

It is not hard to imagine what these people were like during their first years in the capital: wealthy, but still acting like provincials, dressed in a style very far from aristocratic, speaking Russian but with a pronounced, distinctive accent, and out of place among fashionable nobles and ladies. They must have irritated the high-society St. Petersburg aristocracy and even the intelligentsia. Sentiments of this sort were penned by Nekrassov in these malicious anti-Semitic lines:

> If in the boxes your eyes will rest
> You'll see the bankers' wives who choose
> Hundreds of thousands of rubles on each breast,
> And with them their husbands — the Jews.

and further:

> Valor, youth, strength, captured
> A woman's heart in days of old.
> Our lassies are more practical, they're enraptured
> By their ideal — the calf of gold,
> Incarnate in the gray-haired Jew,
> Whose filthy hands rake through
> His chests of gold.

And Dostoyevsky in his *Diary* (1877) writes directly that even Bismarck, Beaconsfield, the French Republic, and Gambetta were all an illusion compared with the "real rulers of Europe, the Yids with their banks."

Whatever was written at the time, however, it is quite clear that Jews invested considerable energy and resources in the development of Russian business life in the second half of the nineteenth century. In this sense they continued the tradition begun by Zundel Hirsh, Borukh Leibov, Nota Notkin, and others.

WE COME NOW to the Supreme Ruling Senate on Ploshchad Dekabristov (formerly Senatskaya Square). What can be the connection between that and Jewish history? What indeed! By the end of the nineteenth century, Jewish legislation (which means, of course, anti-Jewish legislation) had reached such a pitch in Russia that it was almost impossible to obey it all to the letter even if one so desired. Who could live where was very far from being just an idle question. For example, pharmacists had the right of residence in St. Petersburg so long as they practiced their profession, but they lost it once they became, shall we say, dealers or merchants. Others had permission to reside so long as they were in business, but they lost it once they took a job in some other profession. The following anecdote is from those days:

> Two Jews met on a train leaving St. Petersburg. Both were called Haim Rabinovitch. They started up a conversation.
> "What are you being evicted for?"
> "I'm a dentist, but I got fed up with it and went into business. What about you?"
> "I'm a salesman, but I got fed up with business and I'm being thrown out because I'm no longer in business."
> "You know, we can get round this."
> "How's that?"
> "Let's change documents; it makes no difference to the Russian government which Haim Rabinovitch is in business and which one's a professional."

Naturally such confusing legislation gave rise to an enormous amount of bribery and corruption in the villages. Jews suspected of violations were evicted. They appealed to the Senate. There were so many appeals that in 1908 the Senate had to double the staff of the First Department and divide it into two sections. Many careers were made using the Jewish question as a ladder. Some of the appeals were even considered by the Council of State, whose decisions were ratified by the tsar.

The Senate considered, for example, the semimystical affair of "the rights of the Jewish deceased." In Vitebsk the Jewish cemetery became full, but Jews continued to die in total disregard of the established *numerus clausus*—the percentage quota. The community acquired a piece of land next to the new cemetery, but the governor refused to ratify the purchase since the May Laws prohibited Jews from acquiring land outside the town limits. But what could they do? Another law forbade burial inside the towns. An appeal was sent posthaste to the Senate. There the question was discussed at length. The "liberals" recalled that the ban on Jews buying land outside the town was designed to protect the peasants from being exploited by them. But in a cemetery there was no one, apart from the few gravediggers, and certainly no peasants. And a dead Jew could hardly exploit them, however cunning and wily he may have been when alive. The right-wing senators opposed this argument and simply declared that the restrictive laws were not open to such wide interpretation. The necessary two-thirds majority was not obtained when it came to the vote. The case dragged on for many years. The Jews of Vitebsk buried their dead on top of the dead. Finally the "liberals" gained a majority in the First Department of the Council of State, and the purchase of land next to the cemetery was sanctioned.

Let us pass under the archway linking the Supreme Senate and the Holy Synod, and we find ourselves in a quiet, narrow street, one of the oldest in St. Petersburg, called Krasnaya ulitsa (formerly Galernaya). The noise of the modern town hardly penetrates to here. The whole street is studded with old buildings and private residences. It is very pleasant to stroll here. There is also much of interest for us to see in Galernaya ulitsa if we are interested in the history of the Jews of St. Petersburg.

☐ HERE IS NO. 20 with a single balcony at the front. Clearly to be seen on the attic is the cartouche or ornamental scroll where once the owner's coat of arms was inscribed. Next door is a huge building, now colored a bright maroon, with three addresses: Krasnaya ulitsa 22, Leonov Pere'ulok 4 (formerly Zamyatin), and Boulevard Profsoyuzov (formerly Konnogvardeisky Prospekt No. 17). This building once belonged to the man who was probably the richest and most famous Jew in St. Petersburg, Baron Horace Yevselevitch Guenzburg. We have already come across his name several times in the first excursion. It is now time to go into more detail about him and his family.

Horace (in Russian, Goratsii) Guenzburg was born in 1833 in Zvenigorodok, in the Kiev province, and died in St. Petersburg in 1909. His parents spent most of their lives in Paris. Horace himself obtained an excellent education at home. The well-known Hebrew scholar Sukhostaver taught him classical Hebrew and Talmud. At the age of twenty, Guenzburg married his first cousin Anna Hesselevna Rosenberg. She was very respected in the family and had considerable influence over her father-in-law Yevsel. While still a young man, Horace became his father's chief assistant and partner in his commercial, financial, and communal activity. Together with his father he founded in 1859 in St. Petersburg the banking house of I.E. Guenzburg, which became the first modern-style bank in Russia. The bank was located here at No. 4 Zamyatin Pere'ulok. The young financier was, in effect, in charge of the bank, where he prospered. He soon managed to acquire for his firm an exclusive position in St. Petersburg and then also in Europe.

From the very start of his career in the early 1860s, Guenzburg emerged as a patron of the arts and as a very great philanthropist. The best writers, scientists, and artists of St. Petersburg began to meet in his house. Here came M. M.

Stasyulevitch, K. D. Kavelin, and V. D. Spassovitch, professors who had left the university after the Polish uprising of 1863. The renowned music and literary critic V. V. Stassov and the famous writer I. S. Turgenev were close to Guenzburg. M. E. Saltykov-Shchedrin, I. A. Goncharov, I. N. Kramskoy, V. Solovyov, and A. G. Rubinstein were often to be seen in the house. Thanks to Guenzburg, the sculptor Antokolski was able to obtain an academic education. Following the Jewish tradition, Guenzburg gave generously to young impoverished people of talent, both Jewish and Russian. He founded the Archeological Institute and the Institute of Experimental Medicine (together with Prince Oldenburg), among others. The only condition he attached to his charitable donations to general Russian institutions was that they were to be open to all, irrespective of religious affiliation.

Baron Horace Guenzburg's houses on Galernaya ulitsa. All three entrances in this photograph were his.

Up to 1892 Horace Yevselevitch Guenzburg was a councillor of the St. Petersburg Duma and a member of the Stock Exchange Council. He also held the rank of full councillor of state (equivalent to an army general) and a number of other high orders and positions. Between 1868 and 1872 Guenzburg was consul of Hesse-Darmstadt in Russia, and there the archduke elevated him, and later his father, to the rank and title of baron.

Guenzburg's main industrial interest was gold mining; he developed the Lena, Zabaikal, Berezovya, Altai, and other Siberian gold fields. His other enterprises included, for example, the chain steamship company on the River Sheksna and the Platina joint-stock company.

For forty years Baron Guenzburg was the acknowledged leader of the Jewish community in St. Petersburg and throughout Russia. It would be a major task to list all the areas of Jewish life in which he was the chief financier, active participant, and tireless envoy. It is therefore not surprising that in these sketches of life in St. Petersburg we frequently mention his name. His was the main cash endowment for the building of the St. Petersburg Synagogue, and his money financed the publication of books in defense of the Jews.

Guenzburg was chairman of ICA (Jewish Colonization Association), although, as we have already stated, he did not favor emigration. He was also chairman of the Society for the Dissemination of Education among the Jews of Russia and various other similar organizations. His wife, Anna Hesselevna, founded the orphanage on Vassilevsky Ostrov. This man always reacted with generous assistance to the yearly outbreaks of fire, bad harvests, and pogroms in the shtetls.

In his will, Guenzburg asked to be buried in Paris, where his father was buried. This request was, to a significant degree, the result of the worsening situation of the Jews in Russia toward the end of his life. The ceremony of conveying his remains to Paris was an extremely solemn one. There were delegations from many towns, and specially appointed deputies accompanied the coffin to Paris.

In general, it could be said that without any doubt Baron Guenzburg was an outstanding person. Why, then, it may be asked, did he not become a deputy for the Jews at the elections to the first State Duma? Why was he not even put forward for nomination as a candidate, and why did no one go to him for advice? Perhaps his services to the Jewish world had been forgotten. Of course not, it was simply that the times were completely different. Guenzburg was too traditional a Jewish leader. In strict conformity with the teachings of the Talmud, he believed that Jews were obliged to fulfill the laws of the land in which they lived. Loyalty to the government of the day and to the tsar was for him a sacred principle. What could he do? Donate money, a great deal of money, somehow or other to placate the bureaucracy, give bribes (as in the story of Ignatiev). And, of course, to plead, to petition. And if he did not obtain what he was asking for, well, there was nothing more that he could do.

Such a leader was no longer needed by the majority of the Jewish people in early twentieth-century Russia. The political situation inside the country was changing rapidly. Anti-Semitism was attacking the Jews with dreadfully fierce pogroms. And the Jews themselves were no longer a monolithic community, but were different groups, fighting among themselves, each one for his own. In order for their voices to be heard, they no longer had to beg—they had to shout and demand. To achieve anything, even to defend their own homes and families, it had become necessary to resort to arms. The government was not intending to defend Jews from lawlessness and itself took part in the spread of violence, seeing the Jews as the main reason for the spread of revolution and, at the same time, as a convenient scapegoat. Nicholas II, in a telegram sent to one of the leaders of the anti-Semitic Union of the Russian People in June 1907, declared: "Let the Union of the Russian People indeed be my reliable support, a service for all and in all an example of law and order."

Well what could Guenzburg hope to obtain from an emperor for whom the basis of law and order was the Union of the Russian People? For any thinking person it was now clear that the salvation of the Jews lay either in emigration or in revolutionary struggle. There was no room for compromise in such an embittered and crisis-ridden society. But Guenzburg had little sympathy for the revolutionaries of the left or the right, and he did not support emigration or Zionism. Therefore, in the elections for the State Duma, the Jews did not vote for him but rather for the new leaders who neither wanted nor knew how to beg, only to demand. The Jewish people, like all the other peoples in Russia, no longer wanted to beg for anything. This was now considered to be both pointless and humiliating. The time of such leaders as Horace Yevselevitch Guenzburg had passed irrevocably. The people needed completely different ideas and a different strategy to be able to live through the present "today" and somehow to prepare themselves for the severe trials that waited for them on the morrow.

THE COUNTRY'S OLDEST Jewish organization of the contemporary type, the Society for the Spread of Education among the Jews of Russia (OPE), was at one time housed at No. 25 Krasnaya (Galernaya) ulitsa and later moved to No. 23 Zagorodny Prospekt. Founded in 1863, the society was well financed and enjoyed considerable fame in many towns and villages (shtetls) of the Russian Empire. The leadership of OPE included some very rich people: Horace Guenzburg, David Guenzburg (his son), I. A. Wawelberg, D. N. Polyakov, and M. A. Warshawski. Among the intellectual and educationalists were L. I. Katzenelson, Y. M. Halperin, L. O. Gordon, A.Y. Harkavy, and M. I. Kulisher. Such a symbiosis was essential: the rich provided the money, and the educationalists brought enlightenment to the people.

When we talk of the Haskala, and of its significance in the history of the Jews of nineteenth-century Russia, we are also referring to OPE, with which it was organizationally and spiritually connected. The society had dozens of branches in towns such as Odessa, Moscow, Yekaterinoslav, and Kovno. It tried to assume the function of a reformer of Jewish customs, culture, and way of life — to a certain extent even religion — and this inevitably stimulated the already partially developed assimilatory feelings of its members, such as Orshansky, and L. Levanda. It should be noted that a significant proportion of the young people who were educated through the auspices of OPE later abandoned Jewry altogether.

The pogroms, and the May Laws of 1882, had a sobering effect on the Maskilim, as they understood that enlightened education was not the universal panacea. The struggle against assimilation was led by Peretz Smolenskin's journal *Hashakhar* (The Dawn). This mood even penetrated into OPE. In an open

The headquarters of the Society for the Spread of Enlightenment among the Jews of Russia (OPE), at 25 Galernaya ulitsa

letter in the journal *Voskhod* of 1884, the treasurer of OPE, L. M. Rosenthal, argued that the reason for the decline of literature in Hebrew (and today we look upon that period as being a "boom" time!) and the loss of interest on the part of educated young people in religion and national affairs was precisely the propagandist activities of OPE, including publishing in Russian language. Since it was impossible to reject education altogether, Rosenthal suggested an "old patch" on the "new suit": to educate "the new Jews in the fundamentals of religious knowledge."

The letter contained another idea that reflected the new trends in public life. The author recommended to OPE, which had hitherto restricted itself to purely cultural and educational activity and had been completely loyal to the government, that it should now take part in the movement for Jewish rights, even if only on a modest scale. One specific proposal that he made was that the Higher Commission for the Review of the Laws about the Jews be requested to give more assistance to scientists, to remove Pale of Settlement restrictions from those with secondary education, and to provide relief for old teachers.

OPE also bequeathed to succeeding generations a mass of sociological statistics on the condition of the Jewish people at that time (the collection of statistics was actively undertaken by ICA). There were frequent lectures, speeches, and seminars on every conceivable topic at the Society's premises, but probably the greatest service performed by OPE was its contribution to the education of a whole generation of a new type of Jewish intelligentsia. Even though part of this intelligentsia forsook its people, the rest, in a short time, in the lifetime of one generation, were able to ensure the rapid development of Jewish historical study, ethnography, philology, literature, music, and art. It must not be forgotten that most of these zealots did not earn their livings through cultural activity. As a rule, they were doctors, lawyers, engineers, or bank officials. It remains a mystery to many of us how this relatively small group managed in its "spare time" to achieve so much many-sided and fruitful activity — to conduct research; to publish newspapers, journals, and books; to support so many various cultural societies; and to found new ones.

NO. 61 KRASNAYA ULITSA belonged to Horace Guenzburg's son Baron Alfred Guenzburg, the managing director of the Lena Gold Mining Company. The Society for Hygienic Cheap Apartments for the Jewish Population was located here, with Alfred Guenzburg as chairman. ICA was directly involved in the organization of the society in 1900. It issued shares and had a semiphilanthropic and semicommercial status. The society operated mainly not in St. Petersburg but in the towns and villages of the western provinces of Russia, where it provided the not-so-well-off self-employed Jews with cheap accommodations, places for workshops, and small plots of land for market gardens and vegetable plots. In general, the society tried to reduce the number of people without a basic income, without a specific occupation or profession, and even without basic accommodations—a large category, alas, among the inhabitants of the numerous Jewish shtetls.

Of course, this problem could not be completely solved against a background of pogroms, lack of legal rights, lawlessness, restrictions on place of living, education, and so on. Nevertheless, the Society for Hygienic Cheap Apartments for the Jewish Population did much to ease the critical situation, as did the Society for Craft and Agricultural Labor among the Jews of Russia (ORT) and ICA itself, although with different methods.

◻ MOST OF THE odd-numbered houses on Krasnaya ulitsa have their counterpart on Naberezhnaya Krasnogo Flota (Red Fleet Embankment). They were designed so that the buildings with the more impressive facades faced the embankment and the more modest-looking buildings looked out onto Galernaya ulitsa. Between them there was an inner courtyard. Houses here were usually acquired in pairs. Two such pairs belonged to the brothers of Samuil Polyakov, Lazar (No. 12 Naberezhnaya Krasnogo Flota and No. 11 Krasnaya ulitsa) and Yakov (Nos. 62 and 63). These houses are best viewed, naturally, from the embankment.

Yakov Solomonovitch Polyakov (1832–1909) was the oldest of the famous trio. He began his career in the traditional way with tax farming, and then with his brothers, he went into railway construction and banking.

Lazar Polyakov (1842–1914) was based mainly in Moscow, where he established and managed several banks, including his own personal bank, and several industrial enterprises. He was also chairman of the Moscow Jewish community and took an active part in its affairs. In particular, he gave financial and organizational assistance to the building of the Moscow Choral Synagogue on Arkhipova ulitsa. He also had his own synagogue. Lazar hardly lived in St. Petersburg at all, maintaining his house on Angleeskaya Naberezhnaya (as it was then called) purely as a status symbol.

As a result of this and the previous excursion, we can now judge how the once monolithic Jewish community (monolithic in the ideological and not the economic sense, of course) became stratified toward the late nineteenth and early twentieth centuries.

There were still people with the traditional Talmudic outlook on the world and understanding of the relationship between the Jewish people and the governmental power in the Diaspora (galut). This entailed the aspiration to maintain the traditional autonomy in their religious and national life, while conducting a policy of coaxing and compromise with the authorities, unconditionally obeying the laws of the host country. This point of view was founded on habit, religious tenets, and the experience of national survival over the centuries. Baron Guenzburg is an example of this line.

Another idea that had not yet died away at that time was Haskala, that is, the preservation and even the revival of national life through the reform of

The house of Yakov Polyakov. The first Institute of Higher Jewish Studies was also established here in 1919.

Judaism and participation in the values of European civilization. The Maskilim held that the spread of education among the Jews would be sufficient to solve the problems of national alienation, anti-Semitism, the distorted occupational structure, poverty, and so on. This view favored cooperation with the governmental authorities or, at the very least, mutual toleration. This idea was shared by Yehuda-Leib Gordon, Lev Katzenelson, Lev Levanda, and others, all those who were grouped around OPE and similar organizations. However, even this circle began to understand that "pure" education was impossible without civil rights for the people.

The third group comprised the assimilators, who saw no way in which to solve the Jewish problem in the immediate future or who refused to solve it. It might appear at first sight that these people chose the easiest path of transition to the other, dominant, culture, and even sometimes to religion, namely the rejection of everything Jewish. They offered their people physical and social salvation through national suicide.

The fourth group was made up of Social Revolutionaries from whom the leftist parties recruited members (Uritsky and Martov, for example). They refused to recognize anything unique in the Jewish national question. The revolutionaries, especially the Marxists, considered that such "superstructural" phenomena as religion and nationality were the outcome of a specific economic base — capitalism. With changes in the social structure of society and the abolition of private ownership, religions and nations would disappear. Therefore, it was not anti-Semitism as such that should be fought but capitalism, which gave rise to it. It was not only useless but also harmful to try to preserve national upbringing and culture, since national consciousness would be replaced by class consciousness and then classes, too, would disappear.

There was finally yet another view: the Jews are a people doomed to endure national oppression up to the time that they have what every nation has — its own territory and state. Whatever the social system, the Jewish question could not be solved while the Diaspora endured. Zionism was one of the last national movements in Europe, and on the ideological level it offered nothing new. By the time it appeared, powerful national movements had already led to the formation of a united Germany and Italy, as well as independent Serbia, Bulgaria, Rumania, and Greece. The victory of nationalist forces in Czechoslovakia, Hungary, Ireland, Poland, Finland, and other countries was not far off. The Jewish national movement of the new type was retarded by the difficult legal position of the majority of its people and the absence of a common territory. Therefore, many saw no future in Zionism, and even the nationalistically minded intelligentsia sought compromises that would secure the nation's survival in the Diaspora and simultaneously the achievement of civil and political rights.

There were many such quests in search of a solution to the Jewish question on a national basis, for example, the "autonomism" of Simon Dubnow, who believed that Jews could maintain their internal independence as Jews only within the framework of the existing national systems. He opposed both Zionism and assimilation, favoring the preservation of the Jewish social system and communal ideology as autonomous (self-ruling) groups. He thought that these groups should be loyal to the states in which they lived and that their autonomous rights should be protected by those states, in which they would live as full and equal citizens. His elder brother Ze'ev, at first an assimilationist, then a Zionist, went to Palestine in 1882, at the age of twenty-four. He returned to Russia three years later, still, according to his own account, a "fervent nationalist." Ze'ev died in Moscow in 1940.

Like Simon Dubnow, with his belief in "autonomism," the Bund also had its own modest program for national autonomy and was opposed to Zionism. The twentieth century was destined to resolve which of these heterogeneous groups, fighting both each other *and* their common external enemy, had chosen the right path.

EXCURSION THREE

VASSILEVSKY OSTROV

And so, let us set to work! Our work will take place on the soil of the past, but its harvest will belong entirely to the present and the future. We shall show that we, the Jews of Russia, are not only a branch of "the most historical people," but we ourselves have a rich past and we know how to appreciate it. An ancient people, grown gray with age, made wiser by the experience of many centuries, and with an unparalleled past — is it possible for such a people to turn away from its own history?

S. M. Dubnow

As we stroll around the town, in excursion after excursion, we are slowly reconstructing for ourselves an important aspect of its history, the history of its Jewish life. Many enthusiasts of Leningrad's history have a profound knowledge of its architecture. They know what was built by whom and when, when such and such a street was paved, what the facade of this building looked like up to the year eighteen hundred and something. This one is reminiscent of "Baroque," that one is "Russian neoclassic," and that is not even worth looking at — it is nothing but "eclecticism." Thus, for some people, the history of the town imperceptibly becomes the history of its architecture, which, from the point of view of Jewish traditions, is the least important aspect.

But we again return to what, for us, is most important: the history of our people. For though it may not now be known to us, that history was written down in hundreds of monographs and preserved in the memories of thousands of people. We are trying to reconstitute its minute fragments with these, our walking excursions about the town.

Vassilevsky Ostrov was, in the past, very far from being the most densely populated Jewish area of St. Petersburg. According to the census of 1868, its Jewish population was only 139 Jews — 82 men and 57 women — and ranked only eighth among the Jewish population of the capital's districts. Nevertheless, here too many interesting events have taken place.

It is best to begin our excursion around Vassilevsky Ostrov from the Strelka. From here we can see what official and ceremonial St. Petersburg looked like, with its major palaces, cathedrals, the admiralty, and the tsarist political prison — the Fortress of St. Peter and St. Paul. All sorts of people were imprisoned here, from the Tsarevitch Alexei to the members of the provisional government! The last prisoners in the Fortress were the sailors who took part in the Kronstadt uprising in 1921. The Fortress is not actually on Vassilevsky Ostrov, but since we shall not be conducting a special excursion there, let us stop for a moment and recall that one of the first Jewish prisoners of the Fortress of St. Peter and St. Paul (Petropavlovskaya Krepost) was the founder of one of the best-known currents in Hasidism — the Habad. This was the Lubavitcher rebbe, Shneur-Zalman Borukhovitch.

But first a few words about Hasidism.

Hasidism was born in the eighteenth century in Podolia (Ukrainian Transdniestria) and became the basis for a revival of spiritual life for the Jewish population of Galicia and the Ukraine, which had suffered severely in the seventeenth century as a consequence of both the ravages of Khmelnitsky and the movement in support of the false Messiah Shabbetai Tzvi. Hasidism did not in any way reject the fundamentals of Judaism but shifted the emphasis of certain aspects within it, insisting that genuine prayer was more important to God than formal knowledge of the Torah.

Hasidism tried to overcome the psychological inequality between the educated Jews of Lithuania and their almost illiterate co-religionists in the southern, mainly rural areas. Moreover, it taught that worship with a joyful heart was more acceptable to God than worship with tears and suffering. The founder of Hasidism, the Besht — Ba'al Shem Tov — known as B'Sh'T — Israel ben Eliezer (1700–1760), lived in Medzhibozh, in Podolia. He and his followers gave to the simple people hope and comfort in their hard lives, filling the surrounding world with the presence of God and a feeling of the possibility of a miracle. The very appearance of this new religious tendency and its rapid spread among the faithful at a time when Europe had already entered the age of rationalism, and when the religious spirit was everywhere declining, were extraordinary phenomena. This is not to mention the striking fact that the ideas of Hasidism were not born in the head of a university professor or a famous theologian but came literally from the people themselves.

If the enlightenment of the Europe of those days had been delayed by one hundred years, then we may all well have been Hasidim. The triumphant onward march of Hasidism was halted not so much by the forces of traditional orthodoxy (Misnagdim) ranged against it as by the emergence and spread of Jewish Enlightenment, the Haskala.

But at that time in the eighteenth century, traditionally educated Polish and Lithuanian Jews greeted the ideas of the Besht and his followers not only with grave suspicion but also with hostility. There was every reason for this. In Hasidism they saw only schism, sectarianism, apostasy, false messianism (in the special role given to the "Tsadik," or spiritual leader), that is, everything that had already many times inflicted tremendous damage on Jews and Judaism.

The struggle against Hasidism was led by the Vilna Gaon and the Gaon's disciples. Sad to say, the latter did not eschew the assistance of St. Petersburg officialdom, which was not by any means the friend of either side but aimed to destroy Jewish traditions in general. An example of such unpalatable actions was the denunciation made to Tsar Paul I by one of Gaon's followers, the former rabbi of Pinsk, Avigdor Khaimovitch, against the leader of the Lithuanian and Bielorussian Hasidim, Shneur Zalman, who had been responsible for Avigdor losing his post. The denunciation severely blackened the character of the Hasidic leader and portrayed him as immoral and opposed to the government. In particular, it was claimed that Hasidim were transferring large sums of money to hostile Turkey with criminal intentions. In fact, it referred to the regular collection of money from all of Europe's Jews to support the Jewish community in Ottoman Palestine. This accusation, coming on top of the unfavorable evaluation of Rabbi Shneur Zalman by the senator and poet Derzhavin, who had come into conflict with him in Bielorussia, forced the government to bring the "Tsadik" to St. Petersburg in 1798 to investigate the affair. Shneur Zalman's accuser, Avigdor Khaimovitch, also went to St. Petersburg.

Rabbi Shneur-Zalman was forced to defend himself, his disciples, and Hasidism in general. This he did successfully. His first, forced, visit to the capital was not a long one, but the Misnagdim continued to send complaints to the government, and on November 9, 1800, the "Tsadik" was arrested for the second time and again imprisoned in the Fortress of St. Peter and St. Paul. There he again endured a formal investigation and had to refute both orally and in writing the great number of accusations made against himself and his supporters. The Emperor Paul was able to appreciate the true reasons for the hostility and permitted the Hasidim to coexist alongside the orthodox Jews. Rabbi Shneur Zalman was released from the Fortress but was compelled to remain in St. Petersburg until the accession to the throne of Alexander I in March 1801.

We have noted that orthodoxy fought against Hasidism, seeing in it schism and false messianism. However, the main reason for the popularity of Hasidism with the people was that from the very first it declared its aim to be *not* schism, *not* the rejection of tradition or of Judaism, but the strengthening and renewal of tradition by reviving a number of half-forgotten ideas that already existed in Judaism—in the mysticism of the Kabbalah for instance. Shneur Zalman, seeking a compromise with the orthodox, introduced aspects of traditional intellectualism and respect for learning into his variety of Hasidism (Habad).* This middle path was so successful that Habad remains to this day one of the most vigorous and stable tendencies in the Jewish religion.

---

* Habad is an acronym formed by the Hebrew initial letters of Hokhma, Bina, Da'at "חוכמה, בינה, דעת" meaning "wisdom, understanding, knowledge."

The founder of Habad is mentioned in different sources under various names. To avoid confusion we shall list them: Rabbi Shneur (Shneor)-Zalman ben Borukh, Zalman Borukhovitch, Rabbi Zalman Ladier, Rabbi Zalman from Liozno, Alter Rebbe, and Harav Hazaken. He was born in the shtetl of Liozno in the providence of Mogilev in 1747. He died in Peny near Kursk on December 28, 1812, and is buried in Gadyach in Poltava province. As the residence of the Tsadikim following Shneur Zalman often moved (Liozno, Lyady, Lubavitchi, and even Rostov, Leningrad, and New York), the "Habadniks" are often called the Lubavitcher Hasidim and occasionally the Lyady Hasidim.

The lives of the Hasidic Tsadikim are always wreathed in legend. Here is one, associated with the imprisonment of Shneur-Zalman in the Fortress of St. Peter and St. Paul.

One day the Chief of the Gendarmes went to see Rabbi Shneur-Zalman in his cell. The Chief Gendarme, a perceptive man, understood at once who was before him, from the majestic and peaceful face of the Rabbi, so lost in thought that at first he did not notice his visitor. He spoke with the prisoner and asked many questions about the Holy Scriptures. Toward the end he asked: "How are we to understand that God, the omniscient God, asked Adam 'Where are you?' "

"Do you believe," answered the Rabbi, "that the Scriptures are eternal, that they cover all times, all generations, and all people?"

"I do," answered the other.

"So," continued the Tsadik, "in every epoch God asks of every man 'Where do you fit into your world? So many years and days of your allotted span of life have passed. How far have you advanced in your world?' God speaks something like this: 'You have lived forty-six years, how far have you gone?' "

Realizing that his exact age had been stated, the Chief of the Gendarmes, with considerable restraint, put his hands on the Rabbi's shoulders and exclaimed "Bravo," but his heart was trembling.

Well, a legend is a legend.

What is important in this one is not historical accuracy but the idea and the moral. (In fact, the Tsadik was indeed visited by the prison governor. During the reign of Paul I the gendarmes had only just been formed.) What *is* important is something else, namely that Rabbi Shneur's words expressed the fundamental idea of the meaningfulness of man's existence and the purposefulness of his life, whose main point is clearly not transitory success, not a career (let alone in the police), but the service of God and the fulfillment of his commands. And even a prisoner who lives according to these precepts will prove stronger than his captor.

☐ THE FORMER KUNSTKAMERA (at No. 3 Universitetskaya Naberezhnaya) was built from 1718 to 1734 by the architects G. Matarnov, N. Gerbell, G. Chiaveri, and M. G. Zemstov. In the mid–eighteenth century, the

Imperial Academy of Sciences was situated here. At that time the Academy consisted almost entirely of foreigners. The first prominent Russian scientist, Mikhail Lomonosov, who worked here from 1741 to 1765, was the rare exception. It was about this time that Antonio Nunes Ribeiro Sanchez, a famous Portuguese emigré doctor, became an honorary member of the academy.

This is what the *Yevreiskaya Entsiklopedia* has to say about Sanchez: he was born in 1699 into a prosperous and educated family in Pegna Makor in Portugal. On completing his medical studies, he worked with the famous Dr. Bourgava, who recommended him to the Russian government, which was then looking for qualified physicians. Sanchez lived in Russia from 1731. He became a physician at the Medical Chancellery in Moscow, a surgeon in the field army on active service, and then a medical officer at the landed-gentry corps in St. Petersburg. There he became known as an excellent doctor, and he was appointed Second Physician in Ordinary to the Empress Elizabeth. In 1744 he cured the dangerously ill fiancée of Prince Pyotr Fyodorovitch, who was later to become the Empress Catherine II (Catherine the Great).

In 1747 Sanchez left his post because of an eye ailment and went to Paris. In that year, at his request, the Academy of Sciences elected him an honorary member with an annual emolument of two hundred rubles. But suddenly, within a year, the president of the academy, Razumovsky, on Elizabeth's orders, revoked his honorary membership. Sick, and with no means of support, the physician wrote a letter of vindication to the academy, thinking that he had been expelled on suspicion of unreliability. In fact, however, the reason was completely different: his suspected Jewishness. Razumovsky discovered this from the chancellor, Bestuzhev (or Shuvalov?), and passed it on to Sanchez thus: "She (the Empress) considers that her conscience does not allow her to keep in her Academy a man who has forsaken the banner of Christ and has decided to fight under the banner of Moses and the Old Testament prophets."

Sanchez answered:

> The accusation [of Judaism] was false — and it is even more of a calumny since I am of the Catholic religion, but I will not concern myself with refuting the charge since from birth it was fated that Christians would take me for a Jew, and Jews for a Christian, and moreover, Providence destined this in the blood that flows in my veins, that same blood which the first saints of the church had, and the holy apostles, humiliated, persecuted and tortured during their lives, honored and worshipped after their deaths.

This correspondence gives substantial grounds for thinking that Sanchez was of Portuguese Marrano stock and even perhaps took an interest in Judaism and possibly observed certain Jewish rituals. Clearly something in his behavior must have aroused that suspicion, which led to his expulsion from the academy. We know that even after baptism, many Marranos secretly still adhered to Judaism.

On ascending the throne in 1762 Catherine II remembered the old and disgraced physician who had some time before saved her life. She had him reinstated as a member of the academy and awarded him an annual pension of a thousand rubles for life. Sanchez died in Paris in 1783 and left a number of works on medical research, in particular a once famous book on the treatment of syphilis, as well as a work on the curative properties of Russian baths. In translation from French the title is *On Russian Steam Baths: And on the Extent to Which They Facilitate The Strengthening, the Preservation and the Restoration of Health.* And, finally, he left an unpublished manuscript entitled "The Origin of the Persecution of the Jews," the contents of which leave no doubt as to the author's Jewish origins.

A bald skull, a thin neck, strained cheekbones, very expressive arched brows, this is the face of Antonio Sanchez as potrayed by a small illustration in the book *Akademiya Na'uk SSSR* (The Academy of Sciences of the USSR), the face of an outstanding man for whom not even his Jewish origins were forgiven by the religious fanaticism of the eighteenth century.

☐ AS WE APPROACH the former building of St. Petersburg University (No. 7 Universitetskaya Naberezhnaya), we recall that eminent figure of early Russian Haskala, L. Y. Mandelstam, who was the first Jew to graduate from a Russian university. Lev Yosifovitch (Leiba Yosselevitch, Leon-Arye-Leib) Mandelstam (1819 – 1889) was born in the township of Novye Zhagory, midway between Kovno and Riga. He received a traditional Jewish education but also studied the works of the followers of the German-Jewish educationalist Moses Mendelssohn and foreign languages. This is how Mandelstam himself recalls his childhood:

> I come from a simple family, every day and every night I studied the Talmud and at the age of twelve I received the distinction "Ila'i" [from Hebrew עִלָּאִי , meaning superb] and the symptoms of consumption. I read much of Mendelssohn's followers, thanks to my father and my older brothers, and then the philosophy of Maimonides and Spinoza. The officers who came to play billiards taught me languages.

Mandelstam married at seventeen, but he soon divorced owing to conflict with his parents-in-law. His reading encouraged him to continue his studies. He failed the entrance examination for the Vilna Gymnasium (secondary high school) but his second attempt was more successful. The administrator of the Bielorussian educational district wrote to the rector of Moscow University:

> At the second attempt the Board of the Vilna Gymnasium, even though they found his knowledge inadequate for the full course of the Gymnasium, nevertheless found it sufficient for university entrance. . . . Basing myself on this conclusion and taking into account the natural abilities of Mandelstam, who is an unusual phenomenon among his fellow believers, his love of learning and so on, I [the Administrator] have decided to send him to Moscow University as an external student.

Is this not strange? A Jew reveals a level of knowledge in examination below the minimum required, and yet an official bureaucrat provides him with a testimonial and even gives him a letter of recommendation for entry to the university. To understand this state of affairs, we have to look at the internal policies of the Russian government with respect to Jews at that time.

Nicholas I, on the throne from 1825, was a zealous persecutor of any heterodoxy in the country and consequently of Judaism as well. In his attempts to turn the country into a military barracks and his subjects into faceless soldiers, he chose force as the chief means to attain his goal. For the Jews, this meant the dissolution of the "Kahals" (autonomous communal institutions), the introduction of military conscription with the category of "cantonists" (intending forcibly to baptize Jewish children), intensified censorship of the Jewish press, and even the burning of books designated as "harmful" and the imposition of supplementary taxes on traditional clothing, Sabbath candles, and other items.

However, after 15 years, even Nicholas I and his officials realized that the citadels of the Jewish religion could not be stormed with cavalry charges. The Talmud was yet again identified as the "root of all evil," and it was decided to subvert the traditional Jewish system of religious education from within. To this end, a network of transitional "Christianizing" schools was created. The prime mover of this new course was the minister of public education, Sergei Uvarov.

As they were accustomed to expect nothing good from the government, the Jewish communities looked upon Uvarov's "educational" campaign as only a new method of influencing Jews to change their religion. It was commonly and openly stated that, whereas previously the military barracks had been used to enforce baptism, now the schools were being employed to this end. It was not surprising, therefore, that no parents even considered sending their children to the new schools, and the "educational" reform soon collapsed. (Moving ahead to the 1880s, we can see that it was only under Alexander II that education in Russian schools and universities began to become popular among Jewish youngsters, when an educational diploma began to grant certain civil rights without requiring a change of religion.)

At that time, in 1840, it was important for the government to breach the passive resistance of this "stubborn people" and to entice at least a few individuals into the Russian system of education so that they could stand as examples to the rest. This policy of the Russian government coincided with the aspirations of the first of the Maskilim (Jewish enlighteners), who saw in secular education the panacea for a better future for their people. At this time the Maskilim often cooperated with the government. The government pursued its own aims and supported the newly emerging Jewish intelligentsia, so long as it fought for the reform of Jewish life but did not demand civil rights for its people.

The motives and attitude of the Russian officials are now clear, as are the views of Mandelstam himself, which we find in his *Zapiski* (Reminiscences): "Three ideas have governed my soul and my heart: education, the motherland, and my nation." As he set out on the long and unexplored journey to Moscow, he sensed the exceptional significance of his action for the future of his people with an almost messianic sense of destiny, but he worried about the lack of understanding of his role on the part of his brothers, for whom he desired only good.

> This is how I stand at present — a wild, strong, free son of nature, loving my motherland and the language of my native regions but unhappy because of the unhappiness of my brothers in faith. I am infuriated by their bitterness, the waste of their talents, but I am bound by the ties of kinship and feeling for their suffering. The aim of my life is to vindicate them before the world and to help them be worthy of this vindication. They are not evil and are not incurably corrupted, but they lie recumbent like the desperately ill man who clenches his teeth and refuses to take the healing drops from the hands of the doctor. But perhaps their native-born son, part of their soul, who suffers together with them, will be able to win them over.

It is easy to understand the mistrust, the barely hidden disquiet, with which traditional Jewry reacted to the government's "new course" and to the appeals of the Jewish educationalists who cooperated with them. Here is an excerpt from a letter to Mandelstam from his brother, also not raised in the most orthodox of families. How powerful is the sad prophecy in it about the new generation of youth:

> Father gave you a suit of clothes, you will change it. Mother played with your curls, you will cut them off. You will speak a language incomprehensible to us, and you will soon be writing in a script which is unknown to us. Only do not betray your childhood love of our father and mother. . . . O! my brother, my brother, do not forget your kith and kin.

On his way to Moscow the youth met a cantor, who, on learning the purpose of the journey, asked: "Why are you going? You could be the first among your own people and you are leaving everything to become the least among the learned Christians." Mandelstam answered: "The Talmud says 'Better to be the last among the lions, than the first among the hares.'"

Mandelstam studied at Moscow University and then transferred to St. Petersburg University, from which he graduated in 1844 with the degree of candidate of philosophy (general philology). True to his youthful aspirations, he devoted his life to the education of his native people. He published his articles in the *Yevreiskaya Biblioteka* (Jewish Library). While abroad, he translated the Pentateuch and Psalms into Russian for Jews, with a parallel Hebrew text. The books were issued first in Vienna and only after several years, in 1869, in Russia. While still abroad, Mandelstam conducted research work and studied philosophy and the cuneiform script. Following the departure to America of Lilienthal, Uvarov's chief Jewish assistant in the implementation of the educational reforms (it was rumored that he took flight when the ministry proposed that he be baptized), Mandelstam was appointed the Jewish adviser ("Learned Jew") at the Ministry of Public Education. He helped implement Uvarov's plan of opening state schools for the Jews, and he even compiled a number of textbooks for these schools. In one of these, he translated some lines of Pushkin into Hebrew — the first time Pushkin's verse had appeared in Hebrew. When the plan for the Jewish state schools collapsed, however, Mandelstam left his post, in 1857, and once again left the country. He spent his last years in destitution in St. Petersburg; his library was sequestered by bailiffs while he was still alive. He died on the boat between Vassilevsky Ostrov and Petrogradskaya Storona (the Petrograd side). He was not recognized as a Jew and was buried among the Russian Orthodox. Only later were his remains reinterred in the Preobrazhensky Cemetery.

Mandelstam's contemporaries described him as a man full of the feeling of his personal dignity, sensitive to the sufferings of others, a dreamer and a romantic. He made possible the publication of many books (often at his own expense), which, even if there was no possibility of them being sold at a profit, were in his opinion useful to his people. Ending his days in poverty, forgotten by all, he did not complain to anyone of his plight. His memoirs, entitled *From the Notes of the First Jewish Student in Russia,* first published in 1909, are full of interesting and witty observations on the life of the Jews in mid–nineteenth century.

The educational situation changed dramatically during Mandelstam's lifetime. The Jewish youth of the 1880s took the universities by storm, since a diploma promised a better life and permission to reside outside the Pale of Settlement. But now the universities by no means took all who applied. The quota system imposed in 1887 allowed Jews to make up no more than 10 percent of the total student number entering institutes of higher education in the Western provinces, 5 percent outside the Pale of Settlement, and 3 percent in the universities of St. Petersburg and Moscow. Moreover, higher educational establishments such as the Institute of Railway Engineering and the Academy of Medicine and Surgery were closed to Jews, and in the Pale of Settlement itself there were very few higher educational establishments at all. Those who were unable to enter a Russian university went abroad to be educated, if their parents could afford it. A special handbook issued by *Rassvet* (Dawn) for 1910 had a section on the entrance requirements of European educational establishments.

After the 1905 Revolution, the professorial councils of higher education establishments were accorded the right of making independently their own conditions for acceptance of students. This led to temporary abolition of the quota system. Together with the liberal teachers there were many students who supported the abolition of discrimination. At one of the student meetings of St. Petersburg University in 1906 it was resolved: "to recognize the principle of open doors to the University, i.e., the admission without distinction as to nationality, religious affiliation, age or sex; to abolish the percentage limitation on Jews; to admit at the present time all Jews in the order of their application."

In 1908 the quota system was reimposed by law. This at first caused a steep reduction in the acceptance of new Jewish students, since the overall percentage of undergraduates exceeded the quota as a result of the indulgences of the years 1906 to 1908. In general, it was considered in the Ministry of Education that Jewish students went to university to avoid military conscription and to obtain the right to live in university towns for purposes unrelated to studies. Moreover, no one doubted that the competition provided by Jewish students brought pressure on the non-Jews in many matters of university life while "the influence of Jewish students is supported by the mutual aid that is characteristic of their race."

According to OPE figures, in St. Petersburg University in 1886 (before the imposition of the quota), 268 Jews were studying (11.4 percent), and in 1911 (three years after the reintroduction of the quota) there were 661 (7.8 percent). The figures for the Novorossiisky University in Odessa for the same years were 172 (29.8 percent) and 513 (19 percent), respectively. The number of students from Russia studying abroad in 1913 was 12,000, of whom 60 percent were Jews. Of all these students, 35 percent were studying in Germany and 25 percent in France.

From 1911, Jewish communal organizations tried to organize in Russia a private polytechnic institute with no quota, to alleviate the problem of higher education for Jews. These efforts were increased when, as a result of World War I, going abroad to study became impossible. Finally, January 21, 1917, the Polytechnic Institute was opened in Yekaterinoslav (now Dniepropetrovsk). It admitted its first three hundred Jewish students. The staff of the institute offered courses on the history of the Jews, Jewish literature, and other subjects. Saturday was designated as the free day. Later the institute became part of the governmental network of higher education establishments.

It is obviously impossible to list all the notable persons of Jewish origin who graduated from St. Petersburg (Petrograd-Leningrad) University. We will mention only a few of those who were well known in Jewish education and culture in St. Petersburg and who are a part of our excursions: Baron David Guenzburg, orientalist, Candidate of the University, and chairman of the St. Petersburg Jewish Community; I. H. Eisenbet, founder and director of the Jewish Gymnasium (secondary high school) on Teatralnaya Ploshchad, who graduated from the faculties of law and Oriental studies of the university; I. Yu. Markon, orientalist, editor of the journal *Ha-Kedem* (Faculty of Oriental Studies); M. I. Sheftel, chairman of the Association of Academic Jewish Publications (Faculty of Law); and Solomon Mikhoels, the famous actor-director of the Jewish Theater (Faculty of Law). Among the university professors were the ethnographer, L. Y. Sternberg; the historian, S. N. Valk; and one of the first conscientious historians of the Jews of Lithuania and Poland, a non-Jew, S. A. Bershadsky.

The embankment—Universitetskaya Naberezhnaya—of Vassilevsky Ostrov is studded with architectural masterpieces, but particularly noteworthy, from every point of view, is the massive building of the Repin Institute of Painting, Sculpture, and Architecture (formerly the Academy of Fine Arts). The architects for the academy, which took from 1764 to 1788 to complete, were A. F. Kokorinov and Jean-Baptiste Ballin de la Motte. The stone staircase leading from the academy down to the River Neva is guarded by Egyptian sphinxes. A song in praise of the sphinxes was composed by David Shimonovitch, one of those poets who helped to rejuvenate the Hebrew language. He wrote "The Sphinxes" in 1910, and it was translated into Russian by Samuel Marshak. The first two stanzas read:

> This midnight is filled with a magical charm.
> The marble building with radiance is sown,
> The Neva has a dream that disturbs its calm
> And splashes the black and unmoving stone.
> From the depths of the dark blue night there appear
> Two giants—two sphinxes by the water that clings.
> In silence they listen to Neva's murmur, so near,
> And the snow-white North a song to them sings.
>
> I go to them in the radiance hushed,
> In the realm of a white, restless magic spell.
> The town sleeps, from the weight of sin it is crushed,
> And its sleep is stifled in a nightmarish hell.
> Above the palaces a host now gathers
> Of light clouds—a shimmering icy blue.
> Here are those who've been evicted—my brothers—
> The sphinxes doze and the Northern waters, too.

These sphinxes may still, perhaps, remember the generation of the Exodus, but a hundred years ago they witnessed a hitherto unknown phenomenon, the emergence of famous Jewish painters and sculptors. In our first excursion (the section on Maimon), we discussed the attitude of Jewish orthodox tradition toward the fine arts, so we shall not repeat ourselves. But as we are now at the Academy of Fine Arts, it would be appropriate to recall those Jews who worked and studied here. Apart from the two already mentioned, Antokolski and Maimon, these included I. Ya. Guenzburg, L. I. Asknazi, Y. M. Penn, L. S. Bakst, I. I. Brodsky, and Y. G. Gewirtz. Let us say a few words about some of them.

The sculptor Ilya Yakovlevitch Guenzburg was born in 1860 in Vilna and died in Leningrad in 1939. When he was eleven, the talented boy was noticed by the still young Antokolski, who took him to St. Petersburg to study. Guenzburg studied at first with Antokolski himself, then at the Academy of Fine Arts (1878–1886), and finally abroad at the expense of Baron Guenzburg. Ilya Yakovlevitch obtained fame and honor because of his long gallery of sculptured portraits of his great contemporaries: composers, writers, scholars, and political figures of the time. They included statuettes of Leo Tolstoy, Anton

Rubinstein, Pyotr Tchaikovsky, Nykolai Rimsky-Korsakov, Ivan Shishkin, Leonid Pasternak, Dmitri Mendeleyev, Horace Guenzburg, Mark Antokolski, F. Roditchev, P. Milyukov, and Feodor Chaliapin. He carved the heroic sculpture of the famous critic Vladimir Stassov on his tombstone in the Alexander Nevsky Monastery, the sculptures of the head of the dying Antokolski in the Preobrazhensky Cemetery (1909, no longer extant), and the Gogol statue in Poltava province (1910). Two of his bronze statues were erected in Leningrad under the Soviet authority: G. V. Plekhanov (1925) in front of the Institute of Technology and Dmitri Mendeleyev (1932) next door at the Institute of Metrology.*

Guenzburg has left in his memoirs, *Iz Proshlogo* (Out of the Past), a remarkable description of his Jewish childhood in Vilna, his friendship of many years standing with Mark Antokolski, and his meetings with Lev Tolstoy, Prince Kropotkin, Horace Guenzburg, S. Botkin, V. Stassov, V. Vereshchagin, and V. Serov. He also took part in the work of Jewish organizations, being deputy chairman of the Jewish Society for the Encouragement of the Arts and later director of the Jewish Historical-Ethnographic Museum. In 1904 he lived near the academy at House No. 11 on 2nd Liniya, Vassilevsky Ostrov.

The artist Isaak Lvovitch Asknazi was born in the shtetl of Drissa in the Vitebsk Guberniya in 1856 and died in Moscow in 1902. Today he is almost completely unknown, even though he was the first Jew to be made a member of the Academy of Fine Arts before the age of thirty and in his lifetime enjoyed great popularity. Asknazi studied at the academy between 1870 and 1880. His work usually had a profound Jewish theme, including biblical and historical topics and scenes from daily life.

Asknazi's best works are considered to be *Abraham Expels Hagar and Ishmael, Moses in the Wilderness, The Ecclesiast* (The Preacher), *The Death of Yehuda Halevi, A Jewish Wedding, The Eve of the Sabbath,* and his most famous work, *The Drowning of the Jews in Polotsk by Ivan the Terrible in 1563.* This picture is based on a historical fact, the capture of Polotsk by Ivan the Terrible during the Russo-Polish War, which was the first time that a Russian tsar took possession of a town with a large Jewish community. In reply to the request of the town governor as to what was to be done with these Jews, Ivan ordered them all to be baptized, and any who refused were to be drowned in the river. This was done. The picture was part of S. L. Guryevitch's collection in St. Petersburg, but we do not know where it is now. In 1894, before moving to Moscow, Asknazi was living on Vassilevsky Ostrov at No. 10 Maly Prospekt.

Yuri (Yehuda) Moiseyevitch Penn was born in Novoalexandrovsk, in the Minsk province of the Pale of Settlement, into a poor Jewish family. In 1879, on the advice of Asknazi, who was then a student at the academy, he applied for admission but was unsuccessful. He reapplied in 1882, and this time was admitted. His closest friends in the academy were A. Serov and M. Vrubel. In

---

* Metrology is the science of weights and measures, not to be confused with meteorology, the study of weather and climate.

1891 Penn went to Vitebsk, where he settled and set up his art studio, which became the very first school of painting and sculpture in the whole of Bielorussia.

It was this studio that made Penn famous as an artist. Among his pupils, Marc Chagall stands out. Other outstanding artists who passed through Penn's studio as his pupils were Solomon Yudovin, Z. Azgur, and Solomon Gershov. It was not just by chance that in 1919 Chagall, on the basis of the Penn studio, chose Vitebsk as the place to open the Academy of Painting, whose teachers, in addition to Chagall himself and Penn, included K. Malyevitch, Lazar Lissitsky, and A. Kuprin. Penn lived in Vitebsk until his death in 1937. Many artists took pride in the fact that they had been his pupils.

Many of Penn's own paintings have been preserved, many of them in the Vitebsk Museum. Among the characters portrayed in his paintings, we frequently come across simple Jewish folk: a tailor, a watchmaker, a seamstress, children, old men, old women. We also find a self-portrait, a portrait of Chagall, landscapes, everyday scenes, subjects of common life, and views of Vitebsk. Penn's paintings remain long fixed in the mind and memory of the viewer, as does every real artistic creation. The style of his brush indicates the strong tradition of Russian realism, but one can clearly see the presence of new trends in his work.

Leon Bakst (Lev Samoilovitch Rosenberg) was born in 1866 in Grodno and died in 1924 in Paris. He held completely different views and aesthetic principles, representing a new generation of artists. He studied at the academy from 1883 to 1887 and was an extremely assimilated Jew. Both the period and his talent tied Bakst to the group of artists who were to a significant extent responsible for the success of the Russian school of painting. Together with some colleagues from the academy — Alexander Benoit, B. Anisfeld, M. Dobuzhinsky, and others — he formed a creative union called The World of Art. Who now has not heard of this group?

The works of Konstant Somov, E. Lancer, A. Benoit, and Igor Grabar hang in the Russian Museum in Leningrad and the Tretyakov Gallery in Moscow, as do Bakst's own pictures. He created many successful book illustrations and easel paintings, but his main achievement lies in the theater. Bakst staged performances at the Imperial Alexander Theater in St. Petersburg, in the Greek style; of particular note was the *Hippolytus* of Euripides in 1902 and 1903. There then followed a journey to Greece, and his interest in ancient Greek as well as Oriental art can be found in all his work.

When Bakst, as a convert to Christianity who had returned — demonstrably — to Judaism, was evicted from St. Petersburg in 1909, he joined Sergei Diaghilev's ballet troupe and moved to Paris. There, he became the chief artist for all of Diaghilev's productions, including the *Egyptian Nights* by Arensky (1909), *Scheherezade* by Rimsky-Korsakov (1910), and *Firebird* by Stravinsky (1910). Leon Bakst's powerful influence on the European theater is generally recognized, making his well-designed, bright, stylized costumes and stage decorations an essential part of a theatrical performance. His costumes heightened the effect of the spectacle, stressing the movements of the actor's dance. Apart from his work with Diaghilev, Bakst also staged several productions in the theaters of Paris, London, Rome, and New York. In St. Petersburg, Bakst lived at No. 22 Zvenigorodskaya ulitsa. In his youth, Chagall was a pupil of Bakst as well as of Penn.

Many artists, sculptors, and architects lived on Vassilevsky Ostrov, close to the academy. The architect Yakov Germanovitch (Hermanovitch) Gewirtz, the designer of the prayer house at the Preobrazhensky Cemetery, lived at No. 11 Sredny Prospekt. He was a professor at the academy for many years.

Mark Antokolski (of whom I will speak in detail in the Preobrazhensky Cemetery excursion) lived from 1870 to 1872 immediately opposite the academy in Voronin's house at No. 4 5th Liniya. His apartment was on the third floor. When he brought the eleven-year-old Ilya Guenzburg to St. Petersburg, the boy lived at first in that apartment. Antokolski's own studio was actually in the academy itself, on the third floor. It was there that the sculptor was honored in 1871 by a visit from Tsar Alexander II.

For a short time in 1922, Nathan Isayevitch Altman lived at No. 4 1st Liniya, in the former house of David Guenzburg, near the Rumyantsev Gardens. He never studied at the St. Petersburg academy but received his professional training in Odessa and Paris. In addition to his famous portraits of Lenin, Lunacharsky, and Akhmatova, the artist did much work for the Jewish theater. He produced the scenic designs for *The Dybbuk* at the Vakhtangov Habimah Theater (1922), Gutskov's *Uriel Akosta* (1921), and the film *Yevreiskoye 3hchastye* (Jewish Happiness) based on a story by Sholem Aleikhem. As a book illustrator, Altman drew the designs for S. Galkin's *Bar-Kochba* and Y. L. Peretz's *It's Burning* (1940). His portrait of Solomon Mikhoels is outstanding. The list could continue—Altman never lost interest in Jewish art.

We have just had occasion to mention the house of Baron David Guenzburg on 1st Liniya. This address is also closely connected with the history of the first Jewish secular institute of higher education, with courses of Oriental studies. In 1907 the magazine *Ha-Kedem* published an announcement that "in accordance with the decree (ukase) of 15th September this year . . . permission is granted to Baron D. von Guenzburg to open a High School for Jewish Learning under the title of 'Courses of Oriental Studies' in St. Petersburg." It would be desirable to present here, in this excursion, the full program of courses, but within our excursion framework this would not be possible. If it were so, however, we could take the opportunity to explain in broader terms the meanings of the words *Masorah, Exegetics, Midrash, Aggadah, Targum, Possuk, Kabbalah, Pseudepigrapha, Homiletics, Novellae, Responsa,* and more. Even those terms, which superficially seem familiar, are hardly known to the contemporary reader. What, for example, is meant by Jewish paleography, or Hebrew rhetoric? And so far we have mentioned only the titles!

In short, and as we shall see later, a great deal was taught in these courses. First, there was a scholarly analysis of the Bible and the Talmud with all their translations, apocryphas, glosses, commentaries, and commentaries on the glosses, as well as the historic and archeological information that was available on the subject. Second, the students were taught general Jewish history, the history of Jewish culture, literature, philosophy, and Jewish languages, as well as the history, philosophy, and languages of the peoples who had come into contact with the Jews, and an indication of the mutual influences of their cultures. Special subjects were offered, for example, the history and geography of Palestine, Arabic language, rabbinic literature, medieval Hebrew poetry, the influence of Oriental literature on Russian literature, psychology, and pedagogics. It will be obvious that the graduates of these courses had a well-grounded erudition.

The course teachers included David Guenzburg himself (linguistics and religious philosophy), who was nominated as rector; Dr. A. Zarzowsky (linguistics, Bible, and Apocrypha, the history and geography of ancient Middle-Eastern civilizations); Dr. Katzenelson (Talmud and Midrash); Candidate of Oriental studies I. Guenzburg (linguistics, Talmud and Midrash, religious philosophy); Candidate of Oriental studies Isaak Markon (history of Jewish literature); Simon Dubnow (Jewish history); and V. Ashkenazi (pedagogics and didactics).

The courses at first were held in David Guenzburg's house at No. 4 1st Liniya, but in fact much of the tuition was carried out in Eisenbet's Gymnasium (secondary high school) at No. 7 Nikolsky Pere'ulok (now ulitsa Myasnikova). Soon after, they transferred to No. 35 (formerly No. 33) 8th Liniya on Vassilevsky Ostrov, where a student's hostel was established. Simon Dubnow also lived here.

From 1911 to 1913 the courses were held at No. 5 6th Liniya, and in July 1913 they moved to their final address, the building of the Jewish Almshouse at No. 50 5th Liniya. Nevertheless, some studies still continued in David Guenzburg's house, where he himself was the tutor, until his death in 1910. As related in Dubnow's memoirs, the baron did not follow any precise syllabus but lectured "as the spirit took him." He would invite the students into his enormous library, where the tables were littered with rare folio manuscripts and ancient printed books, pick up some medieval book — say, Maimonides' *Moreh Nevukhim* (The Guide of the Perplexed) — tell one of the students to read aloud, and then himself explain in detail the passage that had just been read.

Among the students were recent graduates from yeshivahs, self-taught provincials. Some of them already knew what they were being taught, as they were well grounded in religious literature and Hebrew language. The ones who stood highest in the level of their previous training were those from Odessa, students of Joseph Klausner, who had written history in Modern Hebrew. One of these, Zalman Rubashov, was later a leader of the Jewish workers' movement in Palestine and still later became president of the State of Israel (for two terms, from 1963 to 1973), when he was known as Zalman Shazar, an acronym of the initial letters of *Shneur-Zalman Rubashov.*

The exact number of students is not now known, but in his memoirs

Dubnow recollected that in his class on medieval Jewish history there were about forty students. Among those attending lectures were some students of the St. Petersburg University or the Bestuzhev courses, about which I shall speak shortly. The young people spent much of their time together, walking about St. Petersburg; none of them at that time ever thought that one of them, David Shimonovitch, would write about it in his poems.

Of them all, one stood out by virtue of his erudition: Yechiel Ravrebbe. This tall, stooping blond man came from a Hasidic family of the small town of Baranovka in the Novograd-Volynskaya province of western Russia. He had a splendid knowledge of Hebrew grammar and wrote poetry in modern Hebrew. He translated into Hebrew the libretto of *Samson and Delilah,* the first opera to be performed in Russia in Hebrew. It was staged at the Tenishevsky School on Mokhovaya Street.

The majority of the students at the High School for Jewish Learning did not have residential permission to live in the capital, and those who gave small bribes to the janitors and doorkeepers found difficulty making both ends meet. In the hostel on 8th Liniya they were accommodated two to a room, but Ravrebbe had a room to himself, which everyone considered reasonable. Many of the students earned a little on the side with private Hebrew lessons. Ravrebbe, as the most outstanding, was invited to be Hebrew teacher to the children of Rabbi Katzenellenbogen, the spiritual leader of St. Petersburg. The evenings in the hostel were lively with arguments: Klausner's students argued with Dubnow's, the Socialist-Zionists with the Zionists. The delicate, reserved Yechiel Ravrebbe did not join in these discussions. He studied earnestly, wrote poetry, and worked in both the Society of Lovers of Ancient Hebrew Language and Society of Lovers of Hebrew Literature. The future seemed to be beckoning him to be a great scholar of history and Oriental studies, to be the author of many scholarly works, and to decipher ancient manuscripts found in archeological excavations in Syria. Unfortunately his star, a star of great magnitude, rose just at the time in Russia of a steep decline in Jewish learning in general.

The courses of Oriental studies came to a close with the beginning of World War I. Although they were sometimes referred to in handbooks as higher courses of Jewish learning, and even as the Jewish Academy, it was still only a small private institute of learning, surviving on the financial support of the family of Baron Guenzburg and intended for the tuition of a small number of students. Everything, from the curriculum to the appointment of teaching staff, depended on the choice of the patron, the baron himself. He even had influence on the selection of students, sometimes helping with obtaining residential permits. However, the courses did not become a real Jewish institute of higher education.

The next step in that direction was the foundation in 1919 of the so-called Jewish University.

☐ **NOT FAR FROM** David Guenzburg's house, in a beautiful three-storied building on the corner of 3rd Liniya and Bolshoi Prospekt (3rd Liniya No. 4/8 in apt. 8), lived Full Councillor of State, Merchant of the First Guild Lev Pavlovitch (Arye-Leib Faivelyevitch) Friedland (1826–1898). He was a notable personality in the Jewish community of St. Petersburg and was elected a member of the Board of Management in the 1870s. The Friedland family burial vault is preserved to this day in the Preobrazhensky Cemetery. Friedland comes into this story mainly because of another man — a bibliograph and fanatical book lover— Samuel Yeremeyevitch Wiener (1860–1929), who lived nearby at No. 23 Solovyevsky Pere'ulok, now ulitsa Repina.

Dubnow described Wiener as "a man with a face of parchment who was himself a living parchment with the imprint of the titles of every ancient Jewish book." It was Wiener who persuaded Friedland to set up a memorial to his late wife in the form of an archival library of ancient books and manuscripts. With Wiener's help, the widower dug out complete libraries of manuscripts and books and then bequeathed the entire collection to the Russian Academy of Arts for it to be housed in the Asiatic Museum (Universitetskaya Naberezhnaya No. 5) on condition that Wiener was employed to catalog it.

Wiener had had no formal education. He was a typical Jewish "wunderkind." While still a boy, he became renowned for having cataloged every library in his hometown. He was therefore given temporary residential permit for St. Petersburg, conditional on his completing the catalog. It is not surprising that he did not rush this task. In thirty years he had published less than half the catalog.

From the Asiatic Museum the library passed to the Institute of Oriental Studies of the Academy of Sciences of the Soviet Union, where the work on the catalog was still proceeding as of 1986. Prior to 1888 the library was housed in the owner's apartment.

☐ **IT IS UNLIKELY** that today's students and teachers at the Publishing and Printing Technical College at No. 28 5th Liniya on Vassilevsky Ostrov know that in this modest two-story building a similar professional-technical institution was located from 1917 to 1922 — the Jewish publishing house Kadima (Hebrew for Eastward or in modern Hebrew, Forward). The publishing house had a Zionist orientation. This is apparent even from the list of books that issued from it: for example, Theodor Herzl *The Jewish State,* Max Nordau *Collected Articles,* and Leo Pinsker *Auto-Emancipation.* Incidentally, one of the most valuable books for the historian of Jewish St. Petersburg, is the *Jewish Year Book* for 1918 to 1919, published by Kadima. From the preface we discover that up to 1912 the *Year Book* was published in Vilna, but the fourth edition published there, covering 1912 to 1913 (the Jewish year 5673), was

The Kadima publishing house at 5th Liniya 28

confiscated by the government, and the publisher and editor were taken to court. The Vilna court permitted the publication of the *Year Book* on condition that 120 pages devoted to Palestine were removed. The preface to the 1918 to 1919 (5679) edition ends on an optimistic note: "Only in 1917, after the downfall of the autocracy, has it become possible to prepare a new edition." And indeed, in 1918 in Petrograd the book was published without any restrictions.

The book is a treasury of all sorts of statistics and information about Jewish life. It gives, for example, the number of Jews in all countries and in many individual towns. We learn that in the old Pale of Settlement of European Russia in 1917 there lived 3,305,000 Jews; outside the Pale, 532,000; and in Poland and Lithuania, 2,448,000. The total in European Russia within the prewar borders was 6,321,000, with a further 177,000 in Trans-caucasia, Central Asia, and Siberia—a grand total of 6,498,000.

Jews formed a large proportion of the population in towns such as Kovno and Warsaw (40 percent), Minsk (50 percent), and Berdichev (78 percent). The

Year Book also contains interesting information on the education of Jews in Russia. We discover that in St. Petersburg in 1910 there were thirty-three cheders with 176 boy pupils, 21 girl pupils, and 35 teachers. For the most part, Jewish children obtained their secondary education in commercial or private institutions, where in St. Petersburg the Jewish children comprised 30.4 percent and 37.3 percent of all students, respectively. From 1909 to 1910 there were 7,241 Jewish students in Russia's higher educational establishments, 11 percent of the total number.

A table of mortality by age group and religious affiliation for 1896 to 1897 is revealing. For every thousand children in Russia up to the age of twelve months, the number of Russian Orthodox children who died was 282.8; Lutheran, 178.5; Catholic, 149; Moslem, 166.4; and Jewish, 130.4.

On this excursion it is impossible to go into all the statistics in the *Year Book,* but it contains much more interesting information about criminality among Russia's Jews, about emigration, and so on. A list of most Jewish societies in Russia and abroad, along with their addresses and an indication of their interests and activities, provides the researcher with valuable material. It is also interesting to look at the list of the main events in Jewish history at the end of the *Year Book.* Indeed, an appreciable part of the book is devoted to the subject that led to the court case in Vilna—information about Palestine.

THE NEXT STOP on our excursion is House No. 50 on 5th Liniya, a not large but nevertheless impressive building, built between 1905 and 1913.

This house, about which we will have much to say, was erected from the funds provided by Moisei Akimovitch Ginsburg, a generous philanthropist and member of the financial administration of the St. Petersburg community. He financed the building of the prayer house at the cemetery. The building contained the Jewish almshouse, which until the Revolution bore the name of its benefactor and chairman of its Board of Guardians—that same Ginsburg. Until the Revolution the superintendent of the almshouse was A. P. Tinyanov, and the old people had medical care provided by Grigory Isaakovitch Dembo, the second representative of a celebrated dynasty of doctors. In the 1920s the superintendent and medical officer was Yefim Yevseyevitch Klionsky (1892–1961), later professor and specialist in the treatment of tuberculosis. His family occupied an apartment on the top floor. In those days the almshouse was maintained by the Leningrad Jewish Committee to Provide Help to the Victims of War (LEKOPO).

The Board of Guardians and the Lady Patronesses arranged fund-raising social gatherings to support the almshouse, with performances by the then very young Freidkov, future bass at the Mariinsky Theater; the pianist Perelman, who later became professor at the Leningrad Conservatoire; and the Jewish folksinger Golubyova. Living conditions in the almshouse were very comfortable, two or three to a room, with a large kitchen providing the residents with kosher food.

In 1913 courses on Oriental studies, organized by the Jewish Historical-Ethnographic Society, were held in this same building. On the first and second floors were set aside halls for lectures, a strong room for the archives, and a large room for a museum.

The Historical-Ethnographic Society (the Russian initial letters are IEO), to which we shall return in our next excursion, was created in 1908 by the efforts of several enthusiastic people. At the end of the nineteenth century and early in the twentieth century they gathered material on the history, ethnography, and folklore of Russian Jews. Their achievement, though incomplete, is invaluable because the traditional Jewish "shtetl" has not survived to our day; that life has now gone, and even then it was rapidly disappearing.

Indeed, the increased interest in the creative legacy of the people and its scientific study, the foundation of ethnography, the preservation of the memorials of antiquity — all these tendencies were highly characteristic of the end of the nineteenth century. The Russian and Ukrainian intelligentsia conducted similar work in studying the life of the minority peoples of Siberia, the Far North, and elsewhere. The movement was stimulated by the rapid advances in science, the heightening of national awareness, and the fear that the morrow would probably be too late to study the traditional life of the people. The last point was particularly relevant to the national life of the Jews.

It all began with several articles in the press by Orshansky, I. Lerner, and An-sky on the need to collect and study Jewish folklore. Simon Dubnow led the way in the collection of historical documents, and S. Ginzburg and P. Marek began to gather Jewish folk songs. It was from this that the Society for Jewish Folk Music was born. This led to the formation of the Jewish Historical-Ethnographic Society (IEO) in St. Petersburg in 1908. The society changed its address several times: it was at No. 25 ulitsa Kalyaeva (formerly Zakharyevskaya) in Mikhail Vinaver's apartment up to 1910; ulitsa Nekrassova (formerly Basseinaya) No. 35 in Gessen's apartment until 1912; then 7th Sovietskaya (formerly Rozhdestvenskaya) No. 6, apt. 24; then ulitsa Kalyaeva No. 25, apt. 13 until 1917; 5th Liniya No. 50 in 1918; and ulitsa Ryleyeva No. 8 until 1927.

The constitution of the IEO stated that its aim was to gather, study, and analyze historical and ethnographic materials about the Jews in Russia and Poland from the appearance of the first Jewish settlements to the present day. Meetings were organized on academic topics, public lectures were given on Jewish history and ethnography, and systematic collections of legal deeds and registry entries were published, as were scholastic research works and so on. The chairman of the society was the famous Russian lawyer, Russian and Jewish public figure, and a cadet deputy to the first State Duma, Maxim Moiseyevitch Vinaver. The two vice-chairmen were the historian Simon Dubnow and the educationalist Mikhail Kulisher. The society's active members included S. Goldstein, M. G. Syrkin, L. Y. Sternberg (IEO chairman from 1924), M. I. Sheftel, G. B. Sliozberg, S. G. Lozinsky, I. A. Kleinman, and S. L. Zinberg.

Simeon (Shimon) An-sky

From January 1909 the society published the journal *Yevreiskaya Starina* (Jewish Antiquity). It contained many valuable documents, memoirs, and articles on the history of the Jews of Lithuania, Poland, and Russia. The society gathered a large collection of manuscripts and other memorabilia of the past. It functioned only in St. Petersburg and had no branches elsewhere. Following the emigration of M. Vinaver and then of Dubnow, Professor L. Y. Sternberg became chairman of IEO and editor of *Yevreiskaya Starina,* and after 1927, S. L. Zinberg. By 1925 the Society for the Study of Social Biology and Psychophysics of the Jews had merged with the IEO. In 1922 the commission still maintained its independence and was located at No. 20 ulitsa Furmanova (formerly Gagarinskaya) with A. M. Bramson as chairman. In 1916 the IEO had a museum with academician I. Y. Guenzburg as curator, and he also headed the museum committee. The society existed until 1930.

A considerable role in organizing the Jewish Museum, which was in the same building, was played by Simeon An-sky the renowned writer in Russian and Yiddish, a former Narodnik,* secretary to Pyotr Lavrov (the revolution-

---

* A Narodnik was a member of the People's Will Party. The Social Revolutionaries were successors to the Narodniks.

ary), author of the famous play *The Dybbuk,* and composer of the hymn of the Bund called "Di Shvueh" (The Oath).

Between 1911 and 1914, An-sky led an ethnographic expedition to Volhynia, Podolia, and the Kiev province funded by Baron Vladimir Guenzburg, one of the sons of Horace Guenzburg. The expedition, which was named in honor of Horace Guenzburg, included two specialists in Jewish musical folklore — Yuri Engel and Zusman Kisselgoff — as well as the artist Solomon Yudovin. The outbreak of war brought the expedition to a halt.

In 1916, on the basis of materials collected as a result of An-sky's efforts, the museum was opened in the almshouse building. The museum was closed in 1917 and then reopened in the early 1920s. It had several departments: ethnography, history, music, art, and ancient arts. There were about a thousand items on exhibition: phonograph musical cylinders, on which folk songs had been recorded; collections of popular legends, tales, and myths; manuscripts, old books, and incunabula; photographs of old synagogues, and scenes from everyday Jewish life among the people; synagogue utensils and vestments, some very skillfully crafted; specimens of the clothing of past centuries; wedding decorations; tableware; and so on. By the 1920s the museum had been restocked with pictures on themes of Jewish life painted by N. Altman, Y. Penn, S. Gershov, A. Tischler, and Yudovin, who became curator and lived on the premises together with his family. The museum was open to visitors every Saturday and Sunday for three hours. After the death of I. Guenzburg, the museum committee's chairman was A. M. Bramson, and its members included V. Klionsky, Yudovin, and I. Ravrebbe. Ravrebbe also lived there in the 1920s, as his wife was the housekeeper of the almshouse. The demise of the museum coincided with that of the IEO, in about 1930.

It is interesting that An-sky lived for a while in the almshouse building. There is a remarkable mention of this in the memoirs of Mark Rivesman, who describes how they once met there:

> An-sky was once in St. Petersburg without a permit to be there, either as a "political" or as a "deprivee," and with nowhere to spend the night. In fact he was living illegally in the capital, going from place to place to sleep. The last time I met him was in the morning in a little room on Vassilevsky Ostrov at the almshouse, and in the evening in the Zoo. When I saw him in the morning he was lying on something or other that did not even remotely resemble a bed. It would take the pen of a Gogol to describe the "furnishings" of that room. I will merely say that every single thing there, seemed to be in the wrong place. Only a real "Bohemian" could live that way. He stood up, sat down on the "bed," rubbed his eyes and when he recognized me he said:
>
> "It's a good job a thief didn't break in. . . ." and he burst out laughing at his own joke with such gleeful laughter that for a moment he even infected me.
>
> "Well don't put the evil eye on me. You see I was beginning to yawn. . . . What's the time? Someone stole my watch a couple of days ago."
>
> "About twelve," I said.
>
> "Not bad! I promised to meet Dubnow at eleven, and at twelve. . . . I'd

better not tell you that. You must have been hoping to have a glass of tea with me. . . ."

"I've already had tea."

"You're a lucky chap. Now look. Will you fetch me that writing pad off that shelf. Thanks. Sit down and listen. Only, when I've read it to you don't start being critical."

And he started to read the first scenes from his mystic play *The Dybbuk*. He read splendidly and I listened with bated breath. When he finished reading Act One he asked me:

"What do you think? Is it a well-formed baby? No rickets, no other infantile ailments . . . ?"

"My dear S. A.—do read on."

"Ah, it's got you has it. . . . I'd like something to eat."

"I'll slip out and get some rolls and a few things."

"Now you're talking sense. Run like the wind."

I ran, spurred on by the prospect of hearing from the very lips of the gifted author himself the second act of his marvellous dramatic poem. An-sky was very pleased with his breakfast and carried on reading but not forgetting the rolls, butter, and cheese. The more he read, the more interesting it became. At last he stopped and said:

"Up to now we've been reading on Shabbat Hagadol (Holy Saturday) and I've not written any more. I hope I'll finish the play before my own glorious demise."

IT WAS MAXIM VINAVER who, in 1915, founded the Jewish Society for the Encouragement of the Arts in the same building at No. 50 on 5th Liniya. The vice-chairman was the famous sculptor Ilya Yakovlevitch Guenzburg. In 1917 the society moved to Vinaver's house at No. 25 ulitsa Zakharyevskaya. With the emigration of its chairman after the 1917 Revolution the society probably disintegrated. While it was still active, the society organized several art exhibitions and competitions, even though the initial aims of its founders had been much more ambitious: to publish books and journals, to support young talent, and to promote other aims.

In the half-century from 1880 to 1930 in St. Petersburg, at least forty Jewish cultural, educational, philanthropic, and other societies can be identified. Some were unrealistic and barely survived. Others such as ORT (The Society for Craft and Agricultural Labor among the Jews of Russia), OPE (Society for the Spread of Enlightenment among the Jews of Russia), ICA (Jewish Colonization Association), and IEO (Jewish Historical Ethnographic Society) played an important part in the history of the Jews of Russia.

Leningraders remember that on 10th Liniya in House No. 33 there was until recently the Mathematics-Mechanics Faculty of Leningrad State University. Before the Revolution this was the house of the Higher Women's Courses, better known as the Bestuzhev Courses. Without delving too deeply into the history of these courses, which in itself is very interesting, we must mention that they have a connection with Jewish history.

The well-known lawyer L. M. Eisenberg, in his article "Plehve and the Jewish Bestuzhev Course Graduates," recalls that a certain Devorah Rafailovitch, on graduating from the courses in 1902, set up home on her own away from her father. But the right to live in the capital, as the possessor of a diploma of higher education, was not recognized by the police as only a short while previously the minister of the interior, Plehve, had instructed the commissioner of police not to be lenient to the Jews. Eisenberg took up Devorah Rafailovitch's case and fought it for *eight* years, until eventually, in May 1910, the Council of State recognized the Bestuzhev Courses as a higher educational establishment. Until then, for all those eight years, the grade of the courses had officially been kept low in order to evict some of its Jewish women graduates from St. Petersburg.

Sophia, the daughter of Simon Dubnow (and later the wife of Henryk Erlich, member of the Central Committee of the Bund), studied here for a while in 1904, but in the same year she was expelled for her part in the student disturbances. It was then that she wrote her prophetic poem about Plehve — the persecutor of the Jews. In these verses she compares Plehve with Haman, the Japanese with Cyrus of Persia, and, for some reason, tsarist Russia with Babylon. The poem was printed in *Voskhod,* but the entire edition was confiscated by the police. Then Sophia Dubnovna's prophecy came true: the minister of the interior was shortly afterward shot and killed.

In 1910, and for some years later, the Bestuzhev Courses included a class on the study of Jewish history given by Professor Kartashov. In the 1920s the building formerly used by the courses was given over to a Rabfak (Rabotchi-Fakultet or Workers' Faculty), under the direction of Shulman. The Rabfak prepared its students for entry to higher education, and they had three years of study. The faculty also had "national" departments, including a Jewish one, whose head was Gitlitz. The tuition was conducted in Yiddish. Zinovy (Zusman) Kisselgoff taught mathematics, and Solomon Yudovin taught drawing and sketching.

The first Jewish educational establishment on Vassilevsky Ostrov appeared no later than 1879. An announcement was published in the paper *Ha-Melitz* on October 16, 1879, stating that the private Jewish Gymnasium (secondary high school) and the Weideman Commercial School would now be directed by Dr. Erdel and had moved to 9th Liniya No. 44, apt. 17.

During the succeeding years the small but cohesive Jewish community on Vassilevsky Ostrov maintained without a break some sort of educational establishment, chiefly cheders at the small synagogues and prayer houses. One of these synagogues was, in the early years of this century, at 3rd Liniya No. 48 (entrance in the courtyard). It contained a Jewish school for children from poor families. The headmistress was Sophia Afanasyevna Zeltser. The school was maintained by the Society for the Assistance of Poor Jews on Vassilevsky

Ostrov and Galernaya Harbor (Tsedoko G'doilo), whose chairman was Dr. L. I. Weingerov; its address was No. 33 Sredny Prospekt. The children attended the school for three to four years. Side by side with religious subjects, they were taught modern Hebrew (Ivrit) and elementary Jewish history (in Russian). In the years 1918 to 1920 there was also another prayer house at No. 16 Sredny Prospekt, which had a cheder.

Next door to the building of the former Bestuzhev Courses at No. 37 on 10th Liniya on Vassilevsky Ostrov is a small building with a garden, surrounded by a high fence. For more than half a century this building was associated with the upbringing and education of Jewish children. In the last century, not later

Zinovy Kisselgoff's school on the 10th Liniya, Vassilevsky Ostrov

than 1890, Anna Gesselevna, the wife of the famous Baron Horace Guenzburg, founded here a Jewish orphanage. Later, her son, the gold-mine owner Alexander Guenzburg, took the funding of the institution upon himself. Management of the home passed to a Ladies' Committee of Guardians, chaired by Baroness Matilda Yurievna Guenzburg. G. I. Dembo looked after the health of the children.

With the 1917 Revolution the day of charitably funded orphanages passed. They were replaced by children's homes funded by the state. During the war and the Revolution the Jewish population of the former Pale of Settlement lost several hundred thousand people at the battlefronts, during all sorts of pogroms, and from starvation. Everywhere there were countless orphans.

In the early 1920s a train with ten coaches arrived in Petrograd. It brought Jewish children from Bielorussia and the Ukraine who had seen a great deal in their short lives. Among them were future mathematicians and musicians, Komsomol (Communist Youth League) activists, and heroes of the coming war. The children arrived to begin a new happy life, free from horror and nightmares. They were brought here to 10th Liniya, where No. 93 (later renumbered 76) Children's Home was established. The manager of this home, Zinovy Kisselgoff, became their common father. The writer Doivber Levin later wrote a book about this Children's Home entitled *Ten Coaches*.

Kisselgoff was an outstanding personality and a pedagogue in the highest sense of the word. He was already known in the community of St. Petersburg in the 1910s. We come across his name as a committee member of the Society for Jewish Folk Music and as a teacher at Eisenbet's Gymnasium and the Jewish Trade and Craft School run by the OPE at No. 42 Offitserskaya ulitsa. He is known to have been a gifted teacher, an organizer of Jewish education, a talented musician, a collector of Jewish folk music, and a brilliant connoisseur of folklore.

In 1917 Kisselgoff, together with the other leading Jewish teachers of Petrograd, formed the Petrograd Jewish Teachers' Association, and he became a member of the committee. The association's appeal stated:

> The moment has finally arrived when much of what we have dreamed about for many years can, and must be put into practice. Now, comrades, the chains of slavery have been broken. Great opportunities have been created and the horizons of our work have been broadened and deepened. Now when the country as a whole and each group separately is organizing its forces . . . it is absolutely essential for us Jews as quickly as possible to implement and consolidate our natural cultural rights. . . .

The founders of the Petrograd Jewish Teachers Association were determined to establish Jewish school education of the proper type. The association itself never functioned, but, as Director of the Jewish Children's Home, Kisselgoff had the opportunity to bring at least some of its, and his, plans to realization. Later No. 14 Fully Jewish National School was founded on the basis of

One of the classes of the Jewish National School. Kisselgoff is in the center.

the Children's Home and then from 1938 the Second (not fully) National School. Kisselgoff was appointed headmaster of the school. Judith Mikhailovna Dvorkina was put in charge of the Children's Home. By 1931, there were 267 pupils registered in the school in classes of thirty to thirty-five. Most of them were nonresidents, but boarders made up about 10 percent. It was they who spoke Yiddish and represented the national nucleus of the school. The great attraction of the school for the day pupils living in town was the quality of the teaching of the general subjects and the high success rate of its pupils. The Jewish language, which the pupils studied together with other foreign languages two or three times a week, was treated by the native Leningraders as rather a burden, and to get top marks in it was even considered to be a bit of a disgrace. In the early 1930s the school managers tried to have most subjects taught in Yiddish, but the attempt was abandoned when it became clear that many spoke the language badly and the success rate began to decline rapidly. No Hebrew was taught at all.

The first graduates of No. 11 Jewish National School. This picture was taken soon after Kisselgoff's arrest. For this reason, Director of Studies Lev Yokhelteuk's photo was placed in the upper center instead of Director Kisselgoff's.

The second group of graduates of No. 11 National Jewish School. A new director (non-Jewish) is in the center.

As if in compensation, the extracurricular Jewish cultural life thrived. Kisselgoff encouraged artistic, musical, and drama groups. The school had its own choir, and many of the youngsters were discovered to be fine musicians. Kisselgoff himself played the concertina. Outstanding concerts often took place on the top-floor assembly hall, where the synagogue had been when it was an orphanage. In this favorable atmosphere many of the children developed their creative talents. Frieda Yudborovskaya, who was killed during World War II, had a beautiful soprano voice. She performed Russian classical romances and Jewish songs equally well. Former pupils still remember to this day the unsophisticated lullaby that she often sang:

Shloff, shloff, shloff,	Sleep, sleep, sleep,
Dien tatte vet for'n in dorf	Your daddy is going to the country
vet er brengen a neeselleh	He'll bring back some nuts
vet zein gezunt di feesselleh	So that your feet will be healthy
Shloff, shloff, shloff,	Sleep, sleep, sleep,
Dien tatte vet for'n in dorf	Your daddy is going to the country
Vet er brengen en eppelleh	He'll bring back a little apple
vet zein gezunt di keppelleh	So that your head will be healthy

Minya Weissman, Aron Rubinstein, Syoma Zharovsky, and others acted in the drama group. Lyova Schmidt, the most talented of them, was taken by Solomon Mikhoels into his troupe. Life was full of activity also among the young artists working under the direction of the drawing teacher Boris Yefimovitch Tsirlin. They organized exhibitions in Russian and Yiddish on the life of the school and published a wall newspaper called *Detdomovets.** One of the youngsters, Katzman, became a professional artist but, like Frieda Yudborovskaya, was killed during the war.

For Kisselgoff, folklore was not a dead memorial of times past but an inheritance to be used as a contemporary resource. He generously shared it with his pupils. Famous Jewish actors of the time often visited the school, many of them personal friends of his: Eppelbaum, Mikhoels, Zusskin, and Markish. The group of Jewish vocalists known as Yevokance† also visited the school. Even the children themselves performed at concerts in the Jewish Educational Club, the Leningrad branch of the Society of for the Promotion of Jewish Settlement (OZET), or at the Leonov Tramcar Depot, which had taken the school under its patronage.

Kisselgoff succeeded in making the Children's Home a home not only for orphans but also for the nonresidents. This he achieved through his great erudition, and experience, his gifts as a teacher, and his sincere love of children. The school absorbed all his time. He also lived here with his family in a small

---

* *Detdomovets* means "a resident of a children's home."
† *Yevokance* is an acronym from the Russian words "Jewish Vocal Ensemble."

flat consisting of one room and a kitchen, situated next to the teaching staff's common room. The teachers visited the flat no less than the common room itself. Kisselgoff chose the teachers very carefully and very diligently. Once appointed they remained on the staff for a long time. Relations between the teachers were close, friendly, and informal. Like the headmaster, the majority were outstanding specialists with irrepressible enthusiasm. The teaching ranged far beyond that of a normal school program. Not surprisingly, nearly all the pupils went on to higher education, many obtaining a master's or a candidate's degree and some even a doctorate.

All that has been said still does not fully convey all that was remarkable about this group of people. Other schools, after all, also had qualified teachers and able pupils. As for Jewish culture, it existed at the school in a rather limited form, without modern Hebrew (Ivrit), Jewish history, or basic religious knowledge, and even Yiddish was taught somewhat half-heartedly. Then why do the eyes of former pupils still light up even today when they remember those times? Why do they still look for each other and for their teachers, maintain contact

Zinovy Kisselgoff

and meet each other, phone and write to each other? The reason is probably to be found in the atmosphere of goodness and brotherliness, the "spirit of the lycée" that Kisselgoff, who was imbued with the "mercy of God," was able to inspire into the small group. They all remember his stooping figure (he had a spine defect), his hands behind his back, his bald skull, and his small mustache. He was hot tempered and sometimes even shouted at his pupils, but no one was frightened since they knew his good nature. It was not a telling-off that the children feared so much as the most severe punishment, when the headmaster took the wrongdoer by the arm and led him from class to class the whole day (he taught mathematics), made him sit at the front facing the class, and in the break took him to the staff room, gave him his dinner in his kitchen, and so on until the evening.

Many of the pupils, especially the boys, have not survived. During World War II their age group was the most called up. Those who had entered artillery schools by special callup even before the war died at the very beginning. These included the boarders Aron Rubinstein and Yefim Hamburg and the day pupils Yasha Hershkovitch and Rolik Hellberger. Hershkovitch was exceptionally erudite and a splendid orator, and a shining career in the sciences was forecast for Rubinstein. These hopes were not to be fulfilled. But some at least did survive. Among them are chemists, biologists, lawyers, and art critics. The former Pioneer leader Isaak Spielberg subsequently graduated from the Jewish Rabfak (courses for workers located in the Leningrad University physics faculty) and then the university's law faculty. He is now a Jewish writer in Smolensk and publishes in *Sovietish Heimland,* the only Yiddish-language monthly in the Soviet Union.

There was an unfortunate opportunity for the former pupils to prove their feelings for their adored teacher when Kisselgoff was arrested in 1937. The pupils wrote a collective letter in his defense. Whether the letter had any effect, or whether it was because of other reasons, is not known, but about a year later the aged and sick teacher was released.

On Kisselgoff's release, Solomon Mikhoels went to Leningrad and arranged a celebration for his friend or, as they called it in those days, a "triumph." At the celebrations, Kisselgoff caught a cold and died within a fortnight. Many of his former pupils attended the funeral at the Preobrazhensky Cemetery. The old pupils all remember also, with much tenderness, their other teachers: Dina Grigorievna Mikhailovskaya (biology), Maria No'evna Rosenblum (school secretary and music teacher), Mark Davidovitch Domnitz (history, killed in the first year of the war), Mark Yakovlevitch Schnitzer (physics), Lev Markovitch Yokheltchuk (director of studies and Yiddish), Isaak London (geography), and above all, of course, Zinovy Aronovitch Kisselgoff. When he died, together with him also ended the story of the school on 10th Liniya on Vassilevsky Ostrov, the last Jewish school in Leningrad.

EXCURSION FOUR

THE HOUSE
ON 5TH LINIYA

THE OBJECT OF our interest is on Vassilevsky Ostrov, a building we have seen before, No. 50 on 5th Liniya. For twenty years this house was one of the chief places of interest in Jewish St. Petersburg. The list of organizations, events, and personalities connected with this one building is a very long one. Some we have already mentioned or passed by briefly during one of our previous excursions. Between 1913 and 1935 there were no less than five institutions located in this one house:

1 The Moisei Akimovitch Jewish Almshouse
2 The Baron David Guenzburg Courses on Oriental Studies for Jews, or the Courses of Higher Jewish Studies, or the Academy of Jewish Sciences
3 The Jewish Historical-Ethnographic Society
4 The Jewish Historical-Ethnographic Museum (or the Museum of the Jewish Historical-Ethnographic Society)
5 The Jewish Society for the Encouragement of the Arts

We will begin with No. 50 itself, the whole building. The house is not very large, but it is an impressive-looking four-story building erected some time before 1913. It was designed by Yakov Gewirtz, who also designed the prayer house at the Preobrazhensky Cemetery. The ground floor is a semibasement, with narrow apertures of windows and the main entrance door, whereas another entrance symmetrical with it is in the courtyard, faced with gray granite. The large windows of the first and second floors are decorated with grilled lattice-work frames. There are six windows in a row. On the third (top) floor to both left and right are semicircular windows with modest but delicate decor. There are no Jewish symbols to be seen anywhere.

In the courtyard, parallel to the main building, is a secondary building of the same height and dimensions. The main building housed the communal organizations as well as a prayer hall, a lecture and concert hall, and living apartments for the administration.

The secondary building housed the residents of the almshouse. It is also possible that some of the old people lived in the main building. The building itself was erected from funds provided by Moisei Akimovitch Ginsburg—"Port Arthur Ginsburg"—a generous philanthropist who had made his fortune in 1904 and 1905, from the Russo-Japanese War. Moisei Ginsburg was a member of the financial administration of the St. Petersburg community. He was the main benefactor to finance the building of the prayer house at the Preobrazhensky Cemetery, and a memorial tablet there had his name on it. He himself was chairman of the Board of Guardians of the almshouse, which bore his name. Clearly he was not averse to having his name immortalized during his lifetime. Later, however, the vox populi played a cruel trick on him. It took all the St. Petersburg Ginsbergs, Ginsburgs, Ginzburgs, and Guenzburgs and put them into one general "Baron Guenzburg," to whom they ascribed all good deeds: the building of the synagogue, the cemetery prayer house, the almshouse, and so on. And as for Moisei Akimovitch—it was as if he had never existed.

Before the revolution the superintendent of the almshouse was A. P. Tinyanov, and medical care for the old people was provided by Professor Grigory Isaakovitch Dembo (1872–1959), the second representative of the celebrated St. Petersburg dynasty of doctors. His father, Isaak Alexandrovitch Dembo (born in Kovno in 1846, died in St. Petersburg in 1906), became well known for his efforts to protect Shekhita, the Jewish method of ritual slaughter of cattle. He was for some time an elder of the synagogue. Grigory, his son, was very active on behalf of the Society for the Protection of the Health of the Jewish Population (OSE) and edited the collection *Questions on the Biology and Pathology of the Jews* (Leningrad, 1926). Before the Revolution he practiced not only in the almshouse but also in the Jewish Orphanage not far away. In accordance with the medical ethics of those days, the doctor gave his services to individual old folk and orphans free of charge. He also gave free treatment to all patients in the hospital named in honor of Her Imperial Highness the Grand Princess Maria Fyodorovna. There is a memorial in the Preobrazhensky Cemetery to the three generations of Doctors Dembo: grandfather, son, and grandson.

In the 1920s the superintendent and senior medical officer of the alms-

The House on 5th Liniya

house was a young doctor from the Vitebsk Guberniya, Yefim Yevseyevitch Klionsky. According to the eyewitness P. S., Klionsky also gave medical treatment without any charge. At the same time, Klionsky was studying medical research in the clinic of the Leningrad Institute of Tuberculosis under the guidance of Professors A. Y. Sternberg and M. R. Borok. After the war he was for many years in charge of the Tuberculosis Department of the Metchnikov Hospital. He was also a professor at No. 2 Leningrad Medical Institute, and he wrote more than fifty scientific papers.

The Klionsky family occupied a three-room apartment in the main building of the almshouse, on the third (top) floor, just opposite the staircase. The windows of the apartment, including one semicircular one, overlooked the street. Klionsky lived there with his wife Nehah Aronovna (from whom he was soon divorced) and his small daughter Nora. Nehah Aronovna became one of the lady patronesses of the almshouse, which housed cripples and victims of the war and pogroms, as well as homeless old men and women who had no means of livelihood and no one to care for them.

In his published letters, Simon Dubnow also makes reference to the almshouse:

> 7th August, 1915. Yesterday I visited a shelter for refugees from Malkin (a small Polish town) in the almshouse here on Vassilevsky Ostrov next to the archives of our Historical-Ethnographic Society. The exhausted men and women told of an unheard-of atrocity in the nearby village of Zaremba-Kostselna. The inhabitants were told to get out by a certain time and when some of the unfortunates had not got out on the expiry of the time limit, the Cossacks surrounded the settlement and set fire to it from all sides. They let the Poles out, but many of the Jews trapped in the fire were burned to death.
>
> Oh! Life in that almshouse with its regulations, its customs, internal laws, righteous persons and sinners, public opinion, rumors, objects of respect and scorn, it was full of personal tragedies and senseless recollections of past events and of events that never did occur in that closed, squalid-sublime semivillage type of small world that had something of Bialik, something of Babel, something of Sholem-Aleikhem.

Nehah Aronovna later recalled:

> Sometimes among the inhabitants of the Almshouse one occasionally came across younger people, young in age but somehow on the decline, broken by life. Most of these were women. There were several dozen, never more than a hundred, supported by charity.

According to the eyewitness P. S., then a young boy, a resident of the building, ninety-four people lived in the almshouse.

According to Nehah Aronovna:

> The entrance door was opened by a uniformed commissionaire—Uncle Misha who lived on the ground floor. A nonresident Russian [non-Jewish]

woman named Olga cooked kosher food for everyone in the kitchen on an enormous stove. Those residents who had a little personal money could buy their own food and cook meals for themselves separately. They lived two, three, or four to a room. The rooms were clean. They were all called to breakfast, lunch, and supper by the imbecile Faivka (who was over forty and whose parents were dead). He rang a large handbell and called out: "Koom to dinna." Faivka had a "girlfriend"—a wretched hunchback, Taibele, who was about forty. After the evening meal they often sat together in the courtyard. Among the inmates one stood out from the rest. She was a deaf, middle-aged woman nicknamed Champagne. In the past she had been a needle-woman in a private shop and rumor had it that she had been raped by the proprietor's son. In the Almshouse, Champagne helped to repair clothing for the linen-keeper, Alexandra Vladimirovna, the only Russian [non-Jewish] woman resident of the home. Champagne lived alone in a room that people passed through and that had a wash basin. She lived there by choice, refusing to live with Taibele because, as she declared, she couldn't bear to see Faivka stroking Taibele's belly.

Another woman—"the Estonian"—had lost her husband and son in a pogrom. Nehah Aronovna also remembers a blind old man. It was said of him that when his grandson was taken away from him and conscripted into the army, he was so distressed that he banged his head against the doorpost to such an extent that he blinded himself. The old fellow was educated and spoke several languages. One could often see the motionless figure of a woman standing on the staircase, incessantly looking at the main entrance door as she waited for her brother, a very successful and prosperous engineer who had put her in the home "as no longer required" and hardly ever visited her. Her surname was Kopylova.

The residents were usually visited at breakfast by the housekeeper Esfir (Esther) Markovna Ravrebbe. She and her husband, the scholar Yechiel Ravrebbe, occupied two rooms next to the Klionskys' apartment (with windows also facing the street). The Ravrebbes had no children of their own. Esfir Markovna died in 1930 from extrauterine pregnancy. Her nephew Pinkhas, who later took part in the Jewish historical-ethnographic expedition of 1927, lived with them in the almshouse. Esfir Markovna was an intelligent, refined, caring person. Part of her responsibility was to supervise the daily running of the almshouse.

Bed-ridden patients had their food brought to them in their rooms, and after breakfast they were seen by the visiting district nurse, Yulia Lvovna Gordon. Patients who were up and about came to see her in her office. In difficult cases the doctor, Yefim Klionsky, was called in, and he was treated with the greatest deference by all the inmates.

Many of the old people were God-fearing; for them one of the large rooms on the first floor was fitted out as a synagogue.

Private donations were the main source of income for the maintenance of the home. There was a sort of care committee that was made up in part of the lady patronesses, who also took it upon themselves to raise funds. A photograph has been preserved, which Nehah Aronovna, who is over ninety, believes was taken of a number of people connected with financial assistance to the almshouse. On it can be seen a group of well-dressed individuals — twenty-six men and ten women — sitting or standing at a table laid with a cloth. The photograph is dated May 19, 1928. Nehah Aronovna does not remember where it was taken or who the people are, but Bertha Ioffe, who is eighty-five, was able to identify in it Semyon Moiseyevitch Lessman, chairman of the Board of Management of the Leningrad Jewish Community (third row, seventh from the left, holding a glass). The eighth from the left is Zeibert, a Jewish public activist. The man wearing glasses sitting third from the left in the second row is probably Mikhail Kulisher, professor at the Leningrad Institute of Higher Jewish Studies, a specialist on the economic history of the Jews. Klionsky is also in the picture — sixth from the right in the third row. Both Bertha Ioffe and Nehah Aronovna believe that some of the people depicted are wealthy NEPmen,* benefactors of the almshouse.

Apart from direct donations, one method of raising funds was the holding of charity social gatherings (soirées), organized by the lady patronesses.

An eyewitness, A. B., recalls that he himself as a child took part in such soirées as a member of the choir of the Jewish Elementary School for Poor Children (at 3rd Liniya No. 48) run by the Tsedoko G'deilo Society. That was in 1916. In the 1920s among those who performed at such concerts were Freidkov, the future well-known soloist of the Kirov Theater (his mother was one of the patronesses of the almshouse); Perelman, the pianist, then a boy and now professor at the Leningrad Conservatoire; and Golubova, who sang Jewish folk songs. Collections from these soirées went to support the almshouse. Here, too, were organized auctions at which everyday items were sold at fantastic prices. NEPmen, desirous of demonstrating their generosity, would sometimes pay scores or even hundreds of rubles for a bottle of wine, a cake, a bouquet of flowers.

The Board of Guardians, as some eyewitnesses agree, received some support from the Leningrad branch of EKOPO (Jewish Committee to Provide Help to Victims of the War), which miraculously survived in the city until the late 1920s.

THE COURSES OF ORIENTAL STUDIES

☐ IT WAS IN November 1906, in the private house of old Baron Horace Guenzburg at Konnogvardeisky Boulevard (now Boulevard Profsoyuzov) No. 17, that the first meeting was held for the foundation of an institute of Jewish studies, or "Jewish Academy," that became the first Jewish secular institute of

---

* NEPmen were people who made money during the period of NEP (Lenin's New Economic Policy), from 1921 to 1929.

higher learning in Russia. Among those present were the baron himself, Horace, his son, the orientalist David Guenzburg, Doctor Lev Katzenelson, the historian Simon Dubnow, the official from the Ministry of Justice, Yakov Galperin, and several "notables." Dubnow recalled later that "the sick old man, with the imprint of imminent death already on his face, half-sat and half-lay in a deep armchair at the table, silently listening to his son's report and to our discussions."

David Guenzburg had spent a whole year petitioning and running about the ministry. Finally, in the late autumn of 1907, the magazine *Ha-Kedem* carried an announcement to the effect that "in accordance with the decree (ukase) of 15th September this year, permission was granted to Baron D. von Guenzburg to open a High School for Jewish Learning under the title of 'Courses of Oriental Studies' in St. Petersburg." The Jew-hating government could not bring itself to permit the word *Jewish* to appear on the signboard of the high school and covered the "sin" with the fig leaf "Oriental." The curriculum of studies for the courses was published in the paper in German. It was as follows:

Section One

A 1. Hebreo-Aramaic (Syriac) grammar
    2. Bible and Apocrypha with an account of Eastern translations; medieval commentaries on the Bible
B 1. Grammar and methodology of the Talmud
    2. Talmud and Midrash
C 1. General history of the Jews and Semitic peoples
    2. History of the Jews in Russia:
      (a) The Crimea: the Khazars, Krimchaks, Karaites
      (b) Lithuania and Poland
      (c) The Caucasus
      (d) Jews under the Russian tsars
    3. History of Jewish literature and liturgy
    4. Jewish-Arabic medieval philosophy
    5. Medieval literature of the Jews
D 1. The history of philosophy with an exposition of the influence on it of Jewish religious philosophy
    2. Psychology and pedagogics
    3. General history, especially that of Eastern peoples
    4. Russian history and its connection with the Near East
    5. Russian literature and its influence on Oriental literature
    6. Modern languages

A 1. The Masorah (collection of critical notes on the text of the Old Testament), exegetics, and biblical archeology
    2. Medieval Jewish commentaries
    3. Senior course on Hebrew grammar, stylistics, and metrics
    4. Apocrypha and Pseudepigrapha

B 1. History of oral tradition
   2. Babylonian and Jerusalem Talmud
   3. Targum, Aggadah, and Midrash
   4. Introduction to Pesahim
   5. Rabbinic literature: codices, responsa, and novellas
C 1. General history of the Jews against a background of history of the East
    (study of sources)
   2. History of Jewish literature and liturgy (Piyyutim)
   3. Jewish paleography and numismatics
   4. History of Semitic languages
   5. History and geography of the ancient East
   6. History and geography of Palestine
D 1. Arabic language: grammar and study of selected texts
   2. Syriac and Arabic idiom: grammar and study of selected texts
   3. Optional choice of Assyrian or Ethiopian language
E 1. History of ethical-religious philosophy of the Jews, Babylonians, and Arabs
   2. Jewish homiletics and rhetoric
   3. Kabbalah
F 1. Modern languages

There was also a third section, designed for specialization in certain spheres of the profession of Oriental studies. The course of study was for five years. The fifth year was set aside for specialization.

In thus setting out the curriculum of the courses in full, as a rather historical source, it is our aim to draw the reader's attention to the fact that graduates of courses with such a syllabus had to be highly erudite.

Correspondingly, the founder of the courses placed considerable hope in the graduates, seeing the task of the courses to be "to create an intellectual element among the Jews that will be able to respond to the spiritual and academic demands of Russian Jewry, and will be able to serve its interests as community rabbis or teachers, and be concerned with the preservation intact of the inheritance of the past."

The following were recommended as teaching staff: David Guenzburg himself (linguistics and religious philosophy and rector of the courses), Dr. A. Zarzovsky (linguistics, Bible and Apocrypha, history and geography of the ancient East), Dr. L. Katzenelson (Talmud and Midrash), I. Guenzburg (Arabic language), Y. Markon (history of Jewish literature), S. Dubnow (Jewish history), and V. Ashkenazi (pedagogics and didactics). At a later date the teaching staff was joined by M. Goldstein (archeology), A. S. Kamenetsky (Bible and Hebrew-Syriac grammar), A. Karlin (Talmud), G. Sliozberg (history of Russian legislation about the Jews), and M. Vishnitzer (economic history of the Jews in the Middle Ages).

The participants in the courses began to arrive in St. Petersburg after the autumn festivals (of Rosh Hashana, Yom Kippur, Sukkot, and Simhat Torah) of 1907, and the courses commenced in January 1908. They were "registered" at first in the home of Baron David Guenzburg (1st Liniya No. 4), but in fact they operated on the premises of Eisenbet's Jewish High School at Nikolsky Pere'ulok No. 7 (now ulitsa Myasnikova—the building is extant). Soon the courses were transferred to 8th Liniya No. 33 (now 35), where a students' hostel was established. It was in this building that Simon Dubnow lived with his family in a four-room apartment (entrance from the courtyard). From 1911 to 1913 the courses were housed at 6th Liniya No. 5 (the building is extant), and in July 1913 they moved for the last time to the building of the Jewish Almshouse on 5th Liniya.

To start with, some of the courses were held in David Guenzburg's house (until his death in 1910) when he was tutor. As related in Dubnow's memoirs, the baron did not follow any precise syllabus but lectured "as the spirit took him." He would invite the students into his enormous library where the tables were littered with rare folio manuscripts and ancient printed books, he would pick up some medieval book, say, Maimonides' *Moreh Nevukhim* (The Guide of the Perplexed), tell one of the students to read aloud, and would then himself explain in detail the passage that had just been read.

Just who did take part in these courses? Dubnow writes:

> Our student body was made up mainly of provincials, self-taught or experts, former members of yeshivahs, well versed in specialist Jewish subjects, but without sufficient background of general education. Only a small number of them could satisfy this latter requirement, apart from the university students who turned up for our evening lectures. There were also a few women students from the Higher Women's Courses.

The students who already had a good knowledge of traditional Jewish sources found much of interest in the academic commentaries to them. The *Yevreiskaya Entsiklopedia* says that twenty-five to thirty students were attending each lecture. Dubnow, however, mentions that at the lectures on medieval history there were always about forty present.

Some of the best students later became outstanding figures in Jewish studies, philosophy, and Hebrew literature. Among them were Yehezekiel Kaufman, Zvi Voislavsky, Joshua Gutman, and Solomon Zeitlin. One of the students, Zalman Rubashov, who later, as Zalman Shazar, was president of the State of Israel, quickly became a professional historian, took part in the publication of the *Yevreiskaya Entsiklopedia* and wrote several articles for *Yevreiskaya Starina*. His future wife, Rachel Katzenelson, studied with him. The secretary of *Yevreiskaya Starina*, Itzhak Lurye, also visited the courses. One of the most erudite was the tall, stooping, blond, Yechiel Ravrebbe, already at that time a poet and destined to be an outstanding Jewish scholar. Several lectures were attended by David Shimonovitch, a student of St. Petersburg University who later, as we have seen, wrote about his stay in the capital in Hebrew verse in his poem "The Sphinxes."* Later, he became a known Israeli poet under the name Shimoni.

---

* Printed on page 83.

Most of the students were poverty stricken; moreover, many of them did not have the right of residence in the capital. The latter were living there illegally or, as they jokingly put it, "on the courtiers" or "on commission"; that is, every month they paid a ruble each to the courtyard porter or to the commissioner or doorman for him not to give them away to the police. The lucky ones shared a room for two in the hostel. They had their meals in the Jewish students' dining room on 6th Liniya. (The courses were moved into this building in 1911.) Many of the students earned some money part-time giving Hebrew lessons. In the evenings the hostel blazed with arguments. The Yiddishists quarreled with the Hebraists, the supporters of Dubnow opposed the pupils of Klausner, the Zionists quarreled with the socialists.

In his book *Kniga zhizni,* Dubnow is frequently scornful of the standard of teaching in the Jewish Academy. In his opinion only he himself, Katzenelson, and Vishnitzer were good teachers and "as for the rest, it was absolute chaos." David Guenzburg considered Dubnow's "critical approach" to ancient history to be heretical, and Dubnow refused to acknowledge the baron as being scholarly, looking upon him only as an erudite dilettante and probably feeling "class hostility" toward him. Nor must it be forgotten that Dubnow was not distinguished for the mildness of his character. When David Guenzburg unexpectedly died in the prime of life from cancer, Dubnow did not even then fully make peace with the deceased. He wrote in his diary:

> For his own circle he was a phenomenon; he loved Jewish scholarship, he was in his own way loyal to his people and he wanted to do something for them. But in truth scholarship did not love him: he was devoid of the gift of clear thinking and of passing on his thoughts; he was just as unsuccessful also in his handling of public affairs and, when I worked with him I frequently could not bear his chaotic manner . . . and yet, a man of spiritual treasure has died before his time. Now on the agenda is a reorganization of the academy.

Lev Katzenelson took over as rector of the courses. But with the death of the baron there disappeared also the scanty means that provided for this great beginning. Where now could they obtain the ten thousand to fifteen thousand rubles per annum that was needed to support the courses? Katzenelson could hardly collect the small sum for the rent of premises and for the provision of help to the poorest of the students, while, at that time, the teachers received no pay at all. However, it now became easier to carry out a reform of the curriculum and a reorganization of the teaching methods that the conservative baron had put the brakes on. In 1913 the courses finally obtained more suitable premises in the almshouse building, where they carried on for another four years. And although in the guidebooks and directories it was called a "Jewish Academy," it was really no more than a small private educational establishment, subsisting on means provided by the family of the Barons Guenzburg and other "notables" and reserved for the tuition of a very limited number of students.

To this must be added the ideological and personal conflicts between the teachers, the administration, and the patrons; the problems with residential permits for the students; and the pressure applied on the administration by St. Petersburg officialdom. All of this did not help the Courses of Oriental Studies to be transformed into a real Jewish institute of higher learning.

JEWISH HISTORICAL-ETHNOGRAPHIC SOCIETY

The earliest ethnographic expedition to study the life of the Jews of Eastern Europe was organized in 1850 by Moses Berlin, adviser on Jewish affairs to the governor-general of Bielorussia and a member of the Imperial Geographic Society.* There was also the work of Mikhel Greim (1828–1911)—printer and photographer—whose studio was open in Kamenets-Podolsk in 1860. Greim acquired a reputation as a brilliant photographer of anthropological and historical types, including Jews. His pictures appeared in albums and at exhibitions, and he was given an award by the Imperial Academy of Sciences in St. Petersburg. These photographs and other materials collected haphazardly on the history and ethnography of the Jews did not of course constitute a basis for a systematic scientific study. With the passage of time, the new Jewish intelligentsia began to take a serious interest in its past. In 1891 *Voskhod* published an appeal by Simon Dubnow "for the study of the history of Russian Jews and for the establishment of a Russo-Jewish historical-ethnographic society." The result was the founding of a historical-ethnographic commission with OPE, headed by Mikhail Vinaver; there were of course other articles, appeals, speeches, and concrete initiatives in this direction undertaken in connection with the names of I. Orshansky, I. Lerner, S. Ginzburg, P. Marek, S. A. An-sky, and others.

Then, one autumn day in 1908, Vinaver received permission to set up the Jewish Historical-Ethnographic Society (IEO). There followed organizational meetings in his apartment on Zakharyevskaya ulitsa, where only recently the arguments of the Union for Equal Rights had been seething. The founding meeting of the society took place on November 16, 1908, in solemn circumstances in the Alexandrovsky Hall (now the Wedding Hall) of the Choral Synagogue on Bolshaya Masterskaya ulitsa. The chair was taken by Professor Mikhail Kulisher, with Vinaver and Dubnow on the platform. That evening Dubnow was affected by two conflicting emotions—joy at seeing the foundation of the institution and sadness at the thought of how long it had taken: seventeen long years after his own personal initiative.

* From 1856 to 1866 Moses Berlin was in St. Petersburg as adviser on Jewish matters at the Imperial Department of Foreign Relations. He died in 1888, having been active in the St. Petersburg Jewish community.

Vinaver made an inspiring speech. He recalled how carefully the old registers had been collected, he told of how young Jewish lawyers and writers had read papers addressed to the Historical-Ethnographic Commission on how they had worked on the programs of Bershadsky and Dubnow and of how, during the process of this work, their feelings of the ties between them had grown together with the community of their fates and the fate of their people whose past they were studying. He spoke about the founding of the society as the realization of an age-old dream. "The dream is a modest one, it does not match up to the dream that so recently gripped us, but at least it has its own priceless fascination; it is a dream of youth."

The IEO constitution stated that its aim was to gather, study, and analyze historical and ethnographic materials on the past of Jewry in Russia and Poland — from the appearance of the first Jewish settlements up to the present day; to organize meetings on the imparting of academic information and public lectures on Jewish history and ethnography; and to publish systematic collections of legal deeds and registry entries, scholastic research works, and so on. As we have said, Vinaver was the chairman of the society. The two deputy chairman from 1927 to 1930), Y. I. Gessen, M. L. Vishnitzer, and Zinovy An-sky, S. Goldstein, L. Y. Sternberg (IEO chairman from 1924 to 1927), I. I. Sheftel, G. B. Sliozberg, S. G. Lozinsky, I. A. Kleinman, S. L. Zinberg (IEO chairman from 1927 to 1930), Y. I. Gessen, M. L. Vishnitzer, and Zinovy Kisselgoff.

From January 1909 the society issued *Yevreiskaya Starina* (Jewish Antiquity), which published many valuable documents, memoirs, and articles on the history of the Jews of Lithuania, Poland, and Russia. The society's activity was limited almost entirely to St. Petersburg. Branches were opened later in other towns but were of little importance. The society became moribund in 1917, reviving its activities in 1923 (the so-called "Second" IEO).

The society frequently changed its address; in 1913 the lectures frequently took place at No. 50, 5th Liniya. According to Dubnow, both the Courses on Oriental Studies and the IEO moved here in 1913. "We were given rooms for lectures on two floors, an 'iron room' for the archives and a large hall for the museum of ethnography to start off with, where An-sky deposited his collection. Here, then, were read the frequent reports, usually followed by a discussion."

It was here at No. 50, on 5th Liniya, that Dubnow himself read his reports on "The Jewish Reformation in Germany" (1913), and "Summary of Jewish History in Poland" (1915).

The Society existed until 1930.

S. A. AN-SKY AND THE JEWISH MUSEUM

Semyon Akimovitch Rapoport, who wrote under the pen name of An-sky, was born in 1863 near Vitebsk in Bielorussia. The family was orthodox, and he was given a traditional Jewish education. He taught himself to read Russian when he was seventeen. As a young man he was attracted by the ideas of the populist movement — the Narodniks. But because, according to the thinking of the Narodniks, the Jews were not really a people per se, as a result of their lack of a peasantry, An-sky, like many of his contemporary Jewish revolutionaries, "went out to the people," which meant, of course, the Russian people. He did not, however, as did others, adopt Christianity for the convenience of revolutionary agitation, and as a Jew he was expelled from the village, so he went among the miners in Yekaterinoslav province, then emigrated; from 1894 he became secretary to the revolutionary Narodnik Pyotr Lavrov, until the latter's death in exile in 1900.

An-sky returned to Russia during the 1905 Revolution. His return to Jewry took place at this point. He wrote a great deal on Jewish themes in Yiddish and Russian. He is the author of the hymn of the Bund — "Di Shvueh" (The Oath) — and of the famous play *The Dybbuk,* which has become a classic of Jewish drama. His six volumes of collected stories in Russian are avidly read, with their brilliant tales of colorful people and events, written by a talented storyteller who had been everywhere, knew everything, took part in everything personally. He was a Narodnik and a Socialist Revolutionary correspondent on the Duma commission set up to inquire into the Bialystok pogrom, and deputy to the All-Russian Constituent Assembly and was friendly with Mark Antokolski, Peter Kropotkin, Father Gapon, and Joseph Trumpeldor.

But our present concern with An-sky is his decisive role in organizing the famous ethnographic expedition to Volhynia, Podolia, and Kiev Guberniya between 1911 and 1914, funded by the family of the Barons Guenzburg. An-sky acted as its leader, and the expedition included a number of specialists. We have already described the expedition together with details of the museum that resulted from its findings, as well as recounted an amusing anecdote on the first reading of *The Dybbuk* by its author. On the evening of the day on which An-sky had read Rivesman the first act of *The Dybbuk,* Rivesman met An-sky at the zoo, and they went to have a drink of beer. This time, An-sky began talking of the horrors suffered by the Jews during World War I.

"Here, come with me and I'll show you some photos — I've got quite a collection."

Then he suddenly changed the conversation and started to talk about the valuable Jewish museum pieces that he had collected during his travels together with that celebrated collector of Jewish folk songs, Kisselgoff.

"We'll create a wonderful museum!" he exclaimed enthusiastically. "It will be an academy for the study of folklore. I've got hundreds of wonderful tales and legends, marvellous synagogue relics — you'll see what we're going to do!"

And his face, always beautiful, but so sad only a few minutes before, was beaming with delight.

The members of the expedition had, in fact, collected a very impressive amount of material, and this wealth they proposed to publish in two volumes. Volume One, containing 238 pages of large format and edited by L. Sternberg, was published in 1914. It was called *Tchelovyek* (Man) and had five sections:

1 From birth to cheder — 54 pages, 304 questions
2 From cheder to marriage — 64 pages, 633 questions
3 Marriage — 26 pages, 231 questions
4 Family life — 56 pages, 518 questions
5 Death — 38 pages, 401 questions

This first volume was in the form of answers to questions that had been asked by members of the expedition to inhabitants of the shtetls. There were in all 2,087 questions. The second volume was already in print but was never published. Rechtman actually saw some uncorrected proof copies. The volume was scheduled to have the title *Shabboss and the Festivals*.

In 1916 An-sky visited Kiev, Moscow, Kharkov, and Odessa, where he lectured on ethnography and folklore. He became ill, however, during his lecture tour and went to the Caucasus to be treated for diabetes. In October 1916, after he had recovered, he returned to Vassilevsky Ostrov and to the almshouse building. Here is an extract from a letter he wrote to Rechtman from that address:

Vassilevsky Ostrov, 5th Liniya 50 (Petrograd). October 1916. My dear Abram, I have been all summer in the Caucasus having treatment for the sugar illness that has been diagnosed. . . . It looks as if I'll settle down in Petrograd where I'll occupy myself with work on the materials, to get them ready for print. We're getting ready for the opening of the museum, and have already prepared a special cupboard that's worth a thousand rubles. We've received many new exhibits and I've been thinking of you a great deal. There's no other worker like you. I'm writing some short stories about Hasidic life. My play *The Dybbuk* has been accepted for presentation in the Arts Theater Studio ("Habima," Moscow).

Simon Dubnow also mentions the organizing and opening of the museum. According to him, the museum was closed and sealed on April 9, 1918, by representatives of the Commissariat for Jewish Affairs (the future Yevsektsia, or Jewish Section of the Communist Party) "because of rumors about misappropriation of items from the museum archives." In the Cultural Section of the Commissariat, where Dubnow was given this explanation, two men were known to him: I. Berlin, editor of the section on rabbinics of the *Yevreiskaya Entsiklopedia* and a book kleptomaniac (he never returned scholarly works to

The participants in the ethnographic expedition, 1911. From the right: Simeon An-sky, Yuri Engel, and Solomon Yudovin

libraries), and I. Bukhbinder, who later wrote a good book on the history of the Jewish workers' movement.

Dubnow protested; he wrote to the Academy of Sciences and went to the Commissariat that was housed in the building of the Ministry of Education by Chernishevsky Bridge. In his diary on April 15, 1918, he wrote:

> The last few days there has been an unusual bustle. A lot of bother about the archives, explanations from the Assistant Commissar for Education, a certain young fellow named Greenberg, who, after I protested, promised to have the seals removed from the archives and the museum. I had a strange feeling while I was sitting in that same waiting room where seven years before I had been waiting to see the Deputy Minister to plead for Yasha to be allowed to take the exam after he had been expelled from the university. On that occasion I had been kept to the last and made to wait for five hours and had been seen by a dried-up bureaucrat-professor, whereas now I had been interviewed after a wait of only a few minutes, without waiting in a queue, by a talkative young man who was overflowing with compliments to the "historian" who had protested against the action of the Bolshevik government. So far, however, the archives have not been unsealed. An-sky has arrived and I've put the entire matter in his hands as it's something he is capable of dealing with.

Rechtman has written as follows about this event, in the third person:

> Once when he was in Moscow he heard that the authorities had sealed up the museum. He immediately returned to Petrograd, broke open all the locks and the wax seals, then went to the authorities and announced that he understood and accepted full responsibility for what he had done, but that he had been obliged to do so because the closure of the Jewish museum was an insult to the whole Jewish people and to him himself as the person responsible for that institution.

Nevertheless, the museum remained closed until 1923.

In September 1918 An-sky fled from Russia to Vilna disguised as a priest. There he founded a historical-ethnographic museum and a Jewish cultural association. In 1919, during the pogrom in Vilna, a close friend of An-sky, the Bundist writer and journalist, A. Weiter (Eisik Meir Devenishki) — born near Vilna in 1878), was shot and killed by a Polish legionnaire. An-sky took the death of his friend very badly. He became ill, and his heart was affected. He moved to Warsaw. On October 11, 1920, he wrote: "I've got nothing cheerful to tell you about myself. My legs are swollen and I can't walk. I intend to go to Berlin."

On November 9, 1920, An-sky died. The Jewish press throughout the world — from Zionist to Bundist — reacted to the news of his death with grief. Even the Russian Jewish publications, which were not yet functioning in 1920, somewhat later referred to the death of An-sky, at a time of so many deaths, with very much sorrow, even though with considerable delay. A. Gornfeld wrote that "An-sky had been dreaming of being able to strengthen the historical basis of the Jewish psyche by conscious and determined education. He had been dreaming of an affirmation of Jewish life in the ancient Jewish homeland."

To conclude, we must return to Rivesman's remarkable character study of An-sky:

> He had a beautiful soul; as for his eyes — they were Jewish eyes, thoughtful, wise, questioning and appealing for love toward humanity. He was as much an idealist, as he was a Narodnik and a revolutionary, as he was a Jew, a Jewish writer, and — toward the end — a Zionist. Educated, though to a great extent self-taught, at forty he already gave the impression of being old, which was helped by the premature gray in his curls. But as those curls became progressively grayer, so he seemed to become younger in spirit. Nobody else was capable of such carefree laughter, of such selfless rejoicing among the very greenest of young people, as was this old fellow, and no one else was capable of arousing such fiery inspiration over some action that called to mind a heroic feat, to inspire others and to inspire himself.

We must make, at this point, a brief mention of An-sky's nephew Solomon Yudovin. As I have sometimes reflected, "Leningrad was filled with Vitebsk culture!" Solomon Borisovitch Yudovin was born in Vitebsk in 1892 into the family of a petty craftsman. He studied painting in school under Penn. He came to St. Petersburg in 1910 and continued to study in the School of Painting of the Imperial Society for the Encouragement of the Arts (Director N. K. Rerikh, address Moika 83). From 1912 to 1914 he joined in An-sky's ethnographic expedition, and according to some accounts, not only were they from the same area of Bielorussia, but he and An-sky were also related. An exhibition of Yudovin's work was set up in 1917, consisting of the drawings he made during the expedition, and in 1920 he published an *Album of Jewish Ornaments*. In 1919, he returned to Vitebsk, where he studied with M. Bernstein and M. Dobuzhinsky. In 1924 he again arrived in St. Petersburg, took up residence in the Jewish Almshouse, and was made curator of the Jewish Museum, filling it with his own paintings and pictures of other Jewish artists, mainly those coming from Vitebsk. He devoted much attention to graphics and book illustration, illustrating among others Leon Feuchtwanger's *Jew Suss*. In 1927 an exhibition of Yudovin's work was displayed in Milan; in 1928 it moved to Los Angeles. Simultaneously with his work in the museum Yudovin was teaching painting and sketching in the Jewish section of the Rabfak (Workers' Faculty) in the building of the former Bestuzhev Courses (10th Liniya 33). After the museum was closed down in 1935 he moved to Isaakievskaya Ploshchad (St. Isaac's Square) 5, where he concentrated on graphics and book illustration. Among his best works are views of Leningrad. He died in 1954.

Our last institution at the house on 5th Liniya is the Jewish Museum, the story of which continues after the revolution, well into the twenties. Apart from printed sources such as *Yevreiskaya Starina, Yevreisky Vestnik,* and the German *Encyclopedia Judaica,* there are a number of personal recollections of the existence of the museum in Soviet times. There are here several contradictions, however. It has been stated that the IEO and its museum were reopened in 1923, but the guidebook *Vyes Petrograd* for 1922 informs us that there existed three Jewish historical-ethnographic organizations: (1) The Society for the Study of the Social Biology and Psycho-physics of the Jews (Chairman A. M. Bramson), at Gagarinskaya ulitsa (now ulitsa Furmanova) 20; (2) The Commission for Research into the History of the Jews (Chairman G. A. Krasny-Admoni) at Pushkinskaya ulitsa 4; and (3) The Jewish Historical-Ethnographic Society (Director L. Y. Sternberg) at Vassilevsky Ostrov 5th Liniya 50.

If the (new) IEO was already functioning at 5th Liniya 50, then we must assume that in all probability the museum was also open. The museum was on three floors and occupied three rooms. According to two eyewitnesses, S. M. and D. N., both of them artists from Vitebsk and friends of Yudovin both as artists and as "zemlyak" (originating from the same district or town), Yudovin lived in a room attached to the museum or even in one of the museum rooms. Klionsky maintains that Yudovin lived with his family on the third (top) floor, which is where the administration was housed. In any case, all agree that Yudovin was curator of the museum and that the museum had a large collection of important objects of cultural and financial value. In addition, it had a large number of paintings on various themes of Jewish life—Shekhita (ritual animal slaughter), bar mitzvah, wedding ceremonies, and so on—that the museum authorities had commissioned from the artists on Yudovin's initiative. In particular, the museum acquired seven or so of S. M.'s own works. He remembers receiving a letter from the director, Bramson, with warm recommendations about his work. D. N. was requested by Yudovin to make for the museum a series of six pencil drawings on one quarto sheet, which he did as a gift without making any charge, and they were put on display. *Yevreiskaya Starina* for 1928 (Vol. XII) states that the museum was continually acquiring single items and small collections. Of items of everyday life, the museum had cultural and artistic objects—around 1,000 exhibits, 1,500 photographs, 340 cylinders with phonographic recordings of folk melodies, and 350 books and music scores.

Of some interest, although rather sparing in real information, are the recollections of P. S., the nephew of Ravrebbe's wife, who became secretary of the museum in 1926 and stayed in that post until the museum finally closed. He remembers, for example, the music committee, whose chairman was once again Abram Moiseyevitch Bramson and whose members were Ravrebbe, Zinberg, Vinnikov, Pulner, Klionsky, Milner, and Lyubov Lvovna Streicher, a composer and pupil of Gnessin.

In 1927, P. S. took part in a Jewish ethnographic expedition authorized by the Yevsektsia. Funds, which were provided by IEO, were in short supply and were sufficient only for the expenses of the journey. In the Institute of Russian Literature, Pushkin House, those going on the expedition managed to get some few cylinders for recording folk songs (they were returned to the Institute and are still there); they also bought some extra cylinders on the black market at

A silver goblet presented to Baron Horace Guenzburg by one of the Jewish towns of the Pale of Settlement

their own expense. There was only one other person with P. S. on this expedition—its leader, Sofia Davidovna (Maggid) Etmetchki, the daughter of the Jewish scholar David Maggid, who worked in the manuscript department of the Public Library. The expedition lasted one month, during which time they visited Polonnoye, Lyubar, Sudlikov, and Labun—in the border region between the Oblasts of Zhitomir and Khmelnitsky. On their return they deposited their trophies in the Jewish Museum and returned the cylinders to Pushkin House. Sofia Davidovna kept the personal cylinders that she had bought.

The exact date of the final closure of IEO and the museum is not certain. There still exists a letter of information from the presidium of the Leningrad Jewish IEO to members of Friends of the Jewish Museum. The letter is dated December 16, 1929. It begins with the words "Dear friends, this letter is the last we shall be sending you. On the instructions of the organs of governmental authority, the Jewish IEO and its museum have been closed."

There can be little doubt that the museum closed in 1930. Nevertheless, it may have taken a year or two more to transfer its exhibits elsewhere, dividing books, paintings, and other possessions among different institutions. We do not know how many years this phase took. Nevertheless, there is some basis for believing that the museum did operate for another couple of years. A committee was appointed for the liquidation of the museum, which included a former member of the Yevsektsia, Matz and Yudovin himself. The committee worked for several months. According to P. S., the ritual objects of the collection — scrolls, lamps, candlesticks, silver — went to the Soviet Government Museum of Ethnography in Leningrad, where they exist today (in storage), and the museum archives were sent to the Institute of Jewish Proletarian Culture in Kiev.

Moreover, there is official evidence that in 1938 a significant portion of the museum exhibits was transferred to the Jewish (Mendele Moikher-Seforim) Museum in Odessa, but there is no subsequent information as to the fate of the contents of the Odessa museum during the war.

As we turn away from this house on 5th Liniya, we can reflect that, however much seems to be lost of knowledge and history, we can still find out much of our past and of those who peopled it, if we want to do so.

EXCURSION FIVE

CULTURE AND POLITICS

I don't want to depart this life just yet,
O Petersburg, I still have the numbers of your phones,
O Petersburg, I still have all the addresses,
From which I'll find the voices of the dead.

Osip Mandelstam

We are setting off on the most extensive excursion in size and scope of fortunes and events. It has two main themes: the development of Jewish art, literature, music, and theater and the social life of Jewish St. Petersburg and its place in Russian public life. We shall see the sights of three districts of the city—Moskovskaya (along Zagorodny Prospekt), Liteinaya, and Rozhdestvenskaya (Sovietskaya ulitsa). This was once the focal point of Jewish cultural life, where journals and newspapers were published, parties fought, and schools and clubs operated. And this was not so very long ago.

The Jewish population of these three districts of St. Petersburg, according to the census of 1868, is listed in Table 5-1.

TABLE 5-1. POPULATION OF THREE DISTRICTS OF ST. PETERSBURG IN 1868

Rayon (District)	Men	Women	Total	Number of Literate Persons	
				Men	Women
Moskovskaya	209	214	423	43	84
Rozhdestvenskaya	67	79	146	26	18
Liteinaya	129	100	229	95	46

☐ OUR NEW EXCURSION begins at No. 70 Zagorodny Prospekt, on the corner of ulitsa Bronnitskaya. Here is the house where Osip Mandelstam lived as a child. He was to become one of the great Russian poets and was a member of the Acmeist group of such well-known Russian poets of the early twentieth century as Gumilyov and Akhmatova. He was born in Warsaw in 1891 into the family of a Merchant of the Second Guild, Emil Veniaminovitch Mandelstam. He studied at the Tenishevsky School and then in the Romano-Germanic department of St. Petersburg University. He was first published in 1910. He died in 1938.

Mandelstam's poetry is known both in Russia and abroad. There have been many biographers and students of his work. We shall discuss only one aspect of his life — his Jewishness, from which, it seems, he himself tried to escape throughout his life. One would have to be very prejudiced, however, not to see in his work Jewish motifs that expressed a perception and understanding of life that is peculiarly Jewish. He did not deny this influence. Let us look at his book of autobiographical sketches, *Shum Vremeni* (The Noise of Time), in which he wrote: "Just as a crumb of musk fills a whole house with its aroma, so the smallest influence of Judaism overflows all of one's life. Oh, what a strong smell it is!"

It was, in fact, no more than a whiff, since his father had a German education and his mother a Russian education, and they did not try to, nor indeed would they have been able to, pass on to the boy any genuine national traditions. Those traditions, together with their custodians, the people, con-fined somewhere far away beyond the Pale of Settlement, were quite incompre-hensible and alien to Mandelstam. They disturbed his imagination, dragging him toward the chaos and the bottomless abyss from which, not very long before and with such difficulty, he had torn himself. They were like "the central core of a hard-labor convict," like the hand of a dead body grasping the night in an old cemetery:

> The whole tissue of mirage-like St. Petersburg was only a dream, a brilliant shroud thrown over the abyss, and all around stretched the chaos of Judaism, not a motherland, not a home, not a hearth, but just chaos, the unknown fetal world from which I had emerged, which I feared, which I vaguely sensed and from which I fled, I always fled.
>
> The Judaic chaos penetrated every chink in the walls of the St. Petersburg apartment, with its threat of destruction, with the hat of the provincial guest in the room, the curly lettering of the unreadable books of Genesis thrown onto the dust of the bottom shelf of the bookcase beneath Goethe and Schiller, and with the scraps of black and white ritual.

In his memoirs, his father's study springs to life, crammed full of odd bits of furniture and above all, "the glass-fronted bookcase covered in green baize." "The bookcase of earliest childhood — a man's traveling companion for life" appears as a symbol of a past overcome, the biography of a family that had traveled the onerous and tortured path of the "enlightened" Jews of Russia, from the "bottom shelves" of the Jewish religion through quasi-Germanic culture to an idealized perception of Russian life and culture gained through Russian literature.

> I remember that the bottom shelf was always in a state of chaos; the books did not stand side by side, cover to cover, but lay scattered like ruins; rust-colored Bibles with torn bindings, a Russian history of the Jews written in the clumsy and timid language of a Russian-speaking Talmudist. This was the chaos of Judaism thrown down into the dust. Here also soon fell my Hebrew language reading primer, which I never did study. In a fit of national repentance, a real Hebrew teacher was hired for me. He came from his Torgovaya (Mercantile) Street, and did not take off his cap, which made me feel uncomfortable. . . . There was one striking thing about this teacher, though it sounded somewhat unnatural, and that was his sense of Jewish national pride. He spoke about the Jews as a Frenchman would of Victor Hugo and Napoleon. But I knew that he hid his pride when he went out into the street and that was why I did not trust him.

In contemplating that Jewish bottom shelf, with no conception of what an effort it had been for a "Russian-speaking Talmudist" to write down, at last, the history of his people, and that moreover in a foreign language, at that moment Mandelstam unwittingly looks like a barbarian standing over the ruins of an ancient culture, conquered and destroyed, but still beyond his reach.

Nevertheless, this culture, this "crumb of musk," appearing now in the form of a teacher from Torgovaya Street, now as the joyless September New Year, or as the long-coated bearded men and the women with false hair encountered in the quarters behind the Mariinsky Theater—this world again and again returns to him in half-real, obsessive, and sometimes painful recollections. This is how he describes his visits to the Choral Synagogue, where he was occasionally taken as a child.

> The synagogue with its conical hat and onion domes is lost like a luxuriant alien fig-tree among the squalid buildings. Velvet berets with pompons, exhausted lay-brothers and choristers, clusters of menorahs, tall velvet kamelaukions (priests' hats). The Jewish ship sails ahead under press of full sail, split by some ancient storm into male and female halves. Lost among the female singers I slipped through like a thief, hiding behind the pillars. The cantor, like mighty Samson, brought down the huge building and he was answered by the velvet kamelaukions, and the marvellous balance between vowels and consonants in clearly enunciated words told of the invincible power of the psalms.

The boy's keen ear detected the false tone, the discord of the main, official Gloria.

> The rabbi's sermon sounds so insulting and so vulgar when he says: "His Majesty the Emperor." How banal is all that he says.

But of course it is banal. A banality that, incidentally, sounded also from the pulpit of the Russian Orthodox cathedral, and the Lutheran church, and the mosque. But for the poet, this observation is cause yet again to register his alienation and isolation from what unconsciously still attracts him. When he talks of the "marvellous balance" in the cantor's singing, it forces his memory to return once again to the fragmentary impression of childhood, to that very thing from which, for some reason, he has to flee all his life, and from which it is so difficult to escape.

Mandelstam did not always try to escape from Judaism. A sense of pride in his origins emerges several times in his works: his life itself, without a permanent roof or steady income, but nevertheless full of the sense of a high purpose of his mission on earth. Is not this life reminiscent of the classical fate of the eternally wandering Jew? In 1920, the poet returned to this topic in these words:

> To the mixing hearth return once again,
> 'Twas from there, Leah, that you came,
> For, not the sun of Iliona,
> But yellow twilight you preferred.
>
> Depart now, no one here will touch you,
> In dark of night on father's breast
> The daughter now whose blood is mixing
> May wearily lie down to rest.
>
> But now a fateful alteration
> Within your nature must take place:
> You must be Leah, no more Helen.
> It's not because you are betrothed,
>
> That heavily the royal blood flows
> Than any other through your veins,
> No, you will come to love Judaea,
> God be with you — you'll vanish there.

In his earliest years Mandelstam lived also on Kamenno-Ostrovsky Prospekt (now Kirovsky Prospekt), on ulitsa Zhukovskogo and on ulitsa Herzena (formerly ulitsa Bolshaya Morskaya). At the present time we can give only one more of his addresses with any certainty: No. 49 ulitsa Herzena (next door to Nabokov's house), where he lived in 1926.

Here at the end of Zagorodny Prospekt we can stop to look at two statues by Academician I.Ya. Guenzburg (see Excursion Three): the first, of G. V. Plekhanov (1925), is by the Technological Institute; the second, of D. I. Mendeleyev (1932), is nearby in the square in front of the Institute of Metrology.

The Technological Institute itself is also associated with Jewish history.

Between 1872 and 1876 Aaron Liebermann, one of the first activists of the Jewish revolutionary movement of Russia, studied here, but he did not complete the course because of financial difficulties. He was born in 1844 and committed suicide in New York in 1880.

Liebermann came to St. Petersburg after the collapse of Zundelevitch's Narodnik (Populist) group, which was based in 1872 in the Vilna rabbinical seminary. Whereas the majority of Jewish Narodniks considered their main aim to be "to go to the people," that is, to work among the Russian population (arguing that since the majority of Jews were petty traders and artisans they did not represent the people), Liebermann was the first who decided to conduct revolutionary work among the Jewish population as well, taking into account their specific national and cultural peculiarities. Liebermann emigrated, and in 1876 he founded in London the first-ever Jewish Socialist Workers' Union, which lasted just eight months. He himself wrote the Union's program in a refined biblical style of language of which he was particularly fond. Here are some extracts from it:

> Because we have become permeated with the awareness:
> That while private property still exists, economic want will remain; while people are divided into nations and tribes, enmity will not cease between them;
> That the liberation of us, the Jews, as a part of mankind, can only take place with the liberation of all of mankind;
> That the liberation of all of mankind can only be achieved by the efforts of the toilers themselves once they unite in open struggle to destroy the present system and to replace it with the kingdom of labor, justice, freedom, and the brotherhood of all people;
> We, the sons of Israel, have resolved: fraternally to make ourselves at one with the sacred union of the workers.

A year later, in Vienna, Aaron Liebermann issued the first socialist Hebrew-journal, *Ha-Emess* (The Truth). Only three issues were published. The journal was banned in Russia, and its publisher spent nine months in a German prison. Later, this same name "Truth" — in Russian *Pravda* — was used by the Bolsheviks for their newspaper.

Liebermann's undertaking clearly showed that Hebrew, which was at that time little known among the common people, could not be used to spread revolutionary, let alone socialist, propaganda. Yiddish was much more suitable for this purpose and was later chosen by the Bund as the language of the common people.

☐ TWO IDENTICAL LARGE houses, Nos. 21 and 23 on Zagorodny Prospekt, can be found directly opposite the beginning of ulitsa Sotsialisticheskaya. In the 1910s and 1920s, one of them (No. 23, apt. 35) was occupied by the oldest Jewish educational organization in Russia, the OPE, Society for the

Spread of Enlightenment among the Jews of Russia. Since we have already discussed this organization, here we shall only add some supplementary information.

OPE played a major role during World War I in providing education for the children of refugees. In those years the society established 370 schools for thirty thousand pupils on an annual budget of one million rubles. Following the Revolution, the major Jewish educational personalities in St. Petersburg were S. L. Zinberg, S. M. Ginsburg, and I. G. Frank-Kamenetsky. Lectures on a broad range of subjects were regularly delivered to meetings of the society. They included talks by S. M. Ginsburg on "The Decembrists and the Jews," "The Fiftieth Anniversary of Jewish Theatre," and "Jewish Humor"; by S. L. Zinberg on "The Rationalists — The Freethinkers of Medieval Jewry," "The Jewish Dramatic Repertoire from Goldfaden* to the Present Day," "The Literary Works of L. I. Katzenelson," and "The Fiftieth Anniversary of the Jewish Socialist Press"; by I. G. Frank-Kamenetsky on "The Prophet Jeremiah and the Party Struggle in his Times"; by V. V. Struve on "New Facts on the History of Assyria"; and N. I. Vinnikov on "The Cult of Cedar Wood in Talmudic Literature."

Today we know almost nothing about the content of these lectures and sometimes have only the title, even though in the 1920s a great deal of intensive work on Judaica was carried out. OPE had at its disposal an excellent library. Occasionally, journals or anthologies were published in Leningrad with such titles as *Yevreiskaya Letopis* (Jewish Chronicle), *Yevreiskaya Mysl* (Jewish Thought), *Yevreiskaya Starina* (Jewish Antiquity), and *Yevreisky Vestnik* (Jewish Herald). The results of academic research into Jewish history were published, in Russian, as separate books: M.I. Kulisher, *The Great French Revolution and the Jewish Question* (1927); Yu. Gessen, *The History of the Jewish People in Russia* (vol. 1, 1925; vol. 2, 1927); N. A. Bukhbinder, *The History of the Jewish Workers' Movement in Russia* (1925); V. V. Struve, *Israel in Egypt* (1920); and S. G. Lozinsky, *The Social Roots of Anti-Semitism in the Middle Ages and in Recent Times* (1929).

Between 1910 and 1917 OPE published a monthly journal called the *OPE Bulletin* (from 1912 *The Jewish Educational Bulletin*) edited by Ya. B. Eiger. Its editorial offices were located here at No. 23 Zagorodny Prospekt and the journal pursued the same aims as the society: to spread education among the Jews of Russia, to give news about the achievement of the new Jewish schools and colleges, and to organize schools of higher Jewish studies. Later the journal began to publish supplements in Yiddish and Hebrew.

OPE survived until the end of 1929. In its last years it was more concerned with scientific research and archival and bibliographical matters than with teaching and educational work.

---

* Abraham Goldfaden, born in the Ukraine in 1840, was the founder of the Yiddish Theater in Rumania in 1876. He died in New York in 1908.

☐ ON ULITSA DOSTOYEVSKOGO (formerly Yamskaya ulitsa), not far from Vladimirskaya Ploshchad between Svechny Pere'ulok and Malaya Moskovskaya ulitsa, there is a fairly small, plain building at No. 16. Here, for several years just before and just after the Revolution, was located one of the oldest and most famous of the Jewish communal organizations in Russia, The Society for Craft and Agricultural Labor among the Jews of Russia, well known by its Russian initial letters ORT. We have already mentioned this organization in our excursions, but we shall now look at it in more detail.

ORT, like OPE, was founded with the aim of transforming the life of Russian Jewry in the spirit of the ideas of the Haskala. But whereas OPE took upon itself to conduct cultural and educational work toward this end, ORT concentrated principally on changing the occupational and economic structure of the Jewish shtetl. Its slogan was: "From trading and acting as middlemen, to craft work and agricultural labor." The Society for Craft and Agricultural Labor was founded in 1880, in St. Petersburg, thanks above all to the efforts of the celebrated S. S. Polyakov. The training of Jews in craft work meant the emergence of a skilled work force in the Pale of Settlement, and consequently the possibility of the rapid development of capitalist production there.

The society achieved a great deal in the half-century of its existence.* The first study into the economic conditions of the Jewish population was conducted in 1887. By 1906 ORT had become a substantial organization with its own constitution and reserve capital of 400,000 rubles. Initially the society concentrated on the vocational training of young Jewish people. Its activities gradually expanded into more varied fields: granting of credits and loans to craftsmen and peasants; assistance in the retailing of handmade craft products of cottage industry; the development of a network of craft schools; the establishment of classes in craft work at Jewish primary schools; and the foundation of various training courses. (For example, the two craft schools in Dvinsk and Tsekhanovets [Grodno Province] and the electrotechnical courses in Vilna in 1910.)

As time passed, the society became very popular among the people, since graduation from a school or college and passing professional examinations carried with them the entitlement to reside in the central guberniyas (provinces) of Russia.

The society was also involved in publishing. I. S. Zak's book *Methods of Economic Self-Help in the Field of Craft Work* was published in 1911, followed by H. D. Gurevitch's pamphlet, in Yiddish, "Self-Help for Craftsmen." Other books were published. From 1916 to 1917 a monthly Russian-language journal, called *The Bulletin of Labor Assistance for Jews,* was published in Petrograd. Its

* In Russia. It is still active as the World ORT Union, with headquarters at No. 1 rue de Varembé, Geneva, Switzerland. Some 120,000 students are currently being trained in eight hundred centers in twenty-seven countries, and it is particularly successful in Israel.

editorial offices were in the ORT building: No. 16 Yamskaya ulitsa. L. M. Bramson, M. Urielev, and B. D. Brutskus were among the contributors.

In 1914 ORT organized a loans department named after Y. M. Galperin (a former chairman of the society) to provide Jewish craftsmen in Petrograd with small, interest-free loans. The society's annual budget reached twenty-five thousand to fifty-thousand rubles.

ORT played a very important part during World War I, straining all its resources, as did the other Jewish organizations, to alleviate the sufferings of the Jewish people caused by military activities. By late 1914 a special Workers' Aid Department had been established, which, together with EKOPO (the Jewish Society to Provide Help to the Victims of War) and ICA (The Jewish Colonization Association), developed an extensive network of labor offices and industrial workshops for the unemployed. It also provided schooling for children. In all, seventy-two labor offices and twenty-three industrial workshops were set up. In 1917 ORT began to organize market-gardening cooperatives in Petrograd, but we have no information on whether the capital's Jewish market gardeners did in fact unite.

Apart from S. S. Polyakov, ORT's active members included Y. M. Galperin, M. Bomze, Wawelberg, D. G. Guenzburg, Meyerson, D. S. Polyakov, G. B. Sliozberg, and L. M. Bramson — in the main, people who were also known in other fields of Jewish public life. The chairmen of the society were, successively, S. S. Polyakov, D. S. Polyakov, Y. M. Galperin, G. B. Sliozberg, and Y. Golde (in the 1920s).

In the 1920s the central committee of ORT moved to Berlin, where it became an international organization, participating in certain projects in the Soviet Union. In Leningrad, instead of the chairman, we come across the name of the representative, L. Y. Hoffman. The expertise of ORT was used in the organization of vocational training. Moreover, with the launching of the campaign to organize Jewish agricultural settlements in the Crimea and in the Ukraine, ORT unexpectedly became involved in an enterprise that had been planned long before, but that could not be put into practice before the Revolution: the assisting of the transfer of Jews to agricultural occupations. There was even a Jewish kolkhoz, a collective agricultural settlement, in the Kherson region. It was called Nai ORT (New ORT). Yet another of the functions of ORT was revived: the conducting of research and the publication of the findings on social changes among the Jewish population of the USSR. We know of five such research projects, published before 1930, of which four were published by the Board of ORT.

Research into the social changes of the Jewish population of that time was clearly important. Literally, in the course of just a few years, the percentage of office workers and laborers among the Jews rose sharply, while the proportion of merchants and entrepreneurs fell. This pattern was particularly noticeable in Moscow and Leningrad. In the 1920s Jewish families poured into these cities since the traditional economic structure of the small settlements (the shtetls)

The Society for Craft and Agricultural Labor among the Jews of Russia (ORT) was located here in 1917 and 1918.

TABLE 5-2. NUMBER AND PERCENTAGE OF JEWISH WORKERS IN LENINGRAD IN 1926

	Laborers	Office Workers	Liberal Professions	Self-Employed	Employers with Hired Labor	Unemployed	Occupation Not Known
% of total number of Jews in each group (in thousands)	13.3	40.1	2.5	9.0	2.5	15.5	11.9
% of Jews in each group	2.0	7.2	23.9	8.2	23.6	6.0	4.8

had been destroyed. A change of residence was usually accompanied by a change of profession. Migrants in a big town during Lenin's New Economic Policy (NEP), which began in 1921 and ended in 1929, could become laborers or office workers or, if unlucky, unemployed. The figures on Leningrad for 1926 that were published by ORT appear in Table 5-2.

THE STREET ON which we now find ourselves is so named because here, on the corner of ulitsa Dostoyevskogo and Kuznechny Pere'ulok at Kuznechny Pere'ulok 5/2, Dostoyevsky spent his last years. During that time he was editor of *Grazhdanin* (The Citizen) and a highly conservative individual. A house-museum is now devoted to the writer there. Because we have to pass this house in the course of our excursion, let us take the opportunity to touch on a theme that concerns us not a little: Dostoyevsky and the Jews. This subject has been frequently discussed by specialists, so we do not expect to say anything new; we shall simply mention the matter for those who are not acquainted with it.

It might seem that this has nothing to do with us. What of it if someone does not like Jews? We cannot write about them all. We are not talking of just anyone, however, but of Dostoyevsky. We cannot deny that many of the professional researchers of Dostoyevsky's art in our country are Jews who know perfectly well that they have devoted their creative lives to an anti-Semitic writer.

The writer himself consistently disavowed this label. In his diary, in March 1877, he wrote:

> It is most surprising to me how and from where I fell among the haters of the Jews, both as a people and as a nation. . . . When and in what have I declared any hatred toward the Jews? For in my heart I have never felt this hatred. . . . On the contrary, I say and write that everything that humanitarianism and justice require, everything that humanity and Christian laws demand, all this should be done for the Jews.

It might seem that there is nothing more to add. But most regrettably it is not quite as simple as that. Read the diary once more and you will find in it banal tunes about "the eternal gold business" of the Jews, about their "state within the state," and that the "Yids and their banks" control the fate of the world. In general, it irritates to come across these threadbare "arguments" advanced by a great writer. In declaring that the common people of Russia do not offend the Jews on account of their faith but that the Jew himself keeps his distance — that he does not eat or drink with Russian people — Dostoyevsky is here making far-reaching assumptions. In his diary for March 1877 he wrote:

> Meanwhile a fantasy sometimes enters my head: What would the situation be if, instead of there being three million Jews in Russia and eighty million Russians, it was the reverse? What would happen to the Russians — and how would they treat them? Would they not quite simply treat them as slaves? And worse, would they not utterly fleece them? Would they not beat them to pulp and completely exterminate them as they dealt with other alien peoples in ancient times, in their ancient history?

When we talk of Dostoyevsky's anti-Semitism, we usually refer to the caricatured picture of Isai Fomich Bumstein in *Notes from a Dead House,* in which the Jew is compared to a chicken, a dog, a parrot, a trained animal, and so on. But it seems to me that the preceding quotation is much more powerful. It inescapably leads to the conclusion that "what we do not do, they would do if they were in our place."(!) Is there not in this thought a veiled threat of a "blood-libel," not to mention a sense of national superiority? And this, after all, was written four years before the mass Jewish pogroms.

Then why is it, even after having read about Isai Fomich Bumstein and knowing about that most unfortunate diary, that we are all madly in love with Dostoyevsky? One of the main reasons for this phenomenon may be that in Dostoyevsky's novels (if we leave out the Jewish question) we encounter not rationalism, not faith, not "expediency," but ethics; not the cult of the strong but an apologia for the weak. In other words, it is all that distinguishes Judaism from Hellenistic-Nietzschean philosophy. Let us recall Ivan Karamazov's reasoning about the impossibility of achieving universal happiness at the price of the blood of a single innocent child. And Raskolnikov? A philosophy that is much more Judaic than Christian permeates all of Dostoyevsky's works; his ideas are not in conformity with the Christian ideals, in which the theory of "Love thy neighbor" is so far from the practice ("the end justifies the means"). It is no wonder that his favorite reading was the Book of Job. Even the structure of his works — in which content, thought, philosophic reasoning, and subtle spiritual feelings are much more important than descriptions of nature or the appearance of the heroes — all this undoubtedly corresponds to the Jewish view of the world and unconsciously attracts the Jewish reader. Therefore, Dostoyevsky himself, so apprehensive of the "Jewish gold business" and the "international Jewish conspiracy," acquired through Christianity certain essential features of the philosophical outlook of Judaism.

Ulitsa Rubinshteina (formerly Troitskaya) is short and quiet, but it deserves special study from the point of view of Jewish history, not because of its name, but because in the 1910s and 1920s it happened to be the home of a host of Jewish institutions and organizations—mainly in two buildings.

THE FIRST IS NO. 34 ulitsa Rubinshteina. From 1915 to 1917 the Moskovsky rayon (district) synagogue was located here (its other address at that time was Zagorodny Prospekt No. 6). In 1917 the building also accommodated the Society for the Provision of Elementary Education for the Jewish Children of the City of Petrograd (IVRIO). In all probability these two organizations had close links, since the chairman of the Board of Management and treasurer of the synagogue, D. E. Khavkin, was simultaneously the treasurer of the society. They also shared the same secretary, M. M. Brumberg. The education society's chairman was M. R. Krever, and the vice-chairman was Daniel L'vovitch Ziv, a wealthy manufacturer.

The Petrograd Jewish Teachers' Association was formed here in mid-1917. Its committee was made up of well-known activists in the field of Jewish education: H. H. Fialkov, S. L. Kamenetsky, Zinovy Kisselgoff, M. E. Motyleva, G. L. Aronovitch, E. S. Alexandrova, B. A. Halperin, M. M. Chernin, V. L. Gendler, and L. L. Golomb. The association lasted only a short time, but precisely how long we do not know. In 1925 the building was taken over by two Jewish technical schools that moved in at the same time. They merged in 1927. The school had a metal-working and lathe-turning department and one for garment making.

IVRIO maintained a Jewish primary school at No. 6 Zagorodny Prospekt (1915). In late 1918 a requisitioned building at No. 14 ulitsa Rubinshteina (which has been rebuilt) accommodated the Institute of Higher Jewish Studies (see later). Following the transfer of the institute to ulitsa Stremyannaya in 1925, the same building was occupied by the Sverdlov Jewish Club. The Hasidic religious organization IVRIO (1925–1927), under the chairmanship of S. A. Maryashkin, co-existed peacefully next door on the first floor of No. 12 (also rebuilt). Later, in 1928, the Hasidim were displaced by the Jewish Educational House, which soon after moved to No. 10 ulitsa Nekrassova.

It remains to be added that the nearby house at No. 6 Zagorodny Prospekt accommodated yet another organization between 1912 and 1917: a department of the Courses on Biblical Language and Biblical History for Jewish Students of Higher and Secondary Educational Establishments. The courses themselves were run at the Jewish community building at No. 42 ulitsa Dekabristov. They were founded by the St. Petersburg community rabbi and OPE activist, Moisei Eisenstadt. The courses were apparently organized in an attempt to stem the rapid movement away from Judaism of youngsters studying in Russian educational establishments. Today we can see quite clearly that this initiative had no positive results whatsoever.

The Institute of Higher Jewish Studies was located at No. 14 ulitsa Rubinshteina and No. 18 Stremyannaya ulitsa. Over several decades many people had become involved in the question of contemporary Jewish education in Russia. In this, OPE played a special role and even published a special pedagogical journal *Vestnik Yevreiskogo Prosveshcheniya* (The Herald of Jewish Enlightenment). However, by the start of World War I, things had not progressed beyond secondary education (if we do not include the Courses in Oriental Studies conducted by Baron David Guenzburg, in which only about thirty students participated), even though the need for a Jewish secular higher school had been clearly recognized. In his article on "The Immediate Perspectives and Organization of OPE Work," H. Fialkov writes:

> One cannot but be heartened by the fact that the appropriate circles are at last becoming interested in the question of a Higher School of Jewish Studies. It is shameful and painful to admit that the six-million-strong Jewish population of Russia has, up to now, had to make do without a nursery ground of higher Jewish studies. We are at least a quarter of a century late in this matter. The result is apparent in our extreme spiritual impoverishment in the field of Jewish studies.

In short, the years leading up to the 1917 Revolution were spent in laying the foundations for the first Russian Higher School of Jewish Studies. Teachers were selected and a curriculum worked out (mainly by Mikhail Kulisher). No. 18 Stremyannaya ulitsa was acquired from the former member of the State Duma, L. N. Nisselovitch. The husband and wife M. G. and M. N. Kreinin donated the money for the purchase of the building (200,000 rubles) on condition that it should accommodate the Higher School of Jewish Studies, a library with a reading room, a publishing house and a bookstore, a pedagogic museum, the offices of the central committee of OPE, and the editorial offices of the *Vestnik Yevreiskogo Prosveshcheniya*.

The Revolution prevented the full implementation of these plans, but the idea itself did not die. In February 1919 the Jewish University was opened at Naberezhnaya Krasnogo Flota No. 62, in the former mansion of Yakov Polyakov. In August of that year it moved to ulitsa Rubinshteina No. 14, apt 1, and then to Nisselovitch's house on Stremyannaya ulitsa. Shortly afterward the university was renamed the Institute of Higher Jewish Studies. It had two faculties, literary-philological and historico-social. The courses were of three years' duration. Samuil Lozinski was the rector, and Srul (Israel) Zinberg was the academic registrar. The main aim of the institute was to train teachers as well as qualified people for all fields of Jewish studies. At the same time, lectures were delivered on various aspects of Jewish studies for all who wished to attend, with the building acting as a sort of reading room.

Both the teaching staff and the level of instruction were of a very high standard. Until 1922, Simon Dubnow taught Jewish history. Professor Yosif Mikhailovitch Kulisher (1878–1923), the son of OPE Central Committee member Mikhail Kulisher, taught economics. Aaron Zakharovitch Steinberg

S. L. Zinberg, with his daughter Tamara

lectured on the philosophy of Judaism. His brother was the Left Social Revolutionary, I. Z. Steinberg, head of the People's Commissariat of Justice in the first post-October (that is, Bolshevik) government. Aaron Steinberg was also a board member of the Institute of Higher Jewish Studies.

Ravrebbe was a teacher specializing in modern Hebrew (Ivrit) and its history. At the same time he was translating into Yiddish the ancient Pinkasim (Record Books) of Nesvizh, Lutsk, and Sudilkov, as well as the rabbinical "responsa" on the Pospolita Discourses. At the Jewish University he lectured on the affinity between the Hebrew and Arabic languages.

The rector, S. H. Lozinsky, taught the history of the Jews in the Middle Ages. He was also the author of a book on medieval and contemporary anti-Semitism. His academic registrar, Sergei Zinberg, played a key role in the life of the institute. It seemed as if Zinberg succeeded in everything he put his hand to. He was an outstanding chemical engineer and head of the main research laboratory of the Putilov Works. He achieved much in the field of Jewish education, history, and culture, was an active participant in OPE before the Revolution, and wrote articles on the Jewish workers' movement for the *Yevreiskaya Entsiklopedia* (Jewish Encyclopedia) and for the anthology *Perezhitoye* (Experiences). After the Revolution he joined the editorial board of the journal *Yevreiskaya Starina* (Jewish Antiquity) and became the chairman of OPE. This small, lively, energetic man, though himself not religious, was devoted to Jewish traditions and often attended synagogue. He spent much of his free time at the Asiatic Museum (which later developed into the Institute of Oriental Studies), delving into the history of Jewish literature. The fruit of this effort was a large work on the history of Jewish literature, published in Yiddish in Vilna in the late 1920s and early 1930s.

Other teachers at the Jewish University included S. M. Ginsburg, I. Guenzburg, G. Y. Krasny, M. L. Maimon, S. Rozovsky, I. Y. Maimon, Y. Gessen, M. Eisenstadt, E. Gurlyand-Elyasheva, and other Jewish scholars and cultural activists who at that time still remained in Petrograd. In addition, the former owner of a corset workshop on Gorokhovaya ulitsa—Zaks—acted as the institute's bursar. An important factor in enabling the university to survive was that both lecturers and students received bread rations.

The institute was divided into sections (then called commissions), in which it was possible to study such topics as law in the Bible and the Talmud, medicine in the Bible and the Talmud, and ethics (and even agriculture) in the Bible and the Talmud.

The Institute of Higher Jewish Studies was closed in about 1925. It broke up gradually. Some of the lecturers emigrated. Others transferred their activity —up to a given moment—to OPE, IEO, or the Public Library. In 1928, the *Yevreisky Vestnik* (Jewish Herald), in its academic chronicle section, made no

Advertisement for a meeting of the Society for Jewish Upbringing and Education, to be held at the Zabalkansky Auditorium (Zabalkansky Prospekt, 37/1) on February 7, 1914. S. L. Zinberg was to speak on "The Principal Currents in the New Jewish Literature."

mention of the existence in Leningrad of any Jewish higher academic establishment, although it did list similar institutions in other towns.

Between 1918 and 1929, Stremyannaya ulitsa No. 18 accommodated the OPE library, which was founded by Abram Harkavy in 1878 and moved here from the community building at ulitsa Dekabristov No. 42. The *Yevreisky Vestnik* states that in the 1920s this was one of the richest libraries in Europe in its section on Hebraica and Judaica; it contained a very large collection of manuscripts. In later years the library expanded its holdings mainly with collections of books donated by the descendants of Y. M. Galperin, L. M. Kamenetsky, S. E. Weisenberg, and others. The valuable collection of Hebraica donated by Y. H. Yanovsky's heirs contained more than four hundred volumes. The library exchanged books with the Institute of Bielorussian Culture (Jewish Department), the faculty of Jewish culture of the Ukrainian Academy of Sciences, the library of the Jerusalem University, the Jewish Libraries of Berlin, and others.

The indefatigable Zinberg labored in the library's manuscript department, studying and listing more than nine hundred manuscripts and fragments, including excerpts from the poems of Solomon Gabirol (among which were some unpublished verses), the historical works of Lekhno, the compositions of the Karaite Solomon ben Yerukhim, and extracts from the works of Moses ben Ezra. *Yevreisky Vestnik* notes the increasing number of people using the reading room, which in 1927 was open three days a week for ten and a half months and was used by 4,050 readers.

☐ THE COMMITTEE OF the Society for the Protection of the Health of the Jewish Population (OZE) was located not far from Vladimirskaya Ploshchad at ulitsa Kolokolnaya No. 9. This society was founded in St. Petersburg in 1912, and even though it survived for only a few years, it played a very important role in the life of Russian Jewry. The OZE rules stated that "the society has as its aim to study the sanitary and hygienic conditions of Jews, to disseminate accurate information about hygiene among them, to promote social medicine on a scientific basis, and in general to further the cause of the health of the Jewish population."

We have mentioned in a previous excursion that despite the extreme poverty and unemployment among many Jews of the Pale of Settlement, on average they had a lower infant mortality rate and longer life expectancy than did other Russian religious groups. This phenomenon can be explained by the moral traditions of Judaism (care for children and an extensive network of philanthropic institutions that prevented even the poorest from dying of hunger) and the lower incidence among Jews (in comparison with that among the surrounding rural population) of alcoholism and venereal diseases, which is also in one way or another associated with morals, religion, and culture.

Nevertheless, even in the Jewish shtetls there was quite enough dirt and ignorance, and the way of life of urban Jews over many generations put them "at the head of the league table" for typical industrial illnesses — tuberculosis and certain psychiatric maladies. So the OZE had plenty to do.

In its early years OZE circulated information about hygiene and public health care through pamphlets in Yiddish, public lectures, and so on. It collected figures on the availability of medical assistance for Jews and organized children's medical camps in Yevpatoria and Druskininkai, children's playgrounds, and so on. But it only really came into its own with the onset of World War I, when the refugees and wounded needed urgent medical help of all sorts. OZE provided those in need with free medical help and medicines and opened outpatient clinics, children's centers, nursing centers for suckling mothers and babes, sanatoria for tuberculosis sufferers, and hostels for war cripples.

Almost a third of the society's outgoings were met by government grants,

The activists of The Society for the Protection of the Health of the Jewish Population (OZE). Standing: (third from the right) Yakov Eiger, (eighth from the right) Raphail Botvinnick. Sitting: Grigory Goldberg. In uniform: Abram Bramson.

and the rest was obtained from private donations. The society's budget grew rapidly during the war: to 300,929 rubles in 1915; 1,200,336 rubles in 1916; and 2,027,613 rubles in 1917.

Attached to the society were the following commissions and departments:
Medical and hospital commission
Department for cripples
Nursing centers
Tuberculosis prevention department
Mother and child welfare department
Sports and gymnastics commission
School medical commission
Literature and publishing commission
Prisoners of war assistance commission

During its existence, OZE established a total of eighty-five outpatient clinics, fifteen hospitals, eighty-one nursing centers, and two sanatoria for tuberculosis cases — one in Alushta for lung cases and one in Yevpatoria for children with bone and lymphatic tuberculosis. Thousands of Jews owed their health or their lives to the society.

IN 1910 THE Society for the Regulation of Jewish Emigration was located in Nevsky Prospekt No. 65, apt. 30, not far from the library on Stremyannaya ulitsa and next to the present-day cinema Khudozhestvenny. For about half a century after 1881, emigration was one of the most important aspects of Jewish life in Russia. We have already touched on this question in Excursion One in discussing the work of the Jewish Colonization Association (ICA). Emigration was a spontaneous process over which social organizations had little control. At the same time, the very scale of emigration, the seriousness of the factors that gave rise to it, and the expected grave consequences of the phenomenon meant that emigration could not be ignored by any Jewish public personality.

TABLE 5-3. JEWISH EMIGRATION FROM RUSSIA TO THE UNITED STATES

Year	No. of Emigrants	Year	No. of Emigrants	Year	No. of Emigrants
1881	8,193	1891	42,145	1901	37,660
1882	17,497	1892	76,417	1902	37,846
1883	6,907	1893	35,626	1903	47,689
1884	15,122	1894	36,725	1904	77,544
1885	16,603	1895	33,232	1905	92,388
1886	17,309	1896	45,137	1906	125,234
1887	28,944	1897	22,750	1907	114,932
1888	31,256	1898	27,221	1908	71,978
1889	31,889	1899	24,275	1909	39,150
1890	33,147	1900	37,011	1910	59,824

**TABLE 5-4. COMPARATIVE EMIGRATION FROM RUSSIA TO
THE UNITED STATES FROM 1904 TO 1908**

Nationality	% of Total Number of Emigrants
Jews	50.2
Poles	24.7
Lithuanians and Latvians	8.6
Finns	6.3
Germans	5.0
Russians	4.7
Others	0.5

TABLE 5-5. EMIGRATION FROM RUSSIA TO PALESTINE

Year	No. of Emigrants	Year	No. of Emigrants
1905	1,230	1910	1,879
1906	3,459	1911	2,376
1907	1,750	1912	1,182
1908	2,097	1913	1,600
1909	2,495	1914	6,000

We cite here some figures from the Jewish annual *Kadima* (Forward) and from N. A. Bukhbinder's book *The History of the Jewish Workers' Movement in Russia*. Table 5-3 reveals the clear connection between peaks of emigration and the incidence of pogroms, as well as intensified anti-Jewish legislation, the Revolution of 1905 to 1907, and so on.

Between 1880 and 1914 a total of 1,369,412 Jews emigrated from Russia to the United States. If we add those who left for Canada, Britain, Argentina, South Africa, and other countries — including Palestine — we obtain a figure approaching two million. For example, in only six years (1907 to 1912), 28,242 persons left Russia for Britain. Between 1900 and 1916, 75,808 left for Canada, and between 1904 and 1906, 25,000 went to Argentina.

The age structure of emigrants between 1899 and 1910 was as follows: under fourteen, 25 percent; fourteen to forty-five, 70 percent; over forty-five, 5 percent. In other words, the most able-bodied section of the Jewish population was leaving Russia. Jews composed the overwhelming majority of all nationalities that were leaving Russia for the United States, as Table 5-4 clearly shows.

We should add that the Jewish emigrants were usually the poorest among those who arrived in America during this period. As they disembarked in New York, each had, on average, no more than twelve dollars.

Emigration to Palestine played an important part in the emigration movement, even though at about one thousand each year it represented only an insignificant proportion of the total flood of refugees (Table 5-5).

ICA (Jewish Colonization Association) was the first organization to undertake the regulation of emigration (primarily to Argentina) and to provide the emigrant with money, legal advice, and vocational training. The Palestine Committee in Odessa assisted those who wished to go to Palestine.

As time passed, reference materials were published, giving would-be Jewish emigrants essential information about the journey. For example, a handbook issued with *Rassvet* (Daybreak) had a section detailing what documents had to be obtained for emigration; which were the cheapest and easiest routes to given destinations; how to avoid the extortions of government bureaucrats, speculators, and smugglers; which addresses abroad should be approached to obtain assistance, and so on.

The Society for the Regulation of Jewish Emigration was founded in St. Petersburg in 1907, with the aim of assisting migrants to improve traveling conditions and to help them settle in a new place. The society defended migrants from abuses by individuals and institutions, organized canteens and lodging houses en route, published advice manuals, and acquainted migrants with living conditions in various countries. It also maintained contact with foreign institutions concerned with helping migrants.

The society was run by a board of twelve. The annual subscription was ten rubles for full members, six rubles for associate members, and two rubles for donor members.

All this indicates that even though relatively few emigrated from St. Petersburg, it was the Jews of the capital who, through the organization of societies, the publication of brochures, the collection of money, and so on, undertook the main burden of caring for the migrants. But already some of the more farsighted people, such as Simon Dubnow, were worried about what would happen later. Would the migrant Jews landing in the New World remain Jews and retain their national traditions? And what would happen to those who remained?

Indeed, even though the wave of emigration absorbed only the natural increase in the Jewish population and therefore did not substantially alleviate the problems of those who remained in Russia, all the same it was the most energetic and active part of the population that left. In conjunction with other important and tragic events tending in the same direction, such as pogroms, wars, the later separation from Russia — after the Treaty of Riga in 1921 — of the more cultured Jews of Lithuania and Poland, and the breakdown of the social and economic life of the Jewish shtetl, emigration led to the loss of an enormous part of the cultural heritage for the remaining Russian Jews. Put more simply, the emigration of Jews from Russia led to a tremendous spiritual impoverishment of those who remained. The then "dominant influences" left the country: Sholem Aleikhem, Chaim-Nahman Bialik, Ahad Ha-am, Saul Tchernichowsky, Shneur Zalman, Sholem Asch, and Simon Dubnow. This list could be extended indefinitely and even more so if political figures are added. For example, the declining influence of the Bund among the Jewish masses during the period between the two revolutions was, to a significant degree, associated with the emigration of many of its members to the West.

In conclusion, here is a list of the documents that a Jew needed to obtain a passport for travel abroad at the turn of the century:

1 Ordinary citizen's identity card (called a passport)
2 Certificate from the chief of police or the police superintendent confirming that there was no objection to the applicant leaving the country
3 Certification of registration with military enlistment registration office, or of completion of military service, if this was not already stated on the passport (that is, the identity card)
4 Treasury certificate showing payment of fifteen rubles

In the border town of Libava (now Liepaya), for example, on presentation of these documents, the foreign travel passport was issued on the day of application.

☐ BETWEEN ULITSA NEKRASSOVA and ulitsa Zhukovskogo there lay a quite little street, ulitsa Chekhova (formerly Ertelev Pere'ulok). Two of the buildings here, Nos. 5 and 6, are associated with Jewish history.

No. 6 is a six-story building of glazed brick, built in the pseudo-Russian style, somewhat reminiscent of a fairy-tale castle. At the end of the last century, the editorial offices of the newspaper *Novoye Vremya* (New Times) were based here. It was one of the first in postreformation Russia, following the emancipation of the serfs by Alexander II in 1861, to join in the persecution of the Jews. In 1880, during Alexander II's relatively liberal reign, the paper published an article entitled "The Yids are Coming," which declared that the admission of Jews into Russian culture strengthened their influence on Russian life and increased the danger of their malign influence on "the indigenous population." The appearance of such an article in an influential right-wing newspaper, signified, in essence, the transition to open government anti-Semitic policies. The publisher of *Novoye Vremya* was the not unknown Aleksei Suvorin. Suvorin (1834–1912) published attacks on several leading Jewish figures in St. Petersburg, including the sculptor Antokolski and the poet Nadson. (It was he, incidentally, who published the directory-guide *V'yess Petersburg* — All of St. Petersburg — from which we have extracted so much information for our excursions.) One of the main contributors to this newspaper was the religious philosopher V. Rozanov, author of a number of anti-Semitic works. A complex character, Rozanov, when he was dying, asked that these articles be destroyed.

The four-story dwelling across the street, at No. 5, is associated with something completely different. The Leningrad committee of the Yevreiskaya Kommunisticheskaya Rabochaya Partiya (EKRP) (Jewish Communist Workers' Party) was based here for two years, in 1927 and 1928. The committee secretary was V. M. Borokhovitch. The party was formed as a result of the disintegration of the Social Democratic Workers' Party (Poalei-Zion) and the departure of its left wing. The EKRP had no links with Zionists on the grounds that the interests of bourgeois Zionism and the Jewish proletariat were incompatible.

The Jewish Theater. Up to 1919 we can find no significant traces of any Jewish theatrical life in St. Petersburg–Petrograd, even though amateur and occasionally professional groups did come to the city on tour. With the upsurge of Jewish cultural activity in the 1910s a first step had been taken in this direction. The rules of the Jewish Literary Society stated that the society had a drama section, and the rules of the kindred Y. L. Peretz Jewish Literary and Artistic Society stated that one of its aims was the creation of a Jewish theater. It seems, however, that no significant results were achieved.

The Jewish Theatrical Society was formed in 1916 in the seven-story building on the corner of Saperny Pere'ulok and Mitavsky Pere'ulok (Saperny Pere'ulok No. 9/1). Its members intended finally to develop the theater in Petrograd, but even this initiative was not destined to produce any visible results. The society barely functioned.

Nevertheless, the idea was on the verge of fulfillment, and soon after the Revolution it was realized in the form of a Jewish studio, formed in Petrograd in 1919 by the Commissariat of Jewish Affairs. In 1921 the studio was transferred to Moscow, where, as a result of its merger with the local Jewish theater studio, the Moscow GOSEKT (State Jewish Chamber Theater) was formed. It was later renamed GOSET (Jewish State Theater) and became the most famous Jewish theater in the history of Russia, managing to survive the longest of all—almost thirty years. Its artistic manager up to 1929 was A. M. Granovsky, an outstanding director who, during a tour of the theater in the West, remained abroad. Famous artists such as Marc Chagall, Natan Altman, Falk, and Viktor Tischler helped stage its performances. But those who remember the theater associate it above all with the name of Solomon Mikhoels, people's artist of the USSR, winner of the Stalin Prize, chairman of the Anti-Fascist Committee, and for twenty years artistic director of GOSET.

Solomon Mikhailovitch Mikhoels was born in Dvinsk in 1890 and was killed in 1948 in Minsk. He was the son of an orthodox Jewish merchant and studied in turn in cheder, the Riga Secondary "Réali" School (a school where the classical subjects were not taught), the Kiev Commercial Institute, and the law faculty of Petrograd University (1915–1918). After graduating he was invited by Proletcult to teach mathematics, but he chose instead to become an actor in the Jewish theater.

Russian Jews certainly maintained some sort of theatrical tradition for at least forty years, but the founders of the Soviet Jewish Theater, who saw in the theater a powerful tool to influence the masses, were loath to draw on these traditions. As Liubomirsky wrote in his book *Mikhoels* (published in Moscow in 1938): "The pioneers of the new Soviet Jewish Theater were naturally wary of carrying out these tasks with the assistance of the old-time Jewish stage performers, the professional actors, preferring to deal with amateurs or inexperienced arts students. It was necessary to train a new generation of actors who had nothing in common with the old Jewish acting milieu." With this aim in mind, GOSET was organized.

The performances were in Yiddish, and the theater staged classical tragedies such as Gutskov's *Uriel d'Acosta* and Shakespeare's *King Lear* as well as plays by traditional Jewish writers such as *200,000* by Sholem Aleikhem, *The Witch* by Goldfaden, and *The God of Vengeance* by Sholem Asch; a large amount of the new Soviet Jewish literature and drama was also presented — David Bergelson's *The Deaf Man*, Peretz Markish's *The Ovadis Family*, and I. Dobrushin and I. Nusinov's *The Specialist*. The leading parts were generally played by Mikhoels.

While in Petrograd, the theater did not have its own premises; therefore, it is difficult to give it a precise address for those years. Later, in the 1930s and 1940s, GOSET visited Leningrad several times and usually performed in the Narodny Dom (People's Palace), later in the Velikan (Giant) Cinema or the Promko'operatsiya Palace of Culture (now the Lensoviet Palace of Culture), and also (in the 1930s) in the Musical Comedy Theater.

Many older Leningraders recall the theater's last visit in the summer of 1948. The company performed in the Gorky Bolshoi Drama Theater (No. 65 Naberezhnaya Fontanki). Mikhoels was no longer alive,* and GOSET, which was to survive only a few more months, was named after the great man who had devoted his whole life to the theater. V. L. Zuskin, Mikhoels's close friend and a marvellous actor, took on the job of artistic director. (In the famous GOSET production of *King Lear* in 1935, Mikhoels had played Lear and Zuskin, The Fool.) Among other plays, the theater performed Z. Shneer's *Freilekhs*, Peretz Markish's *The Uprising in the Ghetto*, M. Gershensohn's *Herschele Ostropoler*, and Sholem Aleikhem's *The Revolving Planets*. All the plays were well attended and highly praised. Perhaps these audiences sensed that Leningrad was not destined to see a Jewish theater for a long time to come.

It is difficult to track down where precisely in Leningrad the studio-theater Habimah performed. (*Habimah* is Hebrew for "the stage.") This Jewish theater, performing in Hebrew, came into existence after the 1917 Revolution and lasted until 1927 under the direction of N. D. Zemach. The fact that the theater really did perform in Petrograd is confirmed by the program for the famous performance of the play by Simeon An-sky, translated into Hebrew by Hayim Nahman Bialik, *The Dybbuk (Between Two Worlds)*. The performance

---

* He was killed in Minsk on January 13, 1948, ostensibly by hooligans in a car accident, but as admitted many years later in the Soviet press, it was by the order of the Soviet Secret Police.

was staged by the famous Russian director Yevgeni Vakhtangov, and the scenery and costumes were designed by Natan Altman. The bold undertaking was destined to have a great future. Habimah left Russia in 1926, and went to Palestine in 1931, where it has remained and flourished.

The memory of two other ghostly Jewish theaters is preserved in the Petrograd-Leningrad Directory. No literary evidence or even a memoir about these theaters can be found other than in the directory. The first, the Jewish Drama Theater, is mentioned in 1922 under the address Prospekt Volodarskogo (Liteiny Prospekt) No. 42. The theater was located in the former palace of Princess Z. Yusupova, built by the architect L. Bonshtedt between 1852 and 1878. This is now the Central Lecture Hall. The theater was managed by P. Verkhovtsev.

In 1927 the Leningrad Jewish Theater (LET) was at No. 13 Rakova ulitsa (now the Musical Comedy Theater). A. D. Tikhantovsky was the manager, M. T. Stroyev the director, and I. I. Kaganovitch the producer; A. S. Rabiner and D. I. Sokolov were on the administrative board. Both groups performed in Yiddish.

That is all that we know so far about these theaters.

There was also a Jewish national club until 1927 at No. 7 ulitsa Nekrassova. It then moved, at some time between 1928 and 1930, to the building of the present Bolshoi Puppet Theater at No. 10 on the same street. In the 1920s many national minorities in Leningrad (Germans, Finns, Poles) had their own national clubs and schools, so the Jewish club was no exception with its amateur groups, national choirs, and so on.

Any critic who has ever studied the way that Jews are portrayed in Russian literature must admit that Russian writers usually either did not write about Jews or else wrote badly of them. See, for example, the articles by D. Zaslavsky, V. Jabotinsky, and B. Gorin. One does not necessarily have to read these articles but can turn to the Russian literature itself to prove this point. Take, for example, Dostoyevsky's *Notes from a Dead House,* Turgenev's *The Yid,* or Nekrassov's *Ballet,* not to mention Gogol's *Taras Bulba.* This was so up to the beginning of the twentieth century, by which time the Jewish question had become a burning one as the role of the Jews had increased sharply in all spheres of Russian life. Two opposing camps that emerged among Russian intellectuals were reflected in the pages of Russian literature and journalism: the Judophiles and the Judophobes. At the same time, since the tsarist government conducted openly anti-Semitic policies, hatred of Jews became a distinguishing feature of the reactionaries. It consequently became embarrassing in "respectable" Russian literary society to express one's hostility toward the Jews, since there was then the danger of being taken for a monarchist. It is also possible that some writers realized that in the western guberniyas the bulk of the reading population was Jews and hence the success of the books depended on them.

The Jewish House of Cultural Enlightenment, located at Nekrassova 10 (from 1930 to 1935)

In any case, many Russian writers and cultural figures of the early twentieth century such as Gorky, Korolenko, and Kuprin began to express sympathy and compassion for the Jews, and some even genuinely began to fight for Jewish equal rights. By 1915 these tendencies led to the formation of the Russian Society for the Study of Jewish Life, located in Simeonovskaya ulitsa No. 11, apt. 9 (now ulitsa Belinskogo). The following is an extract from the society's rules:

1. The aim of the society is to study Jewish life, past and present. To this end the society will engage in the study of and research into Jewish history, literature, art, folklore, daily life, and the economic and legal status of the Jews.
2. To achieve these aims the society will:
   a. organize meetings of its members for information and lectures;
   b. organize, with the appropriate authorization, public readings and exhibitions on topics within the field of this study, as well as concerts;
   c. publish, in conformity with existing laws, books, anthologies and periodicals;
   d. propose themes for essays and provide prize money and awards.
Subscriptions: Five rubles a year.

The rules went on to list the names of the officials of the society:

President of the Society: Steward of the Royal Household I. I. Tolstoy.
Committee Members: M. Gorky, Honorary Academician D. N. Ovsyaniko-Kulikovsky, Professor A. V. Kartashev, State Duma Members N. V. Nekrassov, A. M. Kalmykova, N. I. Korobka, Professor V. I. Semevsky, and Professor M. V. Bernadsky.

There still exists an announcement about a musical evening organized by the society, of which the participants included Leonid Andreyev, A. N. Benoit, Z. N. Gippius, A. K. Glazunov, M. Gorky, A. I. Kuprin, Professor N. O. Lossky, D. S. Merezhkovsky, State Duma Member P. N. Milyukov, A. N. Rimsky-Korsakov, State Duma Member F. I. Rodichev, and F. I. Chaliapin.

In 1916 the society promoted the publication of a literary anthology in defense of the Jews called *Shcheet* (The Shield). The contributors included Artsebasheva, Gippius, Merezhkovsky, Sologub, Milyukov, Korolenko, and Bunin. This anthology is very uneven both in terms of literary merit and in the outlook of the authors. There is, for example, the sentimental and sickly sweet eulogy, full of incomprehension of Jewish problems, written by Zinaida Gippius, someone who was only by chance temporarily sympathetic. It repeats the popular concept that because Jesus was a Jew, so there should be sympathy for the Jews:

He accepted the sorrow of life's sad road,
He was first, and all alone,
Stooping to bathe the weary feet that strode,
Servant — yet King on a throne.
He joined in our weeping — Master and Preacher

Over land and over sea . . .
Emperor, our brother and also our teacher
Yet he's a Jew, you see . . .

"The Jewish Question in Russia," an article by P. N. Milyukov, one of the leaders of the Cadet Party, reflected the point of view that was more typical of the Russian intelligentsia of the time. Milyukov did not see any special Jewish needs and considered the Jewish question to be only part of the general problem of the lack of rights in Russia. He wrote:

The question of Jewish equality in Russia is a question of equality for all citizens in general. This is why it can be seen that anti-Semitic parties in Russia have far greater political weight and significance than anti-Semitic parties in the West. Here they practically merge with parties that are in general anti-constitutional, and anti-Semitism serves as the standard of the old order from which we have been trying so carefully to distance ourselves. This is why the Jewish question occupies such a prominent place in Russian society and political life. The momentum of the struggle for equal rights in general and for national equality, here coincide. This is why the Jewish question takes pride of place in our political life.

We should note here that this Cadet leader wanted the attainment of equality by the Jews to be followed by their rapid assimilation.

Of all the authors contributing to this anthology, Korolenko sounds the most sober and mature. In his story "Mr. Jackson's Opinion on the Jewish Question," he affirms that Jews require neither love nor sympathy nor compassion — only equal rights.

In the fierce arguments over "The Jewish Question and the Russian Intelligentsia," Maxim Gorky's role is particularly noteworthy. He frequently and very sharply condemned anti-Semitism and its extreme expression, the pogrom. Not only was he one of the major figures in The Russian Society for the Study of Jewish Life and the author of numerous articles and speeches defending the Jewish people, but he also spoke many times as the champion of all that was best in Jewish literature, culture, and the revolutionary movement. Many Jews owed the greater part of their success, and sometimes even their lives, to him. His article "The Jewish Question and the Russian Intelligentsia" characterized the role of Jews in history as follows:

Throughout the hard path on the road to progress, towards the light, at all stages on this exhausting journey, the Jew stands as a living protest, an explorer. He was always the beacon from which proudly and on high there flashed to the whole world the undiminished protest against everything dirty and low in human life, against the crude acts of violence of man against man, against loathsome vulgarity and spiritual ignorance.

Gorky sees the Jewish question in Russia as above all a question of politics, and he concludes his article with an appraisal of the Russian intelligentsia, to which he himself belonged. What sort of an evaluation does he give?

The intellectual stratum of Russian society is not infected with the poison of anti-Semitism at all. But here I must, to my great sorrow, note that Russian intellectuals, as a whole, have nevertheless never treated the Jews as justice would require. Herein lies their great sin.

☐ THE LARGE FOUR-STORY building on the corner of ulitsa Pestelya and Liteiny Prospekt (No. 21 Liteiny Prospekt) was designed by the architect du Tel in 1876 and 1877. Samuil Yakovlevitch Marshak lived here from 1927 to 1938. We all remember him from our childhood. Marshak is associated with the Children's Publishing House (Detgiz), with marvellous translations, and with the Lenin Prize of 1963. Everybody remembers "Children in a Cage," "Mister Twister" (the story of Oliver Twist), "The Tale of the Foolish Young Mouse," and "The Little Girl," in which the character played and sang so light-heartedly.*

Even bearing in mind our main aim, which is to describe Jewish St. Petersburg, we could not pass this building by, since Marshak never rejected his origins; did not change his surname, first name, or patronymic; and translated into Russian not only Shakespeare and Burns but also Bergelson and Markish.

In his autobiographical sketch *About Myself* the poet writes of his childhood, describing how difficult it had been for him to enter the Gymnasium (secondary high school) at Ostrogozhsk (near Voronezh) because of the "numerus clausus," a quota on the number of Jews allowed to enter. He says that without the support and patronage of Vladimir Stassov and Maxim Gorky he would never have been able to move to St. Petersburg, or live in Yalta, and indeed he would not have been able to complete his education in England at London University (Faculty of Arts).

Marshak recollects how, between 1915 and 1917 in Voronezh, he helped Jewish refugees who were driven away from the area of the frontline fighting by the savage military laws:

> I remember one of the buildings in Voronezh in which an entire "shtetl" had taken shelter. Here, bunks were houses, and the passages between them were the narrow alleyways. It seemed as if an ant-hill had been moved from one place to another together with all its inhabitants. My work consisted of looking after the children of the refugees.

The *Bolshaya Sovietskaya Entsiklopedia* (The Great Soviet Encyclopedia) recommends Marshak's autobiographical tale *V nachale zhizni* (At the Beginning of My Life) (1960) for a more detailed acquaintance with the poet's life. It states that he was first published in 1907. It would therefore come as a surprise to the reader to open the anthology *Yevreiskaya Zhizn* (Jewish Life) for 1904

---

* Four well-known lines of Marshak read: "I am a young girl, I am playing and singing, I never saw Stalin, But I love him." (An earlier version named Lenin instead of Stalin.)

and find there a poem by the seventeen-year-old Marshak! The anthology is devoted entirely to the memory of Theodor Herzl, who died that year. Marshak was also moved by Herzl's death to write a long poem "Over His Grave," from which we give here an excerpt:

And we'll throw a clod of earth, and mournfully stand up,
Ane on the road we're off again. But to deaden the grief
And comfort the people — within my chest there is no strength.
In the cemetery, by the sweet, dear grave
I'll speak of nothing else but death.
Chorus of the People! Oh, like a dark, ominous cloud
May your song be borne over the sorrowing land.

Our leader is dead, Derisively sobbing
The tidal wave swirled, wailed and swooped down,
The abyss, greedily stretched wide its jaws,
And seemed to be waiting for us.
We could not weep, wrapped up in sorrow
We trembled, shaking all over. . . .
Oh who will grasp the helm with his strong right arm
And save us from the wave that will engulf us?

To the helm! To work, while yet in our veins the blood flows!
And our gloom, like lightning flashing in the night
Is torn apart by Him — although his eyes are closed —
And will not be sewn up again!

Of course, later in life Marshak trod a different path. Although a member of Zionist organizations, he did not remain a Zionist. Nevertheless, he did visit Palestine, and this was reflected in his writing, if only in the poem "Jerusalem," published in the anthology *Safrut* (Literature) in 1922. Thus, to the countless prayers, songs, and verses about the Holy City, yet one more poem was added by a famous Soviet poet. In it Jerusalem serves as a symbol of eternity and stability.

Along the mountain road of kings, so grand
Into Jerusalem I come
And at the holy gate I stand
Bemused, stock-still, as though struck dumb.

I hear again the well-known sounds
Of market trade and money change.
The crowds are on familiar ground,
The traveller's joy to them is strange.
From open taverns where tales are told
Are heard the songs of foreign lands,
Swaying, to enter the town so old,
One after the other the caravans.

The visions of life with all its tears,
Like smoke may cover the past that's told,
And yet unchanging for thousands of years
Are the golden Jerusalem hills, so old!

And the slopes and the valleys will call
To keep the memory of ancient days,
When the last of the ruins eventually fall
Swept into the centuries-old, deep haze.
In every age, in every dress
Jerusalem that all cities has led,
True to herself will be, no less
Than the firmament above her spread.

THE LARGE FOUR-STORY building on the corner of Mokhovaya
ulitsa and ulitsa Pestelya, with gryphons supporting the second-floor balconies,
is undoubtedly of interest to the Lubavitcher Hasidim (address: 22/12 Mokhovaya ulitsa). Here, from about 1924 to 1927, lived their Tsadik, Rabbi Yosef-
Yitzhak (Sholomovitch) Shneerson (known as "Rayatz"). He moved here with
his closest associates (those whom the Hasidim call "the Tsadik's Court") from
Rostov-on-Don, where they had been left stranded by World War I. For a short
time, therefore, Petrograd became something that it had never been before and
never became again, the center of Habad Hasidism.

We have found hardly any literature on the life of the Hasidim in the
1920s, so our information on the Lubavitcher rebbe's stay in Leningrad is
fragmentary and probably not accurate. We only know that the Rayatz rented a
large flat on the first floor of the aforementioned building, with its entrance in
Mokhovaya ulitsa, where sometimes 100 to 150 people gathered for prayers;
and that they published a prayer book a couple of times with official sanction.
M. Gorev, in his book *Against the Anti-Semites,* which is also against religion,
declares that Shneerson with the money received from American Jews placed
shoikhets (ritual slaughterers of poultry and cattle), melameds (teachers of
Hebrew, Bible, Talmud, and so on), and other devotees of the sect in the new
Jewish agricultural settlements. He also cited the then popular slogan: "We are
for Lenin and against Shneerson!" from which we can conclude that a bad
relationship existed between Rebbe Yosif-Yitzkhak and the Soviet authorities.
The conflict ended with the imprisonment of the rebbe in the investigation
prison at ulitsa Kalyaeva No. 6, followed by his expulsion to Latvia.

The rebbe's future son-in-law left Leningrad with him. He is the present
Tsadik (since the death of the Rayatz in 1950), Menachem-Mendel Shneerson.
Born in 1902 into the family of the well-known Kabbalist Levi-Yitzkhok, he
lived before his departure at the same address on ulitsa Mokhovaya.

IN 1884, IN ulitsa Petra Lavrova (formerly Furshtadtskaya) No. 25, lived Simeon Yakovlevitch Nadson, a sad-fated poet who died at the early age of twenty-four. His paternal grandfather had joined the Orthodox Church in Kiev. His father died in a home for the mentally disturbed when Nadson was only two years old. His mother, a kinswoman of a family of the nobility, Mamontov, and a beautiful and warm-hearted person, remarried, but this marriage, too, did not last long. The new stepfather hanged himself in a fit of insanity, and the unfortunate twice-widowed young woman died of consumption at the age of only thirty-one.

Nadson graduated from No. 2 Military Gymnasium. In the short time that fate granted him for creative work, he became a famous Russian pessimist-poet, which is hardly surprising considering his background. Nadson's funeral was attended by a large gathering of reading young people. His grave is in the Volkov cemetery, next to the tombs of Dobroliubov and Belinsky. However, the suffering poet's star, like his life, did not burn for long. A century has passed, and educated Soviet intellectuals know little about him. They have heard his name, but almost no one has read his poems. Critics consider him "a literary misunderstanding." We also know nothing about his influence, disciples, or followers. There is only one poem by Nadson dedicated to the people related to him by blood. It was written not only under the stimulus of the persecutions and pogroms of the 1880s, but also as a result of his personal feelings as the victim of anti-Semitic taunts:

I grew up alien to thee, O people outcast,
'Twas not to thee I sang in times of inspiration,
Thy sorrowful oppression; the world of all thy past,
Are alien to me, as is thy education.
And if, as of old, thou wert happy and strong,
And if by the whole world not rejected —
Burning and fired by other dreams along
'Twould not be to greet thee that I'd be infected.

But nowadays, 'neath the burden of thy grief
Thou lower'st thy brow, cringing, hoping to outlast,
When the word "Jew" resounds like the call of "Stop Thief!"
In the mouths of the mob to reject the outcast,
When like a pack of hounds, thy foes show their hate,
And tear thee apart and roundly they curse thee,
Oh then — desperate people, outcast by Fate —
In the ranks of thy fighters, please modestly accept me . . . !

Well, thanks even for that. In 1914 the poem was included in the anthology *Bar-Mitzva*, published for boys reaching Jewish religious maturity. The poet's name is only rarely mentioned in reviews of Russian-Jewish literature, but perhaps, thanks to these sixteen lines, Nadson will not be entirely forgotten, for some time to come.

☐ ON THE CORNER of ulitsa Kalyaeva and Chernishevskaya ulitsa at No. 25 ulitsa Kalyaeva (formerly Zakharyevskaya ulitsa) there is a large four-story building. At one time, at least from 1906 to 1917, Maxim Vinaver, whom we have already met on a number of occasions lived here. He was born in 1862 in Warsaw, and died in 1926 in France. Vinaver was a lawyer, a public figure, and a writer. This is what the *Yevreiskaya Entsiklopedia* (Jewish Encyclopedia) has to say of him:

> He graduated from Warsaw University in 1886 and moved to St. Petersburg where he practiced law. Later he became involved in politics, mainly through involvement in the founding and leadership of the Party of Popular Freedom (the Cadets). This tall, imposing, cultured man, with a rare degree of charm, was greatly respected by members of the party. In the elections to the First State Duma, in which the Cadets obtained a majority, Vinaver quickly emerged as a brilliant orator. He also became the unofficial leader of the group of Jewish deputies, who managed to unite at least in the voting on matters concerning Jews, though in general these deputies had no single opinion on the tactics that Jews should conduct in the Duma. Largely owing to his extreme tact and negotiating abilities, Vinaver was able to obtain the support of the Cadets on the question of equality for national minorities.

Vinaver considered the Jewish question to be closely linked to the general problem of the lack of possession of rights in Russia. In a famous speech to the Duma, he declared:

> We Jews represent one of the nationalities which have suffered most, yet never once have we spoken only about ourselves, for we consider it to be inappropriate to speak just of this and not of civil equality for all. All that my people requests is for the lives of all citizens of the Empire to be standardized.

When Vinaver sat down the Cadets gave his speech a standing ovation. The First Duma, elected on the crest of the 1905 Revolution, still comforted itself with the hope that its activity, speeches, debates, and votes were important for the future of Russia. In actuality, though, this institution was important only as an official forum in which almost anything could be said — but only while it lasted. Then the revolutionary movement began to wane, and Nicholas II prepared for the counterattack. On May 15, 1906, the Duma for the first time put forward a declaration proposing a law on fundamental civil rights, including national equality. In the western provinces many Jews anxiously followed the debate and prayed for a successful outcome. But, as should have been expected, the tsar dissolved the Duma before a vote could be taken. The deputies, nevertheless, did achieve one thing. They conducted an independent inquiry into the Bialystok pogrom and placed the responsibility for Jewish pogroms in general on the government.* In any other country this would have

---

* In a pogrom between June 1 and 3, 1906, in Bialystok, more than seventy Jews were killed and ninety severely injured.

led to the resignation of cabinet ministers. In Russia they dissolved the Duma.

Maxim Vinaver was an active participant in all aspects of Jewish life. A member of the Board of Management of the St. Petersburg Jewish community, he was also one of the organizers of the Union for the Attainment of Equal Rights for the Jewish People in Russia and of the Jewish National Group. He chaired the Jewish Society for the Encouragement of the Arts, as well as the Jewish Historical-Ethnographic Society, which at one time was located here, in his house. He wrote for the Russian Jewish press, was a member of the Central Committee of OPE, and acted as a lawyer in the trials following the pogroms in Kishinev and Gomel.

Vinaver was certainly not a traditional Jew, and he was also far from both the Bund and Zionism. His energies were directed mainly toward the achievement of civil rights for his people and the battle against anti-Semitism. He continued this struggle, even after his emigration to Paris, through the journal *Yevreiskaya Tribuna* (Jewish Tribune), which he edited there.

As an expert on the law and a talented publicist, Vinaver also produced a number of general works, including *Studies on the Legal Profession* (1902) and *The History of the Vyborg Appeal* (1917).

☐ FROM MAXIM VINAVER'S house we can go to the end of ulitsa Tchaikovskogo No. 56 (formerly Sergievskogo ulitsa), where in a large four-story building exhibiting a luxuriant blending of various styles No. 2 Jewish National School was located in 1925. The head teacher was a man named Goldgor. The school was apparently not open for very long. There are no other entries for it in any other years in any of the directories. In the 1920s, as far as we know, two or three Jewish national schools were operating simultaneously in Leningrad, but in the 1930s there was only one, located on Vassilevsky Ostrov.

What was the general situation regarding education for Jews as a whole in the country? Let us take a look at the population census for 1926 to 1927, analyzed by L. G. Zinger and B. S. Engel and published by them under the editorship of and with a foreword by Z. L. Mindlin in the form of a series of tables and diagrams. On the one hand, in terms of the overall percentage of literacy (71.8 percent, of whom 59 percent were literate in Yiddish), the Jews surpassed the average for the Soviet Union (40 percent literate). On the other hand, there is an obvious tendency for a decrease in literacy in Yiddish among Jews who lived in the major centers, Moscow and Leningrad, where there was a high level of secular education. This can be clearly seen from Table 5-6.

Taking note of the fairly high number of Jewish pupils in the Soviet Union, the authors of the survey comment:

A different situation is to be noted with respect to providing the Jewish population with schools in the Yiddish language. If we compare the figures for this provision in comparison with the figures for the section of the Jewish

TABLE 5-6. LITERACY RATES IN THE SOVIET UNION

Republic or Town	Total % Literate		% Literate in Yiddish	
	Men	Women	Men	Women
Ukrainian SSR	74.0	66.6	65.0	56.3
Bielorussian SSR	72.2	66.0	85.0	78.4
Moscow	88.7	86.0	26.1	21.4
Leningrad	88.7	87.0	30.4	21.4

TABLE 5-7. THE NUMBER OF PUPILS (PER EVERY 1,000) BEING TAUGHT IN YIDDISH (FOR 1927)

Republic	All Schools	Elementary Schools
USSR	10.9	9.6
Russian SFSR	0.8	0.7
Ukrainian SSR	34.2	29.8
Bielorussian SSR	58.9	49.3
Zakavkazskaya SSR	1.0	1.1

population which considers Yiddish to be its mother tongue, then we note a marked disparity. Thus, while for every thousand persons of the total population, 12.9 consider Yiddish to be their native language, for every thousand pupils, 10.9 are being taught in Yiddish. This disparity is present in every republic of the Union, but is especially marked in the Russian SFSR and the Zakavkazskaya (Trans-caucasian) SFSR.

This finding is confirmed by Zinger and Engel in Table 5-7.

ULITSA TCHAIKOVSKOGO GOES as far as the Tavrichesky Sad (Garden). At one time this garden, together with the adjacent strip of land along the River Neva, belonged to Catherine II's favorite, Prince Potemkin Tavrichesky. The architect I. E. Stassov built a palace for the prince here between 1783 and 1789. Both palace and gardens were named from Potemkin's title. The address is ulitsa Voinova (formerly Shpalernaya) No. 47. The palace is one of the outstanding monuments of St. Petersburg architecture of the late eighteenth century.

The Tavrichesky Palace is connected with Jewish history because here were held the sessions of the State Duma—the first Russian parliament. Although its powers were limited and although delegates were chosen on the basis of an unjust electoral law, it was able to speak out on behalf of Jewish equality before the law.

There were twelve Jewish deputies in the First Duma: L. Bramson, Ya. Bruk, M. Vinaver, Ya. Iollos, N. Katzenelson, Sh. Levin, M. Ostrogorsky, S. Rosenbaum, S. Frankel, M. Tchervonenkiss, M. I. Sheftel, and V. Yakubson. The Jewish deputies of the First Duma departed, for the first time, from what I have always considered the shameful established tradition among Jewish deputies throughout Europe of not taking part in the struggle for Jewish rights in a direct manner, but exploiting instead the willingness of Christian parliamentarians to help and act. Their voice was clearly heard in all the debates on Jewish and many general Russian matters. Vinaver was the leader in the fight for a law on civil rights. Yakubson took part in the Commission of Inquiry into the Bielorussian pogroms.

After a total of seventy-two days the First Duma was dissolved. About half the deputies, indignant at the use of force, issued to the public the so-called Vyborg Appeal, calling on the population to pay no taxes, to refuse to serve in the army, and to disclaim responsibility for all foreign loans concluded without the Duma's consent. With the exception of Ostrogorsky, who at that time was in England, all the Jewish deputies signed the Vyborg Appeal and, together with the other signatories, were punished for their disobedience by three months' imprisonment. They were also deprived of all rights and property, including the right to stand for election in a new Duma. Not all managed to get off so lightly. Deputy Iollos and M. Hertzenstein, the baptized Jew from Moscow, who was a professor of political economy and an eloquent spokesman on the question of agrarian reform, were both soon after killed by the Black Hundreds.

Only four Jews were elected as deputies to the Second Duma and only two to the third Duma. The Jewish deputies played no noticeable role in either of these Dumas, which carried out the tsar's policies with little protest.

LET US NOW go along Potemkinskaya ulitsa as far as ulitsa Vosstaniya (formerly Zhamenskaya) and continue to Baskov Pere'ulok and ulitsa Nekrassova, where we shall see a few more interesting sights connected with the Jewish history of the town.

In 1917 and 1918 the Society for Scientific Jewish Publications was located not far from the theatrical society at No. 25/28 Baskov Pere'ulok, on the corner of Baskov Pere'ulok and ulitsa Vosstaniya. The society was formed in St. Petersburg in 1907 (or 1908) by Yuli Gessen, Baron David Guenzburg, B. A. Kamenka, L. I. Katzenelson, M. I. Kulisher, and M. I. Sheftel (president). Its aim was to publish and distribute academic works, in Russian and other languages, on the history, culture, and life of the Jewish people. The society's shareholders each bought shares to the value of a hundred rubles and elected from among themselves a committee of twelve to run the affairs of the society for a term of three years. The society was not a commercial publisher, since the profits from the publications did not go to the shareholders but to the society as a whole. A total of 305 shares was issued to 103 shareholders. The high point of the society's history was the publication of the famous *Yevreiskaya Entsiklopedia* (Jewish Encyclopedia) jointly with the publishing house of Brockhaus and Yefron.

Almost next door to the society, at No. 20 Baskov Pere'ulok, at about the same time lived one of its founders, the famous historian of Russian Jewry Yuli Gessen, who had previously lived in a rented flat at No. 35 Basseinaya ulitsa (now ulitsa Nekrassova). At one time the building hosted three separate Jewish institutions: the Society for Scientific Jewish Publications (to 1910); the editorial offices of the journal *Yevreiskaya Starina* (Jewish Antiquity); and the Jewish Historical-Ethnographic Society (1912).

As we move along ulitsa Nekrassova toward Suvorovsky Prospekt, we leave the former Liteinaya quarter and enter the Rozhdestvenskaya quarter of old St. Petersburg. The district of the Rozhdestvenskaya (now Sovietskaya) streets had earlier had yet another name — Peski. The area was never particularly rich. Here lived, all mixed together, professional artisans, pharmacists, and intellectuals. The synagogue was on Suvorovsky Prospekt at No. 2.

LET US START to explore Peski from an enormous, magnificent seven-story building on the corner of Suvorovsky Prospekt and 9th Sovietskaya ulitsa. It is now occupied by the Iskra cinema, but here in house No. 9, apt. 22, on 9th Rozhdestvenskaya ulitsa, the Jewish Folk Music Society was formed on November 30, 1908. Later, in 1910, the society had another address, Sadovaya ulitsa No. 85, apt. 6. Our information about the society, including the quotations, is found in the diploma thesis on Jewish folk music, submitted in 1983 to the Leningrad Conservatoire by Marina Vainshtein (now Goldina).

The movement for the collection, preservation, and distribution of Jewish musical folklore was inspired by S. Ginzburg, P. Marek, and Yu. Engel. Back in the 1890s Ginzburg and Marek had already appealed in an article "Jewish Folk Songs" for "all persons close to the masses of our people to record and inform us of Yiddish folk songs sung in their locality. This living material, reflecting popular views of the times through which the people have lived, is in danger of being lost irretrievably unless it is registered in good time." One such enthusiast and collector was Yu. Engel (1868–1927), a critic for the paper *Russkiye Vedomosti* (Russian Gazette). From 1898 he began to travel around the towns and villages of the Pale of Settlement with a phonograph, recording and publishing folk songs. As a result, he received many threatening letters from the Black Hundreds.

In 1900 Engel organized the first concert of Jewish music in Russia in the Moscow Polytechnic Museum. The concert, which included lectures on Jewish music, was a great success. "The public crowded into the hall, against the walls, in the aisles, in the corridors and on the stairs. The cause of this was some interesting lectures on Jewish songs."* In his lecture at this concert Engel declared:

> The Jewish song really does exist, and is of great interest in itself, from both the ethnographic and the artistic point of view. . . . In religious music we come across melodies which are undoubtedly ancient and which are sung in more or less the same way by almost all the Jews on this earth. The origin of these melodies is lost in the mists of centuries and perhaps even millennia.†

By 1908 the work of the early enthusiasts led to the formation of the Jewish Folk Music Society. It aimed to promote the study and development of Jewish folk music, both religious and secular, through its collection, artistic rearrangement, publication, and distribution to the public. The society strove to support composers and musicians; to organize concerts and lectures; to publish books; and to organize libraries, choirs, orchestras, and competitions.

It was during this period that many Jewish cultural societies were formed: literary, historical, ethnographic, and others. This can be explained by the fact that in the years of reaction following the suppression of the 1905 Revolution, the active sections of the intelligentsia, finding open struggle for civil rights now no longer possible (and some even lost all hope of success in this struggle), turned to permitted cultural activity. They became involved in the development of education, language, literature, music, and art. It is of interest that some radical parties, such as the Bund, took the same path. The outburst of "Yiddishism" dates from this period.

The activities of the society developed rapidly. If at its formation it had 100 members, by 1913 it already had 884, of whom 410 were in St. Petersburg. In 1913 the society's budget reached 4,606 rubles. A prize was established for the best Jewish opera, and branches sprang up in Moscow, Kharkov, Kiev, Riga, Simferopol, Rostov-on-Don, Baku, and Odessa. In its first five years the society presented 154 concerts in various towns, 16 musical gatherings in St. Petersburg. It also published more than a hundred musical compositions for voices and various instruments, including Yu. Engel's collection "Jewish Children's Songs for Home, School and Family." At meetings there were lectures such as L. Saminsky's "Jewish Music, Its Past, Its Present, and Its Prospects" (1915) and D. Shor's "Jews in Music and Music among the Jews" (1916). Performances were also given of the works of the first professional Jewish composers, A. Krein and M. Gnessin.

The society's committee included M. Gnessin, A. Zhitomirsky, P. Lvov, L. Saminsky, S. Rozovsky, E. Shklyar, Z. Kisselgoff, D. Shor, S. Ginzburg, and P. Marek. The president of the society in 1916 was Benjamin Simeonovitch Mandel.

* Ivan Lipayev, *Russian Music Gazette*, No. 52, 1900.
† Yu. Engel, *Izbranniye Statyi* (Selected Articles), Moscow, 1971, p. 503.

Obviously, all this activity did not take place in a vacuum. The Russian liberal intelligentsia took a lively interest in the work of Jewish composers and musical folklorists. Many of the society's activists were former students of N. A. Rimsky-Korsakov, who in general encouraged the development of national cultures, including Jewish. He declared to one of his pupils (apparently Gnessin) that "I am very pleased to see that you are composing in the Jewish spirit. How strange it is that pupils of mine — Jews — are so little interested in their own native music. Jewish music exists, it is wonderful music, and it awaits its Glinka."*

In his book *Mysli i Vospominaniya O Rimskom-Korsakovye* (Reflections and Recollections of Rimsky-Korsakov) (Moscow, 1956, p. 208), M. Gnessin writes:

> It was with such enthusiasm that he held forth about the distinctive features of these [various national] melodies, he showed such sensitivity in helping to arrange them, in encouraging Russians, and Ukrainians, Latvians and Armenians and Jews. One of my colleagues once brought to the lesson two musical pieces entitled "eastern Melodies," apparently for violin with piano accompaniment. "They are very nice compositions," said Rimsky-Korsakov after hearing the music. "But why do you call them 'eastern Melodies' since they are typically Jewish melodies? They could hardly be confused with anything else."

Not only the Russo-Jewish periodicals but also Russian musical publications constantly referred to the achievements of the society. Here is what G. Prokofiev wrote about a Jewish folk concert in 1910:

> The evening of Jewish folk songs on 6th February lasted until well past midnight. . . . I was not so much struck by the musical originality of the songs . . . what I was sincerely envious of was the joy, the pleasure with which the very large audience [almost exclusively Jewish] listened to every song, demanding endless encores. The performers put on a magnificent performance.†

And this is what Viacheslav Paskhalov wrote about the concert put on by the Moscow branch of the Jewish Folk Music Society on March 28, 1916:

> The words of Jewish folk songs are exceptionally rich and varied. They evoke the whole gamut of moods since Jewish poetry reflects religious ecstasy, the tragic suffering of Jewry, and the feeling of unrestrained spontaneous gaiety. This type of music accords completely with the emotional character of Jewish poetry. That is why stylistic execution is completely dependent on the performer's acquaintance with dramatic art.‡

---

* (Glinka was known as the founder of Russian music.) L. Saminsky, *Ob Yevreiskoi Muzikye* (On Jewish Music): Collected Articles, St. Petersburg, 1914, p. 78.

† *Russkaya Muzikalnaya Gazyeta* (Russian Music Gazette), No. 8, 1910.

‡ *Muzikalny Sovremyennik* (Musical Contemporary), No. 21.

Little by little, folklorist journeyings through the Pale of Settlement attracted not only enthusiastic amateurs but also imposing institutions such as the Ethnographic Department and the Musical-Ethnographic Commission of the Imperial Society of the Lovers of the Natural Sciences, Anthropology, and Ethnography (through L. Y. Sternberg) and the Asiatic Museum of the Academy of Sciences. The expedition, which we have already mentioned, to Volhynia and Podolia of 1911 to 1914, organized by An-sky and funded by Baron Vladimir Guenzburg, played a major role in the collection of Jewish folklore. The musical recordings on this expedition were made by Zinovy Kisselgoff, that remarkable personality of the Jewish and the educational movement.

The Jewish Folk Music Society's activity stimulated not only the collection of Jewish folk music but also active professional creativity. It is worth noting some compositions of A. Krein: *Jewish Etudes for String Quartet and Clarinet* (1910–1911), the cantata *Kaddish* (1922), and *Ten Jewish Songs* (1937). Also noteworthy are M. Gnessin's *Variations on a Jewish Theme for String Quartet* (1916), the operatic poem *The Youth of Abraham* (1921–1923), *The Symphonic Phantasia in the Jewish Style* (1916), the vocal cycle *Jewish Songs* (1927), the *The Tale of Ginger Motol* (1929). D. Maggid, R. Gruber, K. Zaks, and M. Gnessin conducted interesting theoretical research into ancient and modern Jewish music. It was not by accident that L. Sabanayev, in discussing the work of the society in his book *The Jewish National School of Music* (Moscow, 1924, p. 31), writes:

> The Jewish nation was always melodious, always expressed its staggering sorrows, rages and temptations in sounds. And now, when the nation has produced an intellectual stratum it not only can, but it must, give expression to its superlative musical tongue. . . . The group that is now performing, that arrived so suddenly and seemingly out of the blue, that superficially has so much in common with the Russian national school from which it sprang — a "Power Group" — this group has great possibilities of becoming the "Power Group" of Jewry.

It is much to be regretted that this prophecy was not destined to be fulfilled.

☐ HAVING ACQUAINTED OURSELVES with the organization that encouraged the musical life of St. Petersburg Jewry, it is logical to make acquaintance with the work of Jewish literary societies. For this we shall move on to the neighboring 8th Sovietskaya ulitsa.

Before the Revolution, three Jewish literary societies were functioning at the same time. One of them, founded before the others in 1908, is located on the route of this excursion. We mean, of course, not the society itself but its former premises on 8th Rozhdestvenskaya ulitsa No. 25, apt. 12. So there's no need to hurry, we shan't be late for the start of the session, lecture, or discussion. We are talking of times that have long since passed.

Even though the Jewish Literary Society was authorized in the names of State Duma members L. N. Nisselovitch, S. M. Ginsburg, and S. L. Kamenetsky, its president, probably the real leader, was Simon Dubnow. The society declared as its aim the study and development of literature in Hebrew, Yiddish, and Russian through discussions, readings, the publication of books, journals, and newspapers, and the organization of museums and exhibitions. As was the practice at that time, members of the society were divided into full members (annual subscription — ten rubles), associate members (six rubles), and donor members (three rubles). The membership dues were relatively low. In comparison, a full member of OPE paid twenty-five rubles a year. All had equal voting rights, and the committee consisted of eighteen people.

Soon after it began to function, the society expanded, establishing branches in Minsk, Berdichev, Orsha, Nezhin, Kiev, Smorgon, and other towns and villages — a total of thirty-five branches and 850 members in 1910. In 1911 the Jewish Literary Society was closed down in accordance with the circular of Stolypin* against "non-Russian" cultural and educational societies that were considered to be "causing the awakening of a harmful and narrow national political consciousness."

In addition to those already mentioned, the society's activists included N. S. Zeitlin, Yu. Gessen, A. Idelson, A. Rappaport, M. Kreinin, Mandel, Rivesman, Rivkin, and S. L. Zinberg. In the spring of 1910 Y. L. Peretz came from Warsaw and read some of his short stories.† In the autumn of 1911 the Austrian publicist Nathan Birnbaum visited the society and delivered a lecture. An important side of the society's activity was the support that it gave to needy Jewish writers.

In 1911, probably as a result of the closing down of the Jewish Literary Society, a new Jewish literary cum scientific society, close in spirit to the former, was founded in St. Petersburg. At first it was located in Sadovaya ulitsa No. 81, apt. 13 (up to 1915) and then at No. 41 Gorokhovaya ulitsa (now ulitsa Dzerzhinskogo). Among its activists were those already mentioned, namely, Saul Moiseyevitch Ginsburg (chairman), M. A. Kreinin (vice-chairman), A. I. Rappaport, and S. L. Kamenetsky. The society was closed down in 1918.

Finally, for a few years, there was yet another kindred cultural organization, the Peretz Jewish Literary and Artistic Society. It was named after Y. L. Peretz, founded in 1916, and located at Prospekt Ogorodnikova, (formerly Rizhsky Prospekt) No. 48, apt. 99. The society aimed to develop Yiddish literature and to found a Jewish "jargon" theater. (*Jargon* was the popular way of referring to the Yiddish language in those days.) A Leon Peretz Fund was

* Peter Stolypin was minister of the interior, May 1906; prime minister, July 1906; assassinated September 14, 1911.

† A Yiddish and Hebrew poet and author, Peretz (1852–1915) brought both the short story and the symbolic drama into Yiddish and Hebrew literature. In 1925, when his deeply pessimistic play *At Night in the Old Market* (written in 1907) was produced in Rumania by the Moscow State Yiddish Theater, the part of the jester was played by Solomon Mikhoels.

established for the publication of popular scientific literature and the translation into Yiddish of Jewish classics (30,000 rubles).

The society's activities reflected a completely new but definitive phenomenon in Jewish life of the 1900s and 1910s, namely, a heightening of the struggle over the question of which language was the genuine Jewish one—Hebrew (Ivrit) or Yiddish—and, most important of all, which language belonged to the future. In which language henceforth should people write for journals, newspapers, and so on? Or, alternatively, should both be rejected in favor of Russian? The polemics of what might seem to be a purely academic question, in practice fairly accurately reflected the political orientation of the participants, their program of activity, their view of the future, and their own culture. It is obvious that religious circles, the intelligentsia, who were more educated in the national spirit, and the Zionists were on the whole in favor of Hebrew. The left-wing intelligentsia, the popular masses, and the Bund all fought for Yiddish. The partisans of Yiddish were inspired by the great achievements of literature in the vernacular ("jargon") in the late nineteenth and early twentieth centuries by such writers as Sholem Aleikhem, Y. L. Peretz, and Sholem Asch. Moreover, the majority of Jews did not know Hebrew, and it could not be used for the propagation of revolutionary ideas among the masses.

For the rabbis and Talmudists, any departure from Hebrew implied a complete rejection of all religious literature and consequently of religion itself. Since Yiddish was the conversational language of only one part of the Jews, the Ashkenazim, the Zionists considered the development of Hebrew to be a necessary condition for the fulfillment of their hopes; the formation of a united Jewish nation on the soil of Palestine. The new Jewish intelligentsia, still few in number, often held to the idea derived from the early Maskilim that Yiddish was not a complete language in itself but only a sad legacy of the life of deprivation of the Diaspora.

☐ LET US NOW move on to the beginning of the neighboring 7th Sovietskaya ulitsa. Here in 1915 and 1916, in house No. 6, was located the society that has often been mentioned (because of the frequency with which it changed its address), the Jewish Historical-Ethnographic Society (IEO). It existed in St. Petersburg–Petrograd–Leningrad from 1908 to 1930.* There is nothing surprising in the fact that the society was simultaneously both historical and ethnographic, since the history and ethnography of a people are indissolubly linked. Often one and the same object or memorial of the past is studied simultaneously by both disciplines. This is all the more so in the case of the Jews, who always and everywhere as a national minority—in their daily life,

---

* The name was changed at the start of the war with Germany in August 1914 from its Germanic form (*burg*, meaning "town") to its Slavonic form (*grad* is Old Russian, *gorod* is modern Russian for "town"); cf. for example, Novgorod, Uzhgorod, Belgorod, Volgograd, Stalingrad, and Kirovograd. The name of the city was changed to Leningrad in 1924, shortly after Lenin's death.

folklore, and so on — were exposed to the influence of the traditions of the majority people. On the other hand, for the Jewish people, their history has always been an essential element of their daily life, and this has inevitably played its part in the formation and preservation of national identity.

The appeals to preserve the knowledge of the past and to study the life of the mass of the people began to grow ever louder among the Jews of Russia from the 1880s onward, that is, from the time when the traditional forms of that very life were beginning to disintegrate. Such IEO activists as Simon Dubnow, Lev Sternberg, Simeon An-sky, Yakov Eiger, and Abram Bramson did all that they could to somehow record and preserve traces of the rapidly disappearing Jewish world. Their efforts, however, did not altogether solve the problem. On the contrary, it is no less urgent today than it was then.

To illustrate this, let us compare two articles written ninety years apart by different people about basically the same thing. We are referring to Simon Dubnow's appeal *On the Study of the History of Russian Jews and On the Foundation of the Russian-Jewish Historical-Ethnographic Society* and to an article by a contemporary Soviet ethnographer, Igor Krupnik, entitled *Problems of the Ethnographic Study of the Jews in the USSR,* published in *Sovietish Heimland,* No. 8, 1982.

From a few parallel texts, the reader will be able to see for himself or herself just how little the situation has changed in the course of almost a century; how much the inadequacy of Jewish ethnographic knowledge has been a cause for concern across that century.

Dubnow:

The criterion of human consciousness is a conscious attitude to the past. This is the road to self-consciousness. . . . Are there any indications at the present time among the thinking strata of our society of such a historical self-consciousness? No, not the slightest. We not only do not acknowledge and do not understand our past, but we simply do not know it factually and it is as if we do not want to know. We are literally people of yesterday, homeless, with no past behind us.

Krupnik:

The ethnographic study of the Jews has a rich historical tradition. . . . However, the ethnographic study of the Jews in recent times has clearly become inadequate. The most recent general studies on Jewish population groups in the USSR were written in the 1950s and early 1960s. Only very few works have been published during the last decade in Russian and they deal with individual questions.

Dubnow:

It is shameful to admit, but it is no use hiding the fact that all the new Jewish "academic" literature of the last thirty years has given a total of three little books which could be of any use in the systematic research into the history of the Jews in Russia.

Krupnik:

It so happened that, in the cross-threads of the development of Jewish ethnography, the line of academic tradition binding us has been broken in many respects. However much we may desire it, it is often difficult for us to realize that we are the successors of the ethnographers of the first half of the twentieth century insofar as we know little of the works and even the names of our precursors.

Dubnow:

The preparatory work for this historiography has already been partly begun in very recent times through the gathering of materials from the Russian state archives. The public, and even the intelligent ones among them, look on this preparatory work with indifference, and do not understand its purpose. . . . Is this work necessary at all? Was there a history at all? Like Speake and Stanley setting off for Africa, knowing almost nothing, that's how we are. . . . We, too, are faced with a type of "Dark Continent" (as the English call the African interior) which lies before us waiting to be explored and illuminated.

Dubnow:

(On how the old Pinkasim—record books—of the Jewish communities are preserved.) How do we use these natural treasures of our history? In the same way that such riches would be used by the most ignorant, the most primitive of peoples, who had no original past, no literature, and in general no spiritual life. We leave our "memory-books" to rot, wherever they happen to have been thrown by the hand of time: in private homes whose owners have no idea of their value, on dusty shelves with other books, in dark store-rooms, in miserable hovels, pushed away between all sorts of rubbish and junk, in piles of ancient printing paper, resting in some forgotten corner of a synagogue, even in attics, in with rubbish, where real "bookworms" in the form of rats and mice assiduously work on our historical memorials.

Krupnik:

During the Great Patriotic War and in the years following, not only were the fates of individuals forgotten, but whole museums with their collections and resources, archives, libraries, letters, photographs and manuscripts were lost. To this day we still do not know what happened to the collections of the Ethnographic Museum that existed in the 1920s and 1930s under the Jewish Historical-Ethnographic Society in Leningrad and which in the late 1930s were dispatched to the Mendele Moikher-Seforim All-Ukrainian Museum of Jewish Culture in Odessa. It can be assumed that the holdings of both museums were destroyed during the Nazi Occupation, but does anyone know this for certain, and what if something was even saved or taken by the Germans to other countries (as they took the Jewish archives from occupied Europe to Warsaw, and cultural objects and artifacts to Prague)? And where can the very rich archives and library of that same Jewish Historical-Ethnographic Society be held? What was the fate of the Ukrainian Institute and of the Bielorussian section of Jewish Proletarian Culture which existed before the war in Kiev and Minsk, of the collections of the Indigenous-Jewish Ethnographic Museum of the Jews of Georgia, the Jewish Department of the State Historical Museum of the Bielorussian Republic, or the Jewish Section of the Berdichev Museum of Local Lore, History and Economy? Unfortunately we still have no answers to these and similar questions.

Dubnow:

This is how the "ignorant, unenlightened mob" treats our ancient historical memorials. The intellectuals treat them even worse, and don't even want to know about them.

Dubnow, commenting on a prejudice against gathering historical materials, said it was prompted by

". . . the fear that putting on display to the public of the ancient "pinkasim," principally those of the "kahals,"* this would arouse the Judophobic press to redouble its cries about the kahals, about a Jewish "status in statu" ("a state within the state"). How can one conceal one's past out of apprehension that it might be to the distaste of some ignorant rascals and worthless newspaper bellowers who trade in Judophobia!

Krupnik:

There have been cases of falsification, reticence, or distortion of the truth in ethnography and the history of culture, albeit with the "best intentions." We can only hope that the experience of our predecessors, their difficulties and mistakes, can be used to our advantage, the researchers of the '80s, all the more so since many of the problems that seemed to have been solved long ago, continue to rise again and again with each new generation.

Dubnow:

We must openly take up and fulfill the task of gathering, concerned only with the truth and not with how others will look upon this truth. We have no cause to look apprehensively over our shoulders; we are not doing anything wrong.

Krupnik:

Therefore our obligation, our primary moral duty, is to act so that the labors of our precursors, or even their memory, does not disappear forever. We must apply ourselves wholeheartedly to the search for the remains of the lost archives and collections, to ferret out information about what happened to the people associated with them, to describe the conditions of the remaining collections which are often preserved under different names, not sorted out or classified, or are held in a very unsatisfactory condition. The efforts of a few professional ethnographers or museum workers are not sufficient for this task.

* *Kahal* is Hebrew for "community"; the kahals in Russia were ancient Jewish communal organizations. They were abolished by Nicholas I in a decree (ukase) promulgated on December 19, 1844.

Dubnow:

It follows from all that has been said that the groundwork of writing the historiography of the Jews of Russia, the searching out, gathering and publishing of various materials, is extremely complicated and can in no way be achieved through individual efforts.

Krupnik:

Surveys, reviews and popular studies about ethnographic and historico-cultural works will bring us new readers and invaluable new helpers. This cooperation could, in time, result in some sort of popular books on the history, ethnography and culture of the Jews of the U.S.S.R.

Dubnow:

To achieve this great and complicated task we must resort to those methods used in similar cases by all other cultural and historical peoples, namely a special society must be formed to conduct research into the history of the Russian Jews.

Dubnow also proposed the publication of a historical journal, and this was later done and given the title *Yevreiskaya Starina* (Jewish Antiquity).

We can now see that by following the mutually echoing themes of these two articles, separated by nearly a century, we have learned about the first steps (Dubnow's appeal) on the path that, after seventeen years, led to the formation of the Jewish Historical-Ethnographic Society (IEO) and of the unenviable fate of the results of that society's work, its museum, its library, its archives.

We do know, however, that in the 1920s the society was still active. This is what the *Yevreisky Vestnik* (Jewish Herald) had to say about the society and its activity: its museum contained more than 1,000 items of everyday life, religion, and art; 1,500 photographs; 350 cylinders with phonographic recordings of folk melodies; and a large collection of musical scores. The IEO archives contained 43 original Pinkasim, 70 copies of Pinkasim and translations of them, 200 manuscripts, 160 early printed books, a collection of documents and letters in ancient (classical) Hebrew, An-sky's archives, a collection of materials for the compilation of a guide to Russo-Jewish literature covering about 10,000 titles, and much else.

The commission set up by IEO for the study of Jewish antiquities (chaired by director Yakov Eiger with B. D. Shulman as secretary) was concerned with the classification of Talmudic material according to the contemporary academic disciplines (the history of medicine, pedagogics, Bible criticism, law, and history). Academic lectures were regularly organized at the society on the history and ethnography of the Jews, given by highly qualified specialists. They included, for example, Lev Sternberg, on "The Problem of Jewish National

Psychology," and "Current Tasks for the Study of the Jews"; I. A. Kleinman on "Jews during the Polish Interregnum"; Yakov Eiger on "Jewish Physicians in the Middle Ages"; Sergei Zinberg on "Abraham Krimsky and Moses Kievsky" and "The Problem of Love in Medieval Jewish Literature"; Mikhail Gnessin on "Jewish Trends in Music and Their Connection with the Life of the People"; Solomon Lurie on "The Third Book of the Maccabees" and "Jewish Daily Life in Hellenic Times"; and Isaac Vinnikov on "The Contemporary Jewish Shtetl."

We could continue indefinitely with the list of titles of lectures and could mentally calculate the amount of lost historical wealth. Our laments, however, do not have the medium's powers of spiritualism and will not bring back to life the corpse of Jewish culture in this town with a Jewish population of 140,000.

So let us move on to our next stop.

IN 1916, IN the neighboring tall, six-story building with bay windows, 7th Sovietskaya ulitsa No. 4, was located the society called Honest Laborer *(Po'al Tsedek),* which had previously, in 1912, been at Gagarinskaya ulitsa (now Furmanova) No. 34, apt. 6. The society promoted the teaching of craftwork to Jewish children. Its chairman was Grigory Samsonovitch Voltke.

The daily Russian-language organ of the Bund, *Yevreiskiye Vyesti* (Jewish News), was published in the same building from the autumn of 1916 to May 1917.

The Bund — the General Jewish Workers' Union in Lithuania, Poland, and Russia — had been founded in 1897 at an illegal congress held in Vilna. Up to 1903 it was part of the Russian Social Democratic Workers' Party, the RSDRP, and then it left, since the local organizations of the RSDRP were formed exclusively as territorial units whereas the Bund insisted that separate local sections should be formed for the Jewish members of the party in the western provinces.* The party did not consider the Jews to be a single nation and limited its national program to the achievement of civil rights and national and cultural autonomy for the Jews of Russia. For the rest, the Bund usually supported the Social Democrats, and later the Mensheviks. For almost all of the prerevolutionary period the Bund existed underground. In 1904 forty-five hundred Bundists were held as political prisoners. Many of them were executed or killed during pogroms, since they often organized Jewish self-defense. By late 1917 the Bund had forty thousand members in four hundred organizations, and it exerted an enormous influence over the Jewish proletariat of Russia. In

---

* RSDRP was founded in March 1898. In July 1903, at its Second Congress held in London, the party split into two — the Bolsheviks (under Lenin) and the Mensheviks (under Plekhanov). In 1912 the Bolsheviks broke away completely, forming the RSDRP(B), which in 1918 became the RCP(B) — the Russian Communist Party (B) — and in 1925 the VKP (B) — the All-Union Communist Party (Bolsheviks). It remained the VKP(B) until 1952, when its name was changed to CPSU — the Communist Party of the Soviet Union, as it is today.

the cultural field, the Bund was on the side of the Yiddishists. It was locked in an irreconcilable ideological struggle with Zionism.

In St. Petersburg–Petrograd, where there was hardly any Jewish proletariat, the Bund had no real standing. It is therefore all the more surprising to find that there was a Bund publication here, and moreover in Russian language, since the Bund usually published in Yiddish. The contributors to *Yevreiskiye Vyesti* included such noted party figures and journalists as Ben-Noemi, E. S. Brenner, M. Vilner, V. Goldman, T. Geilikman, A. Zolotoreva, V. Stekhletskaya-Tereshkovitch, D. O. Zaslavsky, V. A. Kantrovitch, M. Rafess, Henryk Erlich, and Erlich's wife Sophia (Simon Dubnow's daughter).

The Petrograd section of the Bund did not fare very well, as it was cut off by the war from the provinces that had a fair-size Jewish proletariat. But the *Yevreiskiye Vyesti* managed to continue in existence owing to the persistence of Henryk Erlich and M. Rafess, the only two members of the Central Committee of the Bund who were at that time in the capital.

There already had been a Bund newspaper in Yiddish in St. Petersburg for some time. This is what Bukhbinder has to say about it:

> From 1912 the Bund weekly paper *Di Tzeit* (The Times) began to be published in St. Petersburg, with the close participation of Abramovitch (Rein), Olguin, Frumkina ("Esther"), D. O. Zaslavsky, A. D. Kirzhnitz, and B. Orshansky. The workers welcomed the appearance of *Di Tzeit* with great enthusiasm. Workers wrote from Vitebsk: "Our politically conscious comrades greeted the first issue of the Jewish workers' paper with great joy. On seeing the paper we all experienced an inner spiritual happiness. Everyone thought we should have to wait a long time before we could see a Jewish workers' newspaper. We thought that a Jewish workers' paper in our life-time was a fantasy, a daydream which could not come true in practice but, astonishingly, now in a period of gloom, we have a torch which, from high above, lights our way in the darkness."

From Bukhbinder we also learn that before the Revolution "successful work was conducted in St. Petersburg among Jewish students." At the Psychiatric-Neurological Institute and in the University, Bundist groups were formed (the activists were Weintrauch, Kharit, Hatzkeles, and others) that organized lectures, papers, and meetings and, in 1916, published in Russian a collection called *Nash Put* (Our Path). Unfortunately we do not know the address of the editorial offices of either *Di Tzeit* or *Nash Put,* or indeed if they had any legal addresses at all.

☐ IN PESKI ON 3rd Rozhdestvenskaya ulitsa in house No. 16 there was also before the Revolution a society that, like the Russian Society for the Study of Jewish Life, was concerned with the Jews. It could even be said that it involved Jewish culture, but on a somewhat different level. Called the Society for the Study of the Judaic Tribe, its declared aim was "the universal study of

the harmful attributes of this tribe, its malignant religion, and internal laws."
We even have the name of the society's chairman, Nikolai Nikolayevitch Zhedenov. Since our aim is not "the universal study of the history of anti-Semitism
in St. Petersburg" or of individual representatives of this ever-present phenomenon, we cannot say any more either about citizen N. N. Zhedenov or about
the effectiveness of the "scholarly" investigations carried out by his society.
But since we happen, by chance, to have come across this fact, it might be of
interest to any of today's rare fighters against the Jews. Such fighters, too, might
be interested in searching for their historical roots. In concluding this excursion, I therefore generously make it public for them. Please make use of it, you
fighters against the Jews, if you will.

Yury Kolker (then in Leningrad, now in Jerusalem), a Jewish poet who
accompanied me on my excursions, presented me with a poem that reflected
our mood, expressing our thoughts. These were his words:

> They have all passed on — those figures stoop'd down,
> In "kippa"* and "payus"† — 'tis but an illusion;
> That landscape beyond, a spiritual protrusion,
> Only Jewish ruins lie now in old Peter's Town.
>
> The years of pogroms, the revolutionary dreams,
> When the rate of exchange was blood lying in pools,
> The days of publishers, libraries, schools,
> Are all lost years . . . in Galut's‡ bitter streams.
>
> This house is where the poet used to stay,
> Here the philanthropist, there the scholar could be espied,
> The Lubavitcher rebbe was wont here to pray.
> All's gone! — There remains but a cemetery guide!
>
> Gone, like smelted ore of a golden-red hue,
> Down the funnel of time, and through the cascades,
> Back into the past. Their twilight shades —
> Look! — have blended with the clouds, deep into the blue.

* *Kippa* (Hebrew) is the skullcap worn by religious Jewish males.
† *Payus* (Yiddish, pronounced "pie-us"; in modern Hebrew "peyot") are the side curls worn
by ultra-orthodox Jewish males.
‡ *Galut* (Hebrew), the Diaspora, or dispersion of the Jews.

EXCURSION SIX

THE JEWISH PREOBRAZHENSKY CEMETERY

Jewish graves! Is there a country on this earth,
  Where your headstones have not stood as a watchdog of the ages
And where the names of the fathers have not prophesied to their sons
  Thoughts of joyful triumphs in the midst of bitterest sadness,
Of limitless gloom and reveries of sundrenched distant climes?
  The silver hairs of the centuries fall like unmelting snow,
While the letters cut into the stones are blazing,
  Calling forth from the moss and the dust:
We existed. We were here once.

WITH THESE VERSES, Simeon Frug, whose poetry expresses the spiritual crisis through which Russian Jewry was passing — especially the new intelligentsia — in the 1880s, and the simultaneous first timid hopes of the then newly reborn love of Palestine, Simeon Frug wants to start a tour around the old Jewish cemetery of Leningrad.

Why old? Is there then a new one?

No, simply, there are no more burials here.

It is difficult to imagine a more Jewish place than a Jewish cemetery.

What will you not recall to mind, and what will you not think about here? Walk among the graves and it will seem to you that all around are your relatives or your friends. But let me start with a few words about just what a Jewish cemetery is.

In essence it is simply a plot of earth for the burial of the dead. In religious literature there are several ways of referring to a cemetery.

House of Burial	בֵּית קְבָרוֹת
House of Eternity	בֵּית עוֹלָם
House of Life	בֵּית חַיִּים

Because a dead body and a grave are the source of spiritual uncleanliness, cemeteries are usually placed outside of town. At the same time, a cemetery was, to a certain extent, a holy place. Anything, therefore, that could be considered as an activity disrespectful towards the dead, was not permitted. In particular it was forbidden to eat or drink or discuss worldly affairs. Plots of ground under the grave were set aside, usually alike to all and sundry, as a reminder of the fact that Death is the great equalizer. Exception was made in the case of well-known rabbis, who were granted a plot of ground for all their family, or a place for a family vault. Sometimes this honor was granted to specially respected members of the community and well known philanthropists. Suicides, apostates, and people of ill-repute were buried outside the cemetery or by its remotest walls.

During the Talmudic era, the Jews took meticulous care over the neatness of a cemetery. It was then that it was said: "Jewish graveyards are cleaner than royal palaces." In the middle of the 14th century, when European feudal overlords granted muniments (documents as evidence of rights or privileges) to the Jews, and accorded them definition of their legal status, they invariably included clauses referring to the preservation of Jewish graves. For desecration of graves they not infrequently invoked the death penalty. Polish-Lithuanian legislation was hardly any softer in its approach to this question. In the charter of the Grand Prince of Lithuania granted to the Jews of Brest-Litovsk in 1388, there is one clause: "If then any Christian shall desecrate any graves of the Jews, it is our wish to punish him in accordance with the custom of the land, and his property shall be confiscated."

Visiting the cemetery is an accepted practice on the anniversary of the death of relatives, as well as on Fast Days, during the Hebrew month of Ellul (prior to the Jewish New Year) and before the Day of Atonement.

As a cemetery is a ritually unclean place, it is considered compulsory after a visit to wash one's hands. Orthodox tradition even imposes a ban on cemetery visits to the privileged caste of Cohanim (Cohens, or priests), except on occasions of the funerals of relatives.

The first Jewish dead of St. Petersburg were buried in the Volkovsky Lutheran cemetery, in which the Jewish community had bought a small plot of land in 1802. This Jewish plot was in the narrow strip of land between the road to the village of Volkovka and the Volkovka River itself. The road is now transformed into Volkovsky Prospekt, a much wider road that completely covers the area of the Jewish graves.

In this now-hidden plot was buried the first unofficial head of the St.

Petersburg community, Nota Notkin, well known as a philanthropist and intercessor on matters affecting the Jews, a tax farmer from the town of Shklov, and a contractor and victualler to the army of Potemkin.

For every funeral in this plot, the Lutheran community was paid ten silver rubles.

It is said that some twenty-five years ago, during the building of the Prospekt, Volkovsky, a number of gravestone fragments were unearthed, with inscriptions in an ancient "square" lettering.

The next plot of land for Jewish burials was bought in 1859 in the same cemetery. This time it was a corner at the opposite side of the same cemetery, between two ditches and the wall facing ulitsa Samoilovoi (formerly Nobelevskaya ulitsa). Among the bushes, rubbish, and crosses it is possible even now to find in this corner several destroyed Jewish tombstones with inscriptions in Hebrew, German, or Russian. The oldest surviving tombstone, of Dr. Henrich Kuritsky, is dated 1867.

Only in 1874, during a period of relatively liberal attitude on the part of the government, was the new administration of the St. Petersburg community able to acquire a portion of ground for the new Jewish cemetery. In the gazetteer *Petersburg Necropolis*, published by the Grand Prince Nikolai Mikhailovitch in 1912, there is the following information:

> The Preobrazhensky Cemetery (the Cemetery of the Transfiguration) together with the Church of the Transfiguration of our Lord, situated along the Nikolayevsky Railroad at 10 Versts (approximately 6⅔ miles) from St. Petersburg. It is divided up into Russian Orthodox, various other Christian sects, Jewish and Karaite sections. In addition there is a separate military section.

Thus it was that the Jewish cemetery was given a Christian designation in honor of the miracle that happened to Jesus on Mount Tabor. The Christian part of the cemetery has long since been renamed "In memory of the victims of January 9,"* and the word, *Preobrazhensky* (transfiguration) is firmly associated in the minds of the inhabitants of Leningrad with the Jewish graves.

Now burials no longer take place in this cemetery. It is possible only to bury an urn with the ashes of a deceased, after a cremation (in a crematorium elsewhere), in the same grave where lie the remains of the nearest relative of the deceased. The Jews of Leningrad have the choice: either to be buried in a communal nondenominational cemetery or to be cremated and have the ashes placed among the bodies of Jews (something, ironically, forbidden by Jewish law).

The cemetery prayerhouse, in the form in which it appears today, was built only in the twentieth century. At the entrance to the prayerhouse are

---

* "Bloody Sunday" in 1905, when tsarist troops fired on a great crowd that had assembled outside the Winter Palace in St. Petersburg. Many of those gathered there were killed. The lowest estimate, according to the tsarist government at the time, was ninety-six dead.

placed two memorial plaques honoring the events connected with its opening. The right-hand plaque states:

> The foundation stone was laid on 15th day of September in the year 1908. The building was consecrated on 23rd day of September, 1912. It was constructed under the chairmanship of the committee for furnishing the building: Baron D. G. Guenzburg, M. A. Ginsburg; under the supervision of the building commission: Chairman — Engineer G. A. Bernshtein; members: M. A. Warshawski, A. A. Kaplun, N. A. Kotler; according to the design and the instructions of the architect — artist Y. G. Gewirtz.

The left-hand memorial plaque is dedicated to those who financed the construction.

> Erected by arrangement with the Financial Management of the St. Petersburg Synagogue with means provided by the St. Petersburg Jewish community through the generous offerings of Moissei Akimovitch Ginsburg.

To celebrate the opening of the prayerhouse, the printing press of I. Lurie & Co (No. 48 Gorokhovaya Street) produced a brochure: "Order of Service for the Ceremony of the Consecration of the House of Funeral Prayers at the Preobrazhensky Jewish Cemetery of St. Petersburg."

The brochure consists of parallel Russian and Hebrew texts and describes in detail the procedure for the consecration of the prayerhouse. Thus, the Financial Management, the Rabbinate, the members of the Committee of the Building Commission, and honored guests gather in front of the building. The chairman of the Building Commission hands over the key of the main door of the building to the chairman of the Committee, who opens the door leading

The Preobrazhensky Cemetery Prayerhouse. This photograph was taken soon after its construction in 1912.

The Consecration ceremony for the House of Funeral Prayers (Prayerhouse) at the Preobrazhensky Cemetery, 1912

into the prayerhouse. Meanwhile the choir sings the Hallelujah Chorus; the sacred scrolls of the Torah are carried inside in solemn procession. The rabbi delivers a sermon for the occasion of the opening ceremony, which is followed by the then compulsory prayer for the welfare of the tsar. It is of interest to note that, together with a eulogy of Nicholas II and his family, the prayer includes an appeal to God to direct the actions of the sovereign emperor in favor of the Jewish people. The following quotation is a brief extract:

> King of kings, inspire mercy in his [Nicholas's] heart, and in the hearts of all his peers and princes, that they may deal kindly with us and with all Israel. In his days and in ours may there come salvation for the Jews and a secure life for every member of the House of Israel. And may the Redeemer come unto Zion. May such be His will. And let us say "Amen."

The cantor then continues with a hymn of praise for the Almighty. This is followed by short speeches pronounced by G. A. Bernshtein and H. B. Sliozberg, and then comes the memorial service for the dead, which refers to the transitoriness of human life.

Incidentally, the house that we see in the cemetery is not a synagogue in its broadest sense. No one comes here on Saturday, nor do they dance here on the festival of Simhat Torah. Neither is it a place of study (Beit Midrash). A house for the memorial prayer for the dead is a more appropriate designation. Therefore, the architectural style is severe, and there is no unnecessary decoration inside. However, it is nevertheless a synagogue in the literal sense of that word — a place of gathering, albeit on a sad occasion.

A man died. He was brought here, his body was washed, half-a-score old men gathered and read the traditional prayer over the deceased.

Another funeral prayer, for the martyrs who perished for their faith, contains the following lines:

> May He take vengeance for the spilt blood of His servants as it is said in the Torah of Moses, man of God: Sing the praises of His People, O you tribes, for he will avenge the blood of His servants and will take vengeance on His enemies and He will cleanse the Land and purify his people. For is it not written by Thy prophets and Thy servants: "I will give due recompense for the yet unavenged blood."

However, the imperial censor wrote in the prayer book a note to the effect that: "These lines cannot be considered acceptable at the present time."

Let us proceed to the left through an archway in the left wing of the

The Preobrazhensky Cemetery Prayerhouse. The Interior.

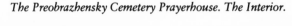

The Preobrazhensky Cemetery Prayerhouse. Columns of the left wing of the building.

prayerhouse and a little further forward. We will see an old memorial in the form of a sarcophagus on a raised stand. This is the tomb of one of the last rabbis of the St. Petersburg Choral Synagogue, David-Tevel Katzenellenbogen.

On the raised stand is an inscription in Hebrew lettering, which is, however, difficult to read as it contains Hebrew mixed with words in Aramaic. There is no Russian-language inscription. From the example of this memorial it is possible to learn what a typical Jewish tombstone looked like. At the top there was usually incised a Star of David. In this instance there is none, but there are two Hebrew letters, *pe* and *nun*. These are the initial letters of the traditional expression *po nikbar,* which means "here is buried," and these two letters are at the beginning of every inscription on a Jewish tombstone. There follows the name of the person who lies beneath the stone and what sort of services the deceased rendered to man and to God.

There are not, and there may not be, either photographs or portraits. One is not allowed to break the second commandment and compete with God in creation. Therefore, the appearance of photographs on later memorials is a categorical departure from tradition. On the lower part of the memorial are five letters תנצבה .

If we examine carefully we shall find that this combination of letters appears on almost every stone. It is an abbreviation of the blessing:

תְּהִי נִשְׁמָתוֹ צְרוּרָה בִּצְרוֹר הַחַיִּים

which may be translated as: "May his Soul be bound in the bond of eternal life."

And where are the dates of the life of the departed? The fact is that it was not done to put the date of birth on Jewish memorials. Birth, in traditional understanding, is not to the merit of the person who is born. Therefore, they did not celebrate birthdays (other than bar mitzvah). When a person is born he has not yet accomplished anything, and it is not known how he will live his life. It depends on him himself, not only on God. However, after his death it will be possible to say whether he was a good person or a sinful one, whether he should be remembered or given over to oblivion. Therefore, in Jewish families they note only the date of death of near relatives, and on that day they pray and light candles.

Let us pause for a more detailed look at the personality of Rabbi Katzenellenbogen himself, a character quite out of the ordinary, whose biography naturally calls for special attention and exceptional investigation. David-Tevel (Tuvia) Katzenellenbogen came from an aristocratic line of rabbis, whose family tree can be traced back to the fourteenth century. One of his ancestors was the well-known Liva ben Bezalel, rabbi of Prague, who created and breathed life into the clay idol, the Golem. The inscription on the tombstone makes reference to this. It also states that Katzenellenbogen was a genuine Gaon, and the sun in the corona of the rabbinate.

Born in 1850, Katzenellenbogen was one of the large family of the dayan (religious judge) of the small townlet of Taurogen, near the border between Lithuania and East Prussia (today Taurage in the Lithuanian Soviet Socialist Republic). Each of his seven brothers also became rabbis. He was given a deeply traditional orthodox education. One of his teachers was the famous zealot, Yisroel Salanter, founder of the religious-ethical study of "Mussar" (Morals) and a champion of the fight against the Enlightenment movement. When Salanter noticed that the boy was showing signs of outstanding intelligence, he advised him to study German (a concession to the demands of the times). In fact, while still young, David-Tevel distinguished himself with considerable erudition in Talmudic writings. In the glosses of Weissman to the abridged publication of the Jerusalem Talmud (1866) many comments have been added in the name of the then still very young, and as yet quite unknown, Katzenellenbogen. In the works of the famous Rabbi of Lvov, Yosef-Saul Natanson, one comes across responsa of Katzenellenbogen. The erudition and devotion of the young man were noticed; in 1876 he was called to take up the appointment of rabbi in the town of Virbalis and then in Suvalki (an important town on the then religious map of Poland). From Suvalki he was invited to become the spiritual leader of the Jewish community in the capital city (1908).

With the death of their former rabbi, the Board of Management, or Council, of the St. Petersburg Jewish community hotly debated the question of whom to choose in his place. The orthodox wing, led by the aged Horace Guenzburg, insisted on a traditional rabbi to strengthen the faith in a St. Petersburg that was being corrupted by Europe. Others who were more assimilated, led by the advocate-barrister G. Sliozberg—those who already did not keep a kosher table at home, and even here during the session of the council, made so bold as to sit without having their heads covered—insisted on the choice of a modern rabbi, who could read and preach his sermons in Russian, and would attract into the synagogue young people who did not know the language, a rabbi who would be able to conduct negotiations and discussions with governmental officials, and who would not look ridiculous in the presence of guests from abroad who belonged to Reform Judaism.

The conservatives won the day thanks to the pressure applied by the baron, who threatened to walk out of the meeting. It was agreed to send to Suvalki the synagogue elder and orientalist Isaak Yulyevitch Markon. Markon, who as a result of his education and kinship with the Polyakovs was a man of influence in the community, was given the task of getting to know Katzenellenbogen more intimately and, if he liked him, to recommend him for the position of rabbi. In Suvalki he was met by an educated man, deeply attached to tradition, yet who was, at the same time, tolerant toward others, a man who had an excellent knowledge of modern Hebrew and was fluent in German, with a classical exterior of noble appearance, high forehead, and deeply penetrating eyes. Markon was so enchanted by all this that he not only took Katzenellenbogen back with him to St. Petersburg, but remained his ardent admirer for the rest of his life.

Before his departure from Poland, the rabbi paid a farewell visit to the district governor, who asked him: "What have they arranged as your salary? — 500 rubles a month? Well that's not less than I am paid in my position as governor!"

Katzenellenbogen and his family of eleven children settled down in Usatchevy Pere'ulok (now No. 2 Makarenko Pere'ulok), then moved to No. 8 in the same street. Two other addresses are known: No. 8 Lermontovsky Prospekt and No. 2 Teatralnaya Square (after 1924).

In the capital it was necessary for the rabbi from the provinces to get used to a new way of life and to settle a whole series of problems of a religious nature. His knowledge of the Russian language was poor, and on each occasion that he went to a meeting with government officials he prepared his statement in writing beforehand. Markon gave him worldly advice. And there was one purely personal family problem: What should he teach and for what sort of life should he prepare his own children?

Naturally all eleven children were taught Jewish knowledge and language by home-tutors (it was customary also to invite children of poor families as participants in the lessons). Sholem Aleikhem, who wrote in "jargon," was not looked upon as serious reading. The only one to read him was the Rabbi's wife. One of the daughters even attended courses on the Talmud, run by David Guenzburg, becoming the first and only female student there. However, in spite of his high status and esteem in the St. Petersburg community, Katzenellenbogen felt very keenly that with his way of life and his world-outlook he belonged to a previous century, to a bygone age, that he was a white raven in this secular capital city. That is why none of his sons took up the calling of rabbi. They registered as external students for courses at the gymnasium and prepared themselves to become advocates, bank employees, and so on. The daughters went to private gymnasia (apart from Saturdays). Only once did the father display firmness when one of his sons declared his desire to become a physician. The Rabbi could not bring himself to permit a violation of the religious ban on the conducting of autopsies.

The situation in Tsarist Russia often compelled Katzenellenbogen to intervene in internal politics. Following the abortive revolution, the years 1905 – 1907 were not favourable for the achievement of any sort of civic rights for the Jews. The Black Hundreds press circulated its anti-Semitic printed material in editions of hundreds of thousands of copies. The Jews suffered from monstrous pogroms. Some fled abroad whilst others went to St. Petersburg for material and legal assistance from their comparatively well-to-do co-religionists.

Representatives were sent on behalf of numerous village communities and on arrival in the capital came straight to the Rabbi's home. To each of them he had to say something and give some sort of help. But for Katzenellenbogen the most pressing questions were those of the faith and the situation of believers. On one occasion he called on the banker Sieff: "I need a large sum of money to support the students of a Yeshivah." "How much? 500 roubles? That would be only pin-money for my wife." Sieff was at that time still a *nouveau riche* and was gaining prestige in the community with his generous philanthropy.

Questions of religion were dealt with by the Minister of Internal Affairs, Maklakov, who was very far from being a liberal. Katzenellenbogen went to see him on several occasions, either being summoned by the minister or on his own initiative, if the situation called for it. For example, at the request of the Jews of Finland he petitioned for a change in the law forbidding the practice of *shechita* (the ritual slaughter of cattle) in Finland. And he won the day. On another occasion, he submitted a request for Jewish soldiers to be allowed home on leave for Passover, so that they would not be obliged to eat bread.

On one occasion Maklakov, knowing the "freethinking" inclination of St. Petersburg Jewish intellectuals, said confidentially: "You know in the Bible there are also quite a few contradictions and obscure passages." Katzenellenbogen became very nervous, went red, and stood up indignantly. "If there are any morals on this earth, they come from the Bible. And you, you are not in a position to condemn it." (He intended to say "discuss it" but because of his faulty Russian he used the wrong word.)*

The minister had the grace to apologize. The obvious sincerity of the rabbi had penetrated even the skin of this highly placed bureaucrat, who for the next two years contacted the rabbi at home to send him his good wishes for Passover on the night of the first seder.

Relationships between the rabbi and the powerful layer of Europeanized Jewry in St. Petersburg did not, and could not, settle down. The traditional Jew who kept a kosher household and spoke Yiddish was more to his liking. He was still able to find things in common and subjects for discussion with Dr. Katzenelson, the brilliant expert on the Talmud and Hebrew language, but Zinberg, the historian of the Jewish socialist workers' movement, never once entered the rabbi's home, although he lived in a house on the opposite side of the very same street, Usatchevy Pere'ulok. Of the many periodicals and magazines in the capital, the only ones that came into the rabbi's home were the moderate Yiddishist paper *Der Haint* and a review of religious-literary publications, issued in Lithuania by Widow Romm and Sons.

Nor did matters in the synagogue itself run smoothly. The service was conducted in three separate places. The main hall was opened for use only on Saturdays and holy days and festivals. Among the truly religious worshippers this place was considered to be a "goyish" hall. The orthodox prayed in a small hall off the main building, in the right wing seen from the front of the synagogue. It had its own separate entrance. The ultra-orthodox Hasidim occupied a small prayer room in the courtyard. The leader of their small community was Shmuel Trainin, a wealthy industrialist, and they had access to their own sources of finance and were administratively independent.

After the death of David Guenzburg (the rabbi went to visit him as he lay

---

* "осуждать" instead of "обсуждать"

on his death bed), the Board of Management moved more in the direction of reform Judaism. Once someone arrived from Berlin and informed them that in the synagogue there (reform, of course) he had seen an organ. Well, naturally the Jews of Germany were an example for all to follow. We must not lag behind, we shall also buy an organ. But here David-Tevel did not give way. So long as he was rabbi, there would be no organ in the synagogue.

Conditions of life in St. Petersburg and the untypical composition of the Jewish community in the capital called, however, for a more moderate religious leader. In 1912 they found their man, Moisei Grigorievitch Eisenstadt, a doctor of philosophy, whom the Board of Management invited to take up the post of community rabbi, while Katzenellenbogen remained as chief rabbi and spiritual leader. Eisenstadt conducted the services in the main synagogue hall, took over youth affairs, participated in activities for education and enlightenment, and was a member of many cultural societies. He read his sermons in Russian. From then on Rabbi Katzenellenbogen devoted more of his time to questions of

The first page of a list of Jews, formerly converted to Christianity, who converted back to Judaism immediately after the February 1917 revolution. There were more than 200 such reconversions. No. 8 on the list is Solomon Yakovlevitch Lurie, the distinguished historian of the ancient world and author of a book on anti-Semitism in the ancient world. This list was found among the archives of the Leningrad Choral Synagogue.

ritual, prayed almost exclusively in the small hall, and attended services in the main hall only at Passover and Sukkot (Tabernacles). He even occasionally looked in at the Hasidic service, where the simplicity of their behavior and the entire lack of decorum never failed to shock his aristocratic nature. The rest of his time he devoted to the study of theology and the writing of theological works.

After the revolution, two of Rabbi Katzenellenbogen's books were published: *Ma'yan Mei Neftoah* (1923) and *Divrei David* (1927). In those years, he suffered a great deal, as he witnessed the destruction of Jewish national life in Russia. But he still could not bring himself to emigrate, as this would mean leaving his community without a spiritual leader at a difficult time. Some of his children had left the country even before the revolution. His youngest son, Iliahu, emigrated to Berlin in 1923, after he had been expelled from Petrograd University for being the son of a rabbi. Later on, Iliahu was to play a prominent part in building up Jewish education in Palestine. Two other sons of Rabbi Katzenellenbogen—Shaul and Hertz—were arrested in the Soviet Union in 1937, together with other religious activists connected with the Leningrad Choral Synagogue; both of them died in a labor camp. The rabbi's daughter, Bertha, survived; today she still lives in Leningrad.

To return to Rabbi David-Tevel Katzenellenbogen: in 1912, during the building of the cemetery prayerhouse, the architect Y. G. Gewirtz was in the rabbi's home a number of times when they discussed the prayerhouse project together. The rabbi helped in the selection of suitable quotations from the Psalms and advised on their placement in the wings of the prayerhouse. They are there to this day.

The February Revolution of 1917 unexpectedly influenced the everyday life of the synagogue. Many St. Petersburg Jews who had earlier been baptized to try to secure better careers now frequented the synagogue to restore their Jewishness. Although educated Jews in St. Petersburg were in general somewhat indifferent about religion, at least a hundred of them returned to the faith of their fathers. Among them it is worth mentioning Solomon Lurye, the historian of the ancient world and author of the book *Antisemitism in the Ancient World,* as well as Sofia Dymshits, the former wife of the writer Aleksei Tolstoy (himself of distant Jewish descent).*

After 1917, David-Tevel Katzenellenbogen decided to remain in Petrograd, although almost all the upper crust of the community (bankers, merchants, industrialists, lawyers) left the country. In 1923 Eisenstadt emigrated to Paris. Synagogue affairs declined. The main building was not heated and was only opened on rare occasions. In bad times, the number of people attending

---

* The descendants of baptized Jews seldom, if ever, converted back to Judaism. It is on ulitsa Belinskogo (formerly Simeonovskaya ulitsa) that one finds the Church in which a Jewish doctor, Asher Blank, was baptized, changing his first name to Alexander. This otherwise obscure Jewish convert to Christianity—he became a medical doctor—is known to history as the grandfather of Lenin; it was his daughter who married Lenin's father.

synagogue services was very small, although as the Jewish population of the town rapidly increased and times improved somewhat, attendance began to grow again. Although, soon after the revolution, the rabbi was officially declared to be a "*former* minister of religious worship," in fact he carried on with his duties right up to his death in 1930.

Granite from the walls of the Choral Synagogue, where Katzenellenbogen had served as rabbi for more than twenty years, was used to make the memorial to Katzenellenbogen in the cemetery. A flagstone with a new inscription replacing the old one, which was partly worn away, was erected in the 1950s. In the Preobrazhensky Cemetery, most of the tombstones or memorials that are still in a state of preservation have their inscriptions in Russian.

In the Preobrazhensky Cemetery, most of the tombstones or memorials that are still in a state of preservation have their inscriptions in Russian.

In the fourth row from the cemetery wall, which goes out onto the street (Nevskaya Alleya), the fifth grave from the left fence is "adorned" with a plain headstone of light-gray granite, a product of the unification of funeral design of the last decades. The old tombstone was felt to be unfitting and was replaced by a new one in 1967 or 1968 from money provided by one of his relatives, now living in Israel. A marble flagstone made into a memorial preserves the original text of the inscription: "Professor Doctor Abram Yakovlevitch Harkavy. Died March 15, 1919."

Harkavy played an important part in the life of the capital, both as an orientalist and as a historian of the Jews of St. Petersburg. For us to be convinced of this it is sufficient to make a brief acquaintance with an article written in his honor by D. Maggid, published in the collection *Yevreiskaya Mysl* (Jewish Thought), Vol. 1 (1922), in Petrograd. Here, during our walk around the cemetery, it is fitting to recall this article even though in an abbreviated form:

> With the death of A. Y. Harkavy (1835–1919) Russian Jewry has suffered a grievous loss. His activity in the field of social sciences was a shining light for over fifty years. He was an inexhaustible, conscientious worker, equipped with a deep knowledge and a truly critical faculty. From 1864 to 1908 he wrote many scientific papers on the history of the Jews in Russia, Lithuania, and Poland, the era of the Gaonim, and the history of the Karaites and the Khazars. He carried out an enormous amount of research work into the Hebrew and Aramaic manuscripts in the Firkovitch* collection, which are preserved in the Public Library. Using this material he printed a mass of commentary on gnomystic literature, numismatics, epigraphics, art, liturgy, archeology, historical geography, Masoretics, poetry of the Middle Ages, and so on. His most valuable work, some three hundred sheets of print, was a detailed description of the manuscripts in the Firkovitch collection.

---

* Abraham Firkovitch (1786–1874), a Karaite leader who sought to establish the independence of the Karaites from Talmudic Judaism. He was supported in this endeavor (which was largely successful) by the tsarist government. To prove his case, he went so far as to falsify his sources.

Harkavy's works were varied in caliber, but were invariably of high quality. Although he himself did not write any large-scale monographs, there is not, states Maggid, nor, he prophesies, will there be, a historian who will not quote from his works. Harkavy was also a scientist who courageously defended the truth in science. At the beginning of his scientific activity, enormous authority and influence in the field of Oriental studies were wielded by Avraham Firkovitch, considered to be the expert on the Karaites. Firkovitch had published a book on the Karaite gravestones in the Crimea. The young Harkavy himself traveled to the Crimea and, after a thorough examination and research into many of the tombstones described by Firkovitch, showed conclusively that part of them were not Karaite but of Hebrew origin. It turned out that Firkovitch had sometimes deliberately changed certain letters when he quoted the inscriptions, which falsified both dates and the general character of the stones. Harkavy's courageous articles brought Firkovitch's career to an abrupt halt.

Harkavy's public activity was closely connected with the Society for the Spread of Enlightenment among the Jews of Russia (OPE), where, from 1864 onward, almost from the very beginning of the foundation of the society, he was a member and collaborator, and then for a period of twenty-three years also a member of the Central Committee. Harkavy was also a book reviewer and a reviewer of pamphlets and brochures for print or subsidy. His participation helped in the publication of the collection "The Tamudists' Conception of the World," and thanks to his collaboration the Pentateuch was translated by Gershtein and Levando and published in parallel Russian and Hebrew texts in Vilna in the 1870s.

Harkavy was also for a short time the secretary of OPE. It was his idea to consolidate the financial assistance given to Jewish teachers and to Jewish women students. He suggested a broadening of communal activity — the development of artistic trades and of agricultural work. It was in fact Harkavy who established the library in the OPE premises, and from 1876 it was he who organized the addition to its bookshelves of books on Hebraica and Judaica. In 1880, on his advice, the library was moved to a place specially set aside for it in the synagogue building, and eventually in 1893 to a communal building on the corner of Offitserskaya and Bolshaya Masterskaya streets (now No. 42 Dekabristov). And in 1917 he gave over to the library his own collection of books and manuscripts and a large part of his archives.

For many years before his death Harkavy served as an elder (warden) of the synagogue and as a member of the Board of Management of the Jewish Community in St. Petersburg. He was very popular, particularly in the Pale of Settlement, and especially because of his interest in Oriental studies. His adherence to scientific principles and his pride in his national awareness were the reasons for his estrangement from the conservative and at times reactionary circles of St. Petersburg. It was not until the late autumn of 1918, when he lay on his deathbed, that the faculty of Oriental studies at the University of St. Petersburg sent him notification of three vacant professorial chairs in Jewish

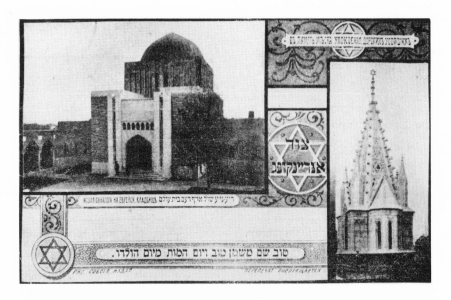

The tombstone of Moisei Maimon

studies, with an invitation to accept any of the three. The dying Abram Yakov-levitch felt the insincerity of the official invitation and sadly predicted that for a very long time not one Jewish specialist on Judaica would be allowed to occupy any of the professorial chairs in the faculty of Oriental studies.

Let us now continue our walk along the facade of the cemetery, next to the synagogue, toward the nearest right-hand corner, where Glavnaya Alleya intersects Nevskaya Alleya. There we shall see a building, not large in size, with peaked domes in a pseudo-Gothic style. It is a vault, now used as a storeroom; the family vault of some rich family or other. But no inscriptions have been preserved on the inside, and there are no inscriptions to be seen on the outside of the building; we have no information as to when or by whom it was built, or how it was put to use. A large stone Star of David, on the top of the vault, disappeared about ten years ago.

If we proceed from the Gothic-style chapel a little forward and to the right, we shall see a modest white marble tombstone in the upper part of which, in carefully formed black letters, is the inscription: "Member of the Academy of Pictorial Arts, Maimon Moisei Lvovitch 1860–1924." The tombstone is in the fifth row from Glavnaya Alleya and in the fifth row from Nevskaya Alleya. In addition, there are two other names on the tombstone, with very much later dates of birth and death. These are probably the artist's daughter and son-in-law. This tombstone was placed there fairly recently. What happened to the original stone, erected immediately after Maimon's death, God alone knows. On our first excursion here we learned that Moisei Lvovitch is the same person

Академик живописи
МАЙМОН
Моисей Львович
1860–1924

Адвокат
КОЛДОБСКИЙ
Борис Матвеевич
1887–1968

КОЛДОБСКАЯ
Александра Моисеевна
1901–198?

A prerevolutionary postcard with the views of the Preobrazhensky Cemetery Prayer-house and the pseudo-gothic vault nearby who achieved recognition and the title of member of the academy with his famous painting *The Marranos* (see *Yevreiskaya Entsiklopedia*). The artist himself related how he came to paint this picture in an article he wrote, which appeared in one of the issues of the *Yevreiskaya Letopis* (Jewish Chronicle — not connected with the London Jewish weekly newspaper, which is published under that name) published shortly after 1917.

It is almost impossible to find the grave of Lev Izrailyevitch Katzenelson, unless one knows precisely where to look for it. It lies along the right-hand wall of the synagogue, approximately about the middle of the wall. One expects to see an imposing, inspiring stone, with a lengthy inscription in Hebrew, and generally to see something befitting the personality of Katzenelson and the position he occupied in the life of the Jewish community. Instead, however, there is a modest concrete stone block, in modern gray style now seen everywhere. A very small marble tablet informs us of his name and the dates of his birth and death (1847–1917). His pseudonym (Buki Ben Yogli) is written in Hebrew lettering. The original memorial stone was also modest, but this be-

The tombstone of Lev Katzenelson (Buki Ben Yogli)

Lev Katzenelson

came quite shabby and cracked. The shell now standing over Katzenelson's grave was erected about eighteen years ago, from money collected by old people who remembered what sort of man he had been.

Lev (Yehuda Leib Benjamin) Izrailyevitch Katzenelson was born in Chernigov in 1847. Until the age of ten he attended cheder and then trained to be a *sofer*, a scribe who copied scriptural parchments. Sitting at his work for twelve hours a day, the boy (already a fatherless orphan) dreamed of one day becoming a great Talmudist. When he was fourteen he secretly ran away to Bobruisk to study in a yeshivah.

For three years, in addition to his Talmudic studies, Lev Katzenelson taught himself German and Russian. Much has been written about the life of this special category of people — not much more than children yet at the same time learned elders — known as *yeshivah-bochers*. It is worth quoting, even though it is a biased view, from L. Grossman's book about Avraham-Urieh Kovner — *Confession of a Jew* (1924, Moscow and Leningrad). Grossman writes:

> Young theologians, roaming from one famous Talmudic School to another, exercising their minds in the most refined casuistry of ancient texts, making

their way on foot, or on rickety horse-drawn carts, from one tiny village to another in order to hear the words of a well-known Bible commentator, their shabby clothing threadbare, half-starved, soaked to the skin from the pouring rains of the western provinces, eternally exposed to sneers, nudges, and insults from the multi-racial poulation of miserable, poverty-stricken, lawless "provinces," but tireless in their determination to acquire the knowledge, mysteriously locked away in the weighty tome with the square letters — they are truly worthy of the penetrating attention of the explorers and artists of the word.

The next lap in Lev Izrailyevitch's life was the Zhitomir Rabbinical School, which he completed in 1872, following which he again settled down to study, this time at the Academy of Medicine and Surgery. Then came the Russo-Turkish War, and Katzenelson served as a doctor in the army. When he returned from the war he passed the exams to become a doctor of medicine and moved to St. Petersburg.

All these outstanding achievements, however, would not have made his name so well known, had it not been for his most active participation in public affairs in the field of Jewish communal life and culture, activity that he did not cease to carry out until the very day of his death, combining it with his medical practice. Katzenelson made an attempt to analyze the most obscure parts of the Talmud, those devoted to questions of medicine, and, on the basis of contemporary scientific notions, to make an evaluation of the knowledge acquired by Babylonian Jews in the field of anatomy and pathology. He published a series of articles on this theme, and in particular on "The Knowledge of Hemophilia in the Talmud." He was outstandingly fluent in modern Hebrew (Ivrit), and he wrote part of his works, including works on medicine, in this ancient, but at that time newly revived language. His articles, under the pseudonym of Buki ben Yogli, can be seen in contemporary Russian Jewish periodicals of that time, *Russky Yevrei* (The Russian Jew), *Yevreiskoye Obozreniye* (Jewish Review), and others.

As a physician, Lev Katzenelson took no payment when he treated poor Jewish adolescents in the professional school at No. 2 Bolshaya Masterskaya ulitsa. Simultaneously, he fulfilled a multitude of communal functions: he was a member of the Central Committee of the Jewish Colonization Association (ICA), a member of the committee of OPE (Society for the Spread of Enlightenment among the Jews of Russia), and vice-chairman of the Society of Lovers of Ancient Hebrew (OLDEY).

Together with Baron David Guenzburg and Abram Harkavy, Lev Katzenelson brilliantly completed his most important task, the general editing of the sixteen-volume *Yevreiskaya Entsiklopedia* (the Russian-language Jewish Encyclopedia), published in the second decade of this century by Brockhaus and Yefron. In the encyclopedia, Katzenelson was responsible for the editing of articles on the Talmudic period. Also, after the death of David Guenzburg, the founder of the courses on Oriental studies, Katzenelson himself took on the leadership of the courses. In general he lived his life in such a way that it can with certainty be said that such a man will never be forgotten by his people. "A rare gifted talent, a warm cordiality, a gentle sense of humor, wrapped in mists of lyricism," this is how he was described by one of his contemporaries.

Lev Katzenelson lived at No. 5 Izmailovsky Prospekt.

As we proceed a little further along Glavnaya Alleya, we shall see, to the left, in the first row from the avenue, a small monument of black marble in the form of an obelisk surmounted by a sphere. In the front, near the top, is a photograph of an intellectual of the old type, stern of appearance, with an inscription in German. Below and behind is inscribed in Russian "Professor Lev Yakovlevitch Sternberg 1861–1927."

Lev Yakovlevitch was born in Zhitomir. As a child he had a good Hebrew education but transferred from rabbinic school to the gymnasium, then entered the faculty of law at Odessa University, from where he was sent to prison for his activity in the Narodnaya Volya (The Populist Party). Such a metamorphosis, from Talmudist to Russian revolutionary, was no accident in those days. This path was followed by thousands of young Jews for whom existing legislation closed the road to a secular education or career. Government-financed rabbinical schools (as distinct from yeshivahs), in fact, turned out all and sundry: writers, lawyers, converts to Christianity, terrorists—anyone apart from officials of religious observance.

After a period of three months in solitary isolation, Sternberg was sent in 1889 to the island of Sakhalin, which decided his future. On Sakhalin there were very few educated or even literate people. Therefore, in accordance with age-old tradition, in Siberia and the Siberian Far East qualified work was usually allocated to the political exiles. Young Sternberg, being an energetic person, decided not to waste his time there and undertook a deep study of the local aboriginal population: Gilyaks, Araks, Tungus, and Ainas. He was helped in this by the administration of the island, which needed to have a census of the local inhabitants. Its members provided Sternberg, the student in exile, with a team of harnessed dogs, food, and an experienced local guide, and off he went.

For some reason or other, among ethnographers who have dedicated themselves to a study of indigenous tribes, there are a number of Jews. In Russia these include L. Sternberg, V. Bogoraz, I. Vinnikov, and V. Iokhelson; abroad, F. Boas and others. What is it that drives such people? A protective feeling on the part of a representative of an ancient folk toward those who still stand on the threshold of civilization? Or, on the other hand, is it a feeling of sympathy toward those deprived of rights, as we were once deprived when we were slaves in Egypt? Whatever the reason, Sternberg fell in love with his Gilyaks and Ainas. It could not be otherwise, for an ethnographer of a people can be successful only if he truly loves that people.

His first articles, sent from exile, were received enthusiastically in St. Petersburg and when in 1897, as a result of amnesty, Sternberg received permission to return home, the Academy of Sciences appealed successfully for him to be allowed temporary permission to stay in St. Petersburg to study and take the examinations at the faculty of jurisprudence in the university.

Sternberg's subsequent voluntary missions to the Amur region and to Sakhalin and the publication of his articles "The Non-Russian Minorities" (Inorodtsi), "The Buryats," "Discussion on Sakhalin," and other works of this nature made his name known in scientific circles. He played an active part in the scientific organization of expeditions from the St. Petersburg Museum of Anthropology and Ethnography and himself participated in an expedition to the North Pacific Ocean region of Russia for the study of indigenous tribes (under the leadership of Boas). After the Revolution, Sternberg, as a professor at Leningrad University, devoted a considerable amount of his time to working with students, wrote a methodology on the collection of ethnographic materials, and prepared successors to take his place.

During all this time, Sternberg did not forget his own people. He published articles of both political and ethnographic content on Russian Jewry: "The Tragedy of the Six Million People," "The Problems of Russian Jewry," "The Latest Findings in the Anthropology of the Jews," "Sakhalin Jews," and other works of this nature. Some of them appeared in the journal *Jewish Antiquity*, of which he became editor after the departure of Simon Dubnow to Riga. When it was reorganized by Sternberg and Bogoraz, the Museum of Anthropology and Ethnography in Leningrad contained, in the twenties, a large Jewish section.

Sternberg's political orientation changed more than once. At first a Populist (member of the Narodnaya Volya — People's Will party), he then drew closer to the Cadets (CDs — Constitutional Democrats) and joined the Union for the Attainment of Equal Rights for the Jewish People of Russia. After the collapse of the Equal Rights Union he worked with a number of moderate Jewish CDs to found, at the end of 1906, a Jewish national group that fought against anti-Semitism but dissociated itself from Zionism. Later Sternberg's outlook became much more leftist.

In St. Petersburg, Sternberg lived at No. 10 Sablinskaya ulitsa, and later, when he became professor, at No. 56 Sriedny Prospect.

A very large gathering attended the funeral of Lev Yakovlevitch Sternberg. Among the students his popularity was very high.

[ ] ONE OF THE largest monuments in the cemetery has been erected over the grave of M. M. Antokolski, the noted sculptor who has with justice entered into both Jewish and Russian history. (Glavnaya Alleya, opposite the Sternberg monument.)

Mark (Mordechai) Matveyevitch Antokolski was born in the center of the Talmudic studies, in Vilna, during the period of the very first Maskilim (Enlighteners). As a child he went, as did all the Jewish children, to cheder. He then went as an apprentice to a wood carver. His artistic talent appeared so early and so pronouncedly in the boy that it very soon became clear that he could not long remain within the restrictions of orthodox traditions. The young man moved to St. Petersburg, and in 1862 he became one of the first Jews to enter as a student at the Academy of Arts. Here he quickly attracted the attention of his teachers, and in 1864 he received the Second Class Silver Medal for his high-relief "Jewish Tailor" (in wood) and the following year the First Class Silver Medal for his ivory and wood carving *The Miser.* Other earlier works on Jewish themes included *Argument over the Talmud, Attack of the Inquisition on the Jews,* and *Nathan the Wise.*

One of the first to notice the young Mark Antokolski, and to draw the attention of the public at large to him, was the famous Russian critic V. V. Stassov, who was always outspoken in defense of the Jews and was a regular patron of young talent. V. V. Stassov, leader of "The powerful small group," was the son of the famous St. Petersburg architect, V. P. Stassov, and uncle of the secretary of the All-Union Communist Party (Bolsheviks), E. D. Stassova. It was, in fact, due to the intervention of Stassov that Antokolski received a stipend from the tsar and financial help from Baron Horace Guenzburg, as a result of which he was able to complete his education (including a period at the Berlin Academy) and made his first trip abroad.

Antokolski's statue *Ivan the Terrible* (1871) brought general acclaim. By now the exultation of the press that had begun in the early 1860s in regard to brotherhood with the Jews had already died down, and the sculptor felt the first outbursts of anti-Semitism. To prevent such attacks on him, he succeeded, with the help of the Grand Princess Maria Nikolayevna, in persuading Tsar Alexander II to make a personal visit to his sculptor's studio. The tsar took a liking to the statue and purchased a copy in bronze for the Hermitage. The upper classes of the aristocracy, forgetting for a brief moment their very recent verbal abuse of Antokolski for his Jewish origins, elected him at the early age of not quite twenty-eight to be a member of the Academy of Arts.

In 1872, in order to recover from illness, Antokolski traveled to Italy, where he created several outstanding pieces of work on Russian historical and Christian themes: *Peter I, Yaroslav the Wise, Dmitri Donskoi, Ivan III,* and *Christ before the People's Court.* His turning to such themes in no way implied that Antokolski was deserting his people. In fact, being a believer from his early childhood, the artist remained true to Jewish traditions to the end of his days, although probably he was not entirely strict in his observance. In Antokolski's day, for perfectly understandable reasons, a purely Jewish plastic and pictorial tradition to all intents and purposes did not exist, whereas the Christian tradition was very rich. If the Christian artist wanted to depict the highest degree of suffering, he portrayed the Crucifixion; grief was the *Pieta;* the symbol of treachery, Judas Iscariot.

Of course, the fact that Mark Matveyevitch was raised as a sculptor within the framework of the Russian school, and especially in a general European cultural milieu, must have played no small role in his upbringing. It was only natural that his outlook coincided in many ways with the views of his teachers. Undoubtedly, to no small extent the subject of the sculptor's work was also influenced by the identity of the person who commissioned it, the Russian nobility, and the Imperial Court. He only had to have a change in patron, and Antokolski was already carving his magnificent marble statue of Spinoza (for Baron Horace Guenzburg).

In 1875 Antokolski returned to Russia and completed a series of busts for the imperial family, as well as busts of Turgeniev, Tolstoy, Botkin, and others. He acquired international fame at the Paris World Fair of 1878, where he received the top prize and the Order of the Légion d'Honneur for his statues *The Last Breath* and *The Head of John the Baptist*. His greatest creations in the following decade were *Yermak* (bronze) and *Nestor the Chronicler* (marble).

Meanwhile, in 1881 Alexander II was assassinated by members of the Narodnaya Volya, and very difficult times ensued for the Jews in Russia. Pogroms, restrictive laws, mass evictions followed one after the other. Nor did the Russian chauvinistic press ignore Antokolski. How dare he, a Jew, create images of Russian and Christian heroes? Stassov alone stepped forward to defend him. Depressed both by harassment and by illness, the sculptor left Russia for Paris, and in 1893 settled there for good. His last creations were selected for the highest awards at the World Fair in 1900, and he was given the Cross of the Légion d'Honneur.

In 1902 Antokolski went for treatment to a spa in Germany where he died. His body was transferred to St. Petersburg and was buried with much solemnity in the Preobrazhensky Cemetery, in the city where he had studied and where he had experienced both fame and torment.

The memorial that we now see was erected in 1909. In the center is an enormous Star of David. Above it, a seven-branched candelabrum. Steps lead to two pairs of stone tablets on which are inscribed, in Russian, the names of the artist's principal sculptures. Above them is his name in Hebrew, Mordechai Ben Matityahu. Below are his name and the dates in Russian. There was also a sculpture of the head of the dying Antokolski, done by one of his students and friends, Ilya Yakovlevitch Guenzburg, that same Guenzburg whom Mark Matveyevitch himself had brought from Vilna as an eleven-year-old boy and had made into a sculptor of world fame. The sculpture disappeared during the siege of Leningrad during World War II.

Today it is difficult to imagine the Russian Museum in Leningrad without the creations of this great sculptor. One does not have to be prejudiced to see the obvious superiority of his works over those of his Russian contemporaries, also on exhibition. Take, for example, the bronze, seated figure of Ivan the Terrible. The tsar is wearing the black hooded cassock of a monk, but the look on his face is far from serene, instilling only dread. Or, the solitary hero *The Dying Socrates,* who chose death rather than compromise his principles to the ignorant masses. Then there is the lonely intellectual rebel, Baruch Spinoza. His features filled with inspiration, deep in thought, almost transparent, he sits with an open book on his knees. Here is the embodiment of cunning, Mephistopheles. And all around is the astonishing technique of Antokolski's in marble, when suddenly we come across a bronze statue of a stylishly dressed man of middle age, with a clean-cut beard, a hat, and a cane. His look is confident and resourceful. This is Samuil Polyakov, the famous Jewish banker and railroad builder.

In his works, Antokolski displays considerable variety, but in one respect he is unchanging — in the power of his talent.

In his recollections of his childhood in the book *Shum Vremeni* (The Noise of Time), Osip Mandelstam describes a visit to the St. Petersburg Synagogue:

> And suddenly two men in top hats, splendidly dressed, glistening with wealth, with the graceful movements of people of high society, reach out with their hands to touch the heavy book and, coming out of the circle, on behalf of all those present perform some highly honored and important act. Who are they? One is Baron Guenzburg. The other — is it Warshawski?

The burial vault of the Warshawskis lies next to the grave of Antokolski. But this is not so easy to guess. The edifice is of the most eclectic architecture. In style it is both Moorish (like the synagogue) and also pseudo-Russian. And the inscription! Try to unravel the huge Hebrew letters on the facade, and you will be puzzled. For the words are Russian, written in Hebrew letters, but reading, not in Hebrew style from right to left, but "backwards," from left to right! They read: "To the Memory of Abram Moiseyevitch Warshawski."

The founder of the St. Petersburg branch of the Warshawskis, Abram Moiseyevitch, a man of public affairs and philanthropist, was born about 1821 and died in 1888. Together with other wealthy Jews he was able to settle in St. Petersburg only in the sixties. A. M. Warshawski, well known for the part he played in almost all the large-scale Jewish charitable organizations, was a member of the Committee of OPE. He also gave help to non-Jews. For example, he built a school for the children of the peasants on his estate at Poltavshchina. The *Yevreiskaya Entsiklopedia,* with tenderness and, one might almost say, with emotion, informs us that A. M. was:

> A man with an exceedingly responsive heart, who could never refuse anyone, even when very frequently he was not in a position to fulfill his promise. Warshawski's funeral was attended by a large number of deputations from the provinces in the persons of rabbis and prominent local public benefactors.

Osip Mandelstam, of course, saw Warshawski's son, the chairman of the financial administration of the St. Petersburg community, Mark Abramovitch Warshawski. His name (see the beginning of our tour) is connected with the building of the cemetery prayerhouse. There was also another well-known member of this family, a nephew of Abram Moiseyevitch, the popular St. Petersburg writer Mark Samuilovitch Warshawski.

From the Moscow weekly *Noviy Put* (New Pathway) of 1916, we learn of one incident in the life of the St. Petersburg community in which M. A. Warshawski found himself in opposition to the opinion of the majority. On May 8, 1916, leading members of the community gathered in the small hall of the conservatoire. War was raging. Petrograd was filled to overflowing with refugees from the Pale of Settlement. The Russian Empire was in the last few months of its existence, and the meeting was discussing the question of reduction of membership fees from twenty-five rubles to three rubles per annum. Presiding at the meeting was the famous lawyer, former member of the Duma as a representative of the Cadets — Maxim Vinaver. Another, even more famous, the lawyer Oscar Grusenberg, in a brilliant speech showed the necessity for this step. How, in point of fact, could the community be so out of touch with the times, with the process of democratization of communal institutions? Finally, let every Jewish tradesman and craftsman participate in settling questions of Jewish life and elect the members of the Board of Management. Warshawski and others of the most wealthy Jews were opposed to the motion, insisting that the number of persons paying twenty-five rubles was so small not because of a shortage of money among smaller businessmen, but because of a general lack of interest in questions of religion. In fact, out of the then Jewish population in Petrograd of almost fifty thousand, only five hundred were paying that sum.

Nevertheless, the speeches of Grusenberg, Bickerman, and other supporters of reform were received with considerable enthusiasm and applause, and the meeting reduced the subscription. It seems that not one of those seated in the hall that day was able to foresee that their hot debates, against the background of approaching events, were absolutely meaningless.

Behind the Warshawski vault we see the enormous burial vault of a distinguished citizen, Councillor of State Friedland. Beyond that is the vault of Kaplun, the court tailor, and on the rear side of the Kaplun Vault, almost touching it, there stands, almost unnoticed, a simple monument in the form of two tablets (corner of Garevaya and Glavnaya Avenues). This was the first grave in the Preobrazhensky Cemetery. Here are buried two young soldiers, artillery assistants, Berka Burak and Moshka Frisno. The Russian inscription states that they were "laboratory workers in the Okhtinsky Gunpowder Factory, 23 years of age. They were killed in an explosion in the laboratory on February 28, the 15th of Adar and buried in this cemetery on March 2, 1875." This is followed by the same text written in Hebrew.

The grave of Sergeant-Major Ashanski (Herzen Avenue, section between Lipovaya Alleya and Luzhskaya Alleya) is one of the very oldest preserved in the cemetery. The recently restored inscription, on a gray stone corroded with time, informs us that "Here lie the remains of Sergeant-Major of the Regiment of the Royal Horse Guards of Her Imperial Majesty The Empress Maria Fyodorovna, Abel Aronovitch Ashanski who enlisted on January 11, 1846. . . . "

The remainder of the inscription, including the dates of his life, is illegible, but we know that Ashanski (real first name Abel-Aaron Itzkovitch) was born in 1825 and died in 1899. On the reverse side of the gravestone is an inscription in Hebrew.

How did a Jew become a serving soldier, not merely in a cavalry regiment but, even more remarkable, in one of the most privileged units in the whole army? And not only that, but, as the tombstone tells us, he reached the rank of sergeant-major!

In order to appreciate the significance of this, one has to understand the atmosphere that prevailed in the Russian Army at the time Ashanski served in it. In the year that he was called up, the majority of soldiers serving in the lower ranks of the Russian Army were feudal serfs, peasants torn away from the soil and forced to serve for twenty-five years in the garrisons of Tsar Nicholas's army (Nicholas I reigned 1825 to 1855) with its brutal drill parades, beatings by officers, running the gauntlet, and so on. For Jews, this recruitment was an even

The tombstone of Sergeant-Major Ashanski

greater torment. Nicholas I introduced compulsory military service for Jews in 1827. The Jewish people, who had no privileges, were not forgotten when it came to the distribution of duties for the defense of the motherland. Moreover, the people without privileges were forced to send to the draft more recruits, proportionately, than the "native" population. Simultaneously, Nicholas introduced the system of "cantonists," that is, compulsory camps for "preparatory training, prior to military service" of Jewish children from the ages of twelve to eighteen. The Pale of Settlement received this new edict with horror. Parents hid their children in other villages. Many children fled to the forests, or mutilated their own bodies intentionally to avoid military service. Specially trained press-gangs, known popularly as "Khappers" (Kidnappers) searched through the villages and hamlets, seizing youngsters in their homes, and often seized young boys aged ten or even eight years old, as they were easier to grab hold of.

Did the Emperor Nicholas and his administrators consider that by increasing the forced recruitment of Jews they would strengthen the army and make it invincible? Not at all! The recruitment was devised by Nicholas and his government quite simply as a melting pot where this "obstinate" people would be compelled to assimilate and eventually be converted to Christianity. It would be easiest to do this in the army by forcible means applied to immature young boys, torn from their families and from their national milieu. Thus for Jews, service in the army was a nightmare and parents mourned for their sons taken as recruits, considering them as good as dead. On seeing a group of these children-cantonists, halted on their march at Vyatka, Alexander Herzen in his book *Byloye i Dumy* (My Past and Thoughts) has described the sight as "one of the most awful" he had ever seen.

The number of Jewish soldiers was not inconsiderable, and in the Russo-Turkish war of 1878 to 1879 many of them displayed heroism. In the victorious Vladimirsky and Suzdalsky regiments of the 16th Division under General Skobeliev, Jews made up about half the number.

Ashanski joined the army at the age of twenty-one and refused to be baptized as a Christian. But he became a good soldier. For the first seventeen years he was a stovemaker in a labor-pioneer battalion, then he was transferred to the Royal Horse Guards (Household Cavalry) regiment. He reached the end of his service but he had no home to return to. Abel-Aaron Itzkovitch refused to accept indefinite leave or retirement. He was promoted to the highest non-commissioned rank, sergeant-major (as a non-Christian it was virtually impossible for him to become an officer), and was given all the rewards and advantages accompanying this rank; he continued to serve in the Russian Army, breaking all records for length of service of a Jew.

In 1890, in view of his advanced age (he was 65), Ashanski was appointed supervisor of sick and wounded, a position he held until his death in 1899. He was very popular in the Regiment of Guards. If it had not been so, he would have long since been forced to retire. On the fiftieth anniversary of his enlistment (1896) he was given a special reception and celebration by the entire regiment, and an order of the day was promulgated mentioning Ashanski's devotion to his unit. The funeral service and burial of this old soldier from Nicholas's army took place here in the Preobrazhensky Cemetery to the accompaniment of exceptionally ceremonial circumstances, and a large crowd of people followed the hearse.

In his book *Fifty Years of Military Service* a former tsarist — later Soviet — general, Count A. Ignatiev, who served in the same Royal Horse Guards Regiment as Ashanski, reflected on how amazed he had been to see so many carriages "with rich gentlemen in them" gathering on the occasion of the death of an ordinary stovemaker. As it turned out, the sergeant-major was respected by his community. According to the regimental regulations, his coffin was carried by all the regiment's commanders under whom he had served. At the time of the funeral, some of them occupied senior positions in the army.

The press (especially the Russian Jewish newspapers) were fulsome in pouring out the most tender and patriotic of feelings.

A year earlier, in 1895, Pobedonostsev, the senior procurator of the Holy Synod, who was the right hand of Tsar Alexander III, in replying to the complaints of a Jewish delegation about persecution and harassment, had cynically declared: "Well, so what? One third will die, one third will leave the country, and the remainder will assimilate into the surrounding population."

To the right of the prayerhouse there are several grandiose vaults. On most of them it is possible to read which families they belonged to. But why is there nowhere to be seen the family vault of the Polyakovs, the famous bankers and contractors of railroad construction in Russia? Where is the burial place of, at least, the most famous of them, Privy Councillor Samuil Solomonovitch Polyakov, who owned a palace on the banks of the River Neva? Take a look at some ruins, which today look like a large heap of rubbish. It is about ten to thirteen rows from the cemetery wall, about the thirtieth row to the right of the synagogue (next to Luzhskaya Alleya). This is all that remains of the Polyakov family burial vault. As we have seen, the bronze statue of him (by Antokolski) is standing in the Russian Museum in Leningrad, but the grave has not been preserved. It has been said that in 1945, after the Great Patriotic War, there were some old tombstones and fragments in an underground cave (which had somehow survived and looked something like a concrete pill-box). Today even those fragments have disappeared.

To the rear of the synagogue lies Garevaya Alleya. Beyond it, in the second row, approximately opposite the central boiler of the prayerhouse, can be seen an old granite stone of imposing appearance, lying almost flat on its fundament and decorated with stone garlands. It is surrounded by a massive cast-iron fence, already partly broken down and eaten away with rust, but its design of garlands intertwined with torches is still clearly seen. On the stone there is no sign of any inscription!

What is it? If it is a grave, then why is there no inscription on the tombstone? If it is not a grave, then what is it?

According to tradition, it is not a grave; the stone was placed there in 1909 by the St. Petersburg community in memory of one of its greatest leaders, Baron Horace Yevselevitch Guenzburg. In his time Horace Guenzburg played a tremendous role in the life of Russian Jewry, especially in St. Petersburg. His generous munificence is well known. However, for various reasons, in his will he declared that he wished to be buried in Paris, and this was adhered to. Almost the entire Jewish community of St. Petersburg turned out to follow the coffin to the railway station. Special delegations were appointed to accompany his body to Paris. It is a rather interesting thought that Antokolski's body was brought from Paris to St. Petersburg; Guenzburg's was taken from St. Petersburg to Paris! What sad comings and goings; is it not a terrible symbol of the aimless wanderings of the Jewish people?

Be that as it may, the Board of Management decided to preserve the baron's memory in St. Petersburg as well, with some sort of monument. Ac-

The Guenzburg stone

cording to Jewish tradition, however, it is not permitted to erect a memorial that is not over the grave itself. So they agreed to put the stone in place without any inscription. In this way, people would still remember that remarkable man.

According to another version, it is not a memorial to Horace Guenzburg but to his son David, his successor in public affairs. And in fact David is buried here. It would appear that before he died, he made a last wish declaring that he wanted no inscription on his tombstone: "Let people remember me for my deeds." (Another variation of this is "The monument to my memory will be the cemetery prayerhouse that I built.")

If we proceed from the Guenzburg stone along Garevaya Avenue to the left, and then turn right along Slutzkaya Avenue, in the second row to the right we shall see a gray granite obelisk without photograph and without any star, either five pointed or six pointed. The inscription on it reads: "Vera Klimentievna Slutzkaya, 1880–1917. Member of Communist Party of the Soviet Union from 1912, Professional Revolutionary, active participant in the Great October Socialist Revolution." From the *Bolshaya Sovietskaya Entsiklopedia,* 3rd edition, we learn that Vera Klimentievna Slutzkaya (Bertha Bronislavovna) was born in Minsk and was killed on October 30, 1917, near Tsarskoye Selo (today the town of Pushkin) while transporting medical supplies to Red Guard detachments during the suppression of the counter-revolutionary rebellion of Kerensky-Krasniy. *The History of the Jewish Workers' Movement in Russia,* by M. Buchbinder (1925), states that Bertha Slutzkaya was first arrested in Minsk in 1898, as one of fifty-six members of the Bund of Bielorussia and Poland. In 1901 her case came up officially and she was released but ordered to report daily to the police.

Apparently the Bund, being entirely nationalistic by composition (although not in its program) did not satisfy her; within a year she transferred her allegiance to the RSDRP (Russian Social Democratic Workers' Party). It is of interest to note that according to the *Bolshaya Sovietskaya Entsiklopedia,* Slutzkaya was a member of the Communist Party of the Soviet Union from 1902, ten years earlier than the date shown on the tombstone. The contradiction is related to the development of Soviet historiography. Previously the date of the formation of the Soviet Communist Party was reckoned as 1912, the year of the formal separation into Bolsheviks and Mensheviks. Now they take the year of the actual split at the London Conference in 1902.

Slutzkaya was a dentist by profession. She took an active part in the abortive revolution of 1905 in Minsk and St. Petersburg, was a member of the militant organization of the RSDRP in London (1907), and carried on party work in St. Petersburg. From 1909 to 1912 she continued her activity in Germany and Switzerland until she was arrested and deported back to Russia. After the February (1917) Revolution, Slutzkaya became a member of the Petrograd committee of the RSDRP (B), secretary of the Vassilevsky Ostrov District Committee of the Party, and took part in the work of the Sixth Congress of the RSDRP (B). John Reed mentions her in his book *Ten Days That Shook the World.*

The memorial to five war victims

After the Revolution, the confectionery factory in Petrograd was named after her, and when the towns of Russia had their names changed in honor of the revolutionary Bolsheviks, her name was temporarily perpetuated; Petrograd became Leningrad, Yekaterinburg became Sverdlovsk, Yelizavetgrad became Zinovievsk (now Kirovograd), Gatchina became Trotsk (now again Gatchina), Ligovo became Uritsk (now again Ligovo), and Pavlovsk became Slutzk (now again Pavlovsk). There were, then, two places called Slutzk: one was the old Lithuanian-Bielorussian town from which Vera Klimentievna's family had taken their surname; the other was the little town near Tsarskoye Selo, where she was killed.

Not far from Slutzkaya Avenue, on the parallel Zelenaya Avenue, it is possible to notice a black vertical gravestone with an inscription: "Mikhail Ignatyevitch Kulisher passed away on the 29 of November 1919." There is no other comment. Nor was any further comment needed, as everyone in St. Petersburg knew Kulisher. He was descended from a family of intellectuals that gave several prominent figures to Russia.

Mikhail Kulisher himself was a widely educated person, known as a historian, a sociologist, an ethnographer, a journalist, and a Jewish public figure. He represented a famous generation of Jews to whom Russian Jews and Russia itself are obliged. He was always among the leaders of various societies for enlightenment (for example, OPE, IEO). Recalling his nature, contemporaries usually use such epithets as "effusive," "passionate," "ardent," "enthusiastic," and "devoted to social interests."

On the committee of OPE, Kulisher took up the position of a moderate assimilationist. All his life he wrote articles for the Russian Jewish press, including *Den* (Day) in Odessa, *Rassvet* (Dawn) (1879) in St. Petersburg, and *Zarya* (Dawn) in Kiev. He also made a big contribution to the development of Jewish secular education in Russia — elementary, secondary, and highest as well. He was always busy compiling Jewish textbooks, working out educational programs, and organizing educational activities. Kulisher's ideal was to make a school teach both Jewish knowledge and contemporary European science.

At OPE gatherings, there were frequent lectures on Jewish literature and history. And everyone knew that Kulisher was one of the most interesting lecturers. His energy, and his natural vitality, gave him the strength to work until he was more than seventy years of age, at which time he wrote a book on the emancipation of French Jewry, several articles on the history of Jews in Russia, and many other articles, right up to his death.

At one point in our excursion we come to a tombstone with the following inscription:

In Everlasting Memory

Rosa Lurie-Gelb
Max Gelb
   Auschwitz
Yosef Lurie
   Stalingrad
Moisei Danishevski
   Krasniy Bor outside Leningrad
Yasha Aviosor
   Petsamo

A gathering on Holocaust Memorial Day at the memorial to five war victims, May 1984

Other than that, there is nothing, neither dates nor epitaph; but it is clear that this is the last war, that this is the Holocaust, that this is the six million, that this is that same tragedy that we have lived through. It must never be forgotten. Starting in 1982, the Jews of Leningrad decided to try to commemorate the Holocaust. They now meet each year at this tombstone, as a symbolic memorial to the six million killed. The day they have chosen is Holocaust Memorial Day on the Jewish calendar.

In the far right corner of the cemetery there are two communal graves from the time of the last war. One is of sailors of the Baltic Fleet; the other is of residents of Leningrad who perished during the blockade. As these graves are in the Preobrazhensky Cemetery, it is possible to assume that Jews are buried there. So if you wish to pay homage to the memory of the fallen, you can go to the general memorial at the communal grave in Leningrad, or come here to this metallic network of wire, which perhaps symbolizes barbed wire fences.

By the far right corner of the prayerhouse there is a gray granite obelisk. The Russian part of its inscription reads: "Rabbi Abram Ruvimovitch Lubanov, 1888 – August 20, 1973."

Rabbi Lubanov was descended from the Lubavitcher Hasidim, those who are still known as the Lyadovsky (that is, from Lyady) Hasidim, or as the Habbadniks (Habbad Hasidim), whose "Tzadik" today lives in Brooklyn. After receiving a good Talmudic education in a Hasidic yeshivah, Lubanov became a rabbi at precisely the time when it would be difficult to imagine a worse occupation. During the thirties he was sent to prison and was released in 1943, when the war was at its height. From then on, for thirty years without a break, right up to his death, he was the leader of the Leningrad synagogue.

The Jews at that time were living on the razor's edge. The war, then the murder of Mikhoels in Minsk in 1948, followed by the killing of the Jewish writers, then "The Doctors' Plot"—the list is endless. It was not always possible every year even to get unleavened bread for the Passover. In the post that he filled, Rabbi Lubanov had to be possessed of not only religious erudition but also of strength of character, enormous authority, and great personal courage. Judging from the stories told by those who knew him, Abram Ruvimovitch did possess these qualities. He was tall, gray-haired, with the marble-like features of a fighting man (like Moses), and he had a deep, penetrating look. His word was law for the man in the street. At the same time he had the ability to talk easily with simple folk so that they were able to feel psychological comfort from his very presence, and, inspired with trust in the rabbi, they shared with him their secrets and their needs and sought his advice.

Leningrad rabbi Abram Lubanov

To this day, Rabbi Lubanov's name is famed in legends among orthodox believers. Tales are told of many instances confirming his indisputable authority, his strength of character, his incorruptibility, and so on. In circumstances of difficult living conditions people came to Lubanov for *din-Torah* (judgment through the Torah), although officially he was not empowered to give any judgments. His verdict was not binding on anyone, and in fact the disclosure of the very existence of such a court of judgment could have resulted in the most serious of consequences for both sides. Nevertheless, Lubanov did sit in judgment, giving verdicts according to the Torah, and his decisions were carried out. After his death, but only following strong intervention from American Jewry, the community was able to receive permission from Moscow for Lubanov to be buried in the Jewish cemetery, where no funerals had taken place for a long time. So that his grave here is the very last one, and it is situated not just anywhere, but in a place of honor.

On the fourth grave behind the Warshawski vault there is a tall tombstone of pink marble on which are inscribed the names of a dynasty of doctors: father, son, and grandson, "Doctor of Medicine Isaak Alexandrovitch Dembo. Born 1846, died 1906. Doctor of Medical Sciences, Professor Grigory Isaakovitch Dembo. Born 8. IV. 1872, died 8. XI. 1939. Yosif Grigorievitch Dembo, 1912–1978." The most well known of them was Isaak Alexandrovitch. He was born in Kovno to an orthodox family and given the usual religious education, but then he began to study secular sciences and graduated from the Medico-Surgical Academy (1870). During the Russo-Turkish War Dembo saw active service with the army as a volunteer doctor. From 1881 to 1883 he studied at clinics in Paris, Vienna, and Berlin, and he published his results as "On the Question of the Independence of the Contraction of the Womb from the Cerebro-Spinal Nervous System." He established his own independent center for uterine contraction, the Dembo Center. He was particularly noted, however, for his comparative study of the Jewish method of cattle slaughter (Shechita).

What is the significance of such a question? Why should a scientist, even if he is a true believer, interest himself in such a problem, which at first glance seems to be a private one? Who asks a farmer how he rounds up his pigs or his cows? What is the difference as to who slaughters cattle in what way?

The fact of the matter is that this question has been exploited by anti-Semites in their propaganda. They declared that the Jews torture animals before killing them and that then the meat goes putrid more quickly. They even organized a conference of the Russian Association for the Protection of Animals (1891) to discuss the "humanitarian aspects" of Jewish ritual slaughter.

At that time there were those who believed that it was possible to justify oneself to anti-Semites. Isaak Alexandrovitch was one of these. He applied for permission to carry out experiments on dogs in the laboratory of I. P. Pavlov; he himself carried out a large number of experiments and conducted anatomical dissections, studied methods of cattle slaughter at various abattoirs in Europe, and made extensive reports to scientific bodies as well as to the aforementioned conference. He wrote a series of pamphlets, including one in Russian on the "Anatomical and Physiological Bases of Various Methods of Slaughter." In his many years of gathering evidence, there was practically nothing that he did not do! This work of Dembo is recalled in the inscription in Hebrew on the reverse side of the gravestone. However, it is doubtful whether the scientist managed to convince or change the minds of those who built their opinions not on facts, but on hatred, not on the results of laboratory investigations, but on falsifications of the genre of *The Protocols of the Learned Elders of Zion.*

In St. Petersburg, Isaak Alexandrovitch was a congregation elder during the time of the building of the Choral Synagogue. His son, Professor Grigory Isaakovitch Dembo, also played an active part in the life of the Jewish community. His name is to be found on the staff of the Jewish Almshouse, named after M. A. Guenzburg, and of the Jewish Orphanage, both of which were on Vassilevsky Ostrov.

One must add that apparently questions relating to the humanitarianism of the Jewish method of animal slaughter are still being raised to this day. This is confirmed by the experience of this tombstone, which has frequently been vandalized. What is there to be said? Hooligans are the same the world over. They sneak in, smash and destroy, defile and profane, and slink away. An example of this sort of vandalism is described in the novel of Grigory Kanovitch *Candles in the Wind* (1982, Moscow, Sovietsky Pisatyel). His hero, Daniil, watches while local peasants in the Jewish cemetery of a Lithuanian town occupied by the Germans uproot and smash the gravestones with crowbars. Daniil says:

> I only managed to read on the black granite "Zalman Katzenelson 1876–1936." Where have they taken you, Reb Zalman? I was overtaken with a fit of shivering. Let them steal gold, I thought, let them torment us with hunger, let them hang a yellow patch round our necks, only let them not lay a hand on our dead. The dead are all equal. The dead all belong to one tribe — the tribe of the dead — and there is no counting!

We have looked at a number of tombstones in the Jewish Preobrazhensky Cemetery. We could see even more. We did not stop by the graves of the famous Soviet surgeon, Professor Mikhail Isaakovitch Kuslick (1898–1965), located on Gertsena Avenue between Lipovaya and Luzhskaya Avenues. We could also have stopped at the tombstone of the director of education and Yiddish teacher in the last Leningrad Jewish school on Vassilevsky Ostrov, Lev Marcovitch Yohelchuck (1874–1955), on Lvovskaya Avenue to the right of the communal war graves; or at the tombstone of a historian of Russian Jewry, Yuly Issidorovitch Gessen (died 1939), on Zabornaya Avenue, right side; or one of the first Hebrew teachers in Leningrad after World War II, Leah Lurye, near the corner of Glavnaya and Nevskaya Avenues, to the right; or the tombstone of a famous collector of old Jewish books and manuscripts, Councillor of State

Lev Friedland: his vault is behind the grave of Burak and Frisno. Also in the cemetery is the grave of an outstanding performer of Yiddish songs, Appelbaum, as well as the graves of several actors of the imperial theaters.

Many graves have not been preserved. Some who died were buried elsewhere. Regarding what sort of graves, we cannot even definitely say whether they have any or not. So far they have not been found. And as to the location of the burial place of those who perished during the war, the revolution, pogroms, terror—nothing whatsoever is known.

In Volkov there is no known grave of Nota Khaimovitch Notkin. It long ago disappeared in the Volkov Cemetery.

There is no known grave of the poet Simeon Frug. He died in Odessa in 1916 and was buried there, but his tombstone was removed in the last war by the Rumanian occupying forces. It is now in Israel.

There is no grave here in Leningrad of Horace Guenzburg, who did not want to be buried in the place where so much suffering was borne by the Jewish people. He willed that his body should be borne away from the birthplace of Beilis to the birthplace of Dreyfus and there interred.

There is no grave here, either, of Alexander Isayevitch Braudo (1864–1924), formerly deputy-director of the Public Library, a man of encyclopedic education, and a leading fighter for equal rights for the Jews. He died very suddenly while on a mission to London. Lev Sternberg, at a memorial gathering for Braudo, said of him: "Alexander Isayevitch was, in a moral respect, the complete and perfect representative of human culture, that culture which at the present time, is everywhere going into decline." It is said that Braudo's body was brought to Leningrad and buried here, but so far we have not managed to find his grave.

There is no grave here of Simon Dubnow (1860–1941), who lived a long and fruitful life, the outstanding historian of the Jews of Poland, Lithuania, and Russia, political activist, founder of the Jewish People's Party, author of many books and articles, translated into a very large number of languages. He died a very old man in 1941, in the ghetto of Riga, murdered by the Nazis, not wanting to be saved at the expense of other lives.

There is no grave here of Israel (Srul) Leizerovitch (Sergei Lazaryevitch) Zinberg (1873–1938). He was head of the principal chemical laboratory of the Putilov Factory, as well as a historian and active promoter of Jewish enlightenment and education. After the Revolution, Zinberg continued to work with OPE and became secretary of the Jewish University. He was arrested in 1938, sent to the East, and died shortly afterward in a camp near Vladivostok.

The remarkable Jewish artist Anatoly (Tanhum) Lvovich Kaplan (1902–1976) is buried by a half-ruined church in the neighboring cemetery named in honor of and "To the Memory of the Victims of January 9."* A draftsman and lithographer, Kaplan was inspired by both Jewish tradition and Russian folk-

---

* "Bloody Sunday," the worst of the clashes between the authorities and the people during the 1905 Revolution.

lore. He illustrated the works of Sholem Aleikhem and produced a series of lithographs, *Views of Leningrad,* during the wartime siege.

So there are not many graves here. But far worse is the fact that today people often do not remember, or even do not know some of those who lie buried here.

I would like to round off this tour through the Jewish Preobrazhensky Cemetery with some verses written by Yosef Brodsky about twenty-five years ago, when the cemetery was situated at the very outskirts of the town and even to get to it was no simple matter.

> The Jewish cemetery near Leningrad.
>   A crooked fence of rotting plywood.
> Beyond the crooked fence, lying side by side
>   Are artists, merchants, musicians, revolutionaries.
>
> They sang for themselves.
>   They saved up for themselves.
> They died for others.
>   But first they paid their taxes, and paid their respects to the policeman,
> And in this world of useless materialism,
>   They discussed the Talmud and remained steadfast idealists.
>
> Perhaps they saw more.
>   Perhaps they believed with blind faith.
> But they taught their children to be patient
>   And they remained stubborn.
> And they did not sow any corn.
>
> They never sowed any corn
>   They simply lay themselves down
> Like seed, in the cold, cold ground,
>   And fell asleep forever.
> And then they were covered with earth,
>   And candles were lighted,
> And on the Day of Prayers of Remembrance for the Dead
>   Hungry old men with high-pitched voices,
> Gasping from the cold, called out for tranquility.
>   They sought and they found it — in the decomposition of the body.
> They remembered nothing.
>   They forgot nothing.
> Beyond the crooked fence of rotting plywood,
>   At a distance of four kilometers from the tramway terminus.

Jewish Graves in Leningrad and Its Suburbs

In addition to those in the Preobrazhensky Cemetery and a part of Volkov Cemetery, Jewish graves can be found at many cemeteries in Leningrad and its suburbs. For example, the famous Bolshevik revolutionaries, Uritsky and Volodarsky, are buried on Mars Field in the special necropolis for the victims of the two revolutions of 1917. A sculptor, Ilia Juentzburg, and a pilot, Captain Plotkin,* are both buried in the grounds of the Alexander-Nevsky monastery. The grave of a member of the first State Duma, Mikhail Gertzenstein, killed by the Black Hundreds, is on the Gulf of Finland near Zelenogorsk (former Tereoki).

It is hardly possible to find any cemetery in Leningrad now without at least a few Jewish graves. That is true even more of the communal graves of wars and revolutions, where many people were buried together. The most remarkable place of that kind is the Peskarevsky memorial cemetery in Leningrad.

There are also some specifically Jewish plots in several suburban cemeteries, among them the cemeteries in Sestroretsk, in Luga, in Petrokrepost, and in Pavlovsk, as well as the Jewish plot in the Pushkin cemetery and some important Jewish graves in the cemetery of Komarovo.

The town of Pushkin (former Tsarskoye Selo) is one of the oldest places of Jewish residence near St. Petersburg. Because of the tsar's summer palace, there were always many troops and military barracks here. So, from the first year of the military conscription for Jews (1827), Jewish soldiers lived in Tsarskoye Selo. After the end of their military service, many of them stayed in the town as craftsmen, tailors, and other tradesmen because the closeness to the center of power provided them with many opportunities to earn money.

There was a synagogue here at Tsarskoye Selo, and a piece of land at the Kazanskoe cemetery was set aside for Jewish graves. A few Jewish graves survive at this cemetery. One of them, dated 1865, is possibly the earliest one in the whole Leningrad district. Among other graves are those of Sergeant-Major of the Life Guards, Imperial Family Battalion, Knight of the Order of Saint George Shimon Tcherkassky (1840–1896); the Jewish-Russian writer David Eizman (1869–1922); and Abram Yakobson (1900–1974), once the highly respected director of Children's House No. 2 for orphans (later House No. 49), where he worked from 1930 to 1967. An epitaph on his grave reads: "Your fatherly love and kindness warmed our childhood and youth."

When the Germans occupied Pushkin in 1941, they shot all the Jewish residents. The exact place of the shooting is not yet known.

The town of Sestroretsk was a popular resort on the shore of the Gulf of Finland and a border town on the Russian side of the frontier with Finland. According to the regulations as they existed in Finland, even when a Jew had a residence permit to live in St. Petersburg, he still had to get a special permit from the Finnish authorities even to visit Finland; so Jews usually did not move farther away from the capital, but stayed in Sestroretsk for the summer.

On a prerevolutionary map of the town, a synagogue and a Jewish cemetery are marked. The remains of the cemetery can be seen even now. When traveling along the highway from Sestroretsk to Beloostrov, after crossing the

---

* Mikhail Nikolaevich Plotkin, born in 1912 in Klinsty, served as a pilot in the Baltic Fleet. On the night of August 7, 1941, he headed one of the two squadrons that took part in the first Soviet bombing raid on Berlin. He was killed in action over the Baltic Sea on March 6, 1942.

bridge over the railway, one can see to the left a military cemetery of the war. It is on the site of what was earlier a part of the old Jewish cemetery. Behind a wall surrounding the military cemetery are still visible the remains of the Jewish cemetery. It is in a deplorable state. Most of the tombstones have fallen down and are damaged. The earliest one is dated 1898. The tombstone of the leader of the community, Rabbi Baruch bar Yehuda Gutterman, is also defiled and damaged.

At the Jewish cemetery in Sestroretsk is a special row of gravestones of one family, Klyatchko: Eidel Klyatchko (1832–1910); Moisei Klyatchko (1832–1912); Isaak Rogov (1840–1912), a doctor of medicine; and Lev Klyatchko (1855–1913), another doctor.

The cemetery in Komarovo, near the town of Zelenogorsk, existed long ago. Its importance as a historical place grew after Anna Akhmatova, the Russian poet, was buried here. From that time on, many prominent Soviet scientists, writers, cultural workers, who had their datchas in Komarovo, were buried here. Among them are several prominent Jews: a surgeon-oncologist, Professor Semeon Holdin (1896–1975); a historian and professor at Leningrad University, Semeon Okhun (1908–1972); a writer, Lev Kantorovitch (1878–1958); a poet and translator, Alexander Gittovitch (1909–1966); a theater artist, Semeon Mandel (1907–1974); a Jewish artist, Natan Altman (1889–1970); author of the book *The Truth about Jews* (1928), Yefim Dobin (1901–1977).

In 1963 the Preobrazhensky Cemetery was closed. A new Jewish plot, named "To the Memory of the Victims of January 9," was allowed in the adjoining cemetery. But it too was soon filled up. The next piece of land for Jewish graves was allotted in the Southern Cemetery, but in the early 1980s it too was filled and the authorities refused to allocate any other site until the summer of 1986, when a new plot was given for Jewish burial, this time in the Kovalevo cemetery.

We have now followed the route of the last of our excursions around Jewish St. Petersburg. We are tired, and that is not surprising. A journey several miles long lies behind us. A journey with its successes and its achievements, disappointments and losses. But, truth to tell, we did not have to hurry anywhere; we had no need to hurry for fear of being late for the performance at the Jewish theater, since the Jewish theater is gone, long ago, and the actors are all long dead. We were not pushed by the knowledge that the library, full of precious Jewish books, would close its doors in our faces, since it has been closed for many years, and no one knows the whereabouts of its books. The most recent newspapers and journals with news about the cultural life of the Jews of our town were sold out over half a century ago, so we have no need to hurry to join the queue at the newspaper stand. The route of our excursions has been a journey through the graveyard, past the graves of our forefathers, who lie, unmarked, with no gravestones or memorial plaques. But still it was a journey worth taking.

The Fontanka Canal, from a painting by M. Dobuzinsky, 1909

PART TWO

PERSONALITIES

THREE SPECIAL RESIDENTS

SIMON DUBNOW

During the course of these excursions we have frequently mentioned the name of Semyon (Simon) Markovitch Dubnow, the Jewish historian, publicist, literary critic, and public figure who lived a long and fruitful life. What is implied by these words?

First, as a "historian," he created a new method of recording Jewish history. He collected and published thousands of documents, wrote *A Universal History of the Jews* (in ten volumes) and *The History of the Jews in Poland, Lithuania, and Russia,* participated in creating the *Yevreiskaya Entsiklopedia* (The Jewish Encyclopedia) and the first volumes of the *History of the Jewish People* (the later volumes were never published), edited the journal *Yevreiskaya Starina* (Jewish Antiquity), and did much, much more.

Before Dubnow, there were hardly any historians of the Jews of Eastern Europe, with the exception of Orshansky and Bershadsky. Although his books may now seem rather verbose, still no serious work can be found on the history of the Jews of Poland, Lithuania, and Russia that does not quote Dubnow and use the facts and figures in his works.

Second, regarding the "publicist and literary critic," it would be difficult to find a St. Petersburg Jewish publication from 1880 to 1920, from the moderate *Russky Yevrei* (The Russian Jew) to the Zionist *Rassvet* (Daybreak), that did not contain one of Dubnow's literary or polemic articles. His main journal, however, was *Voskhod,* on which he worked under the pseudonym *Kritikus.* In his articles he fought against anti-Semitism and insisted on the right of the Jews to national autonomy. He fought for the reform of Jewish communal life, argued against assimilation, and promoted the development of a national literature.

Third, in referring to the "public figure," we mean that throughout his life Dubnow closely followed developments in both Russian and world Jewry. He was always an active participant in public life, and there is no hint about him of the professor shut away in his study. In his countless articles and books and in the journals edited by him, he persistently argued with his opponents, convinced, proved, and educated. Though he did not even hold a diploma of formal education, he still delivered hundreds of public lectures on various topics. He was the chairman of the Jewish Literary Society and vice-chairman of the Jewish Historical-Ethnographic Society. He interpreted the past and the present of the Jewish people in an independent way. He developed the theory of "autonomism," which from his philosophical and historical points of view he transformed into a social and political science on which he based the Jewish People's Party.

Fourth, regarding "a long and fruitful life," it is hard to imagine such a rich human life, eighty years long, which began in 1860, in the heyday of the liberalism of Alexander II and came to a sudden end in 1941 with a Nazi bullet on the streets of German-occupied Riga. He lived his life as an active champion of education and the reform of Judaism, hoping for the rapid development of general brotherhood, and ended with a feverish attempt to record the details of the Holocaust in Germany, to which he himself, alas, became a witness and a victim.

Dubnow was born in Mstislavl on the second day of the Jewish New Year 5621 (October 2, 1860). His grandfather, Ben-Zion Dubnow, was the spiritual leader of Mstislavl. His forefathers had lived in Dubno in Volhynia from the middle of the seventeenth century.

Dubnow first came to St. Petersburg in June 1880 to continue his education. From then until 1922 his life was closely tied to the town. And although from 1889 to 1906 he lived for the most part in either Odessa or Vilna, during those years he regularly visited St. Petersburg. He failed to pass the examination for a course at the classical Gymnasium, so he changed his plans and decided to devote himself to the study of history and journalism. In 1882 he became one of the key individuals on *Voskhod,* which for many years had been the only Russian-language journal for the "new" Jewish intelligentsia. Both Dubnow and the journal initially supported the views of the Haskala, which was at that time undergoing a severe crisis because of the events of 1881 and 1882. The assimilated intelligentsia had become disillusioned with the old ideals (that education in itself would bring equality and happiness to the people) and sought the solution in a return to traditional life, or in baptism, or in revolution, or in Zionism. All those who believed in and still maintained the views of the 1860s gathered round *Voskhod*.

In one of Dubnow's earliest articles, "What Sort of Self-Emancipation Do the Jews Need?"—apparently a public rejoinder to Pinsker's Palestinophile pamphlet "Auto-Emancipation," he argues that the Jews had no need of Palestine or of a separate state, but above all required an internal reform of religion and way of life. In this article, he sees the Jews not as a nation, but only as a religious community. And even religion, in his opinion, required renewal, since the Talmud, and in particular the rabbinate, had confused and complicated the Laws of Moses to an enormous extent and thus isolated the Jews from other peoples. It was necessary to "eliminate tribal isolation and aloofness, held sacred by the Rabbinate, which could be achieved by undermining their foundations and, possibly, by full civil assimilation with the surrounding non-Jewish population." This is what the young twenty-three-year-old scholar and cosmopolitan recommended for his people. In the same spirit was his mature article "The Reform of Secondary Education," in which he proposed the abolition of the "cheders," if necessary, by the state and by force.

However, by the end of the 1880s, Dubnow and the journal *Voskhod* had moved over to a nationalistic position. This transition was probably influenced by the deteriorating domestic position of the Jews in Russia, the maturing of the author, and certainly by the intensive study of Jewish history that had already seized him by the early 1880s. His early works, such as "Shabbetai Tzevi and Pseudo-Messianism in the Seventeenth Century," "Yakov Frank and the Christianizing Sect," and several articles on Hasidism, defined the main area of his research as the history of the Jews of Russia and Poland, which had been only little studied at that time. In a pamphlet in 1891 he appealed to the public to collect historical documents. These materials began to reach him, and the finding and publication of documents became an important aspect of his life. Supplements to *Yevreiskaya Starina* (Jewish Antiquity), such as "The Regional Pinkas of the Va'ad of the Main Jewish Communities of Lithuania"* and "Registers and Inscriptions," contained some of the materials gathered by the historian. His life itself also provided new historical material. His diary, *Kniga Zhizni: Vospominaniya i Razmishlenniya* (The Book of My Life: Recollections and Reflections), was justifiably subtitled "Materials for the History of My Time" by the author. These are invaluable memoirs, not least for excursions round the town. Let us look at some extracts from Vol. 2, which covers the years 1903 to 1922:

> We moved from the noisy 8th Liniya to the much quieter 18th Liniya and we found ourselves in one of those pigeon coops of which there are so many in St. Petersburg. The flat was in the courtyard wing of a five-story building looking out onto a narrow, deep courtyard-cum-well, which even in summer lets in

---

* *Pinkas* means "minute or record book"; *Va'ad* means "committee." Both are Hebrew words.

little light; in autumn and winter the days are transformed into perpetual twilight.

In town we found ourselves in a different situation. We moved from the cramped flat on the edge of Vassilevsky Ostrov and rented a spacious flat in the newly built house of my friend the lawyer Mandel, on Petrogradskaya Storona (the Petrograd Side).

In the years 1914 to 1916 Dubnow often reminisced about the 1880s, his youth, his work with *Voskhod,* his friends of that time, and he relived the past.

Yesterday afternoon I was walking about the "Kivrei Avot" (graves of our forefathers). In the gray half-slumbering hours I wandered around the Nikolsky Garden, went along the Via Dolorosa of 1883 and 1885–1886, from the former flat on Srednaya Podyatcheskaya (the old yellow building at No. 16 is still standing there), over the little Lions' Bridge, past the Kazan quarter, and to the *Voskhod* offices. Images of the past flooded into my thoughts as, in the drizzling rain, I hurried past these sepulchers of the past.

I then went with Tch. over the "Kivrei Avot" to that two-story building on Troitskaya Church Square by Ismailovsky Prospekt, where Frug and I spent the autumn, winter and spring of 1883–1884 together. The dilapidated old house still looks the same as it was but it is now occupied by a factory! [The house no longer exists.]

I have finished "Recollections of Frug" and have thus twice "sat Shiva" a two-fold mourning. Today I went once again to the district where we once lived. I crossed the well-remembered Lions' Bridge to Offitserskaya ulitsa, went up the stairs of No. 17 for a few moments to where the offices of *Voskhod* were in 1882–1885, and then went across Bolshoi Theatre Square where the print shop and editorial offices were from 1886. I once again wandered through the graveyard of the past and those minutes were full of wonderful sacred feelings.

As we have already mentioned, by the late 1880s and early 1890s, Dubnow's views had become more nationalistic. We could go further and say that by the end of the nineteenth century the mature views of the historian had ripened, as had also his attitude toward Jewish history, the nation, its literature, the past, and the future of the people.

Dubnow's history of the Jews is not a history of legislation about the Jews, as Orshansky's was, nor is it a history of religion, as with Graetz, neither is it an unbroken chain of suffering and undeserved persecution, as German Jewish historians portrayed it in the nineteenth century, somehow trying to justify themselves to the Christian reader. Dubnow tried to paint a full-blooded picture of the evolution of Jewish life, with all its chiaroscuro of dark times and bright, covering its economy, politics, daily life, religion, and culture. The people itself takes an active part in his history and is not only the victim of powerful neighbors. Even though this approach was not wholly successful, no one after Dubnow has tried to write Jewish history in the old way.

Dubnow's views on Jewish literature, as on the literature of any language, written by Jews for Jews, are similar to modern concepts. He welcomed the revival of Hebrew as the Jewish language from time immemorial, but he also

Simon Dubnow

appreciated the role and significance of Yiddish literature in the Diaspora as accessible to the most poorly educated reader. He accepted Jewish literature in Russian, German, and other languages, provided that they were close to the Jewish reader.

Dubnow's philosophy, his outlook on life, by the beginning of this century, is best described in his *Letters on Old and New Jewry* — a collection of his articles from 1897 to 1907. There, he describes his theory of the development of nations, which, according to him, could be divided into three stages: (1) racial; (2) territorial/political (or social-autonomous); and (3) cultural and historical, or spiritual. In the first two stages a nation can disintegrate and disappear since its existence is dependent on external factors: community, territory, and statehood. The nation of the third type does not disintegrate if the spiritual elements are present in it, that is, culture and history. The further a nation advanced through the stages of its development, the greater would be the role played in its self-determination — not by economic and political factors, but by its spiritual and above all its national awareness. Dubnow considered the Jews to be the only example of the preservation of nationhood, despite the loss of state independence and the loss of their own common territory. They had passed through the second stage long ago — two thousand years ago — and were now a spiritual nation. Here Dubnow quotes the French Socialist reformer, François Fourier (1772–1837): "A nation is first and foremost a conglomeration of people who consider themselves to be one nation."

"Judaism," writes Dubnow, "is a complete phase of culture — an all-embracing philosophy [not only a religion]. One can be a Jew according to the Prophets, or according to the Talmud, or Maimonides, or the 'Shulkhan Arukh,' according to Mendelssohn or the Besht, even Spinoza or Geiger."* That is to say, any Jew, even a nonbeliever, can, as a rule, find ideas close to his own way of thinking inside Judaism." He continues: "If the definitive idea of all history is not inherent to the Jews as a nation, then certainly 'progressiveness' is inherent, an uninterrupted spiritual advancement without any periods of barbarism."

Throughout his book Dubnow stands firm on the right of the Jews to call themselves a nation, against the assimilationists. "Assimilation is not only a renunciation of the national interests of the Jews, it is also a denial of the individual freedom of the Jewish people and a denial of its equal standing among the international family of nations," (letter No. 2). The nationalism of the author's letters is not in any way a disparagement of other nations or disdain toward them but rather is a striving for the equality of his people among other free nations. "Acknowledge the freedom of any national individual as you would the freedom of your own nation, or: respect every other nationality as

---

* Shulkhan Arukh was the standard Jewish judicial code, dating from the sixteenth century; Barukh Spinoza was the Dutch Jewish philosopher born in Amsterdam in 1632, excommunicated in 1656, died in 1677; Abraham Geiger was the German reform rabbi (1810–1874).

you would your own." Dubnow considers that Jews cannot hope for the respect of other peoples unless they are patriots of their own people, "because respect is only accorded to a person who has respect for himself." Whereas "assimilation is a means of salvation of the Jewish people by national suicide" (letter No. 4).

But how can full civil equality be achieved while simultaneously assimilation in the Diaspora is rejected? After all, in Western Europe and partly also in Russia it was considered that emancipation of the Jews was the reward for national self-renunciation. How was it possible to rescue a people who had departed from religion, when it was only religion — that and nothing else — that had, over the centuries, preserved the Jews as a nation? For Dubnow, the answer to both questions was the same — to create a national party, to fight in the common front for national interests, to stand up for national cultural autonomy; that is, the functions of the disintegrating Jewish community must take on organizations of a new type.

In an effort to convince his reader of the justification of his words, Dubnow quotes from the speeches and articles of many public figures, among them non-Jews: the deputy of the Austrian Reichstag, Breiter, the American writer Mark Twain, the Czech professor Thomas Masaryk, and others. All these pronouncements lead to the one conclusion: the reason for the disastrous situation of the Jews lies precisely in the fact that they fight too passively (or even refuse to fight at all) for their national interests.

What does Dubnow understand by national-cultural autonomy?

In letter No. 5 ("On National Education") he defines autonomy as the self-rule of the community, freedom of language, and the autonomy of schools. In his opinion the Jews can and must attain these three elements of national life in whatever country they live. While fighting assimilation, Dubnow at the same time sharply disagrees with Zionism. He accepts the spiritual Zionism of Ahad Ha'am (on the establishment of a national-cultural center in Palestine). But he considers political Zionism (that is, Jewish statehood) to be not only Utopian, but also even harmful to the mass of the Jews. By a simple calculation of multiplying the maximum rate of emigration to Palestine up to 1898 by the number of years, taking into account natural growth and the most optimistic prognosis, Dubnow shows that even in the best circumstances there will not be more than half a million Jews in Palestine by the start of the twenty-first century. And what will happen to the remaining ten million Jews in Europe? For them Zionism would be a disappointment, an unattainable dream that would push them back toward assimilation. If it is only Palestine that can save the nation from oblivion, then "the Zionists do not have a high opinion of the Jewish people . . . , Zionism is a medicine for the weak. But it is a dangerous medicine if Utopia is not transformed into reality" (letter No. 6). And he adds "I do not feel the need to be a Palestinophile in order to remain a Jew." And then, without his realizing it, he comes close to Ahad Ha'am in polemics, and from there, even more sharply, he forecasts the Holocaust:

I readily accept that the handful of Jews in Palestine will live a "more fully national life" than in the Diaspora, and in advance I rejoice at this but I am concerned also with the fate of the mass of Jewry who will remain in the Diaspora. Or perhaps Palestine will be a sort of Noah's Ark where only a remnant of the Jews will be saved from a universal cultural tempest while all the rest will be drowned in the flood? But such a cruel sentence to be passed on the Diaspora does not, of course, come into the program of the spiritual Zionists [letter No. 7].

In his "Letters on Old and New Jewry," Dubnow discusses many other cardinal questions, vitally important for the Jewry of those times. We can find here a review of the Jewish press in Russia for the previous forty years, emigration to America, and a burning, penetrating analysis of the lessons to be learned from the pogroms in letter No. 12 ("The Lessons of Dreadful Days"), in which the author speaks with deep bitterness of the very modest reaction of the Russian public to the terrifying appearance of medieval barbarity.

How differently did the so-called "progressive-minded public" react to the pogroms and to the introduction of martial law in Poland. For the former (one thousand corpses) — a sigh of regret, here and there cries of indignation. For the latter (there were no fatalities) — organized strikes, protests and indignant resolutions, serious representations to the government.

In his book, Dubnow proposes as the first concrete steps toward the realization of national autonomism the formation of a "Jewish People's Party." This he did in fact create in 1906, from several former members of the Union for the Attainment of Equal Rights for the Jewish People in Russia. This party, as it happens, did not play any significant role in the life of Russian Jewry.

In addition to his scholarly and political activity, Dubnow did not stop for one single day from his communal, educational, and literary-critical activity. He wrote articles on the outstanding representatives of Jewish culture, among them "The Jewish Nekrassov" (about Gordon), "Luzzatto,"* and "Immanuil Rimsky." From 1908 he lectured in St. Petersburg at the Free High School of Professor Lesgaft, as well as at the Advanced Courses of Higher Jewish Studies (Courses on Oriental Studies for Jews) of Baron Guenzburg. After the 1917 Revolution he taught at the Jewish University of Petrograd.

One can imagine how hard it must have been for the sixty-two-year-old man to leave the town where he had spent his best years (twenty-five years) and all the more since he was prone to a highly sentimental and nostalgic appreciation of the past. Do you remember his words? "Today I was once again in the district where we used to live. I crossed the well-remembered Lions' Bridge . . . and went up the stairs of No. 17 for a few moments. . . . I once again wandered through the graveyard of the past."

* Moses Hayyim Luzzatto (the "Ramhal") was poet, kabbalist, and author of several ethical works. He was born in Padua in 1707, lived later in Amsterdam, and died in Palestine in 1746.

Dubnow's attitude to the October Revolution of 1917 was strictly negative. In his diaries he called the power of the Bolsheviks "boor-ocracy" *(khamokratiya)*; he was greatly worried by the participation of Jews in the Red Terror and predicted that the Jewish people would be held collectively responsible for that crime. In 1922 he left Russia.

Leaving the city he had lived in for so long, Dubnow went first to Lithuania to teach Jewish studies at Kovno University. Later he went to Berlin, where he published his *Universal History of the Jews* in English, French, Spanish, Yiddish, and Hebrew translations. At first the coming to power of the Nazis did not alarm him, and when he finally fled the persecution and terror in Germany, he left, not for America or Palestine, to both of which he had been invited, but to the Latvian capital, Riga, where he thought he would find it easier to work on the final volume of his Jewish history. It was in Riga that he was murdered at the very beginning of the Nazi occupation, refusing the chance to escape that was offered to him at the last moment. Legend has it that his last words were "Brothers, do not forget, remember everything that has happened! Brothers, commit this to memory!"

Clearly, with Dubnow's views "there was something not quite right," there was "something unforeseen." His "autonomism" disintegrated under the terrible blows inflicted on the Jews in World War II and now exists unconsciously only in the United States. However, the main task of the historian is not to foretell the future but conscientiously and honestly to record the present and to study the past. In that respect, Simon Dubnow's work is invaluable and will long be cherished:

> The ground is slipping away under our forbears' feet,
> In mighty Vilna, in Warsaw once so rich,
> And in the center of Talmudism, renownéd
> Volozhin.* Their grandsons
> Flee from the barbarians, increasing the Galut.
> They are seeking salvation from the legions of Rome—
> Some with fleeting foot, and some with the cunning of baptism.
>
> The poet, abandoned by the fugitive refugees
> Weeps bitterly over the devoted Shekhina
> Before those who have not yet fled
> Through weakness, stupidity, or downright laziness.
>
> The synagogues once thronged with crowds
> Batei-midrash, yeshivas, and yards
> Of boastful tsadikim, just like churchyards
> Now empty stand. No longer GOD, it is many gods
> That now are worshipped by the Israelites.

* Volozhin was a town in Bielorussia that acquired importance in Jewish life in Lithuania and Russia in the nineteenth century from its yeshivah "Etz Hayim."

"One third will die, one third emigrate, one third convert" — *
The oracles in bureaucratic uniforms
Yet more extreme become the orthodox,
This is no time for talmid-khokhoms
To proclaim their prophetic visions.

Deserted now are Vilna-Sura, and Pumbedita†
And no new Gaon has been born.
There occur pogroms after pogroms.
Lithuania had become almost a new Palestine.
But now — the Pale wipes out lives
And victim to the mindless antagonism
Falls not the first temple, nor yet the last.

Having escaped the Pale, the intellectual
In a German suit, in gray St. Petersburg,
Amid the bustle of the Petrogradsky Side
Or perhaps in the quiet of Vassilevsky Ostrov,
Tries to preserve as much as he can,
To collect, to remember, to record, and to leave to posterity.
A Josephus Flavius, but one who did not go over
To Titus's side. No. With his culture,
But not as voracious as that imperial servant.

He knows that even this horror will pass . . .
Sometime or other. Then his work
Will be looked for and for sure it will be read.

Day and night the historian works,
While on the street all is quiet and peaceful.
And there is a moment to sit and write
Of the appearance of the new Maccabees.

Perhaps I could contrast my own poetic lyricism with Dubnow's pessimism. In his book *Kniga Zhizni,* he wrote: "History and other things tie me to hated St. Petersburg," and again, in an entry dated January 29, 1916: "How agonizingly difficult is life in St. Petersburg, the normal Hades transformed by the war into the Inferno!"

We can now go on a special journey, visiting the places where this remarkable man lived and worked. We will start on the very day on which he first arrived in St. Petersburg, June 20, 1880.‡ That night, and for the first few weeks, he lived with his brother Vladimir (Wolf) in a room that they rented from a Jewish merchant, by the name of Malkin, beyond the Narvskaya Zas-

---

* "One third will die . . . ," the remark attributed to Pobedonostsev, the supreme procurator of the Holy Synod of the Russian Orthodox Church (1880–1905), speaking about the future of Russia's six million Jews.

† Sura, in southern Babylonia, a center of Torah studies, lost its preeminence to Pumbedita (on the Euphrates) at the end of the third century of the Christian Era.

‡ All dates prior to 1918 are according to the old-style calendar.

tava (Narva Gate). It was a provincial-style house with a small garden. Then until late September 1880 they lived in a rented room in a flat belonging to a Jewish family from Mstislavl, former neighbors of theirs, the Alexandrovs, at No. 6 Krasnoarmeiskaya (then called Rota Izmailovskogo Polka).

Dubnow soon became a regular reader at the Imperial Public Library on Ploshchad Ostrovskogo (then Alexandrovskaya) No. 1; the building is still there. In that same year, 1880, Dubnow and his brother often ate in the Jewish restaurant Dyeshovaya Kukhnya (literally, "Low-Price Cooking Dining Room"), which was on the corner of Prospekt Mayorova (then Voznesensky Prospekt) and Sadovaya ulitsa. A one-course meal cost seven kopecks; two courses were thirteen kopecks.

Issue No. 37 for 1880 of the weekly *Russky Yevrei* (Russian Jew) published the first report Dubnow sent from Mstislavl, with the subtitle "Public Affairs; Education; the Need for a Craft School."

In September 1880 Dubnow attended the trial in the case of of Ipollit Lyutostansky *versus* Alexander Zederbaum. Lyutostansky, a Jew who had first converted to Catholicism and then to Russian Orthodoxy, was the author of an anti-Semitic pamphlet on "The Use by the Jews of Christian Blood." Zederbaum, a well-known activist in the Jewish press, was the editor of *Ha-Melitz* (The Advocate) and had exposed in the press some shady business dealings of Lyutostansky. The latter took Zederbaum to court, accusing him of libel. The trial was held in the office of the justice of the peace. Zederbaum's lawyer was S. A. Andreyevsky, and the trial was conducted by Judge Trofimov, who rejected Lyutostansky's complaint. On appeal to a higher court, the session of justices of the peace confirmed the decision of the lower court.

That same September, 1880, Dubnow was accidentally caught up in a case of the theft of officially headed note paper, in which the owner of his flat, Alexandrov, was involved. He was arrested and taken to the Criminal Investigation Department (CID) at No. 24 Bolshaya Morskaya (now ulitsa Hertzena). From the CID, Dubnow was taken to the Spasskaya Police Divisional Prison at the corner of Sadovaya ulitsa and Bolshaya Podyacheskaya ulitsa (now Sadovaya ulitsa, 58/26), where he was imprisoned for four days. When he was released from prison in October 1880, he and his brother went to live in the flat of a relative, Emanuil (the steward of a Merchant of the First Guild), in a house on the corner of Sadovaya ulitsa and Pere'ulok Brinko (then Tairov). Now No. 44 Sadovaya, the building still stands. From late October, Dubnow rented a room on his own in a tiny, miserable flat of a worker's family on the third floor of the same house. He left there in the spring of 1881.

Until October 1881 (when he left to go to Mstislavl), Dubnow lived in a small room on the fourth floor of a grandiose house belonging to Likhachov, on the corner of what were then Yekateringofsky and Voznesensky Prospekts (now Prospekt Rimskogo-Korsakova 6/37, no longer extant). Dubnow later wrote in his memoirs:

Today has been a rare Saturday: complete rest. In the morning I visited the old "Pale" on printing business. I wandered along the Yekaterinensky Canal Embankment where I had lived in March–April 1881, near Kokushkin Bridge and walked past Tairov Pere'ulok where I had sheltered before then. It is the graveyard of my youthful sufferings and of my first literary impulses.

On May 11, 1881, Dubnow took the matriculation examination in the Classical Gymnasium No. 5 at what was then Yekateringofsky Prospekt No. 73 (the corner building after Prospekt Maclean). He failed to pass in arithmetic, however. In that same year, 1881, he was several times in the apartment of Mark Warshawski, an employee of *Rassvet*, on 4th Krasnoarmeiskaya (then 4th Rota).

In April 1882, on his return from Mstislavl, Dubnow lived at first in a Jewish hotel on Sadovaya ulitsa, near the Yusupov Garden. In this hotel, Jews were allowed to live for a short time without a registration permit. He then lived for a little while in Emanuil's flat at the corner of Prospekt Mayorova and Sadovaya ulitsa, as, for the purpose of remaining in St. Petersburg legally, he was registered as the "second domestic servant" of a writer, Warshawski. The "first domestic servant" was the poet Simeon Frug.

In 1882 and early 1883 Dubnow and his fiancée Ida moved in with a German family on 11th Rota Izmailovskogo Polka. There he had a large room with a balcony and she had another room, but soon after this they moved to Srednyaya Podyacheskaya ulitsa No. 16 (extant), where they lived as common-law man and wife.

In the autumn of 1883 Dubnow and Ida moved into two furnished rooms in an old house on Troitskaya Church Square, next to the big building on the corner of Izmailovsky Prospekt where the printshop and editorial offices of *Russky Yevrei* (Russian Jew) were located and where Dr. L. Kantor, the editor, lived. Simeon Frug lived in the next room. (The building has not survived.) Then in late April 1884, Dubnow left for Mstislavl.

From 1885 to 1886 Dubnow, now back in St. Petersburg, frequently changed his address: from mid-August 1885 to May 1886 he lived on Srednyaya Podyacheskaya ulitsa; in May 1886 he was on Liteiny Prospekt in Emanuil's flat, in one room together with Chaim Flekser (later known under the pen name A. Volynsky); he spent two days, December 6 and 7, 1886, in a hotel in Tsarskoye Selo; then, and after spending several days sleeping illegally either among relatives or at the editorial offices of *Voskhod* among piles of books and papers (No. 2 Teatralnaya Ploshchad, extant), Dubnow left for Vilna. He was again in St. Petersburg in late January 1888, when he probably lived with the Emanuils. He then left for Mstislavl again, to write the history of Hasidism.

From late December 1888 to the end of February 1889 Dubnow, again in St. Petersburg, lived with the Emanuils on Liteiny Prospekt. From 1888 to 1889, while doing research work on the history of Hasidism, he often worked in L.P. Friedland's bookstore at 3rd Liniya No. 4/8 on Vassilevsky Ostrov, apt. 8. The library itself was in Friedland's flat.

From August 30, 1890, to late September that year, Dubnow was again in St. Petersburg. Not having obtained a residential permit, however, he left for Odessa, where he lived for a while, before traveling back to Mstislavl, and then to Switzerland.

On May 29, 1902, Dubnow arrived in St. Petersburg for a brief stay, lodging with the Emanuils on the third floor of the house at the corner of Bolshaya Podyacheskaya and Sadovaya (then Bolshaya Podyacheskaya 31, extant).

The literary restaurant Maloyaroslavets on Bolshaya Morskaya ulitsa (now ulitsa Hertzena) No. 8 (extant) was the venue for periodic gatherings of the members of the editorial board of *Voskhod*. In May 1902 Dubnow was the guest of honor at such a dinner.

In late November 1905 when he arrived in St. Petersburg he again stayed with the Emanuils at the same address. He had come to take part in the Second Congress of the Union for the Attainment of Equal Rights for the Jewish People in Russia and, in February 1906, in the Third Congress. He again stayed with the Emanuils during his visit in August 1906. Then he discussed the possibility of teaching in the Free High School of Professor Lesgaft; he visited OPE and the grave of Hertzenstein in Terioki (Zelenogorsk). The last time that Dubnow lived on Bolshaya Podyacheskaya with his relatives was during the summer of 1907. Then he was visited by Baron David Guenzburg in regard to his application for a residential permit.

In August 1906 Dubnow attended a meeting of the Union for Equality in the apartment of the barrister G. B. Sliozberg at Kovensky Pere'ulok 17 (extant). The union was slowly dying. "Despondency," he later recalled, "reigned in the executive where not long ago a lively intellectual debate flourished, where an army of fighters was being prepared for the State Duma."

Dubnow often visited the Jewish historian Yuri Gessen in his flat at No. 35 Basseinaya ulitsa (no longer extant), and even stayed the night there in August 1906 after a meeting of the Union for Equality.

On the eve of Sukkot, September 20, 1906, Dubnow and his wife returned from Vilna to St. Petersburg and stayed in a hotel on Izmailovsky Prospekt next to the former editorial offices of *Russky Yevrei*. Then, from October 1906, the couple lived at No. 1 Malaya Podyacheskaya ("near my former place of residence on Srednyaya Podyacheskaya and by Lions' Bridge [Lviny Mostik]").

From October to December 1906, Dubnow held the professorial chair and lectured in the faculty of Jewish history in Professor Lesgaft's Free High School at No. 32 Prospekt Malkina (then Angleesky Prospect — the building is extant). He prepared his lectures on ancient history in the Asiatic Museum of the Imperial Academy of Sciences (Universitetskaya Naberezhnaya 5).

On December 26, 1906, Dubnow went to Terioki and Vyborg for a few days. In Vyborg he stayed at the hotel Belvedere where, five months earlier, the Vyborg Appeal had been signed. He was back in St. Petersburg on January 1, 1907. In each of the summer months from 1907 to 1911, Dubnow and his family lived on the estate of Linki "with a number of good dwelling houses," near the village of Usikirki, a station on the railway line to Vyborg, and next to Lake Kirko-Yarveh. Here he was visited at his dacha by Lev Katzenelson and the rabbi from Odessa, Kh. Chernovits, who persuaded him to stay on the editorial board of the *Yevreiskaya Entsiklopedia*.

In late summer 1907, Dubnow moved to Vassilevsky Ostrov, 8th Liniya No. 35 (then No. 33, extant). "As I was expecting a more or less successful outcome to my application" (for a residential permit), he later recalled, "I decided in advance to rent a new apartment in St. Petersburg. We left the crowded flat in the grubby house on Malaya Podyacheskaya ulitsa and moved to Vassilevsky Ostrov, where we took a four-roomed apartment on 8th Liniya."

The Courses on Oriental Studies organized by Baron David Guenzburg opened in January 1908 in the Jewish Gymnasium on ulitsa Myasnikova (then Nikolsky Pere'ulok) No. 7. Dubnow was one of the lecturers. In 1908 the courses were transferred from the Gymnasium to Baron Guenzburg's house at No. 4 1st Liniya.

It was in the harbor on Gutuyevsky Ostrov, on board a large steamer bound for Stockholm, that Dubnow said farewell, on May 7, 1908, to Ahad Ha'am, the philosopher and Zionist, who was leaving for London in order to take over the management of the firm of tea brokers Wissotzky. Ahad Ha'am was leaving Russia forever. He was later to settle in Palestine.

On August 20, 1908, Dubnow took part at Prachechny Pere'ulok No. 6 in the first discussions on the future of the *Yevreiskaya Entsiklopedia*. The publishers, at whose editorial offices the meeting took place, were Brockhaus and Yefron. Dubnow participated in the editing of only the first volume, after which he decided not to do any more editorial work, in order to concentrate on his own academic work.

The founding meeting of the Jewish Historical-Ethnographic Society took place on November 16, 1908, in the Alexandrovsky Hall (now the Marriages Hall—"Venchalny Zal") of the St. Petersburg Choral Synagogue, at No. 2 Lermontovsky Prospekt (extant). The meeting was chaired by M. I. Kulisher; both Maxim Vinaver and Dubnow were on the platform. Vinaver was appointed chairman of the society, with Dubnow as his vice-chairman.

The Jewish Historical-Ethnographic Society met at first in Vinaver's apartment at ulitsa Kalyaeva No. 25 (then Zakharyevskaya), at apt. 13 (extant). Jewish public figures often met here to discuss pressing matters concerning Jewry and to work out the principles of coordinated action.

Early in 1909 Dubnow took part in the debates on the direction and content of the journal *Yevreisky Mir* (The Jewish World), which were held in the editorial offices at the printing works of Obshchestvennaya Polza (The Public Good). The building projected at a sharp angle onto the Fontanka at Bolshaya Podyacheskaya No. 39 (extant).

In the late spring of 1910 Dubnow moved to 18th Liniya No. 9 (extant).

The editorial offices of *Yevreiskaya Starina* (Jewish Antiquity) also moved there, with Dubnow as editor.

From 1908 to 1911, Dubnow was chairman of the Jewish Literary Society, located at 8th Sovietskaya (then 8th Rozhdestvenskaya) No. 25, apt. 12 (extant). The committee of the Jewish Literary Society usually met in the hall of the OPE school on ulitsa Dekabristov (then Offitserskaya ulitsa) 42 (extant) or in the communal hall of the Choral Synagogue. Dubnow also continued teaching the Courses of Oriental Studies, which were now held at No. 5 6th Liniya (extant).

In December 1911 Dubnow delivered a lecture on the significance of Jewish history to the Bestuzhev Higher Women's Courses at 10th Liniya 31/35 (extant). His daughter Sofia, a student here in 1904, had been expelled for her part in the student protest against professors who had signed a patriotic address to the government.

In late 1912 Dubnow moved to a new flat on the Petrograd side, ulitsa Skorokhodova 29 (then Bolshaya Monetnaya 21, extant). He later recalled:

> In town we found ourselves in a different situation. We moved from the cramped flat on the edge of Vassilevsky Ostrov and rented a spacious flat in the newly built house of my friend the lawyer Mandel. . . . This house is built in the Berlin style, with central heating and even with electric lighting. There was only one cultural convenience I couldn't get used to — the telephone. However hard it may have been to live in a large town without a telephone, I resisted all attempts to install these "ears in the wall" in my dwelling, through which, at any moment, the bustle of the street could burst in and destroy my concentration on my work.

Dubnow's daughter and her family lived in the same building, as did the owner of the building, Dubnow's lawyer friend, Benjamin Simeonovitch Mandel.

At the end of 1912 Dubnow was elected a member of the Central Committee of OPE (Zagorodny Pospekt 23, apt. 35). At the same meeting at which he was elected, a resolution was passed on the reform of "cheder" classes; taking part in these discussions was Chaim Nahman Bialik, who had just arrived from Odessa.

On May 14, 1914, in the hotel Astoria (ulitsa Herzena, then Bolshaya Morskaya 39, extant), Dubnow had his last meeting with Sholem Aleikhem, who had come from Lausanne for a lecture tour in Russia. They sat on the balcony on the fourth floor.

On July 31, 1914, Dubnow took part in a special assembly of Jewish public figures. It was held in Mandel's apartment at Skorokhovoda No. 29, for the purpose of discussing issues connected with the outbreak of war. Henceforth, meetings were continuous. Thus, on September 8, 1914, the first day of Rosh Hashanah 5675, Dubnow noted in his diary "from 3 to 8 P.M. a meeting at Kreinin's to discuss Polish-Jewish relations." This was at Ilyicha Pere'ulok, then

Kazachiy, 13/45 (extant). Then, on the evening of September 17, 1914, Dubnow attended a meeting "in one of the clubs on Nevsky Prospekt" held jointly with Russian opposition deputies to discuss Polish-Jewish relations.

On February 21, 1915, in the building that we know so well from an earlier excursion, No. 50 5th Liniya, Dubnow delivered a lecture to a meeting of the Jewish Historical-Ethnographic Society, in a hall filled to overflowing. His topic was "A Summary of Jewish History in Poland," and he noted in his memoirs how "I developed the following idea: the thesis of extra-citizenship and national autonomy in old Poland, and the opposing thesis of citizenship without national rights in the ideology of the new Poland and the synthesis of civil and national rights in the future Poland."

Dubnow's diary gives us a good guide to his movements and to our own wanderings in search of him. Maxim Vinaver lived at No. 25 ulitsa Kalyaeva. The diary says:

> 24 February 1915. Last night discussion until two o'clock in the morning in a group crowded into Vinaver's apartment on the painful question of the orientation of the hopelessness of the Jewish masses [which meant which side to support during the war]. They all agreed — to support Russia.
>
> 17 March 1915. A few days spent entirely visiting people: meetings, gatherings, and yesterday Passover seder in a large group at Vinaver's. Encouraging speeches were delivered. Vinaver put the question "Ma Nishtana?"— How was this night of horrors and darkness different from previous nights in our history? I replied with historical parallels of the four Egypts — the Pharaonic, the time of the Elephantines, the Judaeo-Hellenic period, and the era of Maimonides — to illustrate the revolving cycle of Jewish history. We read the Haggadah and we were all in a festive mood, but we all felt that everyone was worried about the night of terrors that we were living through.

In March 1915 Dubnow visited A.Y. Harkavy in the old scholar's house at No. 47 Bolshaya Pushkarskaya (extant). "I was with Goldstein," * he wrote, and asked Harkavy about transferring his archives to our Historical Society. . . . [T]his was the first time that I had crossed the threshold of the 75-year-old man's apartment. How lifeless everything is here! This is a graveyard of history!"

Again and again, Dubnow returned to House No. 50 on 5th Liniya, thus:

> 7 August 1915. Yesterday I visited a shelter for refugees from Malkin (a small Polish town) in the almshouse on Vassilevsky Ostrov next to the archives of our Historical-Ethnographic Society. The exhausted men and women told of an unheard-of atrocity in the nearby village of Zaremba-Kostselna. The inhabitants were told to get out by a certain time and when some of the unfortunates had not got out on the expiry of the time limit, the Cossacks surrounded

---

*Salwian Goldstein (1855–1926), one of the founders of the Historical-Ethnographic Society in 1908, organized the Bershadsky archives, published in *Yevreiskaya Starina,* and was a contributor to the *Yevreiskaya Entsiklopedia.*

the settlement and set fire to it from all sides. They let the Poles out, but many of the Jews trapped in the fire were burned to death.

27 November 1915. We have started our courses on Jewish knowledge (Oriental Studies) for students, meeting in a room of the Historical Society, and discussed the opening of the museum from An-sky's collection. I have now finished the outline of the lecture that I shall be delivering to a meeting of the Historical Society: "The struggle of the individual and of the national principle in the history of Judaism."

On February 23, 1916, an OPE Conference was held at No. 23 Zagorodny Prospekt; Dubnow and Bialik both took part. The discussion centered around the competing claims of Yiddishism (Shtiff) and Hebraism (Bialik). It was the calm before the storm:

January 1917. A few days ago I went on business to the district of Offitsers-kaya ulitsa district and Konnogvardeisky Boulevard on a sunny, frosty day. I was walking past Baron Guenzburg's house when I recalled how on a similar day in 1889 I sat behind those illuminated windows and enthusiastically copied a manuscript for the "History of the Hasidic Schism." The secular excitement of youth striving forward, the sacred melancholy of old age looking back over the path traversed.

The first revolution of 1917, breaking out in February, transformed life for all Jews. On June 8, Dubnow addressed a Jewish meeting in the building of the former stock exchange at 4 Pushkinskaya Ploshchad (extant). He wrote in his diary:

Hot sultry days in Petrograd, electrically charged with politics, blazing with scores of congresses, meetings, a flood of inflammatory slogans thrown by demagogues into the dark masses. Yesterday I took part in a large Jewish meeting in the Stock Exchange Hall, where Vinaver, Sliozberg, military delegates, and others spoke. The aim was to protest against the anarchy reigning. I pointed out the deep root of the evil: the dominance of the class struggle in the revolutionary movement which distorted the course of the revolution, since national and state principles are not subordinate to the class struggle.

On August 23 and 29, 1917, in the hall of the OPE school, ulitsa Deka-bristov 42, there was a conference of the Folkspartei, in which Dubnow participated and of which he was elected a committee member.

In October, the Bolshevik Revolution led to the triumph of Communism, first in Petrograd, then throughout Russia. Early in the new year, on January 21, 1918, Dubnow spoke at a preelection rally for the Jewish Congress, held in the hall of the former Bestuzhev Courses. His speech, entitled "The Contemporary Situation and the Jewish Congress," encountered fierce opposition from the Left Socialist Revolutionary, I. Dobkovsky, who was at that time a deputy chairman to Dimanstein of the Evreiski Komissariat (the Jewish Department of the Ministry of Nationalities). Dubnow later recalled:

In view of the break-up of Russia, the recently elected All-Russian Jewish Congress could not meet, but its St. Petersburg delegates, together with the members of the former Political Bureau, decided to form from among themselves a National Council to carry out on a small scale the large tasks of the Congress. All Jewish parties and groups, even, in part, the Socialists, were represented proportionately on the Council. I joined it together with other representatives of the Folkspartei—Yefroikin, Kreinin, Perelman, Shtiff, Grusenberg (temporarily) and others. For the most part we held our meetings in the new Jewish club, the premises of which were in the former club of members of the State Council, near the State Council building by the Seenyi Most (Blue Bridge).

On December 8, 1917, Dubnow took part in the communal elections in the Choral Synagogue. On December 24, 1917, he attended the memorial prayer service, also in the synagogue, for the Jewish writer Shalom Abramovitch (Mendele Moikher Seforim), who had died in Odessa, at the age of eighty-three.

In February 1918 the Jewish University was opened in Petrograd; Dubnow later lectured there. He was also present on April 11, 1918, at a meeting of the Presidium of the National Council, held in G. B. Sliozberg's apartment at Kovensky Pere'ulok No. 17.

In the spring of 1918 the National Council dissolved itself, as a result of the formation in Moscow of a Vaad (Council) of Jewish Communities (Tsevaad) with more extensive authority.

In the summer of 1918 there was an attempt to publish a book *Jews in the Russian Revolution*. Lifshitz was the publisher of the collection, and a meeting was held in his flat on Liteiny Prospekt; the principal supporters of the project were L. Bramson, Yefroikin, L. Sternberg, and Dubnow. Nothing came of this initiative, however.

In the autumn of 1918, within a year of the Bolshevik Revolution, Dubnow went to the Commissariat of Education (formerly the Ministry of Public Education) on Tchernishevsky Bridge (its address was ulitsa Lomonosova 5, and it is extant). The cause of his visit was the unexpected closure of the Jewish Museum on Vassilevsky Ostrov. Earlier, in tsarist times, Dubnow had gone to that same building, when it housed the Ministry of Public Education, to plead in vain on behalf of his son, who had been expelled from the university for taking part in student disturbances.

Despite the Bolshevik Revolution, Jewish activity continued, as Dubnow's diary makes clear: "29 December 1918. Yesterday evening I was at a gathering of lecturers to organize the Jewish People's University. We met in a luxurious private house on Angleeskaya Naberezhnaya (No. 62), the former palatial home of Polyakov, and now belonging to Propper, publisher of the *Stock Exchange News,* where our classes will be held." Propper had offered his house as a home for the university to save it from being turned into a military barracks, with the inevitable destruction of its furnishings and fittings. "The ladies supplied coffee with skimpy little biscuits," Dubnow noted.

On June 21, 1919, Dubnow was present on the premises of the printing press and publishing offices of Brockhaus and Yefron, Prachechny Pere'ulok 6, for a meeting of the Folkspartei. The leaders of the party not having met for a long time, this meeting was held to discuss the dissolution of the Jewish community councils. It was decided to take no action.

On December 5, 1919, the first session of the commission to investigate the documents in the ritual murder trial cases was held in the archives building of the Senate. As well as Dubnow, the Jewish members of the commission were Krasny, Sliozberg, and Sternberg. The Russian members were Professors Platonov, Karsavin, Druzhinin, and Blinov, the Keeper of the Archives. Dubnow noted: "How strange was this meeting, among the records of the Senate." The archives of the Senate were kept in the building of the Synod, Ploshchad Dekabristov, then Senatskaya Ploshchad 1–3. Dubnow considered that some of the Russian commission members themselves (Platonov and Druzhinin) believed the blood-libel.

Food rations were issued at the House of Academics at ulitsa Khalturina, then Millionaya ulitsa, No. 27, formerly the palace of the Grand Prince Vladimir Alexandrovitch. The ration issue was based on a list drawn up by the Commission to Improve Conditions of Academics (KUBU). Dubnow was included in the list as a teacher at the Jewish University. It was necessary to register for these rations once every month and then, once a week, to go on foot to collect the food, stand in a long queue, and carry the package home, without transport, even though the package sometimes weighed up to thirty-five pounds.

On April 29, 1921, there was a special gathering to honor Dubnow, and to celebrate his forty years of academic and creative activity. The gathering was also a party for his sixtieth birthday. It was held in the building of the Institute of Higher Jewish Studies at Troitskaya ulitsa No. 14, apt. 1.

In October 1921 Dubnow spent a few days in a convalescent home for academics called Sandomuch* in Tsarskoye Selo. He soon ran away from there because of the lack of heat, light, and other necessities. Six months later, in April 1922, Dubnow left Petrograd for the last time.

---

* *Sandomuch* is an acronym formed by *san,* meaning "sanatorium"; *dom,* "house"; and *uch,* "academics" (for example, scholars, scientists).

YECHIEL RAVREBBE

I know that I shall vanish
Like a little star into the mist of oblivion
And my grave will be obliterated.

H. N. Bialik

In the little shtetl of Baranovka, in the Volhynia province of western Russia, a child was born, Yechiel Ravrebbe. The majority of the population of the little village were Jews, whose life was a mixture of extreme poverty and extreme piety! All were Hasidim, followers of the Makarov Tsadik. If at that time someone had wanted to see with his own eyes real folk life, deep religiosity, true jollity and to hear songs and fables, Baranovka would have been the place to visit.

When the Hasidim were visited by their Tsadik the whole village was transformed: it was an event, it was a festival, it was really something. When the Tsadik ate, and that itself was a whole ritual, he liked to have one of the children sing to him. As a reward, the selected child was given food at the rebbe's table and a glass of wine to drink. On one of these occasions when the Tsadik arrived, on the Friday evening following the Sabbath evening prayers when the synagogue was crowded, Ikhia (as Yechiel Ravrebbe was fondly called) managed to squeeze his way to the reading desk where the rabbi was sitting and to receive from him the greeting of welcome "Kabboloss sholoim." The rabbi knew the boy—his father was considered to be one of the most ardent fans of the Tsadik and he himself had gained the reputation in the synagogue of being a "massmid"—a most diligent pupil. Suddenly the rebbe took the boy's hand in his and said: "Today, dear heart, you shall sing at table."

"But Rebbe," said the boy in horror, "I haven't got a voice and I can't sing."

"Yes, dear heart, today you shall sing at table" was the reply.

And thus it was—he sang.

The child remembered all his life both his panic and the taste of the fish and the wine that he received as his reward for singing for the rebbe.

Ravrebbe's nephew David Krivitsky has left us an account of his uncle. The boy's parents were Isroel and Beila. The father was a butcher. Until he was ten the boy studied in cheder and then in the beit-midrash. He distinguished himself by his quick grasp and his excellent memory. His grandfather told Krivitsky that in the evenings, lying in bed, Ikhia would read the whole parasha (the Sabbath reading of the weekly portion of the Torah) with Targum Onkeloss (translation into Aramaic) and learn it by heart. In the beit-midrash he helped everyone, and they called him a "walking encyclopedia." Whenever there was any difficulty, they turned to him. His erudition was due not only to his innate talent but also to his tireless assiduity and capacity for work.

Until he was eighteen, Ikhia spent his days and nights in the beit-midrash and acquired the designation of "Ila'i"—exceptionally gifted. He wrote his first verses and his first sayings on the field of Gemarah. Fellow pupils of his in the beit-midrash did the same. They sent their first poetic efforts to the paper *Ha-Tsoifeh* (The Onlooker). Of the three that were sent, only Ravrebbe's poem was published. This first publication brought Ravrebbe into contact with the local provincial intellectuals. He quickly realized, however, that he could gain nothing from these people.

Another matter was the seething life of class struggle in the Baranovka porcelain factory, where they made the most exquisite and expensive china-ware, for the painting of which they brought in experts from all over the world. It is no surprise that there was a vigorous socialist group there and that Ravrebbe had close connections with them. He read illegal literature, and he was subjected to a search by the authorities. It was then that he wrote the Yiddish poem "Di Veber" (The Weavers) that he sent to *Der Fraynd* in St. Petersburg.

Ravrebbe was spared military service because he was an only son. In 1902 he married Esther Lebensohn. Soon after, at the age of twenty-one, he left for Vilna, where he spent two or three years in intensive study, which brought him a certificate of matriculation for the course at the Gymnasium and *semikhah* (recognition as a rabbi) from the rabbinate of Vilna. At that time he broke away from socialist philosophy, joining the circle of Rabbi I. L. Kantor. In 1907 Ravrebbe came to St. Petersburg.

The primary reason for Ravrebbe coming to the capital is not quite clear. David Krivitsky considers that his intention was to join the courses of Baron Guenzburg. In the opinion of the eyewitness L. P., who came to know Ravrebbe much later—in 1932—the young scholar at first took the examinations as an external student in Eisenbet's Secondary High School, where he was awarded the gold medal. He then studied for some time with Khvolson. Another eyewitness, B. T., believes that Ravrebbe's main but unrealized ambition was to enter the St. Petersburg Conservatoire (he was very musical), but this intention he kept carefully hidden.

Zalman Rubashov (later Zalman Shazar) recalls that Ravrebbe did in fact prepare for the examination at Eisenbet's, but he is not sure whether he took the examination. Rubashov mentions Ravrebbe as being among the first students invited to the Courses of Oriental Studies. Apparently Ravrebbe did not, however, study very long at the high school; perhaps he only attended lectures of the courses that were housed there at that time. Nevertheless, he was one of the best students at Baron David Guenzburg's Courses of Oriental Studies. This tall, stooping twenty-six-year-old blond fellow with a delicately featured face, not looking at all like a Jew, surprised everyone with the depth of his erudition and his superb knowledge of the Bible and of rabbinic literature, Hebrew language, and grammar. He made a deep impression both at the courses and in the family of the St. Petersburg rabbi, where he taught the children Hebrew. For the family of an orthodox Talmudist from Lithuania to encounter such an educated man from a little Hasidic shtetl in the Ukraine, far from the traditional centers of Talmudic learning, was particularly unexpected.

Ravrebbe was shy and delicate, quiet and reserved, even reticent. His circle of friends was never very broad. He did not like to talk about himself. B. T., the daughter of the St. Petersburg rabbi, recalls that for a long time no one even knew that he was married (Esther Markovna came to St. Petersburg much later). It is not surprising tht B. T.'s mother could not understand why their home tutor so strongly resisted all her attempts to marry him off.

During his first years of attendance at the lectures, Ravrebbe lived with the other students in the hostel at 8th Liniya No. 33. And no one was surprised that, both as a poet and as the most able student, he had his own room, between the hostel and the building where the lectures were conducted. In any case, he did not feel at his ease in the Russian capital. Moreover, it was a long time before he was given official residential permit. The Hebrew poet Shimonovitch (who later took the name Shimoni), explained in verse that Ravrebbe's stooping posture was due to his lack of the right of residence in St. Petersburg, and the general discomfort that he felt in what was for him a "foreign" city. Finally, the efforts of one of the baron's servants were crowned with success: Ravrebbe received the much sought after permission — as a craftsman working in the manufacture of ink. As, of course, he never made any ink, he, like other students, had to keep out of the way during police raids by walking the streets of the capital all through the night.

Ravrebbe's complete devotion to study, to books, and to Jewish scholarship in no way made him into a communal personality. He not only never took part in political life — although he had his own opinions about everything — but even declined to join in the arguments that flared up between students in the hostel. Only in the debates between the Yiddishists and the Hebraists did he join in to support the latter.

As a poet, Ravrebbe naturally became close to David Shimonovitch (1886, Bobruisk – 1956, Israel), whose general romanticism, as expressed in his poetry, combined in him a love for Palestine, the Land of Israel, and a revolutionary spirit. He translated the popular revolutionary song, *You Fell as a Victim*, as well as many of Lermontov's and Pushkin's lyrical poems, into Yiddish.

For Ravrebbe, the studies at the David Guenzburg courses were most important. But he too, like Shimonovitch, found time for other activities. He visited the Society of Lovers of Hebrew Literature.

Once, because of his musical talent, Ravrebbe was attracted to a communal undertaking. When the idea was born to stage an opera in Hebrew, Ravrebbe shut himself up in his room for a whole month, during which time he translated into Hebrew the libretto of *Samson and Delilah* by Saint-Saens, synchronizing it with the musical score of the original. Dr. Lev Katzenelson, who supported the idea, had the libretto printed; shortly afterward the opera was performed under the direction of Golynkin at the Tenishevsky School.

The entire intelligentsia of the capital came to the premiere. Ravrebbe's happiness knew no bounds. This was the first, and probably the last, presentation in Russia of grand opera in Hebrew. In 1919 there was an attempt to put on a performance at the Operatic Studio in the Conservatoire; it got as far as the printing of notices, but no premiere was ever performed.

Ravrebbe's musical talents were so broad that, so we are told, he was even brought into contact with Chaliapin; it was said that he taught Chaliapin to sing the then popular Jewish song *Od lo avdo.* (Now called *Ha-Tikvah*—The Hope—it is the anthem of the State of Israel and of the Zionist movement universally.) There is in fact an old woman in Leningrad who remembers Chaliapin singing this song in an approximate Russian translation. Chaliapin was indeed greatly interested in Jewish culture; he was a member of the Russian Society for the Study of Jewish Life and took part in its musical evenings, at which he sang Jewish songs; he also more than once attended Kol Nidre on the Day of Atonement at the Choral Synagogue.

In the 1900s Ravrebbe was published more than once in what was then a very sound literary journal in Hebrew, *Ha-Shiloakh,* published in Odessa by Ahad Ha'am, with the help of Bialik. Bialik acknowledged Ravrebbe as a talented poet and gave him his patronage, as he did to all talented young Jews attracted to the newly blossoming national poetry. Rubashov recalls that in 1908 Ravrebbe invited him into his room and, sitting on his bed, read some of his verses to him. There was in Ravrebbe's poetry a romanticism of nature and a searching for his road in life, eastern motifs, and love lyricism, and in one of them—as in Bialik's "I Know that I Shall Vanish Like a Little Star"—there is a foreboding of the Revolution, "the rising, blazing sun . . . "; he very much wanted to prolong the state of morning slumber. It was called "At Dawn":

Hush, Ariel, spread thy wings,
And on my world thy happiness cast.
And while thy brilliance lingers on
Extend o'er me the dreaming vault of heaven.

In much of Ravrebbe's poetry the influence of Bialik is evident. This is not surprising, as Bialik's influence is evident in all Hebrew poets who followed him. Here is another translation, put into English from a Russian translation of the Hebrew, of a poem by Ravrebbe:

When I go down at night to the river's mouth,
    and hear the lapping of the waves,
Over me falls the blessing of silence,
    like a tender mother it comes,
And into my breast a quiet returns,
    and hope to my troubled soul.
And again to visit my poor heart
    there comes for one brief moment,
My long forgotten golden dream,
    that long ago forsook me.

> The dream blossoms in silence within my heart
>> like a silvery moon in a brook;
> Its reflection quietly peers closely at me;
>> for like me it is tired and wan.

The last poems written by Ravrebbe were printed in the Moscow collection *Ha-Tekufah* (The Era) in 1918. He then devoted himself almost exclusively to study, occasionally turning his attention to journalism. He is mentioned between 1919 and 1922 among the teachers of Hebrew philology of the Jewish university. In 1922 there was a comment by him in *Yevreisky Vestnik,* in reply to a review of young Yiddish poets written by Sergei Zinberg (in the article "Jewish Poets of the Ukraine" in the April issue of the *Vestnik*). In his review, Zinberg had welcomed the "joie de vivre" of the poetry of Peretz Markish and his group of "singers of nature and of the Ukrainian soil," calling their verses "a joyful and invigorating wonder." In reply, Ravrebbe expressed his astonishment, and even indignation, over Markish's lofty tone and major key, the "inappropriate" style of his poetry, so incompatible with the tragic reality of Ukrainian Jewry during the Civil War, when tens of thousands were murdered. Ravrebbe writes:

> But if on one bank of the River Dniepr there stretch long columns of Jewish coffins, and on the other bank are sitting the children of those very same murdered Jews, singing the praises of the breadth and length of the Ukrainian expanse, and in their songs there is no grief and on their lips there are no curses — then it is perhaps a wonder, but it is certainly not joyful nor is it invigorating.

Neither the two disputants — Zinberg and Ravrebbe — nor the poet-object of their polemics — Markish — knew then that the new order would make all their fates equal, irrespective of their views on any particular problem. These views, in fact, had little if any influence on the dates of arrest and death of their respective bearers: the pro-Zionist Ravrebbe was arrested in 1938 and died soon after; the anti-Zionist Zinberg was arrested in 1938 and died that same year; the "almost" Communist Markish was arrested in 1948 and killed in 1952. It was enough that all three represented Jewish culture.

In 1924 the Institute of Bielorussian Culture was opened in Minsk; Ravrebbe and Isaac Markon were both invited to lecture in the Jewish department. Markon was made professor of medieval Jewish literature and Ravrebbe was appointed reader. He was there until 1926, when he was dismissed because, in quoting Dubnow to his students, he did not sufficiently criticize the "reactionary, bourgeois, nationalistic" content of Dubnow's writings. Markon left the institute with Ravrebbe, emigrating to Germany. Ravrebbe returned to Leningrad. His address, apart from the Minsk interval, was one we know well, the Jewish Almshouse on 5th Liniya, where his wife Esther Markovna worked as housekeeper. They lived, together with Esther's nephew, in two rooms on the third (top) floor, next to the Klionsky apartment.

Yechiel Ravrebbe

Throughout the twenties, Ravrebbe worked diligently, as he had done before and as he did all his life. He spent days on end in the Public Library and in the Asiatic Museum, which at that time had no central heating, gathering material for the basic research of Zinberg's *History of Jewish Literature*. He also translated into Yiddish extensive extracts from the valuable "Pinkasim" in Leningrad, including those of Nesvizh (seventeenth and early nineteenth centuries), the fraternity of tailors of Lutsk (eighteenth century), and Sudilkov (eighteenth century).

Simultaneously with B. Shulman, Ravrebbe worked on searching for and translating into Yiddish the rabbinic responsas. *Yevreisky Vestnik* for 1928 informs us that this material, more than thirty printed sheets in all, was suggested for publication as a separate collection. At this time, Ravrebbe was head of the department of Hebraica in the Society for the Spread of Enlightenment among the Jews (OPE).

In 1926 Ravrebbe had an article published entitled "Svad'ba Makarovskogo Tsadika" (The Wedding of the Makarov Tsadik), which would seem to be his personal childhood recollections of Hasidic life. In 1928 he published in *Yevreiskaya Starina* an article on the false messianic movement of Sabbatai Zevi called "A Journey in the Late Seventeenth Century — Avraham Kunki"; and in the final, thirtieth issue of *Yevreiskaya Starina,* there is an article by him called "The Mstislav Tumult in Jewish National Creativity." Ravrebbe also published abroad a number of articles on the history of the Jews in the Middle Ages and on ancient history, because the St. Petersburg auditorium in the field of Jewish scholarship was being inexorably reduced and the isolation from knowledge beyond the borders of Russia could be felt also in the quality of research.

As Ravrebbe lived in the building that also housed the Jewish Museum, he joined the Museum Commission, and helped with the preservation and enlargement of the collections. As a scholar, he was entitled to special food rations and salary, but his increased interest in Jewish history was not because of this, nor even despite it. He felt deeply, so he said, that not one minute should be lost in saving what could be saved, asking:

> Is it not time for Jewish historians, ethnographers, composers, and writers of records of daily life to set about analyzing our inheritance and doing it with increased tempo and greater energy than they have been doing until now? Is it not time for us to delve into this storehouse before the world-wide storm disperses the remnants to the seven seas, and from the whole epoch of Jewish life that will perhaps become the epilogue to the period of two millennia of Jewish history not even a trace will remain?

The 1930s found Ravrebbe no longer a young scholar; but he was well known both in the Soviet Union and abroad. The "Almshouse Period" was over. Esther Markovna was dead. Together with his mother-in-law and his wife's nephew, Ravrebbe moved into No. 26 – 28 Kamenno-Ostrovsky Prospekt, where Kirov lived.* He was given a two-room apartment and continued his scholarly way of life as before.

Ravrebbe's small salary as an employee of the Public Library, about 400 to 500 rubles, was quite enough for him. He worked continuously without taking any days off. He hardly ever went to the synagogue. He went regularly to the Public Library, traveling there and back by bus, and he was content to do so. The circle of his friends remained as before: Doctor Nahum Shwartz, a Hebrew-language poet; the Jewish scholar David Shulman; two lifelong acquaintances from the Ukraine; and the family of Dr. Vladimir Ioffer and his wife Bertha. That was all. He had no time to socialize — he had to work. He rejected the suggestion that he remarry, with the excuse that the proposed new wife was a chemist, and this, in his opinion as a convinced humanitarian, was a quite unnecessary profession.

---

* It is now Kirovsky Prospekt.

The eyewitness L. P. remembers that in 1932 he was taken for the first time to meet Ravrebbe, by a friend who was hoping to become an engineer. In the heat of an argument this friend called Ravrebbe a "grave digger" and was in turn called a "blacksmith." A quarrel developed. But L. P., in whose eyes Ravrebbe was crowned with the halo of a *haham* (a sage), continued to visit him. Ravrebbe even suggested to him that he should collect, and make an anthology of, Hebrew proverbs, idioms, and sayings. L. P., whose thoughts were more materialistic, declined, however, when he understood that the task would not be a paid one.

Ravrebbe's own salary was about the same as that of a young worker. It never even occurred to him that scholarly work could bring in an income. He was once asked to draw up a reference list detailing the post-Biblical sources that mention the legendary Sambatyon River, beyond which the ten lost tribes of Israel were taken into captivity. The legend says that the river is very turbulent and unnavigable but that it runs quietly and smoothly on the Sabbath. However, as the Israelites (or Hebrews, for they were not yet called "Jews") were forbidden to travel on the Sabbath, they could not cross the river and thus could not return from exile. Ravrebbe put a great deal of work into the task and drew up the requested details. He was quite astonished when he was then offered an honorarium.

According to L. P., Ravrebbe had a knowledge of twenty languages. During the time of their acquaintance, he compiled a card index on the extensive Firkovitch fund in the Public Library (begun by Abram Harkavy) and, together with I. Vinnikov, did a great deal of work on the compilation of a concordance to the Palestinian (Jerusalem) Talmud, which was later published in part by Vinnikov.

In 1934 Ravrebbe's group issued four brochures (three and four in a single issue) and in 1935 two more brochures (in one issue), entitled "Information Bulletin of the Jewish Group of the National Department of the Miye Saltykov–Shchedrin State Public Library in Leningrad." The first four issues were typed, and the last two were mimeographed. Ravrebbe's articles were still on substantial Jewish themes; most of the other articles concerned Birobijdan and other aspects of Jewish Communist life. Even so, this brochure constituted the last specifically Jewish cultural publications until the *Leningrad Jewish Almanac* of 1982 (now, in 1988, in its seventeenth issue).

However, the greatest effect was produced by Ravrebbe's article "On the Cuneiform Texts of Ras-Shamra," published in 1935 in the *Soviet Academy of Sciences News Bulletin* by the Mar Institute of Language and Thought.

From 1928 to 1932, French archeologists had excavated in Syria on the territory of the ancient Canaanite town of Ugarit (second millennium B.C.). Among the finds were some clay tablets inscribed with a cuneiform text whose alphabet and language had not previously been known. Using their combined efforts, several leading scholars from different countries had completely deciphered the alphabet of the unknown letter. But the language itself, a form of

Canaanite dialect with elements of other unknown tongues, was beyond the comprehension of the Semitologists. The contents of the inscriptions to a great extent still baffled them.

Ravrebbe, through his research, was able to give a grammatical analysis of the language: suffixes, articles, verb forms, and other aspects. Using his considerable erudition in the field of ancient tongues, he was able to make considerable progress in the reading and the interpretation of some of the texts. He evaluated the role of the open cuneiform as being cultic-sacerdotal, as distinguished from the Phoenician alphabet that had existed simultaneously and that was used when it was more convenient to write on parchment (for example, to mark the conclusion of trade agreements).

Considerable interest was also aroused in the analysis of the Pantheon of the Canaanite gods that Ravrebbe produced, as well as his comparison of several biblical subjects with similar subjects in ancient Canaanite mythology. His work gave significant impetus, indeed, to the progress of research into the discoveries at Ras-Shamra and greatly enriched the general study of Semitology. *Izvestiya* published a long article devoted specially to him, together with a photograph, and an American Jewish paper wrote about him: "Where Christian research workers have failed, a Soviet Jewish poet, writer, and scholar has succeeded."

According to the eyewitness L. P., Ravrebbe was rewarded for his Ugaritic work with the offer of a professorial chair, but where this was to be is not known. Once, in 1937, when he was working in the Leningrad Public Library, he was approached by a man in military uniform who offered him a professorship at Tbilisi University, on the recommendation of Professor Nikolsky, with whom Ravrebbe had written a book. Ravrebbe did not recognize the man, who, it seems, was A. S. Bubnov, People's Commissar of Education of the Russian republic. Soon afterward, however, Bubnov was "liquidated" — it was the height of the Stalin purges — and the Tbilisi post was forgotten. Eight months later, L. P. visited Ravrebbe's apartment on what is now Kirovsky Prospekt. The door was opened by Ravrebbe's mother-in-law, who told him that Ravrebbe had been arrested three months earlier. He was held for some time in the Kresty Prison in Leningrad, but then parcels for him were no longer accepted (an indication that he was probably dead).

In Palestine, Ravrebbe's nephew, David Krivitsky, actively helped by Rubashov (Shazar), Bialik, and others, succeeded after many months in obtaining a Palestine immigration certificate for Ravrebbe from the British Mandatory government. The certificate was sent to the British Embassy in Moscow, but it was already too late.

MARC CHAGALL

In the winter of 1906 to 1907, Marc Chagall and his friend Meckler left the city of Vitebsk to go to the capital. There, Chagall found a job as a retoucher with the photographer Yaffe, who was also an artist. The pay was sufficient to cover only his rent, and he did not like the work — what was the point of embellishing reality? Chagall turned for help to the sculptor Ilya Guenzburg, who gave him a letter of recommendation to Baron David Guenzburg, who in turn gave him a little money. This money was sufficient for only a few months of pitiful existence.

Chagall did not have the means to rent a room for himself; he lived in odd corners, not always having a bed to himself. Later, he recalled that at one time he shared a bed with a laborer — the owner of a big black mustache. On another occasion, his room was divided by a curtain, behind which lived a drunkard and his wife. Once, Chagall was arrested and detained for two weeks when he traveled without the necessary "internal" passport from St. Petersburg to Vitebsk. There is evidence that he once did some sign-writing for shops in St. Petersburg, and, it seems, he was even a salesman for a while.

Eventually Chagall came to the attention of a St. Petersburg patron, the barrister and solicitor Grigory Abramovitch Goldberg, who was a committee member in OZE (the Society for the Protection of the Health of the Jewish Population). Goldberg arranged for Chagall to be registered as his personal valet, so that he could receive permission to reside in the capital. For several months Chagall lived in a tiny cubbyhole under the stairs. He often visited Goldberg's apartment at Liteiny Prospekt No. 31, and later at Zakharyevskaya ulitsa No. 11. Goldberg often moved from one apartment to another. Chagall's relationship with his generous host was warm and friendly.

Chagall was not able to enter the Academy of Arts, as he did not have a matriculation certificate. His attempt to join the Artistic-Industrial School of Baron Stieglits at Solyanoi Pere'ulok 9, in the winter of 1906 to 1907, was also unsuccessful: his paintings were looked upon as too untraditional. He managed eventually to get into an art school open to all comers, the one run by the Imperial Society for the Promotion of the Arts at Naberezhnaya Moiki 83. The society itself was located at Bolshaya Morskaya 38 (now ulitsa Herzena). These two buildings, joined by a shared courtyard, are now occupied by the Leningrad Section of the Union of Artists (LOSKh).

Soon after Chagall joined the school of painting on the Moika, Nikolai Rerikh was appointed its director. Noticing the talent of the young artist, Rerikh obtained for him an extension of his permit to live in St. Petersburg, as well as exemption from army service.

On April 17, 1907, Chagall was mentioned favorably in the art school's annual report and was rewarded with a grant of six rubles. In September 1907 this was increased to fifteen rubles per month. The young artist was already extremely sensitive, almost intolerant to any criticism, especially if he thought it was unjustified. One of his teachers, Bobrovsky, a theatrical stage designer, told Chagall at one of the lessons on drawing from life that he was not able to draw a knee correctly. Chagall took offense and walked out of the school; he did not even take the grant for the last month.

Chagall took a hundred of his drawings to be looked after by the photographer Annenkov, who lived on Zakharyevskaya ulitsa. (In 1907 there was only one Annenkov registered on Zakharyevskaya ulitsa — a nobleman and assistant barrister, Constantine Mitrofanovitch. This Annenkov's apartment — No. 25 — was in the same building in which Vinaver lived. In the directory of St. Petersburg for 1907 there is no mention of any photographer Annenkov or Anenkov.) Later, this Annenkov declared that he had not been given anything, and he never returned any work to Chagall.

For some months Chagall studied at S. M. Zeidenberg's private school of art and painting at No. 9 Furshtadskaya ulitsa (now ulitsa Petra Lavrova), where the tuition was in the spirit of Repin. He painted landscapes, copying them from Levitan's paintings in the home of a lover of the arts. There are two paintings that have been preserved from those days — Goldberg's drawing room and his study.

It was due to Goldberg that Chagall was able to make the acquaintance of the leaders of the Jewish liberal intelligentsia of St. Petersburg: Maxim Vinaver; his brother-in-law Leopold Sev, who was active in the Russo-Jewish publishing world; the critic M. G. Syrkin; and the writer Posner. They appreciated that they were dealing with an artist out of the ordinary. Vinaver became very attached to Chagall, who later recalled him with great affection: "I remember his glistening eyes, his rapidly moving eyelashes, the sensitive shape of his mouth, his light brown beard, and his noble profile that — alas — because of my shyness and deference I did not dare to draw. He was very close to me, almost like a father." Vinaver often invited Chagall to his apartment at No. 25 Zakharyevskaya (now ulitsa Kalyaeva), and the artist not infrequently stayed the night, sleeping on a divan in the editor's study (Vinaver was editor of *Voskhod, Novy Voskhod,* and *Yevreiskaya Starina*); during the day he worked in the vestibule among the unsold magazines.

On one occasion, at Leopold Sev's apartment, Chagall was told about Leon Bakst and his lessons in the Zvantseva School. The artist Elena Niko-layevna Zvantseva, on her return to Russia from Paris, had founded an art school in Moscow in 1899, where she hoped to organize tuition in the spirit of the avant-garde of French art. But Serov and Korovin, whom she invited to work in her school, quickly proved to her that they did not have sufficient appreciation of contemporary art. Zvantseva moved to St. Petersburg, where, in the persons of Bakst and Dobuzhinsky, she found what she was looking for. Bakst was in no way a provincial; he was well acquainted with the French school and loved to talk to his pupils about the paintings of Édouard Manet,

Claude Monet, Gauguin, Cézanne, Van Gogh — the masters whom our generation was not destined to get to know until fifty years later. Chagall went with a letter from Sev to see Bakst on Sergievskogo ulitsa (or it may have been at No. 24 Kirochnaya). Chagall later recalled his meeting with Bakst:

> His fame after the Russian season abroad overawed me, I don't know why. . . . Would he find that I had any talent? And what if he didn't? When he looked at my sketches that I handed to him from the floor where they were lying, he said, dragging out his words in a lordly tone: "Ye-es, ye-es, there is talent but you have been corrupted, you are not on the right road — cor-rup-ted."

Nevertheless, Bakst accepted Chagall into the school. It was on the corner of Tavricheskaya and Tverskaya Streets (Tavricheskaya No. 25), in that famous house with the "tower," where in Vyacheslav Ivanov's apartment gathered the then literary elite of St. Petersburg, among them Alexander Blok, Gumilyov, Anna Akhmatova, Osip Mandelstam, Merezhkovsky, and Gippius. They called themselves the Society of Enthusiasts for the Artistic Word or The Academy of Verse.

In the Zvantseva School, Dobuzhinsky taught drawing on Wednesdays and Bakst taught painting in oils on Thursdays. Chagall recalls that his easel stood next to those of Countess Tolstoy and Nijinsky. In 1909 the Zvantseva School moved to Spasskaya ulitsa 23 (now ulitsa Rileyeva), and a year later to Zabalkansky Prospekt No. 1 (now Moskovsky Prospekt).

Already at that time, at the age of twenty-one, Chagall had his own oddities. For example, when he was alone, he liked to work in the nude. In his memoirs, he describes one of his special dreams of that period:

> An empty, square, room; in the corner a narrow bed and I am lying on it. It is getting dark. Suddenly the ceiling opens and a winged being flies in with a crash of thunder, filling the room with movement and clouds of steam. There is the sound of rustling of the spreading wings. I realize that it is an angel! I am unable to open my eyes for the light is so bright, so brilliant. After looking all round the room it flies up again and disappears through the open ceiling, taking with it all the light and the blue air. Once again it is dark. My painting of *The Vision* is a reflection of that dream of mine.

The Zvantseva School held its own exhibition from April 20 to May 9, 1909, in the premises of the recently started artistic and literary journal *Apollon*. The editorial offices of the journal were in the same building as the fashionable restaurant Donon, at No. 24 Naberezhnaya Moiki. Repin, in several articles, tore the exhibition to shreds.

In 1910, Bakst went to Paris as a scene painter with Diaghilev's ballet company. But Chagall's attempt to get taken on as assistant stage painter met with failure. Maxim Vinaver again came to his rescue. He obtained for him a stipend for four years, to continue his work in St. Petersburg, or to travel abroad. In gratitude, Chagall gave him his painting *The Wedding.* Leopold Sev bought the picture *The Deceased.* In spite of his patron's advice that he should go to Italy, Chagall decided to go to Paris, where he arrived with all his pictures in late summer 1910.

Chagall returned to Russia from Paris on June 15, 1914, planning to stay for a mere three months. But this had to be extended indefinitely, first because of the outbreak of war on August 2, 1914. In the summer of 1915 he returned to Vitebsk, where he married Bella (Bertha Rosenfeld), the daughter of a Vitebsk businessman who owned three jeweler's shops. Bella was a graduate of one of the best schools in Moscow, was attracted to the theater, attended lectures given by Stanislavsky, and herself took part in performances. But for us, the most important side of her was her role in Chagall's life.

In September 1915, Chagall and his wife moved from Vitebsk to Petrograd. During this period Chagall made the acquaintance of several future Soviet public figures, including Bonche-Bruyevitch, Demian Bedny, Mayakovsky, Yesenin, and Pasternak. He remained closest, however, to the old group of Jewish intellectuals, especially M. Syrkin and Dr. Elyashev, who published in the Zionist press under the pseudonym of Ba'al Makhshovess (Hebrew for "The Thinker").

To avoid military service, Chagall got himself a job in the Bureau of War Economy, headed by Bella's brother. Until the early spring of 1917, he and Bella lived in a small flat at 7 Perekupny Pere'ulok (the building is extant).

In Petrograd Chagall again drew close to the Goldberg family, who at that time lived at Naberezhnaya Fontanki 86, apt. 14. He had stayed with them in this apartment for about a week in 1915. Grigory Goldberg had kept several of Chagall's works, including a variant of *Jew in Green,* an album of drawings, and others. All were lost or destroyed during the siege of Leningrad in World War II.

There is yet one more address where it was possible to see Chagall fairly frequently: Kaznacheiskaya ulitsa 3, apt. 31. This was the home of his sister Anna and her husband Boris, who had moved from Vitebsk to St. Petersburg in 1911. The other sisters, Mania, Lisa, and Marusia, followed Anna, also gradually moving to the capital. During this period Chagall took part, with success, in a number of exhibitions: in March 1915 in Moscow, in April 1916 in a one-man exhibition in the private gallery of N. E. Dobichina in Petrograd, at 7 Marsovo Polye, and in the same year in another exhibition in Moscow. Then, in December 1916, his paintings were shown in an exhibition of contemporary Russian painting organized by H. Dobichina.

Early in 1917, Chagall made sketches on a Jewish theme for some small wall panels for the Petrograd Jewish School. He spent the summer of 1917 in a dacha outside Petrograd, and immediately after the October Revolution of 1917 he left the capital for Vitebsk. Despite the upheavals of revolution, Chagall had a resounding success at the exhibition of revolutionary art that was held from April to June 1919 in the Winter Palace in Petrograd. It put on display 2,826 exhibits of 359 artists; Chagall's paintings were hung in the first two halls. Twelve of these paintings were bought from the exhibition by the new Soviet government.

Today there are five of Chagall's pictures from his St. Petersburg and Vitebsk periods in the Russky Muzey (The Russian Museum) in Leningrad: *Father* (1914), *A Shop in Vitebsk* (1914), *Mirror* (1915), *Red Jew* (1915), and *Going for a Walk* (1917). Several of his pictures are also in private collections.

Chagall had visited Leningrad in 1974. The news of his death in 1986 reached us here in Leningrad with a special sadness: despite his life in Vitebsk and Paris, for us he will always be a part of the Jewish heritage of our city.

TWO SPECIAL VISITORS

MOSES MONTEFIORE

Moses Montefiore (born in Italy in 1784, died in England in 1885) was an outstanding public figure and philanthropist. He founded the London Banking House of Montefiore Brothers, took part in the Napoleonic Wars with the rank of captain, and founded the first insurance society in England. In fact, it was he who introduced the idea of life insurance. He also formed the first company in England to introduce street lighting by gas.

In 1836 Montefiore granted a loan to the British government to enable it to abolish slavery in the British colonies. In 1837 he was made a sheriff of the City of London and lord lieutenant of the County of Middlesex, to all intents and purposes abolishing capital punishment during his term of office. He was knighted by Queen Victoria and in 1846 given the title of baronet.

Montefiore was a deeply religious, orthodox Jew, and never violated any of the dogmas of the Jewish faith and its traditions. He was distinguished for his generous charity toward Jews, including many donations to the Jewish community in Palestine, which he visited seven times. He was instrumental in halting the case of blood-libel in Damascus in 1840 and made a point of defending Jews throughout the world — in Italy, the island of Corfu, Morocco, Rumania, and Russia. He twice visited St. Petersburg, in 1846 when he appealed for an improvement in the condition of the Jews and in 1872 on the occasion of the celebrations to mark the bicentenary of Peter the Great.

A wealth of biographical literature has been written about Montefiore, and a multitude of folk legends have been made up about him. His first visit to Russia, in 1846, came at a very difficult period for Russian Jewry. Nicholas I and his administration were doing all they could to bring about the assimilation and Christianization of the Jews, to liquidate the remnants of communal autonomy, and to destroy the material and moral bases of life in the shtetls. It was not proposed to grant the Jewish people any sort of civil or political rights. To achieve these goals, the government used all sorts of methods, among them new and restrictive laws, evictions, and transfers of population; compulsory military service for a term of twenty-five years; compulsory state-run secular schools; the fight against the Talmud; censorship; and the burning of Hebrew books.

It is not surprising therefore that the arrival in Russia of their defender, Montefiore, at this very unpropitious moment, was looked upon by the Jews almost as the coming of the Messiah. They expected from the distinguished, exalted philanthropist not only generous charity but also an active approach to the tsarist government to alleviate its anti-Jewish policies.

Wherever Montefiore went he was met by the leaders of the local communities and by great crowds of the wretched suffering people. All sorts of fanciful legends were woven about his wealth and influence. Henceforth, proverbs, sayings, and fables in which Montefiore was the chief hero enriched the folklore of Eastern European Jewry. For many years his portrait, copied and reproduced countless times, hung even in the houses of the most orthodox men and women, who normally avoided being photographed even for documents, not wishing to look upon the representation of the human form — God's creation.

As far as is known, the great philanthropist obtained nothing of substance from the tsar, although he was received with honor. In answer to his request for his co-religionists to be granted rights, Nicholas I replied: "They will receive them when they become something like you."

We learn about the details of Montefiore's visit to the capital in 1846 from his secretary's diary. Here are the relevant entries:

> 1st April, 1846, at 3 P.M. — Montefiore and his wife arrived in St. Petersburg. The accommodation that had been reserved for him in advance was not considered to be satisfactory, so he transferred to the Hotel De Prusse.
>
> 2nd April — Montefiore visited Bloomfield, the British ambassador, and asked him for a letter of recommendation to Count Nesselrode, the minister of foreign affairs.
>
> 5th April — Audience with Nesselrode, who had already been informed by Bloomfield of Montefiore's arrival and of his desire to found a new Jewish school, as well as of his request for the annulment of the decree on the eviction of the Jews from the border zone.

On April 5 Montefiore was received by Nesselrode. That same day, Montefiore was received by the minister of public education, Uvarov, who had created the program of state-controlled education for Jewish children. During the conversation Uvarov declared that the Jews were ignorant and did not even know their own language and that they had to be made first and foremost to learn Hebrew, and then mathematics and other sciences.

The Secretary's diary continues:

9th April—Montefiore took a long walk to the Soldiers' Synagogue, a small, dirty building, filled to capacity, not far from Angleeskaya Naberezhnaya. Several soldiers seemed to him to be ill.

15th April—Montefiore was received by Count Kisselev, who was the leader of the commission for drawing up legislation on the Jews. Later in the day a solemn ceremony of farewell to Sir Moses Montefiore was held in St. Isaac's Square with the participation of outstanding Jewish and some non-Jewish personalities of St. Petersburg.

16th April—Montefiore's departure from St. Petersburg.

Montefiore paid his second and last visit to St. Petersburg in 1872. During this visit he made note of significant changes for the better that he had observed in the life of the Jews in the capital. During this visit he stayed in the Hotel De Klee, on Mikhailovskaya ulitsa (now ulitsa Brodskogo) No. 1. The hotel survives; today it is the Yevropeiskaya.

THEODOR HERZL

Theodor Herzl (born in Budapest in 1860, died in Edlach, Austria, in 1904), journalist, author, and playwright, is considered to be the founder of political Zionism. Until 1896 he was a highly successful journalist with the Austrian liberal press. After 1896, under the influence of the Dreyfus case, he wrote his book *The Jewish State,* in which he formulated the aims of Zionism as a political movement. From that moment, until his death, he was the acknowledged leader of the Zionist movement. In 1897 he organized the First Zionist Congress in Basle, which adopted a program for the creation of a legal refuge for Jews in Palestine. With the aim of founding such a refuge, he met many politicians, statesmen, and monarchs: Sultan Abdul Hamid, Kaiser Wilhelm II, and, in Russia, the minister of the interior, Vyacheslav von Plehve, and the minister of finance, Serge Witte.

Herzl visited St. Petersburg in August 1903, with the object of persuading the Russian government to influence Turkey to bring about more favorable conditions for the realization of the Palestine project. Through an intermediary, the Warsaw lawyer Yasinovsky, he made the acquaintance of Madame Korvin-Piotrovskaya, who lived in St. Petersburg and who was on friendly terms with Plehve.

Arriving in St. Petersburg on August 7, 1903, Herzl went to Korvin-Piotrovskaya on the following day. That same day he also made the acquaintance of Maximov, a Russian liberal who went together with him and the Zionist activist from Libava (Liepaya, in Latvia), Dr. Nissan Katznelson, to the town of Pavlovsk to see General Alexei Alexandrovitch Kireyev, aide-de-camp to the emperor. (Address in Pavlovsk: Sadovaya ulitsa 2.) (Katzenelson, incidentally, accompanied Herzl throughout his entire journey in Russia.)

After lunch with Kireyev, Herzl had a long conversation with Plehve, lasting three quarters of an hour. During this interview, Plehve spoke with unexpected enthusiasm for Zionism, provided, as he told Herzl, that "it worked towards emigration." Furthermore, Plehve agreed to Herzl's request for an "effective intervention" by Russia with the sultan of Turkey, in support of a "charter" for Jewish colonization in Palestine.

On August 9, Herzl went to the islands (Yelagin, or Kamenny Ostrov), to the dacha of the minister of finance, Witte.

On August 10, Herzl received from Kireyev a letter of recommendation to Hartwig, director of the Asiatic department in the Foreign Ministry, which he sent to Hartwig together with his visiting card.

On August 11, Herzl was again with Korvin-Piotrovskaya, who, at his request, wrote to Plehve an eight-page letter. At Herzl's request, she added a remark to the letter to the effect that now, after a Turk had murdered the Russian, Rostovsky, Turkey would probably comply with any request from Russia.

On August 12, Herzl received a long letter from Plehve, which completely satisfied him. To it was attached a personal accompanying note. Plehve's letter read:

> So long as Zionism consisted of wanting to create an independent state in Palestine and undertook to organize the emigration from Russia of a certain number of its Jewish subjects, the Russian government could be completely favorable to it. But once this principal Zionist objective is abandoned, to be replaced by straight propaganda for a Jewish national entity in Russia, it is obvious that the government can in no way tolerate this new direction taken by Zionism. It would only create groups of individuals quite alien and even hostile to the patriotic sentiments which are the strength of every state.
>
> That is why confidence can be placed in Zionism only on condition that it returns to its former program of action. If it did so, it would be able to count on moral and material support from the day when certain of its practical measures would help to reduce the size of the Jewish population in Russia. This support could take the form of protecting the Zionist emissaries to the Ottoman government, of facilitating the work of the emigration societies, and even of providing for the needs of these societies, obviously from sources other than the state budget, by means of a tax levied on the Jews.

It was his hope, Plehve added, that as Jewish emigration from Russia increased, the position of Russia's remaining Jews would improve. Indeed, at their second meeting, on August 13, Plehve went so far as to assure Herzl that what would suit the Russian government best would be the "creation of an independent Jewish State, capable of absorbing several million Jews."

The second meeting, Herzl noted, "went somewhat more quickly than the first."

On August 14, Herzl met Plehve in the evening on Nevsky Prospekt and "combined my speechless greeting with a reminder."

After his visit to Plehve, Herzl had an unofficial meeting in St. Petersburg with a group of Jewish literary figures, among them Ben-Zion Katz (writer and journalist), Doctor Katzenelson (Buki Ben Yogli), Saul Ginzburg, L. Rabinovitch, Y. Brutskus, S. Rosenfeld, Leopold Sev (member of the editorial board of *Voskhod*), and N. Katzenelson.

On August 16 Herzl left St. Petersburg with definite hopes in Plehve, who had produced a deep impression on him. Herzl did not like Witte, however, although he was considered by many at the time to be somewhat more of a liberal.

Herzl's visit resulted in mixed reactions on the part of the Jews in Russia. Many condemned him for his conversations with Plehve, the organizer of the Kishinev pogrom. The Jews of St. Petersburg also had other reasons for dissatisfaction. Herzl had made no attempt to meet the leaders of the community, did not visit any of the wealthy or well-known Jews of the capital, and, as the Warsaw Hebrew-language newspaper *Ha-Tzefirah* remarked, did not even visit the Choral Synagogue.

A DIRECTORY OF
PERSONALITIES

(The names appear in the same order as on the original author's list, which is in strict alphabetical order according to the Russian language Cyrillic alphabet.)

1   **Ahad ha-am (Asher Hirsh Ginsberg)** (1856–1927). Writer, public activist, spiritual Zionist. Came to St. Petersburg in February 1906 to take part in Third Congress of the Union for Equal Rights. Was in St. Petersburg for the last time early in May 1908 on his way to London. Said farewell to Dubnow on May 7, 1908, in the harbor on Gutuyevsky Ostrov.

2   **Aizman, David Yakovlevitch** (1869–1922, lived his last years in Tsarskoye Selo). Russian-Jewish writer.

3   **Alpern, Hirsch**. Resident of Bialystok. Helped the Russian Army by collecting military intelligence in 1811. Was rewarded for exemplary conduct in September 1811 with fifty chervontsi (five hundred rubles) and a ring valued at four hundred rubles. Received in St. Petersburg by the minister for war, Barclay de Tolly.

4   **Altman, Natan Isayevitch** (1889, Vinnitsa–ca. 1970, Leningrad). Lived permanently in Leningrad from 1936. Address (1922): Vassilevsky Ostrov, 1st Liniya 4 (extant). Artist. Scenic designer for the play *The Dybbuk* (Habima) 1922, the film *Jewish Luck*. Painted portrait of Solomon Mikhoels.

5   Amusin, Yosif Davidovitch (1910, Bobruisk, Bielorussia – 1984, Leningrad). Historian, Kumranist (Dead Sea Scrolls), student of S. Y. Lurie and V. V. Struve. Address: ulitsa Orbeli 27, korpus 3, apt. 12.

6   An-sky (Rapoport), Simeon Akimovitch (1863, Chashnik, Bielorussia – 1920, Warsaw). Writer in Russian and Yiddish, folklorist, ethnographer. Author of the play *The Dybbuk* and of the hymn of the Bund "Di Shvueh" (The Oath). Leader of the Jewish ethnographic expedition to the regions of Volhynia and Podolia (1911 – 1914), founder member of the Historical-Ethnographic Society, deputy from the SRs (Social Revolutionaries) to the All-Russian Constituent Assembly (1917), founder of the Jewish Historical-Ethnographic Museum in Petrograd. From 1909 to 1910 he frequently lived in Zelenogorsk (formerly Tereoki) in the Leningrad Oblast. Address in Leningrad (1916 – 1918): Vassilevsky Island, 5th Liniya 50.

7   Antokolski, Mark (Mordechai) Matveyevitch (1843, Vilna – 1902, Bad Homburg, Germany). Sculptor, academician from 1871. Works include *Ivan the Terrible, S. S. Polyakov, Spinoza, Argument over the Talmud, Nathan the Wise, Peter the Great, Yaroslav the Wise, Dmitri Donskoi,* and many others. Address (1870 – 1872): Vassilevsky Island, 5th Liniya 4 (extant). After 1872 he lived mostly outside Russia.

8   Asknazi, Isaak Lvovitch (1856, Drissa, Vitebskaya Guberniya – 1902, Moscow). Artist, from 1885 he was an academic painter. His works include *The Ecclesiast, The Death of Yehuda Halevi, The Drowning of the Jews in Polotsk by Ivan the Terrible in 1563.* Address (1894): Maly Prospekt 10 (extant).

9   Babel, Isaak (1894, Odessa – 1941? in a slave labor camp of Stalin's Gulag). Jewish-Russian writer, in Petrograd illegally from 1915. From 1917 to 1918 he was an official interpreter in the foreign department of the Cheka. His works include *Tales of Odessa, Red Cavalry (Konarmiya).*

10   Bakst (Rosenberg), Lev Samoilovitch (1866, Grodno – 1924, Paris). Lived in St. Petersburg from 1883 to 1909. Address (1904): Zvenigorodskaya ulitsa 22. Artist designer of theater and scenery decors for Diaghilev.

11   Bat-miriam (Zhelezniak) Yokheved (1901 – 1980). Hebrew poet. Born in Keplits, Bielorussia, lived in St. Petersburg in the 1920s, settled in Palestine in 1928. She died in Israel.

12   Benenson, Grigory Osipovitch, Merchant of the First Guild. Address (1916): Naberezhnaya reka Moiki 16 (extant). Director of commercial-industrial company Grigory Benenson; chairman of the Society for the Provision of Primary Education for Jewish Children in the Peskovsky District of St. Petersburg.

13   Bershadsky (Domashevitsky) Isaiah (1871, near Volkovysk – 1908, Warsaw). Novelist; wrote under the pseudonym of Bershadsky — acronym from the Hebrew *Ben Reb Shimon Domashevitsky.* Member of editorial board of periodical *Ha-Zman* in St. Petersburg 1904 to 1905.

14   Bershadsky, Sergei Alexandrovitch (1850 – 1896). Professor at St. Petersburg University. Non-Jew (Russian Orthodox). One of the first historians of Eastern European Jewry. Collected more than two thousand documents. Was published in *Yevreiskaya Biblioteka* and in *Voskhod*.

15 Bialik, Chaim Nahman (1873–1934). Born near Zhitomir, lived in Palestine from 1924; was in St. Petersburg and took part in conferences of OPE on questions of the reform of school education. Also took part in the congress of OPE on February 23, 1916, where he argued in favor of Hebraism against Shtiff, who was for Yiddishism. Address of OPE: Zagorodny Prospekt 23 (extant).

16 Bliokh, Ivan Stanislavovitch (Bloch) (1836, Radom, Poland–1901, Warsaw). Address: ulitsa Brodskogo 1/7 (formerly Mikhailovskaya ulitsa) (extant). Convert to Christianity, Calvinist, but maintained interest in the Jewish question. Economist, railway constructor, pacifist, philanthropist. Contributed to ICA (Jewish Colonization Association). Was a friend of Herzl.

17 Bogoraz, Vladimir Germanovitch (Nathan Mendelevitch). Adopted pseudonym of N.A. Tan (1865, Ovruch, Volhynia–1936, Rostov-on-Don). Address (1917): Bolshaya Obyezdnaya (formerly Lesnoi Uchastok) 6-a (no longer extant). Russian ethnographer; authority on the Chukchee and Yakutsk peoples and Siberian Eskimos; man of letters, member of Narodnaya Volya (People's Will Party). Converted to Christianity at age of twenty. Director of the Museum of Religion and Atheism; professor at Leningrad University.

18 Botvinnik, Mikhail (1911, St. Petersburg–   ). Soviet chess master; three times world champion. Address (from 1940): Borodinskaya ulitsa 1, apt. 29.

19 Brafman, Yakov Alexandrovitch (1825, Kletsk–1879). Convert to Christianity; at the age of thirty-four he joined Greek Orthodox Church. A bitter anti-Semite; author of the *Kniga Kagala* (The Book of the Kahal) (1869). Government-appointed censor of Hebrew and Yiddish books in Vilna and St. Petersburg. Grandfather of the Russian poet Vladislav Khodasevitch (1886–1940).

20 Braudo, Alexander Isayevitch (1864–1924, London). Assistant director of Imperial Public Library, St. Petersburg. Russian-Jewish historian and civic leader. Member of OPE (Society for the Spread of Enlightenment among the Jews of Russia), OGDK (Society for Help to Jewish Victims of War). Address: ulitsa Saltykova-Shchedrina (formerly Kirochnaya) 43 – B. Son, Isai, a violinist.

21 Brick, Osip Maximovitch (1888, Moscow–1945, Moscow). Address (1917): ulitsa Zhukovskogo 7 (extant). Writer and literary critic. Founder of Society for the Study of Poetic Language (OPOYAZ); editor of the magazines *Leff* and *Noviy Leff*.

22 Brodsky, Isaak Izrailyevitch (1883, in the village of Sofievka, Tavricheskaya Guberniya–1939, Leningrad). Address (1922): Bolshoi Prospekt, Petrogradskaya Storona (formerly Prospekt Karla Liebknechta) 57; in the 1930s, Ploshchad Iskusstv 3 (formerly Ploshchad Lassalya). Painter; a pupil of Repin, director of the Academy of Arts, professor of art. As official portrait painter, his subjects included Kerensky, Trotsky, Lenin, and Stalin. Today the Brodsky Museum stands on Ploshchad Iskusstv.

23   Dashevsky, Pinkhas (1879–1934). In June 1903, while he was a student at the Kiev Polytechnic Institute, he assaulted and wounded P. Krushevan, owner and publisher of the anti-Semitic newspaper *Bessarabets* and the chief instigator of the Kishinev pogrom. The assault took place on Politseisky Most (Bridge) now called Narodny Most, in St. Petersburg. Sentenced to five years of hard labor but released in 1906. Died in a Soviet prison in 1934.

24   Dembo, Isaak Alexandrovitch (1846, Kovno—or Ponevezh—Lithuania–1906, St. Petersburg). Founder of a dynasty of prominent physicians, doctor of medicine, initiator of a campaign to defend Shekhita (Jewish ritual slaughter) against accusations of cruelty to animals (1891), elder of the St. Petersburg Synagogue during the construction of the building. Address (1905): Prospekt Bakunina (formerly Kalashnikovsky Prospekt) 9.

25   Drabkin, Abram Notovitch (1844, Mogilev–1909, St. Petersburg). Address (1894): Naberezhnaya Fontanki, 183 (extant). Doctor of philosophy; active in communal affairs. Rabbi of St. Petersburg Synagogue (1876–1908). Studied in Volozhin, Vilna, and Breslau (Wroclaw) (under Graetz). Wrote in *Vestnik Russkikh Yevreyev* (Russian Jewish Herald) and other papers. Initiator of the First and Second Congresses of Jewish Communal Activists in 1881 and 1882. Founded, and supplied with utilities and equipment, many of the St. Petersburg Jewish communal institutions.

26   Dubnow, Semyon (Simon) Markovitch (1860, Mstislavl–1941, Riga Ghetto). Address: 1883–4, Troitskaya Ploshchad 3 (no longer extant); 1883 and 1885–6, 188 Srednyaya Podyacheskaya 16 (extant); until 1910, 8th Liniya 35 (formerly 33) (extant); 1913–1922, ulitsa Skorokhodova 29 (formerly Bolshaya Monetnaya 21) (extant). Historian, publicist, literary critic. Author of *History of Jews of Lithuania, Poland and Russia.* Editor of *Yevreiskaya Starina* (Jewish Antiquity) (1908–1918). Wrote for *Voskhod* under the pen name Kritikus. He wrote *Universal History of the Jewish People* in ten volumes. Founder of Jewish People's Party (1906); propounded the theory of (Jewish) National Autonomism. Author of *Letters about Ancient and Modern Jewry* (1897–1902). Chairman, Jewish Literary Society; Co-chairman, Historical-Ethnographic Society.

27   Eidelman, Boris Lvovitch (1867–1935). Founder of the Kiev Union to Fight for the Liberation of the Working Class; delegate to the First Congress of the RSDRP (Russian Social Democratic Workers' Party). Imprisoned in the Fortress of St. Peter and St. Paul from 1898 to 1900.

28   Eiger, Yakov Borisovitch. Physician, chairman of the Jewish religious community of Petrograd after 1917. Member of OPE (Society for the Spread of Enlightenment among the Jews of Russia), OZE (Society for the Care of the Health of the Jewish Population). Address in 1917: ulitsa Pestelya (formerly Panteleimonovskaya) 7 (extant).

29   Eisenstadt, Moisei Grigorievitch (1869–1943). Lived (1915) at Naberezhnaya Fontanki 159. Doctor of philosophy; community rabbi of the St. Petersburg-Petrograd Synagogue (1911–1923). Member of the Central Committee of OPE (Society for the Spread of Enlightenment among the Jews of Russia); member of ONM (Jewish Folk Music Society), OLDEY (Society of Lovers of Ancient Hebrew Language), and others. Active in public life.

30   Elport, Isaak Izrailyevitch (1878–1942, Leningrad). Address: ulitsa Furmanova 22, apt. 8. Publisher and editor of *Novozemyelnaya Gazetta* (The Novaya Zemlya Gazette) and *Severniy Zhurnal* (The Northern Magazine); organizer of the scientific-industrial expedition to the Kara Sea to open up navigation from London to Tyumen. A self-taught inventor.

31   Erlich, Henryk (Wolf Hirsh) Moshkovitz (1882, Lublin–1941, Kuibyshev). Lawyer; delegate of the Bund in the Petrograd Soviet in 1917. Son-in-law of Simon Dubnow. Arrested in Poland by the Soviet authorities in 1939 and sentenced to ten years of hard labor. Granted amnesty in September 1941, but immediately rearrested; executed, December 1941. Address from 1913 to 1917: ulitsa Skorokhodova 29 (formerly Bolshaya Monetnaya 21).

32   Friedland Arye-Leib Faivelyevitch (Lev Pavlovitch) (1826–1898). Merchant of the First Guild, full councillor of state, donated his enormous collection of Jewish books and manuscripts to the Asiatic Museum. Burial vault in the Preobrazhensky Cemetery. Address in 1892: 3rd Liniya 4/8 (extant).

33   Frug, Shimon (Simeon) Shmuel Grigoriyevitch (1860, Kherson–1916, Odessa). Address: Troitskaya Ploshchad (no longer extant). Russian-language poet; Palestinophile. Author of a collection of poems *Zionides*, etc. Published in journal *Noviy Put* (A New Path), *Yevreiskoye Obozreniye* (Jewish Review), *Voskhod* (Sunrise). He then turned to Yiddish; his poems and songs were extremely popular with the Jewish masses.

34   Gershov, Solomon Moiseyevitch, (1907, Vitebsk–   ). Leningrad Jewish artist; a pupil of Penn. Lives today in one of the southern suburbs of Leningrad.

35   Gershuni, Grigory (Gersh Isaakov-Itzkov) Andreyevitch (1870, Tavrova, Kovno Guberniya–1908, Zurich, Switzerland). Educated in a Russian high school in Shavli (Siauliai). He organized and headed the Fighting Organization (Boyevaya Organisatsiya) of the Social Revolutionary Party. Responsible for a number of assassinations of some of the highest and most hated officials and dignitaries, including the minister of the interior, Sipyagin (1902) and the governor of Ufa, Bogdanovitch (1903). Was in St. Petersburg from 1902 to 1903, especially on February 12, 1903. Address: Nevsky Prospekt 176 (extant). Buried in Montparnasse Cemetery, Paris.

36   Gewirtz, Yakov Germanovitch (Hermanovitch). Address: Vassilevsky Ostrov, Sredny Prospekt 11 (extant). Architect, designer of the prayer-house in the Preobrazhensky Cemetery and, among some twenty houses in St. Petersburg, including No. 50 5th Liniya. Professor of the Academy of Fine Arts (dean of the faculty of architecture).

37 Ginsburg, Saul Moiseyevitch (1866, Minsk – 1940, New York). Jurist, publicist, historian, folklorist. Member of Central Committee of the OPE. Founder and editor of *Der Fraynd* (the first Yiddish daily in Russia). Took part in the work of the Jewish Scientific Institute in Vilna; professor of Leningrad Institute of Higher Jewish Studies; chairman of the Jewish Literary-Scientific Society. Address: Naberezhnaya Krasnogo Flota (formerly Angleeskaya Naberezhnaya) 12 (extant).

38 Goldman, Mikhail Isaakovitch (Lieber) (1880, Vilna – 1937). Member of Central Committee of the Bund (from 1902). Leader of the Bund delegation to the Second Congress of RSDRP (Russian Social-Democratic Workers' Party) (1903). Member of the Central Committee of the RSDRP (1907). Member of the Executive Committee of the Petrograd Soviet (1917). Member of Presidium of Central Executive Committee of USSR, First Session.

39 Gordon, Yehuda-Leib (Leon) Yosifovitch (Lev Osipovitch), also known as J. L. Gordon (wrote under the pseudonyms of Mevakker (Hebrew for "The Critic") and Esol, (1830, Vilna – 1892, St. Petersburg). Lived in St. Petersburg from 1872. Address: Prospekt Moskvina (formerly Troitsky Prospekt) 10 (extant). Hebrew poet. One of the Maskilim (the Jewish Nekrassov). Secretary to St. Petersburg Jewish community and secretary of OPE (Society for the Spread of Enlightenment among the Jews of Russia); editor of *Ha-Melitz* (from 1880). Imprisoned in St. Petersburg's Litovsky Zamok (the Lithuanian Fortress) in 1879, following a false accusation. His works were printed in *Yevreiskaya Biblioteka, Tzion, Dyen* (The Day), *Golos* (The Voice), *Voskhod* (Sunrise). In *Voskhod* he wrote "The History of the Settlement of the Jews in St. Petersburg" (1881, I – II).

40 Grusenberg, Izrail Yosifovitch (Oscar Osipovitch) (1866, Ekaterinoslav, now called Dniepropetrovsk – 1940, Nice, France). Address: Sadovaya ulitsa 123 (extant); (1904) Ligovsky Prospekt (formerly Ligovskaya ulitsa) 63; also ulitsa Nekrassova (formerly Basseinaya) 7, and (1913) ulitsa Saltykova-Shchedrina 34 (formerly Kirochnaya). Legal expert, advocate. Defended Mendel Beilis, Gorky, Korolenko, Anensky, Tchukovsky, Milyukov, the members of the First Duma who signed the Vyborg Appeal; also defended the Soviet of Workers and Deputies of St. Petersburg, and acted as defense counsel in the Armenian case, the Minsk pogrom trial, the Kishinev pogrom trial, the Blondes case, and the Dashevsky trial. His brother S. O. Grusenberg was a writer and a doctor. After the February 1917 Revolution Oscar Grusenberg was appointed senator by the provisional government; when the Soviets assumed power he left the country.

41 Grusenberg, Samuel Osipovitch. Younger brother of the famous lawyer. A doctor of medicine; worked as a journalist, editor, and publisher. Until 1899 he worked on *Voskhod* and edited *Nedelnaya Khronika Voskhoda* (Weekly Bulletin of Voskhod) and *Budushchnost* (The Future). Address: Pushkinskaya ulitsa.

42 Guenzburg, Alexander, Baron. Address: Krasnaya ulitsa (formerly Galernaya ulitsa) 43 (extant); 8th Liniya 43; ulitsa Soyuza Petchatnikov (formerly Torgovaya ulitsa) 17. Son of Baron Horace Guenzburg. Owner of gold mines, banker, philanthropist (especially Jewish Orphanage).

43   Guenzburg, Alfred, Baron. Address (1912): Krasnaya ulitsa (formerly Galernaya ulitsa) 61 (extant). Son of Baron Horace Guenzburg. Owner of gold mines, Chairman of OGDK (Society for Hygienic Cheap Apartments for the Jewish Population).

44   Guenzburg, David Goratzievitch, Baron (1857–1910). Son of Baron Horace Guenzburg. Address: Ploshchad Shevchenko (formerly Rumyantsevskaya) 3 (extant). President of St. Petersburg Jewish community, orientalist, councillor of state, philanthropist, editor-in-chief of *Yevreiskaya Entsiklopedia*; President of OPB (Society for the Relief of Poor Jews), ICA (Jewish Colonization Association), OLDEY (Society of Lovers of Ancient Hebrew Language); founder of the Higher Jewish Studies Courses. Owned a large library of valuable ancient books and manuscripts in Hebrew, bought by Zionists for a university in Jerusalem, but still today in the Lenin Library in Moscow.

45   Guenzburg, Dmitry, Baron. Son of Baron Horace Guenzburg. Address (1915): ulitsa Khalturina (formerly Millionaya ulitsa) 26 (extant). Chairman of the administration of the House of Lovers of Work, near the Alexander Nevsky Monastery.

46   Guenzburg, Gabriel-Yakov, Baron. Another son of Baron Horace Guenzburg, managing director of a chain of steamship companies on the River Sheksna. Address (1913): Krasnaya ulitsa (formerly Galernaya) 18 (extant).

47   Guenzburg, Horace Yevselevitch, Baron (1833, Zvenigorod, Kiev Province–1909, St. Petersburg). Lived in St. Petersburg from 1859. Address: Krasnaya ulitsa (formerly Galernaya) 20 (extant); Pere'ulok Leonova 4 (Bank I. E. Guenzburg); Boulevard Profsoyuzov 17, Krasnaya ulitsa 22 (formerly Zamyatin Pere'ulok 4, Konnogvardeisky Prospekt 17, Galernaya ulitsa 22) one house (extant). Banker, owner of gold mines, philanthropist, president of the St. Petersburg Jewish community, chairman of ICA (Jewish Colonization Association), OPE (Society for the Spread of Enlightenment among the Jews of Russia); founder of ORT, the Institute of Archeology, and the Institute of Experimental Medicine; active councillor of state; made a fundamental contribution to the construction of the St. Petersburg Choral Synagogue. Buried in Paris.

48   Guenzburg, Ilya Yakovlevitch (1859, Grodno–1939, Leningrad). Address (1904): Vassilevsky Ostrov 2nd Liniya 11 (extant). Artist and sculptor, studied under Mark Antokolski; works include the tombstone over the grave of V. V. Stassov; the memorial to G. V. Plekhanov (1925); busts of Pyotr Tchaikovsky, Shishkin, Leonid Pasternak, Antokolski, Roditchev, Pavel Milyukov, and Chaliapin. Chairman of the Jewish Society for the Encouragement of the Arts; Director of Jewish Historical-Ethnographic Museum.

49   Harkavy, Albert (Abram) Yakovlevitch (1835, Novogrudok, Bielorussia–1919, Petrograd). Address: Bolshaya Pushkarskaya 47. Orientalist, historian, scholar of Jewish history and literature, head of the Oriental manuscripts department of the Imperial Public Library. Published works on the Jews of Russia, Poland, and Lithuania; on the Karaites and the Khazars; on archeology; and on other subjects. Made a special study of, and exposed the forgeries in, the Hebrew and Arabic manuscripts in the Firkovitch Collection. Active in public affairs, especially in the Jewish community; member of the Central Committee of OPE. Warden of the St. Petersburg Synagogue.

50   Hertzenstein, Mikhail Yakovlevitch (1859, Odessa – 1905). Convert to Christianity, economist, member of the Constitutional Democrats (Cadets), Deputy to the First Duma (1905), spoke in the Duma on agrarian questions. Killed in 1905 by Black Hundreds in Tereoki (now Zelenogorsk, outside Leningrad), ten days after the Duma was dissolved. Memorial near the place of the murder on the coast of the Bay of Finland, near the convalescent home Tcharodeika. The inscription on it has been erased.

51   Herzl, Theodor. Lived in St. Petersburg from August 7 to 16, 1903. Among those whom he met were V. K. von Plehve (in Pavlovsk and St. Petersburg) and S. Y. Witte (on the islands). The Zionists of St. Petersburg arranged a dinner in his honor.

52   Hessen, Yosef Vladimirovitch (1866, Odessa – 1943). Address (1906): ulitsa Sofia Perovskoi (formerly Malaya Konyushennaya) 1/3 (extant). Advocate, barrister, in 1898 he founded the law journal *Pravo,* and he also contributed to the magazine *Ryetch.* Member of Central Committee of Cadets (Constitutional Democratic Party). Elected deputy to the Second Duma (1907). After 1917 he left Russia for Helsinki and then Berlin.

53   Hessen, Yuli Isidorovitch (1871, Odessa – 1939). Address: Baskov Pere'ulok 25 (extant); ulitsa Nekrassova (formerly Basseinaya) 35. Historian, author of *History of the Jews of Russia* (1914) and *History of the Jewish People in Russia* (two volumes, 1925, 1927). Founder of Society for Scientific Jewish Publications. Initiated publication of *Yevreiskaya Entsiklopedia* (sixteen volumes, 1908 – 1913).

54   Idelson, Abram Davidovitch (1865, Vekshin, Lithuania – 1921, Berlin). In St. Petersburg from 1905. Address: Vassilevsky Ostrov, 6th Liniya, 41 (extant). Member of the Central Committee of the Zionist Organization. Editor of journal *Rassvet* (Dawn); member of OLDEY (Society of Lovers of Ancient Hebrew Language) and of the Jewish Literary Society. Journalist, publicist.

55   Izgoyev (Lyande) A. S. Member of the Central Committee of the Cadets (Constitutional Democrats). Address (1906): 3rd Sovietskaya (formerly 3rd Rozhdestvenskaya) 9, apt. 3 (extant).

56   Kaminka, A. I. Member of the Central Committee of the Cadets (Constitutional Democrats). Philanthropist, financier. Address (1906): Ligovsky Prospekt 87 (extant).

57   Katzenellenbogen, David-Tevel (Tuvia) Hertzelevitch (1850, Taurogen, Lithuania – 1930, Leningrad). In St. Petersburg from 1908. Address: Pere'ulok Makarenko (formerly Usatchev Pere'ulok) 2; then Lermontovsky Prospekt 8 (extant); also Teatralnaya Ploshchad 2. Chief rabbi and spiritual leader of the St. Petersburg–Petrograd–Leningrad community (1908–1930). A descendant of Levi Ben Bezalel. Talmudist; author of many religious works.

58   Katzenelson, Lev Izrailyevitch (Yehuda-Leib Benjamin) (1846, Chernigov–1917, Petrograd). In St. Petersburg from 1878. Wrote under the pen name of Buki Ben Yogli. Address: Izmailovsky Prospekt 5 (extant). Doctor of medicine; Hebrew writer; active supporter of the Haskala. Member of the Central Committee of OPE (Society for the Spread of Enlightenment among the Jews of Russia) and of the Central Committee of ICA (Jewish Colonization Association). Editor *Yevreiskaya Entsiklopedia* (Jewish Encyclopedia); chairman of OLDEY (Society of Lovers of Ancient Hebrew Language). Works published in *Russky Yevrei* (The Russian Jew), *Ha-Melitz* (The Advocate), *Yevreiskoye Obozreniye* (Jewish Review), *Ha-Yom* (Today). Published works on medicine in the Talmud, works on history and religion, and short stories — all in Hebrew. On the death of Baron David Guenzburg, he became head of the Institute of Jewish Studies.

59   Kisselgoff, Zinovy Aronovitch (?–1938, Leningrad). Address (1917): Naberezhnaya Fontanki 21 (no longer extant); from 1925 to 1937, Vassilevsky Ostrov 10th Liniya 37 (extant). Pedagogue, music folklorist, activist in promotion of school education. Member of the Central Committee of OPE (Society for the Spread of Enlightenment among the Jews of Russia); director of Jewish Children's Home No. 93 (1925), No. 14, then No. 11 Jewish National School at the same address. One of the founders of the Jewish Teachers Association (1917).

60   Klionsky, Yefim Yevseyevitch (1892–1961). Address (1920s): Vassilevsky Island 5th Liniya 50 (extant). Senior physician and director of the Jewish Almshouse at the same address. Member of the Museum Commission at the Jewish Museum. Professor at the second Leningrad Medical Institute.

61   Kovner, Avraham-Urieh (1842, Vilna–1909). Yeshivah student, then a left-wing feuilletonist in the St. Petersburg paper *Golos* (The Voice) (1872–1874). In 1865 he published a collection of essays in Hebrew (Heker Davar), attacking the narrow, romantic confines of Haskalah literature. After 1868 he wrote only in Russian and called for the closing of Yeshivot. Arrested in 1875 and charged with stealing 168,000 rubles from the bank where he worked. Known for his correspondence from prison and exile with leading Russian writers, including Dostoyevsky, Rozanov, and Tolstoi. At the age of fifty he converted to Christianity and married a high school final-year student. Address of the St. Petersburg Discount and Loan Bank (established 1869): Nevsky Prospekt 30 (extant).

62   Kreinin, Miron Naumovitch (Meir) (1866, Bykhov, Bielorussia–1939, Jerusalem). Vice-chairman of the Jewish Literary-Scientific Society. Member of the Jewish Literary Society and of OPE (Society for the Spread of Enlightenment among the Jews of Russia). Address (1913): Pere'ulok Ilyicha (formerly Bolshoi Kazatchiy) 13 (extant).

63   Kulisher, Mikhail Ignatyevitch (1847–1919, St. Petersburg). Historian, sociologist, legal expert, ethnographer, journalist; active in communal affairs. Works published in magazines *Dyen* (The Day), *Rassvet* (Dawn) (1879), *Zarya* (Dawn). Author of Jewish school textbooks and of curricula for primary, secondary, and higher education; organizer of education; member of the Central Committee of OPE (Society for the Spread of Enlightenment among the Jews of Russia); member of the Jewish National Group; founder of the Society for Jewish Scientific Publications. Address (1917): ulitsa Mayakovskogo 56 (formerly Nadezhdinskaya ulitsa).

64   Lensky (Steinson) Hayim (1905, Slonim, Grodno District–1942, Soviet prison camp). Hebrew poet. In Leningrad from 1925 to 1934. In the 1920s he joined a group of young Hebrew poets that included Krivoruchko, Bat-miriam, and Shvartz. In 1925 he settled in Leningrad as a worker in the Amal metal factory founded by the Hehalutz organization. In late 1934 he was arrested for writing in Hebrew and sentenced to five years of hard labor in Siberia. Returned to Malaya Vishera, near Leningrad, in 1939 but was again arrested in 1941, and disappeared.

65   Levanda, Lev. Writer, journalist, Maskil, assimilationist; published in journals *Voskhod* (Sunrise), *Yevreiskaya Biblioteka* (Jewish Library), *Yevreiskoye Obozreniye* (Jewish Review), *Russky Yevrei* (The Russian Jew). Author of the novel *The Burning Time.*

66   Levi, Lipman. Reached St. Petersburg from Courland. With the titles of Oberhofcommissar and commercial agent, he was financial adviser at the court of the Empress Anne (Anna Ioannovna) and was a friend of Biren, one of Anne's favorites.

67   Lozinsky, Samuil Hertzevitch (1874 Bobruisk, Bielorussia–1945). Russian historian; rector at the Institute of Higher Jewish Studies. Specialist on the history of the Jews in the Middle Ages and on Western Europe in modern times. Address: 1913, Degtyarnaya ulitsa 39; 1922, Zagorodny Prospekt 34.

68   Lubanov, Abram Ruvimovitch (1888–1973). Address: Lermontovsky Prospekt 2 (lived on the synagogue premises until 1958), then at Altaiskaya ulitsa 2, apt. 5 (1958–1973). Rabbi of the Leningrad Choral Synagogue (1943–1973). A Hasid. A graduate of the Lubavitcher yeshivah.

69   Maggid, David Hillarovitch (1862, Vilna–1942). Son of Hillel-Noah Maggid-Steinschneider; stonemason, book dealer, epitaph writer, and biographer of Vilna. Address in 1917: ulitsa Dekabristov (formerly Offitserskaya) 36. Active in Jewish communal affairs; teacher, bibliographer, epigraphist. Bibliographer for OPE (Society for the Spread of Enlightenment among the Jews of Russia); head of the Hebrew department in the Petrograd Public Library, 1919.

70   Maimon, Moisei Lvovitch (1860–1924, Petrograd). Address in 1904: Sadovaya ulitsa 63 (extant); also Bolshaya Podyacheskaya 24 (extant). Artist; elected to the Academy of Fine Arts for his picture *The Marranos.*

71   Mandelstam, Lev Yosifovitch (1819, Noviye Zhagori–1889, St. Petersburg). A Maskil; entered Moscow University in 1840, then transferred to St. Petersburg University, where he graduated as a candidate of philosophy in

1844. The first Jew to graduate from a Russian university. Counsellor in Jewish affairs at the Ministry of National Enlightenment.

72   Mandelstam, Osip Emilyevitch (1891, Warsaw – 1938 in a Soviet prison camp). Address: Zagorodny Prospekt 70 (extant); in 1926, ulitsa Herzena (formerly Bolshaya Morskaya) 49. Russian poet. Memoirs of childhood in *Shum Vremeni* (The Noise of Time) (1925).

73   Margolin, Moisei Markovitch (1862 – ?). Secretary of the editorial board of the *Russian Encyclopedic Dictionary* and of several other Russian encyclopedias of the publishers Brockhaus and Yefron. Lawyer. A cousin of Eliezer Margolin, who was commander of the Second Battalion of the Jewish Legion (49th Royal Fusiliers) (1917 – 1918). Address: ulitsa Soyuza Petchatnikov (formerly Torgovaya) 28.

74   Markon, Isaak (Dov-Ber) Yulyevitch (1875, Rybinsk – 1949, London). Titular privy councillor. Orientalist; worked in the manuscripts department of Imperial Public Library. Candidate of Oriental languages; professor at Leningrad University. Member of OLDEY (Society of Lovers of Ancient Hebrew Language). An elder of the St. Petersburg Synagogue. In *Perezhitoye* (Experiences), he describes the A. Voznitsyn Affair. Address in 1917: ulitsa Dekabristov (formerly Offitserskaya) 50 (extant). Left Petrograd in 1922 (professor at Minsk — Bielorussian — University, 1922 – 1924). Left Russia in 1926. Fled from Holland in 1940 and escaped to England.

75   Marshak, Samuil (Samuel) Yakovlevitch (1887, Voronezh – 1964, Moscow). Address (1927 – 1938): Liteiny Prospekt 21 (extant). Children's poet; many translations from English. Head of Lendetgiz (Leningrad Publishing House of Children's Books). Lenin Prize (1963). Autobiography: *At the Start of Life* (1960); Verses: "Over His Grave" (A Jewish Life, 1904), "Jerusalem" (Safrut, 1922).

76   Martov, L. (Yuli Osipovitch Zederbaum) (1873, Constantinople – 1923). One of the organizers of the Bund and the RSDRP (Russian Social-Democratic Workers' Party — Mensheviks). Studied at St. Petersburg University (1890 – 1892). Member of the St. Petersburg Soviet (1905, 1917); editor of the paper *Nachalo* (The Beginning). Grandson of the Hebrew, Yiddish, and Russian publisher, A. I. Zederbaum.

77   Mikhoels, Solomon Mikhailovitch (Vovsi) (1890, Dvinsk – 1948, Minsk). Most famous Soviet-Jewish actor; director of the Moscow State Jewish Theater (GOSET). Graduate of Petrograd University (1915 – 1918) faculty of law. Helped in the formation of the Jewish Theatrical Studio in Petrograd in 1919, which developed into the State Theater. Address (1917): Pere'ulok Dzhamboula (formerly Leshtukov Pere'ulok) 2 (extant).

78   Montefiore, Sir Moses (1784, Leghorn, Italy – 1885, England). Anglo-Jewish public figure. Visited St. Petersburg in 1846 and in 1872. In 1872 he stayed at Hotel De Klee (now Yevropeiskaya), ulitsa Brodskogo (formerly Mikhailovskaya) 1/7 (extant).

79   Nadson, Simeon Yakovlevitch (1862 – 1886). Russian poet. Son of a baptized Jewish musician and a Russian-Orthodox lady of nobility. Author of the poem "I Grew Up Alien to Thee, O People Outcast." Address (1884): ulitsa Petra Lavrova (formerly Furshtadskaya) 25 (extant).

80   Nathanson, Mark Andreyevitch (Bobrov) (1850, Kovno – 1918, Switzerland). In St. Petersburg 1868 – 1872 and 1875 – 1879. Revolutionary, member of Narodnaya Volya (People's Will Party), then of the Social Revolutionary Party (SRs). Member of Central Committee Left SRs. (Studied at the Medico-Surgical Academy 1868 – 1872.) Imprisoned in the Fortress of St. Peter and St. Paul (1877 – 1880). Exiled to Siberia in the 1880s, and again from 1894 to 1902.

81   Nevakhovitch, Yehuda-Leib Ben Noach (Lev Nikolayevitch) (1776, Letichev, Ukraine – 1831). One of the earliest Maskilim; founder of the school of Russian-Jewish literature. Author of *The Wailing of the Daughter of Judaea,* which he dedicated to the minister of the interior, Kochubey. Was coopted as a member, in an advisory capacity, on the Speransky Commission to Study the Jewish Question (1803). Was tutor to the children of A. Peretz, in whose house he lived. Address: Nevsky Prospekt 15 (extant). Nevakhovitch's conversion to Christianity (Lutheran) turned many people away from the Haskala.

82   Notovitch, Yosif Konstantinovitch (1849, Kerch – 1914). Address: Canal Griboyedova (formerly Yekaterinensky Canal) 113 (extant). Son of a rabbi, in his youth he converted to Christianity (the Greek Orthodox Church). Published the daily *Novosti* (News) (1876 – 1905). Journalist; doctor of philosophy, he graduated from the St. Petersburg University.

83   Orshansky, Ilya (Elijah) Grigoryevitch (1846 – 1875). Maskil, historian, assimilationist. He was in St. Petersburg in the 1870s.

84   Pasmanik, David (1869, Gadyach in the Ukraine – 1930). Zionist writer and leader; journalist. Wrote in *Yevreiskaya Zhizn* (Jewish Life) and *Rassvet* (Dawn), author of the book *Stranstvuyushchy Izrail* (The Wandering Jew). After 1917 he joined the monarchists and emigrated to Paris.

85   Peretz, Abram (1771 – 1833). One of the first Maskilim and a leader of the Jewish community. Lived in St. Petersburg from about 1800. Address: Nevsky Prospekt 15 (extant). A protégé of Prince Potemkin. Tax farmer. He joined the Speransky Commission to Study the Jewish Question in advisory capacity. Convert to Christianity. His son Grigory was a Decembrist, his son Yegor a senator, governmental secretary and member of the State Council.

86   Peretz, Grigory (Hirsch) Abramovitch (1788 – 1855). Address in 1803: Nevsky Prospekt 15 (extant). Founded the Society for Liberation of the Jews . . . and Their Settlement in the Crimea. Converted to Christianity, together with his father, in 1813. After the revolt of the Decembrists (1825) he was imprisoned and banished to northern Russia but was allowed to leave for Odessa twenty years later (1845).

87   Polyakov, Lazar Solomonovitch (1842, Dubrovno, Bielorussia – 1914). Addresses: Naberezhnaya Krasnogo Flota (formerly Angleeskaya Naberezhnaya) 12 (extant); Krasnaya ulitsa (formerly Galernaya) 11 (extant). Privy councillor. Chairman of the Moscow Jewish community. Banker; builder of railways; active in public affairs; philanthropist.

88 **Polyakov, Samuil Solomonovitch** (1837, Dubrovno, Bielorussia – 1888, St. Petersburg). Address: Naberezhnaya Krasnogo Flota (formerly Angleeskaya Naberezhnaya) 4 (extant), formerly the home of Countess Laval, which he bought in 1870. Privy councillor; large-scale contractor in the construction of railways. Banker, millionaire, philanthropist, founder of ORT (Society for Craft and Agricultural Labor among the Jews of Russia); member of Central Committee of ICA (Jewish Colonization Association). There is a statue of him by Antokolsky in the Russian Museum, Leningrad.

89 **Polyakov, Yakov Solomonovitch** (1832, Dubrovno, Bielorussia – 1909, Biarritz). Address: Naberezhnaya Krasnogo Flota (formerly Angleeskaya Naberezhnaya) 62; also Krasnaya ulitsa (formerly Galernaya ulitsa) 63. Privy councillor, banker, tax farmer, builder of railways. Brother of S. and L. Polyakov. Vice-chairman in Russia of ICA (Jewish Colonization Association).

90 **Propper, Maxim.** Banker; publisher of the newspaper *Stock Exchange News,* published at Canal Krushteina 15 (formerly Admiralteisky Canal) (1913). Home address: Nevsky Prospekt 28 (no longer extant).

91 **Pulner, I. M.** Head of the Jewish section in the government Museum of Ethnography of the Peoples of the USSR. In charge of the Jewish department in the Public Library. Died during the siege of Leningrad (1941 – 1944). The Pulner archives are in the Ethnography Museum, Leningrad.

92 **Ravrebbe, Yechiel I** (1882 – 1938). Address (1920s): Vassilevsky Ostrov, 5th Liniya 50 (extant). Orientalist, Hebraist. Translated ancient Jewish "Pinkasim" of Russia and Poland. Worked in the manuscript department of the Public Library. Had a command of many languages. Taught at the Institute of Bielorussian Culture (Jewish section) in the 1920s.

93 **Rubashov, Zalman (Shazar)** (1889, Mir, Minsk Province, Bielorussia – 1974, Jerusalem). Together with his future wife, Rachel Katznelson, he attended lectures at the Courses of Oriental Studies in St. Petersburg, organized by Baron David Guenzburg. He was third president of the State of Israel (two terms, 1963 – 1973).

94 **Rubinstein, Anton Grigoriyevitch** (1829, Podolia – 1894, St. Petersburg). Address (1887 – 1891): ulitsa Rubinsteina 38 (extant). Composer, pianist; he founded the St. Petersburg Conservatoire in 1862, becoming its director. Converted to Christianity as a child. There is a memorial plaque on the house.

95 **Rutenberg, Pinkhas (Piotr) Moiseyevitch** (1879, Romny, Ukraine – 1942, Jerusalem). Graduated from the St. Petersburg Technological Institute. Worked as an engineer at the Putilov factory. Social Democrat, then a Social Revolutionary, then a Zionist. Participated in the execution of Father Gapon, 1906. When he realized that there was anti-Semitism even in the revolutionary movements he left Russia for Palestine, November 1919. Established the Palestine Electric Corporation in 1923, using hydroelectric power from the River

Jordan. Address in St. Petersburg in 1905: Prospekt Stachek (formerly Peter-hofskoye Chaussée) 48, apt. 1 (no longer extant).

96   Sanchez, Antonio Nunez Ribeiro (1699, Portugal – 1748, Paris). Portuguese Marrano. In St. Petersburg from 1740 to 1747. Physician; second senior doctor of medicine at Court. Treated the Empresses Elizabeth and Catherine II. Honorary Member of the Academy of Sciences (1747 – 1748 and 1762 – 1770). Author of books *On the Treatment of Syphilis* and *On the Therapeutic Qualities of Russian Baths*. Also wrote on the reasons for the persecution of the Jews.

97   Schneerson, Menachem Mendel (1902–   ). Son-in-law of the "Rayyats." Was in Petrograd-Leningrad from 1924 to 1927. Address: Mokho-vaya ulitsa 22/12 (extant). After the death of his father-in-law in 1950 he became (in New York) the seventh successive Lubavitcher rebbe and head of World Lubavitch Movement. Lives today (1988) in New York.

98   Schneerson, Yosef-Yitzhak Ben Sholom (Sholomovitch) (1880 – 1950, New York). Lubavitcher Tzadik who assumed the leadership of the Habad Hasidim during the civil war after the 1917 Revolution. Was in Petro-grad-Leningrad from 1924 to 1927. Address: Mokhovaya ulitsa 22/12 (extant). Known as "Rayyats" (*Rabbi Yosef-Yitzhak*).

99   Sev, Leopold Alexandrovitch (1867 – 1922, Paris). Editor of *Voskhod* (Sunrise), *Svoboda i Raventsvo* (Freedom and Equality), *Yevreiskaya Nedelya* (Jewish Week), *Reguisti I Nadpeesi* (Registers and Inscriptions), and *Yevreis-kaya Tribuna* (Jewish Tribune) (in Paris). Brother-in-law of Maxim Vinaver.

100   Shafirov, Piotr Pavlovitch (1669 – 1739). Baron. His palace was between the Nevsky Prospekt and Kirpichny Pere'ulok; he also lived on ulitsa Herzena and ulitsa Gogolya (neither extant). Vice-chancellor under Peter the Great. His grandfather was a convert to Christianity.

101   Shapiro, Felix Lvovitch (1879 – 1961, Moscow). Author of the only Hebrew-Russian dictionary published in the Soviet Union (1963). Lived in St. Petersburg from 1906 to 1915. Taught at the Yugenburg School. Address: 5th Sovietskaya (formerly 5th Rozhdestvenskaya) 16. His grandson Michael Prestin was one of the leaders of the Jewish national movement in Moscow in the early 1970s.

102   Sheftel, Mikhail Isaakovitch (1858, Zhitomir – 1922, Petrograd). Jurist; a graduate of the faculty of law of St. Petersburg University, he became one of the most noted lawyers in Russia. Chairman of the Society for Scientific Jewish Publications, member of the Central Committee of OPE (Society for the Spread of Enlightenment among the Jews of Russia), IEO (Historical-Ethno-graphic Society), EKOPO (Jewish Society for Aid to Victims of the War), and others. Member of the Bureau for the Defense of Jewish Rights, member of the Central Committee of the League for Equal Rights for Jews, Deputy to the First Duma for the Cadets (Constitutional Democrats), a signatory of the Vyborg Appeal.

103   Shneur, Dr. Zalman Ben Borukh (Borukhovitch) (Zalman La-dier of Liozno, Bielorussia) (1745, Liozno, Mogilev District – 1813, Piena,

Kursk District). Founder of the Habad (Lubavitcher Hasidism). As a result of a slanderous denunciation by the Misnagdim, he was imprisoned in St. Petersburg 1798 and again from 1800 to 1801. On both occasions he was incarcerated in the Fortress of St. Peter and St. Paul.

104   Sholem Aleikhem (Solomon Naumovitch Rabinovitch) (1859, Pereyaslavl, Ukraine – 1916, New York). In May 1914, coming from Lausanne for a lecture tour of Russia, he visited St. Petersburg, staying at the Astoria Hotel. Address: ulitsa Herzena (formerly Bolshaya Morskaya) 39. Dubnow visited him here on May 14, 1914.

105   Simonovitch, Shimon Avelyevitch (1886, Vilna Province – ?). Social Democrat, anarchist, anarcho-Communist. Several times arrested and sent into exile; imprisoned in the Schlisselburg Fortress from 1911 to 1917.

106   Sliozberg, Henry Borisovitch (1863, Mir, Bielorussia – 1937, Paris). Address in 1906: Kovensky Pere'ulok 17 (extant). Lawyer, active in Jewish communal affairs. Member of the Board of Management of the St. Petersburg Jewish Community. One of the organizers of the Society for Equal Rights, members of which met in his home. Member of OGDK (Society for Hygienic Cheap Apartments for the Jewish Population). Member of the Legal Society of the Imperial University of St. Petersburg.

107   Sternberg, Lev Yakovlevitch (1861, Zhitomir – 1927, Leningrad). Addresses: Universitetskaya Naberezhnaya 5 (1922) (extant); Sablinskaya ulitsa 10. Member of Narodnaya Volya (People's Will Party), ethnographer, professor at Leningrad University. Was exiled in 1889 to the island of Sakhalin, where he studied the Gilyak, Arak, Tungu, and Aina peoples. Editor of *Yevreiskaya Starina* (Jewish Antiquity) (from 1924). Member of League for the Attainment of Equal Rights for the Jews in Russia and of Jewish People's Group (1906). Articles: "The Tragedy of the Six Million People," "The Problem of Russian Jewry," "The Latest Findings in the Anthropology of the Jews." Organizer of the Museum of Ethnography.

108   Tchernichowsky (Gutmanovitch) Saul (1875, Mikhailovka village, Ukraine – 1943, Jerusalem). Hebrew poet; translator. Doctor of medicine (physician). His literary life may be divided into five periods: Odessa (1890 – 1899); Heidelberg-Lausanne (1899 – 1906); Russia (1906 – 1922); Berlin (1922 – 1931); and Palestine (1931 – 1943). He lived in St. Petersburg from 1915 to 1922.

109   Trainin, Shmuel (Samuil Aronovitch). Address: Prospekt Ogorodnikova (formerly Rizhsky Prospekt) 48 (extant). Leader of the Hasidic community in the 1910s, owner of the metalwork factory S. A. Trainin in St. Petersburg, Merchant of the First Guild.

110   Trumpeldor, Ioseph (1880, Pyatigorsk – 1920, Tel-Hai, Palestine). Awarded the medal of the Order of St. George and promoted to officer rank, for heroism in action in the Russo-Japanese War (1904). One of the founders of the Jewish self-defense organization, Hagana. Went to Palestine 1912. Deported by the Turks 1914. Helped to found the Zion Mule Corps in Egypt as deputy commander, which later became nucleus of Jewish Legion. In summer 1917 he tried to persuade the provisional government to form a Jewish self-defense military unit (1917) and regiments in the Russian Army to fight Turkey. While in Petrograd, he organized training for settlement in Palestine, 1917 to 1919. He wrote an account of these events in his memoirs. Killed by Arabs in the Upper Galilee.

111   Utevsky, Hirschel (Gershon) Monus-Leibovitch (Grigory Lvovitch). Doctor of medicine, well-known pediatrician, hero of the Russo-Japanese War of 1904. Lived on Krestovsky Island. Address: Konstantinovsky Prospekt 15. He also owned a wooden house at Morskoi Prospekt, No. 39 (no longer extant).

112   Utyussov, Leonid Osipovitch. Originator of Soviet jazz. Lived in Leningrad in the early 1930s. Address: Mayakovskogo 21, apt. 14 (extant).

113   Valk, Sigismund Natanovitch. Historian, archeologist, student of A. S. Lappo-Danilevski. Taught in 1910 at the Eisenbet Jewish Gymnasium. Professor at Leningrad University for thirty years; worked on the encyclopedia *Granat.* A bust of him stands today in the history faculty room of the University of Leningrad. Died in 1975 at age 84.

114   Vinaver, Maxim Moiseyevitch (1862, Warsaw – 1926, Menton – St. Bernard, France). Address: ulitsa Kalyaeva (formerly Zakharyevskaya) 25 (extant). Lawyer, communal worker, and politician. One of the founders of the Constitutional Democratic Party (Cadets) and the Union for Equal Rights, founder of the Jewish People's Group *(Narodnaya Gruppa).* Unofficial leader of the Jewish faction in the First Duma (twelve members). Took part in the Vyborg Appeal and was punished with the rest. Brilliant orator, editor of the magazine *Herald of the Law,* chairman of the Jewish Association for the Encouragement of the Arts, a friend and patron of Marc Chagall. Member of the Central Committee of OPE. President of the Historical-Ethnographic Society.

115   Vinnikov, Isaac Natanovitch (1897, Khotimsk, Bielorussia – 1973, Leningrad). Student of Lev Sternberg. Head of Institute of Oriental Studies at the Academy of Sciences in Leningrad. Dean of the faculty of Assyrian and Middle-Eastern inscriptions at Leningrad University. Published works on pre-Islamic Arab history and culture, and on the customs and language of Arab tribes in Central Asia.

116   Warshawski, Abraham Moiseyevitch (1821 – 1888, St. Petersburg). Banker, railway constructor (Moscow – Brest-Litovsk – Poltava railway), and philanthropist; active in Jewish communal affairs, especially OPE; burial vault preserved in the Preobrazhensky (Jewish) Cemetery. Son, Mark, chairman of the financial management of the St. Petersburg Jewish Community. Address: Bank M. A. Warshawski and Co., Prospekt Macleana (formerly Angleesky Prospekt) 21 (1915) (no longer extant).

117   Wawelberg, Hippolit Andreevitch (1843, Warsaw – 1901). Banker and philanthropist, head of the banking house, Gunne-Nussen, Wawelberg. Bank address: Nevsky Prospekt 25/1 (until 1912), Nevsky Prospekt 7/9 (after 1912). Left Warsaw for St. Petersburg, 1869; member of OPE, one of the treasurers and supporters of ICA (Jewish Colonization Association).

118   Wiener, Samuel Yeremeyevitch (1860–1929). Hebrew bibliographer; in 1887 appointed to work in department of Hebrew and Yiddish books in the Asiatic Museum of the Imperial Academy of Sciences. Helped to acquire and cataloged the Friedland Collection. Address (1913): Vassilevsky Ostrov, ulitsa Repina (formerly Solovevsky Pere'ulok) 23.

119   Yefron (Efron), Ilya Abramovitch (1847, Vilna–1917, Petrograd). Great-grandson of the Vilna Gaon; book publisher; founder of the publishing house Brockhaus and Yefron.

120   Yudovin, Solomon Borisovitch (1892, Vitebsk–1954, Leningrad). Address in the 1920s and 1930s: Vassilevsky Ostrov, 5th Liniya 50 (extant). Graphic artist; a pupil of Penn. In St. Petersburg from 1910. Curator of the Jewish Museum. Author of *Album of Jewish Ornaments* (1920); illustrator for the novel *Jew Suss,* by Leon Feuchtwanger. Nephew of S. An-sky.

121   Zakheim, Moisei Davidovitch (1885, Ruzhani, Grodno Province–?). A weaver by trade, revolutionary, member of the Bund in Bialystok (1903); Social Revolutionary, member of the Fighting Organization (1904); carried out attempts on the lives of the chief of the Okhrana in Bialystok, the police chief, and Police Inspector Samsonov, organizers of the Bialystok pogrom of 1905. He was arrested in St. Petersburg in 1906, but escaped from the convict transport train (étape) while on the way to Siberia. Arrested again in 1908 and sentenced to fifteen years of hard labor. Imprisoned in Schlisselburg, 1910–1917.

122   Zederbaum, Alexander Yosifovitch (1816, Zamosc, Poland–1893, St. Petersburg). Famous publisher of Jewish press in three languages: *Ha-Melitz* (Hebrew) (The Advocate—the first Hebrew weekly published in Russia; 1860); *Vestnik Russkikh Yevreyev* (Russian) (Russian Jewish Herald; 1871); Dos *Yiddishe Folksblat* (Yiddish) (Jewish People's News-sheet; 1881). Address: 3rd Krasnoarmeiskaya (formerly 3rd Rota) 10 (no longer extant). Grandfather of the revolutionary Y. Martov.

123   Zeitlin, Joshua (1742, Shklov–1822). Merchant of Shklov; purveyor and contractor to the government and to Prince Potemkin's army. Father-in-law of Abram Peretz and grandfather of Grigory Peretz. He supported the Vilna Gaon and fought against the Lubavitcher Hasidism. During a visit to St. Petersburg in the 1770s he stayed as a guest of Prince Potemkin in the Winter Palace.

124   Zinberg, Srul (Israel) Leizerovitch (Sergei Lazaryevitch) (1873, Kremenets, Volhynia–1938, Vladivostok). Was in St. Petersburg not later than 1900. Addresses: Pere'ulok Labutina (formerly Pryadilny Pere'ulok) 3, apt. 1; Pere'ulok Makarenko (formerly Usatchev Pere'ulok) 6. Chemical engineer, historian of the Jewish Socialist workers' movement and of Jewish literature. Academic secretary to the Institute of Higher Jewish Studies. Co-editor, from 1924, of *Yevreiskaya Starina* (Jewish Antiquity). Wrote a nine-volume history of Jewish literature (in Yiddish). A leading member of OPE (Society for the Spread of Enlightenment among the Jews of Russia) and of the Jewish Literary Society. Arrested in 1938 by the Soviet authorities and deported to Vladivostok's camp, where he died that same year. Posthumously rehabilitated (1956).

The 7th Rota (now the 7th Krasnoarmeiskaya), Moskovskaya quarter. Painted by M. Dobuzinsky, 1909.

PART THREE

PUBLICATIONS AND INSTITUTIONS

PERIODICALS, COLLECTIONS, AND ENCYCLOPEDIAS

HEBREW

1. *Ben-Ami* (Son of My People) (1887). Supplement to *Ha-Yom* monthly. Four issues published.
2. *Ha-Zman* (The Time) (1903–early 1904, then in Vilna). Nationalist newspaper, twice weekly and daily from 1904. Ed. B. Katz, with close cooperation of L. Katzenelson, D. Frischman, and authors H. N. Bialik and S. Abramovitch. In Vilna—new editors. Supplement (until 1904)—quarterly collection: L. Shulman "The History of Yiddish Literature"; L. Katzenelson "On the Pure and the Impure among the Ancient Hebrews"; B. Katz "History of Jewish Enlightenment."
3. *Ha-Yom* (Today) (1886–early 1888). Nationalist newspaper. Ed. L. Kantor with cooperation of D. Frischman, A. Rosenfeld, L. Katzenelson. First Hebrew-language daily. Supplement—monthly *Ben-Ami*.
4. *Ha-Kedem* (The East) (1907–1909). Quarterly. Scholarly. Address: ulitsa Deka-bristov (formerly Offitserskaya) 50, apt. 3 (extant). Ed.: I. Y. Markon, A. Zarzovsky. On the study of the ancient and Semitic East.
5. *Ha-Melitz* (The Advocate) (1860–1873, 1878–1904). Nationalist newspaper. Founded by A. Zederbaum and I. A. Goldbaum. In St. Petersburg from 1871; weekly until 1886 and then daily. Ed. and pub.: A. Zederbaum (to 1893), then L. Rabinovitch. Other editors were M. Lilienblum (in Odessa), L. O. Gordon (1880–1883, 1886–1889), S. Friedberg (1883–1886). The paper did not appear from 1873–1878, and it

was closed down in 1904. From 1881 to 1902, ten supplements were published. Ed. address: 3rd Krasnoarmeiskaya (formerly 3rd Rota) 10 (1892) (no longer extant); ulitsa Soyuza Petchatnikov (formerly Torgovaya) 17 (1901–1904).

6.   *Ha-Saffa* (The Language) (1912). Monthly educational paper. Address: ulitsa Dekabristov (formerly Offitserskaya) 50 (extant). Organ of the Society of Lovers of the Ancient Hebrew Language.

7.   *He-Avar* (The Past) (1918). Quarterly historical journal. Ed.: S. M. Ginzburg with the close cooperation of M. G. Eisenstadt, Benzion Katz, and S. Rosenfeld. Published by "Khayim" (in memory of Khayim Kogan). Two issues were published.

YIDDISH

1.   *Die Arbeiter Shtimme* (The Worker's Voice) (1917). Twice-weekly newspaper. First issue, March 8, 1917; last issue—November 24, 1917. Central organ of the Bund. Names of editor and publisher not quoted.

2.   *Arbeiter Tzeitung* (Worker's Newspaper). First issue—January 20, 1881. Newspaper of the Narodnaya Volya (People's Will Party). It did not deal with any Jewish questions. Editor and publisher unknown, perhaps Tzukerman or Gelfman.

3.   *Blatter Vokh E Tagebukh* (Newsweek and Diary) (1900–1901). Weekly, nonparty.

4.   *Die Varkheit* (Truth) (1918). Organ of the Bolsheviks and Left SRs (after Nos. 8–9—only the Bolsheviks). From No. 4 published in Moscow. Communist weekly. Ed.: S. Dimanshtein, G. Torchinsky, N. Bukhbinder. Secretary: A. Dobkovsky.

5.   *Dos Vort* (The Word) (1914). Magazine. From May 14, 1914, to June 11, 1914—five issues. Organ of Po'alei Zion.

6.   *Die Yiddishe Velt* (The Jewish World) (1912). Monthly, organ of the Folkspartei. Ed.: S. M. Dubnow, Kh. D. Gurevitch, I. P. Yefroikin, S. A. An-sky, Perelman.

7.   *Der Yiddisher Soldat* (The Jewish Soldier). Zionist newspaper published by Central Bureau of Zionist Wartime Organization, devoted to questions for the All-Russian Jewish Congress. Ed.: M. Blumberg, Shpint, A. Yudelevitch. No. 1—January 1918.

8.   *Dos Yiddishe Folkblatt* (Jewish People's News-sheet) (1881–1890). Weekly, nonparty. Pub.: Levi. Ed.: A. Zederbaum, assisted from 1883 by Sholem Aleikhem. In the last years there was also a regular weekly supplement.

9.   *Dos Yiddishe Folksblatt* (Jewish People's News-sheet) (1917–1918). Organ of the Folkspartei. Pub. and ed.: I. P. Yefroikin and N. I. Shtiff. No. 1—October 3, 1917, with ten issues to the end of the year. The last issues were Nos. 1 and 2, January 20, 1918. Then it was published in Kiev under a different editor.

10.   *Der Yiddisher Emigrant* (The Jewish Emigrant) (1907–1914). Twice-weekly newspaper, nonparty organ of ICA (The Jewish Colonization Association). Ed.: D. G. Guenzburg; from 1910 S. Y. Yanovsky, assisted by Z. Rubashov. Devoted to questions of emigration.

11.   *Yedios* (Information)—Information of the Organizing Committee of the All-Russian Jewish Congress. No. 1—October 4, 1917; final No. 8—January 23, 1918. No signature of editor or publisher. Nonparty, issued irregularly.

12.   *Die Kommune* (The Commune) (1918). Bolshevik weekly. Editorial committee, published by collective of Jewish Communists. From No 2—ed.: Z. Greenberg and S. Rappoport; published by Commissariat on Jewish Affairs. No. 1—September 1918. Nos. 2–5—September 1918.

13. *Dos Leben* (Life) (1905). Literary monthly supplement to the newspaper *Der Fraynd*. Ten issues published.

14. *Dos Leben* (Life) (1906). Alternative title of the newspaper *Der Fraynd,* published under this title to avoid political legal action.

15. *Dos Professionelle Leben* (Professional Life) (1917). Weekly published by the Professional Commission of the Central Committee of the Bund. Nos. 1 and 2 (May 12 and June 4) issued as supplement to *Die Arbeiter Shtimme.* No. 3 issued separately. Final issue — No. 16, October 10, 1917.

16. *Der Tog* (The Day) (1904). Nonparty, daily.

17. *Togblatt* (Daily News-sheet) (Petrograd Togblatt) (1917–1918). Daily. Ed.: Kh. Gurevitch. Pub.: M. Zaks, D. Kagan, I. Oyzerman; from No. 37 — ed.: I. Greenbaum; later pub.: D. Kagan. No. 1 — May 7, 1917. Nationalist with democratic leanings and, on change of editor, Zionist. January 23, 1918, closed for violation of the decree on announcements; began to come out with the same staff and editor under the title of *Unzer Togblatt.*

18. *Unzer Togblatt* (Our Daily News-sheet) (1918), published on closure of *Togblatt* in January 1918. Ed.: R. Rubinstein. Pub.: Kh. Gurevitch. At No. 120 of August 9, 1918, it was closed down as being a bourgeois newspaper.

19. *Dos Folk* (The People) (1917). Newspaper published by organizing committee of the Folkspartei for the All-Russian Jewish Congress. Two issues published in December 1917.

20. *Die Frayer Shtimme* (The Free Voice). Communist weekly. Organ of the Petrograd Commission on Jewish Affairs. Ed.: N. Bukhbinder, Z. Greenberg, S. Rappoport. No. 1, Spring 1918.

21. *Der Fraynd* (The Friend) (1903–1909). Nationalist, daily. First Yiddish daily. Ed.: S. Ginzburg with Kh. Gurevitch and I. Lurye. Fifty thousand copies. From 1905 with monthly supplement "Dos Leben." In 1906 it appeared under the title of *Dos Leben* (because of legal action). Ed. address: Prospekt Mayorova (Voznesensky Prospekt) 53 (1909). From 1909 published in Warsaw with ed. S. Rosenfeld and S. Rappoport.

22. *Die Tzeit* (The Times) (1912–1914). Bund weekly with Abramovitch (Rein), Olguin, Esther Frumkina, D. Zaslavsky, A. D. Kirzhnitz, B. Orshansky.

23. *Der Sheigits* (The Rascal) (1905). Humoristic. Ed.: A. D. Idelson.

24. *Der Shnaider* (The Tailor) (1912–?). Bund.

RUSSIAN

1. *Budushchnost* (The Future) (1899–1904). Nationalist weekly. Ed. and pub.: S. O. Grusenberg. Authors: S. Frug, O. O. Grusenberg, L. I. Katzenelson. Ed. address: Pushkinskaya ulitsa 7 (extant). Twenty-one hundred copies (No. 41, 1903). Supplement (see No. 2).

2. *Budushchnost* (1901–1904). Scientific-literary collection, annual supplement to the newspaper. Four volumes published. Ed. and pub.: S. O. Grusenberg. Supplement to the collection — A Study of the History of the Jews of Russia, Part I, 1904.

3. *Bullyetyen* (Bulletin) of the military section of the Central Committee of the Zionist Organization 1917.

4. *Bullyetyen* (Bulletin) of the Board of Management of the Seventh All-Russian

Zionist Congress, published by the organizing committee of the Board of Management of the seventh Congress (from May 24, 1917, during the days of the Congress).

5. *Bullyetyen Ort* (The Bulletin of ORT). Pub.: M. B. Gurevitch, Ed.: Gurlyand, Elyasheva. One issue in 1918.

6. *Vestnik Yevreiskogo Prosveshcheniya* (The Herald of Jewish Enlightenment) (1913–1917). Before 1913 published as *Vestnik OPE* (The OPE Herald). Monthly educational. Ed. address: Zagorodny Prospekt 23 apt. 35 (extant). Ed.: (1916) M. G. Eisenstadt, N. R. Botvinnik, S. M. Ginzburg, G. A. Goldberg, P. I. Kagan, S. L. Kamenetsky, M. G. Ravvin, Kh. Kh. Fialkov, S. L. Zinberg, M. M. Shteingaus, Y. B. Eiger. 1913: No. 23 (September)–No. 26 (December); 1914: No. 27 (January)–No. 30 (April); 1915: No. 31 (January)–No. 37 (December); 1916: No. 38 (January)–Nos. 47–48 (February 1917). Supplements: 1913—Program of subjects to be taught in Jewish schools. Program of teaching spoken Hebrew. A. Z. Rabinovitch "The History of Pedagogy from Earliest Times to Our Days." 1914—The Jewish Library. Supplements in Yiddish and Hebrew.

7. *Vestnik Yevreiskoi Obshchiny* (Jewish Community Herald) (1913–1914). Monthly. Ed. and pub.: I. I. Perelman. 1913: No. 1 (August)–No. 5 (December); 1914: No. 1 (January)–No. 5 (May).

8. *Vestnik Ope* (OPE Herald) (1910–1913). Monthly educational journal of OPE. Address: Zagorodny Prospekt 23, apt. 35 (extant). Ed.: Y. B. Eiger. Representative of OPE: N. R. Botvinnik. 1910: No. 1 (November)–No. 2 (January); 1911: No. 3 (January)–No. 10 (December); 1912: No. 11 (January)–No. 18 (December); 1913: No. 19 (January)–No. 22 (final no. April). Then it was published as *Vestnik Yevreiskogo Prosveshcheniya*. Supplement: 1911—bibliographical list of old and new Hebrew textbooks. Report on the activity of OPE for 1910 and 1911.

9. *Vestnik Russkikh Yevreyev* (Russian Jewish Herald) (1871–1873). Weekly, assimilationist. Office address: Canal Griboyedova (formerly Yekaterinensky Canal) 56, apt. 2 (extant). Pub.: A. Zederbaum. Ed.: E. P. Karnovitch.

10. *Vestnik Trudovoy Pomoshchi Sredi Yevreyev* (Herald of Labor Aid among the Jews) (1915–1917). Monthly of ORT. Address: ulitsa Dostoyevskogo (formerly Yamskaya) 16 (extant). Authors: L. M. Bramson, M. Urielev, B. D. Brutskus. Ed.: B. D. Brutskus. Pub.: M. B. Gurevitch. 1915: No. 1 (December); 1916: No. 2 (January)–No. 10 (December); 1917: Nos. 11–12 (final). Then published as *Yevreisky Ekonomichesky Vestnik* (Jewish Economic Herald). (See No. 43).

11. *Voprosy Biologii I Patologii Yevreyev* (Questions on the Biology and Pathology of the Jews). Collection (1926, 1928, 1930). Ed.: V. I. Binstock, A. M. Bramson, M. M. Gran, G. I. Dembo. Pub.: *Prakticheskaya Meditsina* (Practical Medicine). Address: Liteiny Prospekt (formerly Volodarskogo) 49 (extant). Three issues published.

12. *Voskhod* (Sunrise) (1881–1899). Nationalist monthly magazine. Ed. address: ulitsa Dekabristov (formerly Offitserskaya) 17 (1881–1885) (extant); Teatralnaya Ploshchad (formerly Ploshchad Bolshogo Teatra) 2 (1886–1899) (extant). Ed. and pub.: A. E. Landau, with help from L. O. Gordon (Mevakker), S. O. Grusenberg, S. M. Dubnow (Kritikus). In 1884–1899 the only Jewish periodical in Russian language. Supplement— *Nedelnaya Khronika Voskhoda* (Weekly Chronicle of Voskhod); then *Khronika Voskhoda*. From 1899 it became the newspaper *Voskhod* with supplement *Knizhki Voskhoda* (Voskhod Notebooks). In all, together with the *Knizhki,* almost three hundred issues appeared. Supplement: Josephus Flavius—*Antiquities of the Jews.*

13. *Voskhod* (Sunrise) (1899–1906). Newspaper that developed from *Khronika Vosk-*

hoda. In 1899 twice weekly, and from 1902, daily. Address: ulitsa Herzena (formerly Bolshaya Morskaya) 29 (1904) (extant). Ligovsky Prospect 36 (1905–1906) (extant). Ed.: M. G. Syrkin, L. A. Sev, M. M. Vinaver, M. Trivus (Sh'mi), Y. Brutskus, L. Zaidenman, S. Ginzburg, M. Posner, L. Bramson. Pub.: M. M. Vinaver, M. G. Syrkin. Supplement—magazine *Knizhki Voskhoda* and also *Protokol* (The Minutes) of the OPE Committee Meetings (1903; S. M. Dubnow *Universal History of the Jews on the Basis of the Latest Scientific Research*. Books 1–3 (1904–1906).

14. *Golos Bunda* (The Voice of the Bund) (1917). Weekly magazine, organ of the Central Committee of the Bund. Ed.: V. A. Kantorovitch.

15. *Dyelo Pomoshchi* (The Case for Help) (1916–1917). Fortnightly. Address: ulitsa Dekabristov (formerly Offitserskaya) 60, apt. 22 (no longer extant). Organ of EKOPO (Jewish Committee to Provide Help to Victims of the War). Ed.: L. Y. Khazan. Pub.: S. G. Polyak. 1916: No. 1 (April 1)–No. 14 (December 20); 1917: ten issues up to June 5. Previously *Pomoshch* was published (see No. 58).

16. *Yevreiskaya Biblioteka* (The Jewish Library) (1871–1880 and 1901, 1903). Appeared at irregular intervals. Educational and historico-literary. Address: Teatralnaya Ploshchad (formerly Ploshchad Bolshogo Teatra) 2 (extant). Pub.: E. Landau. Authors: L. Levanda, I. Orshanksy, L. Gordon, V. V. Stassov, L. I. Mandelstam, M. I. Kulisher, A. Y. Harkavy, S. Bershadsky.

17. *Yevreiskaya Zhizn* (Jewish Life) (1904–1907). Monthly Zionist magazine. Address: Suvorovsky Prospekt 3. Ed.: M. D. Rivkin, I. V. Sorin, A. D. Idelson. From 1905 to 1906 it appeared under the titles *Khronika Yevreiskoi Zhizni* (Chronicle of Jewish Life) and *Yevreisky Narod* (The Jewish People). Authors: D. Pasmanik, B. Brutskus, B. Goldberg, Vl. Jabotinsky, M. Ussishkin, L. Yaffe, Kh. N. Bialik, S. M. Dubnow, S. Marshak. From 1905—a weekly with a monthly supplement. Pub.: S. F. Bussel; from No. 4, 1904—I. V. Sorin; from No. 5, 1905—A. F. Vilkoreisky; from No. 3, 1907—M. S. Glickin. Then *Rassvet* was published. Supplement—*Altneuland*.

18. *Yevreiskaya Letopis* (Jewish Chronicle) (1923–1926). Scientific-literary collection. Only four issues appeared, irregularly. Ed.: L. M. Klyatchko, with help from L. M. Eisenberg, S. G. Lozensky, I. A. Kleyman (Kleinman). Leningrad-Moscow.

19. *Yevreiskaya Mysl* (Jewish Thought) (1922–1926). Scientific-literary collection. Appeared irregularly. Pub.: "Kadima" (Forward) (1922), "Seyatyel" (The Sower) (1926). Ed.: S. N. Ginzburg. Publisher address: Vassilevsky Ostrov 5th Liniya 28 (1922).

20. *Yevreiskaya Nedelya* (Jewish Week) (1910). Nationalist, weekly. Ed.: Kh. L. Gurevitch, L. A. Sev. Pub.: Kh. L. Gurevitch Nos. 1 and 2 (April 16)–No. 11 (June 24). Published instead of *Novy Voskhod,* which was temporarily closed.

21. *Yevreiskaya Niva* (Jewish Cornfield) (1913). Monthly. Pub. and ed.: I. A. Dubossarsky. 1913: No. 1 (April)–Nos. 5 and 6 (December). Devoted to questions of colonization and emigration.

22. *Yevreiskaya Rabochaya Khronika* (Jewish Workers' Chronicle) (1917–1918). Weekly newspaper, organ of the Jewish Social-Democratic Workers' Party "Poalei Zion." From No. 13 twice weekly. Ed.: N. M. Raffalkess. From April 29th to end of 1917, sixteen issues published. In 1918 publication ceased with No. 3–4 (March). Before 1917 the Petrograd Committee of Poalei Zion issued a news sheet.

23. *Yevreiskaya Semyeinaya Biblioteka* (Jewish Family Library) (1902–1903). Zionist monthly. Address: Lermontovsky Prospekt 7 (formerly Bolshaya Masterskaya 5). Forerunner of *Yevreiskaya Zhizn* (see No. 17), twelve issues published.

24. *Yevreiskaya Starina* (Jewish Antiquity) (1909–1918, 1924, 1928, 1930). Scien-

tific-historical quarterly magazine. Address: Vassilevsky Ostrov 18th Liniya 9 (extant), office at ulitsa Nekrassova (formerly Basseinaya) 35 (1911) (no longer extant). Organ of the Jewish Historical-Ethnographic Society. After the revolution it appeared much less frequently. Ed.: S. M. Dubnow, and from 1924, L. Sternberg; from 1927, S. L. Zinberg. In all, thirteen volumes were published: ten volumes in 1918, Vol. 11 in 1924, Vol. 12 in 1928, Vol. 13 in 1930.

25. *Yevreiskaya Tribuna* (Jewish Tribune) (1918). Organ of the Department of Culture and Enlightenment of the Commissariat on Jewish Affairs. Ed.: I. Z. Berlin, N. A. Bukhbinder, Z. G. Greenberg. 1918: Nos. 1 and 2 (April 13), following (and final) Nos. 3 and 4 published in Moscow.

26. *Yevreiskaya Shkola* (The Jewish School) (1904–1905). Monthly magazine devoted to education of the Jews. Ed. and pub.: I. Y. Lurye. 1904: No. 1 (January)–No. 10 (December); 1905: No. 1 (January)–No. 7 (October).

27. *Yevreiskaya Entsiklopedia* (The Jewish Encyclopedia). A sixteen-volume publication. Publisher address: Prachechny Pere'ulok 6 (Brockhaus and Yefron) (extant). Ed.: Baskov Pere'ulok 25 (Society for Scientific Jewish Publication) (extant). General ed.: Baron David Guenzburg, L. I. Katzenelson, and A. Y. Harkavy.

28. *Yevreiskiye Vyesti* (Jewish News) (1916–1917). Weekly of the Bund. Address: 7th Sovietskaya (formerly 7th Rozhdestvenskaya) 4, apt. 29 (extant). Authors: Ben-Noemi, M. Vilner, T. Heilikman, S. Dubnova-Erlich, L. Zaslavsky, M. Rafess. Ed. and pub.: N. T. Grushkina. 1916: No. 1 (October)–No. 9 (December). In 1917 there were seven issues until February 16, when it was replaced by the official organ of the party.

29. *Yevreiskiye Izvestiya* (Jewish News) (1907–1911). Nationalist weekly. Ed. and pub.: D. L. Grace. Eighty-four issues in all.

30. *Yevreisky Almanakh* (Jewish Almanac) (1923). Artistic and literary-critical collection.

31. *Yevreisky Vestnik* (Jewish Herald) (1922). Nationalist, monthly. Address: Baskov Pere'ulok 12, apt. 8 (extant) (No. 1, April); Nevsky Prospekt 34, apt. 3 (extant) (No. 3, June); Naberezhnaya Fontanki 149, apt. 14 (extant) No. 4 (July). Ed.: B. I. Kaufman, I. A. Kleinman. Pub.: "Kadima." Two thousand copies, only seven issues published.

32. *Yevreisky Vestnik* (Jewish Herald) (1928). Scientific-literary collection. Organ of OPE (The Society for the Spread of Enlightenment among the Jews of Russia). Editorial board: S. M. Guenzburg, S. L. Zinberg, I. A. Kleyman. Address of OPE, Stremyannaya 18.

33. *Yevreisky Yezhegodnik Kadima Na 1918–1919* (Jewish Almanac of Kadima (Forward) for 1918–1919) (1918). Ed.: Y. S. Goldberg, Y. R. Klebanov, and others. Address: Vassilevsky Ostrov 5th Liniya 28 (extant). One issue (?). Before 1912 there were three issues in Vilna.

34. *Yevreisky Izbiratyel* (The Jewish Voter) (1906–1907). Twice-weekly newspaper. Ed. and pub.: G. M. Korobochkin. Published in collaboration with the Union for Equal Rights for the Jewish People in Russia, during the elections for the Second State Duma. 1906: No. 1 (December 5)–No. 7 (December 29); 1907: Nos. 8 and 9 (January 4)–No. 15 (February 1).

35. *Yevreisky Mir* (The Jewish World) (1909–1911). Monthly magazine. From January 1911 changed to weekly newspaper. Ed. address: Bolshaya Podyacheskaya 39 (early 1909) (extant); Prospekt Mayorova 20 (formerly Voznesensky Prospekt) (1909); Bolshaya Podyacheskaya 35 (1910). Ed. and pub.: G. M. Portugalov, from No. 12 (1910)—S. M. Trotskaya. In 1909 editorial board was S. M. Dubnow, S. A. An-sky, L.

Sev, M. Tribus, A. I. Braudo; from late 1909: A. Braudo, Y. Sacher, S. An-sky, Perelman. It was closed temporarily by the authorities in 1910. In the interval it appeared as *Yevreiskoye Obozreniye* (Jewish Review). 1909: No. 1 (January)–Nos. 11–12 (November–December); 1910: No. 1 (January)–No. 18 (April) Nos. 19–20 (September)–No. 36 (December); 1911: No. 1 (January)–No. 17 (April). In 1910 the magazine *Yevreisky Mir* was published as a supplement.

36. *Yevreisky Mir* (The Jewish World) (1910). Quarterly magazine. Literary-artistic. Ed. and pub.: S. A. Trotskaya. Supplement to the newspaper *Yevreisky Mir*. Three issues published: Nos. 2 and 3 as a separate book.

37. *Yevreisky Mir* (The Jewish World) (1917). Pub.: Central Committee of the Folks-partei (Jewish People's Party) for the All-Russian Jewish Congress in Petrograd. No. 1 — December 1, 1917.

38. *Yevreisky Mir* (The Jewish World) (1918). Literary collection. Ed.: A. Sobol and others. One issue (?).

39. *Yevreisky Narod* (The Jewish People) (1906). Weekly, Zionist newspaper. Ed. and pub.: A. D. Zaidenman. Produced on closure of *Yevreiskaya Zhizn* and *Khronika Yevreiskoi Zhizni*. Ten issues from October 18 to December 20, 1906. Then it appeared as *Rassvet*.

40. *Yevreisky Proletariy* (Jewish Proletariat) (four issues from March 31 to May 1917). Pub.: Jewish Workers' Party of Zionist Territorialists. Ed. and pub.: M. Shtatz.

41. *Yevreisky Rabochy* (The Jewish Worker) (1905 and 1918). Weekly newspaper, organ of the Bund. In 1905, ed. and pub.: M. G. Kipman. Only one issue on December 30. It was confiscated and publication closed. In 1918 ed. and pub.: B. I. Kagan (from No. 6 — D. Makhlin). 1918: No. 1 (April 5)–No. 10 (July 31). Closed because it contained anti-Soviet propaganda.

42. *Yevreisky Student* (The Jewish Student) (1915–1918). Fortnightly Zionist. Ed. and pub.: Y. R. Klebanov, R. Carmi (1917). 1915: No. 1 (January)–Nos. 11–12 (December); 1916: No. 13 (January)–Nos. 23–24 (December). Final Nos. 29–30 appeared in January 1918.

43. *Yevreisky Ekonomichesky Vestnik* (Jewish Economic Bulletin) (1917). Monthly, nonparty. Published with collaboration of ORT (The Society for Craft and Agricultural Labor among the Jews of Russia). Ed.: B. D. Brutskus. Pub.: M. B. Gurevitch. One issue, May 1917.

44. *Yevreiskoye Dyelo* (Jewish Affairs) (1914). Monthly magazine. Ed. and pub.: G. L. Tzeitlin. One issue.

45. *Yevreiskoye Obozreniye* (Jewish Review) (1884). Nationalist monthly magazine. Address: Izmailovsky Prospekt 7 (extant). Ed.: L. Kantor. Pub.: G. M. Rabinovitch (1884). Authors: L. O. Levanda, A. Y. Harkavy, L. I. Katzenelson, Margulies, Simeon Frug, S. O. Grusenberg. Seven books published.

46. *Yevreiskoye Obozreniye* (Jewish Review) (1910). Nationalist weekly newspaper. Communal-political and literary newspaper. Ed. and pub.: N. I. Dymshitz. Issued during the interval of the publication of *Yevreisky Mir*. Address: Izmailovsky Prospekt 21, apt. 28 (extant). No. 1 (May 27)–No. 14 (August 26).

47. "Informatsionny Bullyetyen Yevreiskoi Gruppy Otdyela Natzionalnostei Gosudarstvennoi Publichnoi Biblioteki imenyi M. Ye Saltykova — Shchedrina v Leningrad-ye" (Information Bulletin of the Jewish Group of the National Department of the Miye Saltykov–Schchedrin State Public Library in Leningrad). Ed.: K. R. Mergelidze and E. M. Pulner. Nos. 1–4, 1934; Nos. 1–2, 1935.

48. *Izvestiya Petrogradskogo Ts. K., OSE* (News of the Petrograd Central Committee of OSE) (1917–1919). Organ of the OSE (Society for the Protection of the Health of the Jews). Fourteen issues in 1917, ten issues in 1918. Printed on a rotator-duplicating machine (mimeograph).

49. *Izvestiya Ts. K.* (News of the Central Committee) of the federation of student Zionist organizations *He-Haver* (Hebrew — "The Friend") (1917–1918).

50. *Izvestiya Ts. K.* (News of the Central Committee) of the popular Zionist faction *Tse'Irei-Tsiyon* (Hebrew — "The Young People of Zion"). Weekly, twelve issues in late 1917 and January 1918.

51. *Izvestiya Ts. K.* (News of the Central Committee) of the Zionist Organization in Russia (1917). No. 1 — April 9, 1917. Then again No. 1 — August 22, 1917; No. 2 (last number) — October 10, 1917.

52. *Knizhki Voskhoda* ("Voskhod" Booklets) (1899–1906). Magazine, scientific-literary and political. Supplement to the newspaper *Voskhod* and, at the same time, supplement to the magazine *Voskhod*. Ed. and pub.: M. G. Syrkin. Address: Same as that of the newspaper *Voskhod*. First booklet No. 11 in 1899 as a continuation of the last booklet No. 10 of the magazine *Voskhod*. From 1901 to 1905 there were twelve issues each year. In 1906 No. 3 (March) was the last. Supplements: (1) 1901 — Israel Zangwill "Ghetto Tragedies"; (2) 1902 — L. Peretz "Jewish Life as Depicted by Jewish Recorders of History" (L. Peretz, S. Abramovitch, Sholem Aleikhem, and others); (3) 1903 to 1905 — S. M. Dubnow "Universal History of the Jews," Books 1–3.

53. *Listok Petrogradskogo Komityeta* (News-sheet of the St. Petersburg Committee) of the Jewish Social-Democratic Party "Poalei-Zion" (1917). Weekly. Ed. and pub.: Nir (pen name of N. M. Raffalkess). From March 11 to April 17 — six issues. Later it was retitled *Yevreiskaya Rabochaya Khronika* (Jewish Workers' Chronicle).

54. *Nash Put* (Our Road) (1916). Collection devoted to the interests of Jewish students. Printed at Mytninskaya ulitsa 11.

55. *Nedelnaya Khronika Voskhoda* (Weekly Chronicle of Voskhod) (1882–1897). Weekly newspaper. Ed. and pub.: A. E. Landau. From the late 1880s the editor was S. O. Grusenberg. Address: same as *Voskhod*. Supplement to the magazine *Voskhod*. Later it appeared as *Khronika Voskhoda*.

56. *Noviy Voskhod* (New Voskhod — Sunrise) (1910–1915). Weekly, nationalist. Ed. address: ulitsa Kalyaeva (formerly Zakharyevskaya) 25, apt. 13 (extant). Ed. and pub.: M. G. Syrkin. Editorial board: L. A. Sev, M. M. Vinaver, G. B. Sliozberg, M. I. Sheftel, M. L. Trivus (Sh'mi), L. M. Eisenberg, S. V. Posner, L. Y. Sternberg, R. M. Blank, M. Y. Pritykin, Kh. A. Krechmar-Kleymance (from 1914). In content and in editorial staff it was a continuation of the newspaper *Voskhod*. From April 5 to July 1, 1910, it was closed down. In its place *Yevreiskaya Nedelya* was published. In April 1915 it was closed down altogether for the duration of the war.

57. *Perezhitoye* (Past Experience) (1908–1913). Collection of historical memoirs. Published irregularly. Pub. address: Prachechny Pere'ulok 6 (Brockhaus and Yefron) (extant). Publication of documents and articles relating to Jewish history and culture in Russia. Ed.: S. A. An-sky, N. R. Botvinnik, A. I. Braudo, Y. I. Hessen, S. M. Ginzburg, S. L. Kamenetsky, P. S. Marek, S. L. Zinberg. Four collections published.

58. *Pomoshch* (Help) (1915–1916). Magazine. Organ of IKOPO (Jewish Committee to Provide Help to Victims of the War). Fortnightly. Ed.: D. Y. Khazan. Later published as *Dyelo Pomoshchi*. Devoted entirely to the question of how to help Jewish victims of the war. 1915: No. 1 (December); 1916: No. 2 (January)–No. 7 (March).

59. *Rassvet* (Dawn) (1879–1883). Weekly, moderately assimilationist, then national-ist. Ed.: A. Zederbaum and Dr. A. Goldenbloom, then Bogrov and Y. Rosenthal. Address: ulitsa Marata (formerly Nikolayevskaya). With close cooperation of M. S. Warshawsky, N. Minsky (Vilenkin), M. I. Kulisher, Y. Rosenfeld.

60. *Rassvet* (Dawn) (1907–1915 and 1917–1918). Zionist weekly newspaper. Ed. address and offices: Pere'ulok Dzhambula (formerly Leshtukov Pere'ulok) 19, apt. 6 (1907) (extant). Ed. address: ulitsa Soyuza Petchatnikov (formerly Torgovaya) 17 (until 1913) (extant); Soyuza Petchatnikov 11 (1913–1915) (extant). Pub. address: Sotsialisti-cheskaya ulitsa (formerly Ivanovskaya) 22 (1912). In 1907 ed. and pub.: G. L. Zeitlin; from No. 28: Z. S. Krais; from No. 32: S. K. Hepstein, then A. D. Idelson (Ibn Daud Davidson); from No. 43 (1907): M. S. Glickin; from No. 43 (1908): L. S. Babkov. Supplement: The *Rassvet* Handbook (1910). Closed by order of the Supreme Com-mander of the Sixth Army in June 1915. From July 1915 it appeared in Moscow as *Yevreiskaya Zhizn*. From July 1, 1917, *Rassvet* was again published, but it was closed on September 7, 1918, after which subscribers were given *Khronika Yevreiskoi Zhizni*. From 1917 to 1918, ed. A. D. Idelson; pub.: M. S. Aleinkov and S. K. Hepstein.

61. *Reguisti I Nadpeesi* (Registers and Inscriptions). Collections of historical docu-ments. Published irregularly, Vol. 1 — 1899, Vol. 2 — 1910, Vol. 3 — 1913. Published by IEO (The Jewish Historical-Ethnographic Society).

62. *Russky Yevrei* (The Russian Jew) (1879–1884). Weekly, moderately assimilation-ist. Address: Izmailovsky Prospekt 21, apt. 28 (Head Office) (extant). Ed.: L. Berman; from 1883, L. Kantor. Authors: L. Levanda, L. I. Katzenelson (Buki Ben Yogli). Ed. address: Izmailovsky Prospekt 7 (1881–1883) (extant).

63. *Svoboda I Ravyentsvo* (Freedom and Equality) (1907). Newspaper, twice weekly. From No. 21 — weekly. Ed. and pub.: D. A. Levin; from No. 22 — G. A. Goldberg. Last issue: No. 46 (September 28).

64. *Khronika Voskhoda* (1898–1899). Weekly newspaper. Issued after *Nedelnaya Khronika Voskhoda* and until it developed into the newspaper *Voskhod*. Ed.: S. O. Grusenberg. Supplement to the original magazine *Voskhod*.

65. *Khronika Yevreiskoi Zhizni* (Chronicle of Jewish Life) (January–September 1905). Weekly Zionist newspaper. Appeared when *Yevreiskaya Zhizn* was closed. Same edito-rial board.

66. *Khronika Yevreiskoi Zhizni* (Chronicle of Jewish Life) (from November 10, 1918 – ?). Zionist weekly. Appeared when *Rassvet* was closed.

67. *Eretz-Israel* (The Land of Israel) (May 1918 – ?). Monthly magazine, published by the Society to Promote the Economic Rebirth of Palestine, for the Petrograd and Moscow Palestinian Societies. From No. 4 it was published by the Council of Palestin-ian Societies Tekhias Ho-Oretz (Hebrew — "The Revival of the Land"). Ed.: B. A. Goldberg.

68. *Altneuland* (The Old-New Land, which was the title of a booklet written by Theodor Herzl). No. 1 (January 1906) – No. 10 (October–November). Monthly Zion-ist magazine. Ed.: Z. Soskin. Supplement to the magazine *Yevreiskaya Zhizn*, it was a translation into Russian of a German monthly magazine that was published in Berlin and was devoted to a study of Palestine.

BOOK PUBLISHERS, DEPOSITORIES, AND SHOPS

1.   The Publishing House Brockhaus and Yefron Book Publishers. Address: Prachechny Pere'ulok 6 (until 1917).

2.   Book publishers and Book Depository Vostok (Russian—"The East") (1910s). Address: ulitsa Soyuza Petchatnikov (formerly Torgovaya) 11.

3.   Book Publishers Kadima (Hebrew—"Forward") (1917–1922). Address: 5th Liniya 28 (1917–1919); Nevsky Prospekt 34, apt. 3 (1922).

4.   Book Depository and Publisher Ezro (Hebrew—"Help") (1910). Address: Sadovaya ulitsa 52. Proprietor: Sofer.

5.   Book Depository and Book Shop Ezro (Hebrew—"Help") (1910s). Address: Prospekt Rimskogo-Korsakova (formerly Yekateringofsky) 1.

6.   I. L. Golovchiner's Book-Store (1916). Address: Ligovsky Prospekt 107, apt. 29.

7.   Jewish Book Shop (1920s), near Nevsky Prospekt.

8.   Poalei Zion's bookstore, Molot (Hebrew—"The Hammer") (1928). Address: Liteiny Prospekt 50.

SOCIETIES AND ORGANIZATIONS

CULTURAL-EDUCATIONAL, LITERARY-ARTISTIC, SCIENTIFIC, AND SIMILAR SOCIETIES

1. *Aktsionernoye Obshchestvo Gigienicheskikh Dyeshovikh Kvartir Dlya Yevreiskogo Naseleniya* (OGDK) Society for Hygienic Cheap Apartments for the Jewish Population (OGDK) (1900–1918). (A joint-stock-holding company.) Address: ulitsa Dekabristov (formerly Offitserskaya) 60 (no longer extant); Krasnaya ulitsa (formerly Galernaya) 61 (extant). Chairman: Baron Alfred Guenzburg. Collaborated with the Jewish Colonization Association (ICA). Capital five hundred thousand rubles. Zone of activity in the Western Guberniyas.

2. *Botei Menukho* (Hebrew—"Rest Homes") (from May 28, 1918–?). A joint-stock-holding company floated to finance the construction of convalescent homes, hotels, rest homes, and so on, for mass emigration to Palestine. It hardly functioned.

3. *Yevreiskoye Istoriko-Etnograficheskoye Obshchestvo* (IEO) (Jewish Historical-Ethnographic Society) (November 16, 1908–1930). Address: ulitsa Kalyaeva (formerly Zakharyevskaya) 25, apt. 13 (1910) (extant); ulitsa Nekrassova (formerly Basseinaya) 35 (1912); 7th Sovietskaya (formerly 7th Rozhdestvenskaya) 6, apt. 24 (1913–1916) (extant); Vassilevsky Ostrov 5th Liniya 50 (1918) (extant); ulitsa Rileyeva 8 (1927). Chairman: M. M. Vinaver. Vice-chair: S. M. Dubnow and M. I. Kulisher. In 1924 to 1927 it was headed by L. Y. Sternberg and in 1927 to 1930 by S. L. Zinberg. Objectives: The collection, study, and processing of materials on the history of the Jews of Russia and Poland. Published: *Yevreiskaya Starina* (Jewish Antiquity)(from 1909); *Reguisti I Nad-peesi* (Registers and Inscriptions) (three vols.). In 1925, Commission for the Study of the Psychophysics of the Jews (Chairman: A. M. Bramson), Museum Commission (Chairman: I. Y. Guenzburg, Museum Director).

4.   *Yevreiskoye Kolonizatsionnoye Obshchestvo* (EKO) Jewish Colonization Association (ICA) (1891, London; and from 1892 in St. Petersburg-Petrograd to 1918). Address: Krasnaya ulitsa (formerly Galernaya) 20 (1910) (extant); Pere'ulok Leonova (formerly Zamyatin Pere'ulok) 4 (1910) (extant); ulitsa Dekabristov (formerly Offitserskaya) 60 (1917) (no longer extant). Chairman of the Russian section — Baron Horace Guenzburg, M. A. Warshawsky (1917). Objectives: The organization and formation of Jewish agricultural settlements in Argentina. Later in other countries as well. Professional training, collection of statistics. In the 1920s the ICA center in Paris, France, collaborated with the Komzet (Soviet Government Committee for Settling Jewish Workers on the Land) in the establishment of Jewish agricultural settlements in the Crimea and the Ukraine.

5.   *Yevreiskoye Literaturno-Na'uchnoye Obshchestvo* (Jewish Literary-Scientific Society) (1911–1917?). Address: Sadovaya ulitsa 81, apt. 13 (1915) (extant); ulitsa Dzerzhinskogo (formerly Gorokhovaya) 41 (1916) (extant). Chairman: S. M. Ginzburg (1916). Objectives: Development of scholarly literature and belles lettres in Yiddish, Hebrew, and other languages.

6.   *Yevreiskoye Literaturnoye Obshchestvo* (Jewish Literary Society) (1908–1911). Address: 8th Sovietskaya (formerly 8th Rozhdestvenskaya) 25, apt. 12. Chairman: S. M. Dubnow. Objectives: The study and development of literature in Hebrew, Yiddish, and other languages. In 1910 it had thirty-five branches and 850 members.

7.   *Yevreiskoye Literaturno-Khudozhestvennoye Obshchestvo imeni Leona Peretza* (The Jewish Leon Peretz Literary-Artistic Society) (1916–1918). Address: Prospekt Ogorodnikova (formerly Rizhsky Prospekt) 48, apt. 99 (extant). Objectives: Development of literature and theater in Yiddish.

8.   *Yevreiskoye Obshchestvo Vospitaniya i Obrazovaniya* (Society for Jewish Upbringing and Education). On February 7, 1913, it met at the Zabalkansky Auditorium, Zabalkansky Prospekt No. 37/1, to hear a lecture by S. L. Zinberg.

9.   *Yevreisky Obshchestvenny Komitet* (Jewish Social Committee) Leningrad Section (abbreviated to "Yevobshchestkom") (1925–?). Address: ulitsa Voinova (formerly Shpalernaya) 4-a. Authorized representative: L. Y. Offman.

10.   *Yevreiskoye Statisticheskoye Obshchestvo* (Jewish Statistical Society) (1916–1918). Address: Petrogradskaya Storona, Bolshoi Prospekt 5, apt. 8 (extant). Objectives: The study of the economic and cultural condition of the Jews in Russia by means of census, questioning, investigating, examining. From 1913 to 1914: The Vilna Statistical Society.

11.   *Yevreiskoye Teatralnoye Obshchestvo* (Jewish Theatrical Society) (1916–1917). Address: Saperny Pere'ulok 9. For the development of theatrical activity. The society hardly functioned.

12.   *Informatsionnoye Byuro Dlya Yevreiskikh Emigrantov* (Office of Information for Jewish Emigrants) with branches in all the major towns and larger villages. Address: Pere'ulok Leonova 4 (formerly Zamyatin Pere'ulok, the home of Baron Horace Guenzburg). Published the following booklets: "America," "Canada," "Argentina," "Syria and Palestine," "Teach-Yourself English."

13.   *Kommissiya (Arkhivnaya) Po Istorii Obrazovaniya Russkikh Yevreyev* (Commis-

sion to Maintain the Archives on the History of Russian Jews) (1918–1919). Based on the Jewish subcommissariat of education. Organizers: S. Lozinsky and S. Ginzburg.

14. *Kommissiya Dlya Issledovaniya Yevreiskikh Pogromov* (Commission for the Study of the Jewish Pogroms) (1918–1920). Chairman: G. Krasny-Admoni. Published: "Materials on the History of the Anti-Jewish Pogroms in Russia." Editor: S. M. Dubnow.

15. *Kommissiya Dlya Razrabotki Arkhivnikh Dokumentov Po Ritualnim Protsessam* (Commission to Examine the Documents Relating to the Blood-Libel Trials) (1918–1920). Chairman: Professor S. F. Platonov. Members: Professor A. P. Karsavin (philologist), V. G. Druzhinin (archeologist), Blinov (keeper of the archives, formerly chief secretary of the Senate). On the Jewish side: G. Krasny-Admoni, S. M. Dubnow, G. B. Sliozberg, S. G. Lozinsky, L. Y. Sternberg. The sessions were held in the Senate Archives Building.

16. *Kommissiya Po Issledovaniyu Istorii Yevreyev* (Commission on Research into the History of the Jews) (1922). Address: Pushkinskaya ulitsa 4. Chairman: G. A. Krasny-Admoni.

17. *Obshchestvo Dlya Dostavleniya Nachalnogo Obrazovaniya Yevreiskim Detyam g. Petrograda "Ivrio"* (ODNO) (Society for the Provision of Elementary Education for Jewish Children in Petrograd) (1917–?). Address: ulitsa Rubinshteina (formerly Troitskaya) 34 (extant). Chairman: M. R. Krever.

18. *Obshchestvo Dlya Dostavleniya Pervonachalnogo Obrazovaniya Yevreiskim Detyam Peskovskogo Rayona g. Petrograda* (ODPO) (Society for the Provision of Primary Education for Jewish Children in the Peskovsky District of Petrograd) (1917–?). Address: Prospekt Bakunina (formerly Kalashnikovsky Prospekt) 9 (extant). Chairman: G. I. Benenson.

19. *Obshchestvo Dlya Na'uchnikh Yevreiskikh Izdaniy* (Society for Scientific Jewish Publications) (1907–1917–?). Address: ulitsa Nekrassova (formerly Basseinaya) 35 (no longer extant). (1910): Baskov Pere'ulok 25 (extant). Chairman: M. I. Sheftel. Objectives: The production of scientific Jewish literature in various languages. Together with the publishers Brockhaus and Yefron, the society produced the *Yevreiskaya Entsiklopedia*.

20. *Obshchestvo Dlya Uregulirovaniya Yevreiskoi Emigratsii* (Society for the Control of Jewish Emigration) (1907–1917–?). In St. Petersburg from 1910. Address: ulitsa Dostoyevskogo (formerly Yamskaya) 32 (1909) (extant); Nevsky Prospekt 65, apt. 30 (1910) (extant). Objectives: To improve the conditions of travel and settling in of the emigrants. The protection of the migrants from abuse and exploitation by individuals and institutions. The administration in 1909 included L. M. Bramson, A. I. Braudo, S. E. Veisenberg, L. Y. Vigodsky, A. V. Zalkind, V. S. Mandel, M. A. Kroll, I. D. Idelson, M. A. Kreinin, A. F. Perelman, I. A. Rozov, M. L. Trivus, I. V. Yashunsky. The society opened an information office for Jewish emigrants (see No. 12).

21. *Obshchestvo Yevreiskoi Narodnoi Muzyki* (Jewish Folk Music Society) (1908–1924). Address: ulitsa Sadovaya 85, apt. 6; 9th Sovietskaya (formerly 9th Rozhdestvenskaya) 9, apt. 22. Chairman: V. S. Mandel (1916). Objectives: The collection, study, development, and propagation of Jewish folk music. In 1913 it had 884 members, with branches in Moscow, Odessa, Riga, Kiev, Kharkov, and elsewhere. In the 1920s it functioned in Moscow.

22. *Obshchestvo Po Zemelnomu Ustroistvu Trudyashchikhsya Yevreyev* (Society for the Promotion of Jewish Settlement). Northwestern provinces administration (SevzapoblOZET) (1924–1931–?). Address: Nevsky Prospekt 23 (1925) (extant); Naberezh-naya Fontanka 34 (1929); ulitsa Nekrassova 10 (1930) (extant); ulitsa Plekhanova 1 (1931) (extant). Chairman: P. O. Petrov-Sokolovsky (1925), S. Rappoport (1930), A. I. Gellner (1931). Objectives: The settlement into kolkhozes (collective agricultural farms) of Jewish poor in the Crimea and in the southern Ukraine. In the Leningrad Oblast (Province) they established the kolkhozes "Yevrabzem" and "Yevselkop." One of them was in Irinovka, and another not far from Kolpino.

23. *Obshchestvo Izucheniya Rodnoi Literatury* (Society for the Study of Native Litera-ture) (1916–1917). A Bund organization, the society existed as a cover for political meetings that were held on Vassilevsky Ostrov.

24. *Obshchestvo Izucheniya Sotsialnoi Biologii I Psikhofiziki Yevreyev* (Society for the Study of the Social Biology and Psycho-physiology of the Jews) (1922). Address: ulitsa Furmanova (formerly Gagarinskaya) 20. In 1925 it was a commission with the Historical-Ethnographic Society.

25. *Obshchestvo Lyubeetelyei Drevne-Yevreiskogo Yazyka* (OLDEYa) (Hebrew—"Agudas Khovevei S'fas 'Ever") (Society of Lovers of the Ancient Hebrew Language) (1906–1917). Address: ulitsa Dekabristov (formerly Offitserskaya) 50 apt. 3 (extant). Until 1907 it was a committee of OPE. In 1917 it merged with "Tarbut." Chairmen: Baron David Guenzburg (1907–1910), L. I. Katzenelson (1910–1917), I. Y. Lurye (1917). Published: magazine *Ha-Saffa*. Objectives: Concern over the teaching of He-brew in cheders, yeshivahs, and so on, and publication of literature in Hebrew.

26. *Obshchestvo Okhranyeniya Zdorovya Yevreiskogo Naseleniya* (OZE) (Society for the Protection of the Health of the Jewish Population) (1912–1919). Address: ulitsa Kolokolnaya 9 (extant). Objectives: To study the sanitary and hygienic conditions, to distribute information on hygiene, and to set up children's convalescent homes and colonies (Yevpatoria, Druzkeniki). After 1914, it provided aid to refugees. In 1917 the expenditure was two million rubles.

27. *Obshchestvo Po-oshchreniya Vysshikh Znaniy* (Society for the Encouragement of Higher Learning) (1912–1917). Address: ulitsa Herzena (formerly Bolshaya Morskaya) 56 (extant). Chairman: M. A. Ginsburg. Objectives: The encouragement of learning and aid to students of St. Petersburg high schools and refugee students. Budget: seventy-five thousand rubles (1916).

28. *Yevreiskoye Obshchestvo Po-oshchreniya Khudozhestv* (Jewish Society for the Encouragement of the Arts) (1915–1917). Address: Vassilevsky Ostrov 5th Liniya 50 (1915) (extant); ulitsa Kalyaeva (formerly Zakharyevskaya) 25 (extant). Chairman: M. M. Vinaver. Vice-chair: I. Y. Guenzburg. Objectives: Development of the plastic arts, exhibitions, lectures, and so on.

29. *Obshchestvo Rasprostranyeniya Prosveshcheniya Sredi Yevreyev Rossii* (Society for the Spread of Enlightenment among the Jews of Russia) (OPE) (1863–1930). Ad-dress: Krasnaya ulitsa (formerly Galernaya) 25 (to 1900) (extant); Zagorodny Prospekt 23, apt. 35 (1910–1917) (extant); Stremyannaya ulitsa 18 (1925–1926) (extant). Chair-men: Barons Yevsel Guenzburg, Horace Guenzburg, David Guenzburg. Members of the Central Committee: I. A. Wawelberg, L. Levanda, D. N. Polyakov, M. A. Warshawski, L. I. Katzenelson, L. O. Gordon, A. Y. Harkavy, Y. M. Galpern, M. I. Kulisher, S. L. Zinberg, and others. Objectives: Encouragement of culture, organization of secular education. Thirty-five branches in various towns. Published: Magazine *Vestnik Yevreis-kogo Prosveshcheniya*. One of the most well-known and respected of Jewish organiza-tions.

30. *Obshchestvo Remyeslennogo I Zemlyedyelcheskogo Truda Sredi Yevreyev Rossii*

(Society for Craft and Agricultural Labor among the Jews of Russia) (ORT) (1880–1929). Address: Krasnaya ulitsa (formerly Galernaya) 3 (1910) (extant); ulitsa Dostoyevskogo (formerly Yamskaya) 16 (1917–1918) (extant); ulitsa Vosstaniya (formerly Znamenskaya) 24 (1925) (extant); ulitsa Dzerzhinskogo (formerly Gorokhovaya) 9 (1928) (extant). Chairmen: Y. Galpern (1910), G. B. Sliozberg (1917), D. Ya. Khazan (1924). Founder: S. S. Polyakov. Objectives: The training of Jewish young people to become agricultural and craft workers. Published: *Vestnik Trudovoi Pomoshchi Sredi Yevreyev* (1916–1917?). Moved abroad after the revolution, when its authorized representative in Leningrad was L. Y. Offman (1925–1928).

31 *Obshchestvo "Tora veda'as"* (The "Torah and Knowledge" Society) (October 2, 1917–?). Objectives: Raising of national consciousness among the Jews; mental, moral, and physical development and improvement of the way of life of members of the Society. Program of activity: (1) The opening of educational establishments, cheders, yeshivahs, kindergartens, synagogues, prayerhouses. (2) The organizing of reports, lectures, excursions, recreation, entertainment. (3) The organization of clubs, theaters, concerts, exhibitions, libraries, bookshops; the publication of newspapers, magazines. (4) Medical, insurance, and legal help, the opening of hospitals, baths, swimming pools, almshouses.

32. *Obshchestvo "Trud i Otdykh"* (Society of "Labor and Rest") (1916–?). Address: At Gatchinskaya ulitsa: Club for adolescents on the premises of the Petrograd Jewish School; and at ulitsa Zhukovskogo 12: Club on the premises of the Women's Commerce School.

33. *Obshchestvo "Chestniy Truzhenik"* — "Po'el Tzedek" (The "Honest Laborer" Society — "Po'el Tzedek" in Hebrew) (?–1912–1916–?). Address: ulitsa Furmanova (formerly Gagarinskaya ulitsa) 34, apt. 6 (1912) (extant); 7th Sovietskaya (formerly 7th Rozhdestvenskaya) 4, apt. 6 (1916) (extant). Chairman: G. S. Voltke. Objectives: Trade and education for Jewish children.

34. *Obshchestvo Ekonomicheskogo Vozrozhdeniya Palestiny* (Society to Promote the Economic Rebirth of Palestine) (1918–?). Address: Pere'ulok Ilyicha (formerly Kazachiy Pere'ulok) 4, apt. 6. Chairman: M. P. Kreinin. Objectives: The economic development of Palestine by means of attracting financial support and labor and technical forces of Russian Jewry.

35. *Peterburgskoye Otdelyeniye Sportivnogo Obshchestva "Makkabi"* (The St. Petersburg Section of the Maccabee Sports Organization). Objectives: Physical development and national education of Jewish young people.

36. *Petrogradskoye Yevreiskoye Utchitelskoye Obshchestvo* (The Petrograd Jewish Teachers' Society) (1917–?). Address: ulitsa Rubinshteina (formerly Troitskaya) 34 (extant). Committee: Kh.Kh. Fialkov, S. L. Kamenetsky, Z. A. Kisselgoff, M. E. Motyleva, G. L. Aronovitch, E. S. Alexandrova, B. A. Alperin, M. M. Tchernin, V. L. Gendler, A. L. Golomb. Objectives: Union of teachers in the Jewish schools for the purpose of raising the standard of the education.

PHILANTHROPIC SOCIETIES

1. *Damsky Kruzhok Po Vznosu Platy Za Utchashchikhsya V Srednikh Utchebnikh Zavedeniyakh* (Ladies' Circle to Provide the Fees for Pupils at Secondary Schools) (1900–1915).

2. *Yevreiskii Kommitet Pomoshchi Zhertvam Voini* (EKOPO) (Jewish Committee to

Provide Help to the Victims of War, later the Leningrad Jewish Committee to Provide Help to the Victims of War—LEKOPO) (1914–1930). Address: ulitsa Dekabristov (formerly Offitserskaya) 60 (1916) (no longer extant); Naberezhnaya Fontanki 19 (1924–1927) (extant). Published: "Dyelo Pomoshchi" (The Case for Help) (from 1917). In 1917 its budget was thirty-one million rubles (of which seventeen million came from the government and ten million from abroad). In 1925 it was also known as the "Komityet po okazaniyu pomoshchi byednim yevreyam" (The Committee to Provide Help to Poor Jews). Chairmen: G. B. Sliozberg, A. M. Bramson, A. M. Lessman, Y. S. Eiger.

3. *Mo'ess Khitim* (Money for Wheat). Commission to provide help to Jews at Passover (Pesah). Under the auspices of the Synagogue Board of Management. Elected annually. In 1907 became part of OPB (see No. 7).

4. *Obshchestvo Dlya Dostavleniya Utchashchimsya Dyeshovoi I Koshernoi Pishchi* (Ma'akhal Kosheir) (Society to Provide Students with Cheap and Kosher Food) (1916–?). Address: ulitsa Petra Lavrova (formerly Furshtadskaya) 16, apt. 1. Chairman: Baroness M. Guenzburg.

5. *Obshchestvo Dlya Okazaniya Pomoshchi Byednim Yevreyam V.O. I Galernoi Gavani* (OPB) (Tsedoko G'deilo) (Society to Provide Help to the Poor Jews of Vassilevsky Ostrov and Galernaya Harbor—Tsedoko G'deilo) (Yiddishized Hebrew for "Charity is Great"). (1916?—1917?). Address: Vassilevsky Ostrov Sredny Prospekt 33 (extant). Chairman: L. I. Veingerov.

6. *Obshchestvo Pomoshchi Bolnim Yevreyam "Bikkur-Kholim"* (Society for Aid to Sick Jews—"Bikkur Kholim") (Hebrew for "Visiting the Sick"). Founded by OPB (see No. 7), it existed until 1907. Annual budget about thirty-five hundred rubles. Accountable to the Board of Management of the St. Petersburg Synagogue.

7. *Obshchestvo Posobiya Byednim Yevreyam* (Society for the Assistance of Poor Jews) OPB (1907–1917). Address: Canal Griboyedova 140 (formerly Yekaterinensky Canal) (extant). Chairman: Baron Horace Guenzburg (1910–1917). Funds supplied from members' subscriptions, occasional donations or bequests, lotteries, social evenings. The Jewish People's Dining Room and Baths were on the same premises. By late 1907 the amount of donations reached twenty-seven thousand rubles.

8 *Obshchestvo Posobiya Byednim Yevreyam "Tsedoko G'Deilo"* (Society for the Relief of Poor Jews—Tsedoko G'deilo) (Hebrew for "Charity is Great"). Just like "Bikkur Kholim" (see No. 6), it was accountable to the synagogue. Budget twenty-five hundred rubles. In 1907 it merged with OPB.

ALMSHOUSES, CHILDREN'S HOMES, HOSPITALS

1. *Dyetsky Sad Yevreiskogo Obshchestva Vospitaniya I Obrazovaniya* (Kindergarten of the Jewish Society for Upbringing and Education) (1917). Address: Lermontovsky Prospekt 14 (extant). Administrator: B. S. Belenkaya.

2. *Dyetsky Dom No. 93* (Children's Home No. 93) (1917–1930). Address: Vassilevsky Ostrov 10th Liniya 37. Administrator: Z. A. Kisselgoff.

3. *Yevreiskaya Bogadyelnya Imeni M. A. Ginsburga* (The M. A. Ginsburg Jewish Almshouse) (1913–1929). Address: Vassilevsky Ostrov 5th Liniya 50. Chairman: M. A. Ginsburg (till 1917). Administrator: E. E. Klionsky (1920s).

4. *Yevreisky Sirotsky Dom* (Jewish Orphanage) (before 1892–1917). Address: Vassilevsky Ostrov 10th Liniya 37 (extant). Founder: Baroness A. G. Guenzburg (wife of

Baron Horace), succeeded by her son Alexander Guenzburg. Supervisor: M. M. Dollner (1892). In 1915 chairman of the Ladies' Committee was Baroness M. Guenzburg. Medical superintendent: Dr. G. Dembo.

5. *Lechebnitsa Lekopo* (Medical Aid Society Hospital) (1920–1930). Address: ulitsa Dzerzhinskogo 10 (extant). Senior medical officer: Dr. P. B. Khavkin. Today the hospital is the medical clinic of the Leningrad KGB.

6. *Priyut Dlya Yevreiskikh Detyei Prinyavshikh Pravoslaviye* (Shelter for Jewish Children Converted to the Russian Orthodox Church). Address: Konnogvardeiskaya ulitsa 39 (1878).

7. *Priyut Dlya Yevreiskikh Sirot* (Shelter for Jewish Orphans). Opened in 1865 in the Araktchev Barracks (ten orphans). Address: at the end of ulitsa Voinova (formerly Shpalernaya) (no longer extant).

POLITICAL ORGANIZATIONS

1. The Bund (General Jewish Workers' Union in Russia, Lithuania, and Poland). Leaders in St. Petersburg: H. Erlich and M. Rafess. Founded 1897.

2. *Gruppa "Vozrozhdeniye"* (The "Rebirth" Group) (1903–1905). Territorial autonomism in the future and national rights while in dispersion. Merged with SERP (see No. 9).

3. *Gruppa Demokraticheskogo Obyedinyeniya* (The Group of Democratic Unity) (1917). Yefroikin, Perelman.

4. *Yevreiskaya Demokraticheskaya Gruppa* (The Jewish Democratic Group) (from 1904). Formed from Byuro Zashchity Yevreyev (Bureau for Defense of the Jews). Leaders: L. Bramson, A. Braudo, Bickerman, Sacher, Shabad.

5. *Yevreiskaya Kommunisticheskaya Rabochaya Partiya* (Jewish Communist Workers' Party)—former left wing of the Poalei-Tzion (Hebrew—"The Workers of Zion") (1921–1928). Leningrad Committee. Address: ulitsa Chekhova 5 (extant). Secretary: V. M. Borokhovitch.

6. *Yevreiskaya Narodnaya Gruppa* (Jewish People's Group). Formed from members of the Union for Equal Rights. Leaders: M. Vinaver, G. Sliozberg, L. Y. Sternberg (1906–1917). Congress was held in St. Petersburg in 1907. On non-Jewish questions they were in agreement with the Cadets (Constitutional Democrats).

7. *Yevreiskaya Narodnaya Partiya* (Jewish People's Party) (Folkspartei) (from December 1906–1917). Formed from the Union for Equal Rights. Leaders: S. M. Dubnow, M. Kreinin, A. Zalkind, V. Mandel, S. Khoronzhitsky. They called for broad cultural autonomy. In general, matters close to the Cadets.

8. *Yevreiskaya Natsionalnaya Gruppa* (Jewish National Group). Leaders: An-sky, S. Ginsburg.

9. *Yevreiskaya Sotsialisticheskaya Rabochaya Partiya* (SERP) (Jewish Socialist Workers' Party) (1905–1917). Socialist program with cultural autonomy. Leader: Kh. Zhitlovsky.

10. *Yevreiskaya Sotsial-Demokraticheskaya Rabochaya Partiya* (Jewish Social-Democratic Workers' Party) (Poalei-Tzion) (Hebrew—"The Workers of Zion"). Leader: Ber Borokhov.

11. *Yevreiskaya Territorialnaya Rabochaya Partiya* (Jewish Territorial Worker's Party).

12. *Obshchestvo "Ahavat Tzion"* (The "Love of Zion" Society). Started in the 1880s. Student Zionist organization.

13. *Rosseeskaya Sionistskaya Organizatsiya* (Russian Zionist Organization) (1917). Congress held in Petrograd in May 1917. Central Committee address: ulitsa Rubinshteina 20 (1917) (extant).

14. *Sionistskaya Sotsialisticheskaya Rabochaya Partiya* (Zionist Socialist Workers' Party) (from 1904).

15. *Soyuz Dlya Dostizheniya Ravnopraviya Yevreiskogo Naroda V Rossii* (Union for the Attainment of Equal Rights for the Jewish People of Russia) (1905–1907). Leaders: M. Vinaver, G. Sliozberg, L. Bramson. M. Ratner. First Congress in March 1905 in Vilna; Second Congress in November 1905 in St. Petersburg. The union broke up on May 16, 1907, after the elections for the Second State Duma. From it were formed the Zionists (in November 1906 at the Congress in Helsingfors), the Jewish People's Group, the Jewish Democratic Group, and the Folkspartei.

RUSSIAN SOCIETIES FOR THE STUDY OF THE JEWS

1. *Liga Borby S Antisemitizmom* (The League to Fight against Anti-Semitism). Established not later than 1915 by M. Gorky, L. Andreyev, F. Sologub. Members: Alexander Kerensky and the Narodniki (members of the People's Will Party), Tchaikovsky, and Vera Zasulitch.

2. *Obshchestvo Izucheniya Iyudeiskogo Plemeni* (Society for the Study of the Judaic Tribe) (1915–1917). Address: 3rd Sovietskaya ulitsa (formerly 3rd Rozhdestvenskaya) 16 (extant). Chairman: N. N. Zhedenov. An anti-Semitic organization whose objectives were "A thorough study of all the evil qualities of this tribe, its malignant religion, and its internal laws."

3. *Russkoye Obshchestvo Dlya Izucheniya Yevreiskoi Zhizni* (The Russian Society for the Study of Jewish Life) (1915–1917). Address: ulitsa Belinskogo (formerly Simeonovskaya) 11, apt. 9 (extant). Chairman: I. I. Tolstoy. Objectives: The study of Jewish life, history, art, economics, legal situation, and so on. The organization of social gatherings, exhibitions, publication of books. Published: the literary-scientific anthology *Shcheet* (The Shield) with the participation of Gorky, Korolenko, Milyukov, Artsebashev, Sologub, Bunin, Gippius, Merezhkovsky. Among those who participated in the musical soirées were Glazunov, Chaliapin, Rimsky-Korsakov, Kuprin, and Roditchev.

RELIGIOUS INSTITUTIONS

COMMUNITY ORGANIZATION

Leningradskaya Yevreiskaya Religioznaya Obshchina (LERO) The Leningrad Jewish Religious Community (LERO) (1927–1928). Address: Lermontovsky Prospekt 2 (extant). Chairman: A. I. Guterman. Vice-chairman and administrator: I. O. Ginzburg.

MEETING HOUSES FOR PRAYER

1.   Artillereeskaya ulitsa 2 (extant) (1920s).
2.   Prayer hall on the first floor of the almshouse at Vassilevsky Ostrov 5th Liniya 50 (1913–1929?).
3.   Ligovsky Prospekt 55 (extant) (1920s).
4.   Ulitsa Nekrassova 46 or 48 (1920s).
5.   Petrogradsky Rayon, ulitsa Shchorsa (formerly Maly Prospekt) 33 (no longer extant) (1915–1917?).
6.   Soldiers' wooden prayerhouse, opened in 1850 not far from Naberezhnaya Krasnogo Flota (formerly Angleeskaya Naberezhnaya). It was visited by Sir Moses Montefiore.

7.   Temporary prayerhouse in Shcherbakovsky Pere'ulok (next to Naberezhnaya Fontanki). The *hazan* (cantor) was Yanovsky, a baritone with the Leningrad Opera Company.

8.   Pavlova Hall at ulitsa Rubinshteina 13 (now the House of Creative Work of the People). In the 1920s during Jewish festivals it was used as a prayerhouse.

9.   Hasidic prayerhouse, Nevsky Prospekt 128 (1920s).

10.   Prayerhouse in the Preobrazhensky Cemetery (from 1912). Address: Alexandrovsky Farm Prospekt, Preobrazhensky Cemetery. Architect: Y. G. Gewirtz. Funds provided by M. A. Ginsburg.

SYNAGOGUES

1.   *St. Petersburg Choral Synagogue* ("Small" from 1886, "Great" from 1893). Address: Lermontovsky Prospekt (formerly Bolshaya Masterskaya ulitsa) 2 (extant). Architect: Shaposhnikov. Artist: Bakhman. Rabbis: A. N. Drabkin, David-Tevel Katzenellenbogen, M. G. Eisenstadt, Olswanger, M. Gluskin, A. R. Lubanov. Elders: A. Y. Harkavy, I. A. Dembo, I. Y. Markon, B. M. Sapotnitsky. Chairmen of the Community: Baron Yevsel Guenzburg, Baron Horace Guenzburg, Baron David Guenzburg, M. A. Warshawski, Y. B. Eiger, S. M. Lessman, A. M. Pechersky. Seating for twelve hundred.

2.   Synagogue on Vassilevsky Ostrov. Address: Vassilevsky Ostrov 10th Liniya 37 (extant), on the premises of the orphanage; also at Vassilevsky Ostrov 5th Liniya 50 (extant), on the premises of the almshouse.

3.   Temporary synagogue on Voznesensky Prospekt (1870).

4.   Synagogue on ulitsa Vosstaniya near where it is crossed by ulitsa Rileyeva (1920s).

5.   Hasidic synagogue on ulitsa Zhukovskogo 51 (no longer extant) (1920s–1932).

6.   Synagogue by Lions' Bridge (L'viny Mostik) across Canal Griboyedova (1870s–1880s) (no longer extant).

7.   Synagogue in the town of Luga (no longer extant).

8.   The Moskovsky District Synagogue (1913–1917?). Address: Zagorodny Prospekt 15 (1913) (extant); Zagorodny Prospekt 6 (1915) (extant); ulitsa Rubinshteina (formerly Troitskaya) 34 (1917) (extant). Chairman of the Board of Management: D. E. Khavkin.

9.   Moskovsky District Synagogue (1930). Address: 7th Krasnoarmeiskaya ulitsa 1 (extant).

10.   The Peskovsky District Synagogue (?–1913–1927–?). Address: Suvorovsky Prospekt 2, second floor (extant). Chairman of the Board of Management (1915): I. M. Kogan.

11.   Semyonovsky District Synagogue (1915–1917–?). Address: Malo Dyetskoselsky Prospekt (formerly Maly Tsarskoselsky Prospekt) 30 (extant). Chairman of the Board of Management: I. Z. Shapiro.

12.   Semyonovskaya area synagogue (1912–1913). Address: Ruzovskaya ulitsa 13 (extant). Chairman of the Board of Management: P. I. Nevelson.

13.   Semyonovskaya synagogue (1904). Address: Malo Dyetskoselsky (formerly Maly Tsarskoselsky Prospekt) 5.

14.   Synagogue in the town of Sestroretsk (1913–1917–?) (no longer extant). Benefactor: I. B. Guterman.

15.   Synagogue in the area of Solyani Gorodok (1910s).

16. Synagogue in Tsarskoye Selo. Address: Gorod Pushkin, Moskovskaya ulitsa 33 (extant).

17. Synagogue at Vassilevsky Ostrov Sredny Prospekt 16. It occupied half of the second floor, including a cheder and a philanthropic society (1918–1922–?).

18. Synagogue at Vassilevsky Ostrov 3rd Liniya 48, second floor (1916–1918–?).

19. Religious Society Medrash-Shmuel (1925). Address: Prospekt Ogorodnikova (formerly Rizhsky Prospekt) 48 (extant). Chairman: E. Faltinovitch.

20. Religious Society of Hasidim Ivrio (1925–1928). Address: ulitsa Rubinshteina 12 (extant). Chairman: S. A. Maryashkin.

21. Oktyabrsky District Synagogue (1917–1931). Address: Prospekt Mayorova 47.

CEMETERIES

1. The Jewish section in the Volkovsky Protestant cemetery. The old section, purchased in 1802, is no longer extant. The new section dates from 1859. A few ruined memorial stones, dating from 1867 to 1874, can still be seen.

2. The Kazan Cemetery in the town of Puskhin, formerly Tsarskoye Selo (The Tsar's Village). It has a Jewish section. The oldest tombstone is dated 1865. Among those buried here are Sergeant-Major of the Life Guards, Battalion of His Imperial Majesty, Holder of the Medal of St. George's Cross, Shiman Cherkassky (1840–1896); the writer D. Y. Aizman; several professors.

3. The Jewish cemetery in the town of Sestroretsk. Partially preserved. There is also a Jewish section in the Russian Orthodox cemetery. Buried here are the families Guterman, Klyatchko, and others. The earliest tombstone that has been preserved is dated 1898.

4. *The Jewish Preobrazhensky Cemetery* (from 1874). Address: Alexandrovsky Farm Prospekt (formerly 10 versts on the Nikolayev Railway) (extant). Supervisor: A. P. Brusnikov (1915). Among those buried here are Rabbi David-Tevel Katzenellenbogen (1930), A. Y. Harkavy (1919), M. L. Maimon (1924), L. I. Katzenelson (1917), L. Y. Sternberg (1927), M. M. Antokolski (1902), L. O. Gordon (1892), Z. A. Kisselgoff (1938), A. M. Warshawski (1888), I. A. Dembo (1906), Sergeant-Major Ashanski (1899), S. S. Polyakov (1888), Baron David Guenzburg (1910), Vera Slutskaya (1917), M. I. Kulisher (1919), Rabbi Lubanov (1973), Y. S. Hessen (1939).

EDUCATIONAL
ESTABLISHMENTS

JEWISH

1. The Vassilevsky Ostrov OPB School "Tsedoko G'deilo" (Hebrew—"Charity is Great") (?–1915–1917). Address: Vassilevsky Ostrov 3rd Liniya 48 (extant). Principal: S. A. Zeltser.

2. The Eisenbet Jewish Gymnasium (Secondary High School) (1906–1917). Address: ulitsa Myasnikova (formerly Nikolsky Pere'ulok) 7 (1906–1908) (extant); Teatralnaya Ploshchad 18 (1910–1917) (extant). Founder and director: I. G. Eisenbet. Teachers: A. S. Dolinin, S. N. Valk, Z. A. Markov, Z. A. Kisselgoff, T. Y. Zeitlin, Desnitsky, A. I. Pinsker. Among the pupils were R. Khitarov, L. Y. Shatzkin, O. L. Ryvkin, Loitsyansky.

3. Jewish Nos. 1 and 2 Technical Professional Schools (1924–1927). Address: ulitsa Rubinshteina 34 (extant). Principals: No. 1 School—A. E. Levinson (1924), A. E. Movshovitch (1925); No. 2 School—S. I. Aviron; in 1927— I. P. Gandelman. Departments: metalworking (fitter and turner) and needlework. In 1927 they combined into one technical professional school.

4. Jewish Elementary School "Ivrio" (?–1913–1917–?). Address: Zagorodny Prospekt 6 (extant).

5. Jewish Elementary School, Peskovsky District (?–1913–1917–?). Address: Prospekt Bakunina (formerly Kalashnikovsky) 9 (1915) (extant); Basseinaya ulitsa 12 (1913).

6. The Berman Jewish School (from 1867). In Tsarskoye Selo. Fifty Jewish children were taught here free of charge.

7. The Jewish School Talmud-Torah ("Magen-David"—Star of David) In memory of

Baron David Guenzburg (1913–1915–?). Address: Ruzovskaya ulitsa 13 (1913). Maly Detskoselsky Prospekt (formerly Maliy Tsarskoselsky) 30 (1915).

8. Jewish Women's School of Commerce (?–1916–1917–?). Address: ulitsa Zhukovskogo 12 (extant). Together with it was the club for adolescents—"Trud i Otdikh" ("Labor and Rest").

9. Institute of Higher Jewish Studies (Jewish University) (1919–1925). Address: Naberezhnaya Krasnogo Flota (formerly Angleeskaya), 62 (1918) (extant); ulitsa Rubinshteina (formerly Troitskaya) 14 (1918–1925), rebuilt; Stremyannaya ulitsa 18 (1927) (extant). Rector: G. S. Lozinsky. Dean of Studies: S. L. Zinberg. Objectives: The training of teachers, historians, philologists. Faculties: Literary-philological, historical-social. Teachers: S. M. Dubnow, I. M. Kulisher, A. Z. Steinberg, Y. I. Ravrebbe, M. M. Tchernin, V. V. Struve, M. G. Eisenstadt, S. M. Ginzburg, I. Y. Guenzburg, M. L. Maimon, I. Y. Markon.

10. "Yevreiskaya Shkola" "The Jewish School" Association (1912). For gatherings of teachers at the OPE School.

11. Courses on Biblical Language and Biblical History for Jewish Students of Higher and Secondary Educational Establishments (1912–1917). Address: ulitsa Dekabristov 42 (extant), with a branch at Zagorodny Prospekt 6 (extant). Founder: M. G. Eisenstadt. Teachers: B. Alperin and F. Shapiro (1912). About fifty students. Lectures were given mainly in Hebrew.

12. Courses on Oriental Studies for Jews (Courses of Higher Jewish Studies), organized and given by Baron David Guenzburg (1908–1917). Address: Vassilevsky Ostrov 1st Liniya 4 (1908) (extant); 8th Liniya 35 (formerly 33) (1908) (extant); 6th Liniya 5 (1911) (extant); 5th Liniya 50 (from summer 1913).

13. Courses on the Study of Palestine (1918). Zionist. Teachers: B. Goldberg, A. I. Idelson, S. M. Dubnow, Brutskus, Joseph Trumpeldor.

14. Boys' and Girls' Professional and Trade School for Jewish Young People (St. Petersburg OPE School) (?–1900–1917). Address: ulitsa Dekabristov (formerly Offitserskaya) 42 (extant). By the beginning of 1902 there were 221 boys and 208 girls. Of them 320 were given tuition free of charge. Tuition fees in 1901 were from eight to eighteen rubles; in 1909 from nine to thirty-six rubles per annum. The general studies courses lasted five years for boys and three years for girls. Courses for trade training were three to four years. For boys: metalwork and machine-shop practice and butchery; for girls: ladies' tailoring and seamstress work. In 1902 the head of the boys' school was A. M. Konshtam, and the head of the girls' school was P. P. Antokolskaya; from 1910 the head of both was M. S. Yugenburg. Teachers: F. I. Bakhalovitch, I. Y. Yoffe, V. S. Rafailovitch, E. P. Tarabardeyeva, E. A. Steinbock, Y. I. Bernstein, M. L. Bolotin, I. B. Goldman, A. I. Kongisser, I. Y. Krasny, S. M. Livshitz, A. E. Markov, L. A. Rabinovitch, M. S. Rivesman, U. S. Rosenzveig, M. D. Rivkin, Y. M. Reznik, E. G. Shally, M. I. Schneider, S. L. Abugov, B. A. Alperin, G. L. Aronovitch, V. L. Gendler, Z. A. Kisselgoff, A. Y. Lipman, V. S. Markova, M. M. Tchernin, F. D. Shargorodskaya, F. L. Shapiro, and others.

15. No. 2 Jewish National School (1924–1925). Address: ulitsa Tchikovskogo 56 (extant). Head: F. S. Goldgor (1925).

16. No. 5 Jewish National School (1918?–1931?). Address: ulitsa Dekabristov 42 (extant). Director: M. S. Yugenberg (1918); T. Y. Tzeitlin (1925–1930); Shakinskaya (1931).

17. No. 14 Fully Jewish National School (?–1928–1937). Address: Vassilevsky Ostrov 10th Liniya 37 (extant). Head: Z. A. Kisselgoff. In 1931 there were 267 pupils.

18. No. 34 Fully Jewish National Secondary School (?–1933–?). Address: Pere'ulok Matveyeva 1-a. Head: T. Y. Tzeitlin.

19. Petrograd Jewish School (?–1916–1917–?). Address: Gatchinskaya ulitsa. With it was the first club for adolescents—"Trud i Otdikh" ("Labor and Rest").

20. School for the Provision of Primary Education for Jewish Children (?1915–1917–?). Address: ulitsa Shchorsa 33 (no longer extant).

21. Art School "Betzalel" (1912).

22. Private Jewish Gymnasium (Secondary High School) (for Commerce) Videman. (?–1879–?). Address: Vassilevsky Ostrov 9th Liniya 44, apt. 17 (1879).

GENERAL EDUCATIONAL ESTABLISHMENTS

1. Lesgaft Free High School. Faculty of Jewish History (October 1906–December 1906). Address: Prospekt Macleana (formerly Angleesky) 32 (extant). Lectures delivered by S. M. Dubnow.

2. Bestuzhev Higher Women's Courses. Address: 10th Liniya 33 (extant). In 1904 Dubnow's daughter, Sophia Dubnova-Erlich, was a student here. In 1911 the group studying Jewish history was in the care of Professor Kartashev.

3. The Medico-Surgical Academy. Among its graduates were L. I. Katzenelson (1872) and I. A. Dembo (1870). M. A. Natanson was a student here from 1868 to 1872. Address: ulitsa Lebedeva (formerly Nizhegorodskaya) 8 (extant).

4. St. Petersburg Conservatoire. Address: Teatralnaya Ploshchad 3 (extant). Founded by A. G. Rubinstein, who was its first rector. Among its teachers were H. I. Wieniawski, L. Auer, N. E. Perelman, S. I. Savshinski, M. Y. Chalfin; its students included Jascha Heifets, Efrem Zimbalist, M. Weiman, V. G. Walter, M. A. Wolf-Israel, M. Gnessin, A. Krein. In 1916 the Jewish community held a meeting in its small hall.

5. St. Petersburg University. Address: Universitetskaya Naberezhnaya 7 (extant). In 1842 L. I. Mandelstam was the first Jew to graduate from the university. Among the professors were L. Y. Sternberg, V. G. Bogoraz, I. Yu. Markon, S. N. Valk; among students were M. I. Sheftel, S. Mikhoels, L. Martov (Yu. Tsederbaum).

6. Russian Academy of Arts. Address: Universitetskaya Naberezhnaya 17 (extant). Students included M. M. Antokolski (1864–1869), I. L. Asknazi (1870–1880), L. S. Bakst (1883–1887), I. I. Brodsky (from 1902), I. Y. Guenzburg (1878–1886), M. L. Maimon (1880s). Director: I. I. Brodsky (1934–1939).

MUSEUMS, THEATERS, CLUBS, AND LIBRARIES

JEWISH

1. Ope Library (Communal Library) (1878–1929). Address: Krasnaya ulitsa (formerly Galernaya) 25 (1878–1880) (extant); Lermontovsky Prospekt (formerly Bolshaya Masterskaya) 2 (in the synagogue, 1880–1893) (extant); ulitsa Dekabristov (formerly Offitserskaya) 42 (community building) (1893–1918–?) (extant); Stremyannaya ulitsa 18 (?–1920–1927?). Organizer: Dr. A. Y. Harkavy. One of the finest collections in Europe of books on Judaica and Hebraica.

2. Goset (Gosudarstvenniy Yevreisky Teatr) (Jewish State Theater) (1919–1948). Developed from the Jewish Studio that existed in Petrograd from 1919 to 1921. Director: Granovsky (Azarkh). Manager-actor: Solomon Mikhoels. Artists: Marc Chagall, Natan Altman, Falk.

3. Jewish Theatrical Studio (1920–1922). Director: A. R. Kugel.

4. Jewish House of Cultural Enlightenment. Address: ulitsa Rubinshteina 14 (1928); ulitsa Nekrassova 10 (1930–1935). Director: S. A. Szidlovsky (1928).

5. Jewish Drama Theater. Address: Liteiny Prospekt (briefly Prospekt Volodarskogo) 42 (1922) (extant). Yiddish language. Manager: P. Verkhovtsev. Now: Central Lecture Hall.

6. Jewish Club. Address: ulitsa Nekrassova 7 (1927); ulitsa Nekrassova 10 (1928–1930) (extant). Directors: S. A. Szidlovsky (1928); T. F. Gillman (1930). Guest appearances from I. O. Dunayevsky, S. Marshak, L. Utyussov, S. Mikhoels, V. Zusskin, Z. A. Kisselgoff. Now: Puppet Theater.

7. Jewish Club (1918–1920). On Isaakiyevsky Ploshchad (St. Isaac's Square), next to the Mariinsky Palace. Now: the club in the name of Volodarsky.

8. Jewish Historical-Ethnographic Museum (Museum IEO). Address: Vassilevsky Ostrov 5th Liniya 50 (1916–1930?) (extant). Organizer: S. An-sky (until 1918). Objectives: The accumulation and exhibition of materials on history and ethnography, including those collected on the An-sky ethnographic expedition through the Volhynia, Kiev, and Podolsk gubernias (1911–1914). In 1930 it had the following departments: ethnography, history, music, artistic and ancient arts. Curator: S. B. Yudovin. Director: Academician I. Y. Guenzburg. Chairman of Musical Commission: A. M. Bramson (1930).

9. Leningrad Jewish Theater. Address: ulitsa Rakova 13 (1927) (extant). Manager: A. D. Tikhantovsky. Chief Producer: M. T. Stroyev. Directors: A. S. Rabiner, D. I. Sokolov. Now: Musical Comedy Theater.

NON-JEWISH

1. Asiatic Museum of the Imperial Academy of Sciences (1900s–1917–?). Address: Universitetskaya Naberezhnaya 5 (extant). The Jewish library in the museum contained more than thirty thousand volumes. It also held the library of religious books and manuscripts donated by the St. Petersburg merchant Friedland. Part of its collection of books was transferred to the library of the Institute of Oriental Studies of the Academy of Sciences of the USSR.

2. The Saltykov-Shchedrin Public Library (formerly the Imperial Public Library). Address: Ploshchad Ostrovskogo 1–3 (extant). Large repository of Hebrew manuscripts and ancient printed books and incunabula (including the Firkovitch collection). Before 1917 it held fifteen thousand books and two thousand manuscripts. Among those who worked in the library were A. I. Braudo (deputy director until 1924), I. Y. Markon, A. Y. Harkavy, Y. I. Ravrebbe, D. Maggid, Piness.

3. The Museum of the History of Religions and Atheism (formerly the Kazan Cathedral). Address: Kazanskaya Ploshchad 2 (extant). It contains a small section on Judaism.

4. The Museum of Ethnography of the Peoples of the USSR. Address: Inzhenernaya ulitsa 4/1 (extant). From 1924 to 1941 there was a Jewish section. The I. M. Pulner materials and archives are kept in this museum. Some objects from the Jewish Museum are kept there.

5. The Russian Museum (Russky Muzey) (formerly Mikhailovsky Palace). Address: Inzhenernaya ulitsa 4/2. Significant collection of the works of Jewish artists and sculptors, including N. Altman, Anisfeld, Bakst, Chagall, Antokolski, Ilya Guenzburg, and Falk.

6. The V. F. Kommissarzhevskaya Theater of Drama. Address: ulitsa Dekabristov (formerly Offitserskaya) 39. From March 30 to April 30, 1908, the A. M. Kaminsky Jewish Repertory Theater Company (from Warsaw) performed here, on tour, in Yiddish. The leading actresses were his wife, Esther-Rokhel Kaminskaya, and his daughter, Ida Kaminskaya.

JEWISH RESTAURANTS, DINING ROOMS, AND SHOPS

1. Jewish Bakery (1910s). Address: On the corner of ulitsa Rimskogo-Korsakova (formerly Yekateringofsky Prospekt) and Prospekt Mayorova (formerly Voznesenskogo).

2. Jewish "Dyeshovaya Kukhnya" ("Low-Price Cooking") Dining-Room. Address: On the corner of Prospekt Mayorova (formerly Voznesenskogo) and Sadovaya ulitsa. In 1880 Dubnow and his brother often ate here. One-course meal cost seven kopecks; two-course, thirteen kopecks.

3. Jewish "Kukhmisterskaya" ("Eating House") (1917). Address: ulitsa Rimskogo-Korsakova (formerly Yekateringofsky Prospekt) 3 (extant). Proprietor: S. N. Ertman.

4. Jewish "Kukhmisterskaya" ("Eating House") (1917). Address: ulitsa Dzherzhinskogo (formerly Gorochovaya) 39 (extant). Proprietor: N. D. Stolyar.

5. Jewish "Kukhmisterskaya" ("Eating House") (1906–1913). Address: Sadovaya ulitsa 36 (1906) (extant); ulitsa Dhzerzhinskogo (formerly Gorochovaya) 46 (1913). Proprietor: Elyash Zelmanovitch Garfunkel.

6. Jewish "Kukhmisterskaya" ("Eating House") (1906). Address: Nevsky Prospekt 73. Proprietor: N. M. Gordin.

7. Jewish "Kukhmisterskaya" ("Eating House") (1913). Address: Nevsky Prospekt 98. Proprietor: B. A. Glicken.

8. Jewish "Kukhmisterskaya" ("Eating House") (1913–1917). Address: ulitsa Rimskogo-Korsakova (formerly Yekateringofsky Prospekt) 5 (extant). Proprietor: Marfa Petrovna Ostukhovitch (1917); S. B. Alshtwang (1913).

9. Jewish "Kukhmisterskaya" ("Eating House") (1913–1917). Address: ulitsa Sadovaya 45 (extant). Proprietor: A. G. Lebedev.

10. Jewish "Kukhmisterskaya" ("Eating House") (1913). Address: ulitsa Sadovaya 49. Proprietor: A. I. Antselevitch.

11. Jewish "Kukhmisterskaya" ("Eating House") (1906). Address: Sadovaya ulitsa 53 (no longer extant). Proprietor: R. I. Levenshtein.

12. Jewish "Kukhmisterskaya" ("Eating House") (1906). Address: Naberezhnaya Fontanki 40 (extant). Proprietor: R. I. Mikhelevitch.

13. Jewish "Kukhmisterskaya" ("Eating House") (1913–1917). Address: Nevsky Prospekt 108. Proprietor: A. I. Znessin.

14. Jewish Dining Room (1930–1948). Address: Nevsky Prospekt 88 (extant). Jewish-style cooking, but not kosher. Now it is a meat-pie-shop attached to the cinema Stereo-kino. The cook was the former proprietor of the Moroz dining room.

15. Jewish Students' Dining Room (1911–1918–?). Attached to the Courses of Oriental Studies. Address: Vassilevsky Ostrov 6th Liniya 5.

16. Jewish Students' Dining Room (1920s). Near the Sitny Market on Bieloozerskaya ulitsa or Kropotkinskaya ulitsa. Lunch cost ten kopecks. It is believed that the dining room was maintained by the Jewish community.

17. Jewish Private (Kosher) Dining Room (1920s). Address: ulitsa Rubinshteina 15?

18. Jewish Private (Kosher) Dining Room "Lakhmaniya" (Hebrew — "Bread-roll") (?–1928–1930–?). Address: Sadovaya ulitsa 32 (via the courtyard, second floor). Good standard dining room of restaurant quality.

19. Eliyashev's Foodshop (?–1917). Address: Sadovaya ulitsa (opposite cinema Smena) (extant). Confectionery, pastry-cook, groceries, dates, figs, and wines and vodka kosher for Passover.

20. Kosher Meat Shop at Co-operative Prices (1946?). Address: ulitsa Dzerzhinskogo 50.

21. St. Petersburg Synagogue People's Low-Price Dining Room (?–1907–1917). (Opened in 1879; from 1907, the Jewish People's Low-Price Dining Room; then, No. 1 Jewish People's Dining Room.) Address: Canal Griboyedova (formerly Yekaterinensky Canal) 140 (extant). In 1907 lunch was six kopecks (instead of ten), fifteen (instead of twenty), twenty-five (instead of thirty). In 1907, 56,327 meals were served, including 22,670 free meals. Patrons: M. Y. Ginzburg, V. A. Guryan, A. A. Soloveitchik, A. R. Nisselovitch, L. V. Berzh, D. L. Weinstein, I. S. Kadinskaya, S. O. Friedland (1907); E. G. Babus, L. V. Berzh, D. L. Weinstein, A. I. Goldarbeiter, I. S. Kadinskaya, A. R. Nisselovitch, S. O. Friedman, R. Y. Yasnaya (1915). Chairman: A. A. Soloveitchik. Director: A. L. Minovitsky.

22. No. 2 Jewish People's Dining Room (?–1913–1915–?). Address: 4th Rozhdestvenskaya 32/9 (1913); Ligovsky Prospekt 61 (1915). Meals were sold for only a fraction of their cost. From 1913 to 1915 Patrons were S. A. Birshtein, A. I. Goldarbeiter, E. R. Grad, A. M. Dymshitz, I. G. Kroll, S. L. Logunova, M. S. Pumpyanskaya, Z. Y. Zilberman, S. R. Logunov; in addition, in 1913: B. Y. Bassyevitch, R. S. Blumberg, A. L. Dembo, A. R. Nisselovitch; in 1915: E. Y. Alper, Z. M. Kovarskaya, R. S. Frank.

23. Restaurant "Akhilas Kosheir" ("Kosher Eating") (?–1912–1915–?). Address: ulitsa Rimskogo-Korsakova (formerly Yekateringofsky Prospekt) 1, second floor (extant).

24. Restaurant "Karpass" (Vegetarian Restaurant). Address: Kuznechny Pere'ulok

(1879). On February 16, 1879, on the birthday of Tsar Alexander III, the rabbinic commission of three hundred people met here.

25. Merchant Vavelberg's Market (1915). Address: Kurlyandskaya ulitsa 33 (no longer extant).

26. Central Jewish "Kukhmisterskaya" ("Eating House") (1922). Address: Sadovaya ulitsa 31/34, apt. 22 (extant). Satisfying, tasty kosher meals.

WORKS BY JEWISH ARTISTS IN THE RUSSIAN MUSEUM (RUSSKY MUZEY)

(According to the official catalog *Aurora*, Leningrad, 1980)

Altman, Natan Isayevitch (1889–ca. 1970)

1. *Self-portrait,* 1911
2. *Self-portrait,* 1911
3. *Wedding Portrait of Esfir (Esther) Yosifovna Shvartsman,* 1911
4. *Canal in Bruges,* 1911
5. *Macquis,* 1912
6. *Pitcher and Tomatoes,* 1912
7. *Portrait of the Poetess Anna Andreyevna Akhmatova, Born in Gorenko (1889–1966),* 1915
8. *Sunflowers,* 1915
9. *Portrait of Nadezhda Kryt,* undated

Anisfeld, Boris Izrailyevitch (1879–1973)

1. *Capri*, undated
2. *The Magic Lake*, 1914
3. *Venice, the Rialto*, 1914
4. *Sailing Ship*, 1914
5. *The Sultan's Palace*, 1916
6. *Vase with Flowers and Fruit*, 1916
7. *In the Tyrol Mountains*, 1917

Antokolski, Leib Movshovitch (1872–1942)

1. *Crockery*, 1894
2. *Interrogation*, 1889

Asknazi, Isaak Lvovitch (1856–1902)

1. *The Whore before Christ*, 1879
2. *Beggar in Church*, 1884
3. *The Parents of Moses*, 1891
4. *Jewish Wedding*, 1893

Bakst (Rosenberg), Lev Samoilovitch (1866–1924)

1. *Courtyard of the Cluny Museum in Paris*, 1891
2. *Haystacks*, 1891
3. *Child in Front of Icon*, 1893
4. *Self-portrait*, 1893
5. *Street in the Rain, France*, 1893
6. *Mountain Lake*, 1899
7. *Advertising Notice for "Puppet Show,"* 1899
8. *Head of a Child*, undated
9. *Supper*, 1902
10. *Church in the Forest*, undated
11. *Portrait of Marina Nikolayevna Gritsenko (1900–1971), the Artist's Stepdaughter*, undated
12. *Portrait of Sergei Pavlovitch Diaghilev (1872–1929) with Nanny*, 1906
13. *Curtain for the V. F. Kommissarzhevskaya Drama Theatre*, 1906
14. *Ancient Horror*, undated
15. *Woman's Head*, undated

Braz, Yosif (Osip) Emanuilovitch (1872–1936)

1. *Mother and Child*, 1896
2. *Doorkeeper*, 1897
3. *Portrait of the Artist Alexander Petrovitch Sokolov (1829–1913)*, 1898
4. *Portrait of Countess Helena Mikhailovna Tolstaya née Tchertkova (1865–1956), Wife of Count D. I. Tolstoi*, 1900
5. *Portrait of Count Dmitry Ivanovitch Tolstoi (1860–1942?), Later Director of the Hermitage*, 1901

6. *Portrait of an Unknown Man,* 1903
7. *Dutch Woman,* undated
8. *Portrait of the Artist Constantine Constantinovitch Pervukhin (1863–1915),* undated
9. *Interior,* undated
10. *Portrait of the Sculptor Ilya Yakovlevitch Guenzburg (1859–1938),* undated
11. *Mountain Landscape, Brittany,* 1911
12. *Landscape with Trees,* undated
13. *After the Rain,* 1915
14. *Landscape with River,* undated
15. *Still-life with Bronze Mortar,* 1920
16. *Still-life with Pitcher,* 1921
17. *Still-life with White Serviette,* 1922

Brailovsky, Leonid Mikhailovitch (1867–1937)

1. *In the Harbor,* 1914

Brodsky, Isaak Izrailyevitch (1883–1939)

1. *Portrait of the Artist's Wife, Lyubov Markovna Brodskaya née Hoffman (1888–1962) on the Terrace,* 1908
2. *A Dull Day,* 1909
3. *Quiet Corner. Fountain in Rome,* 1910
4. *Early Spring,* 1911
5. *Melting Snow, Silverskaya,* 1913
6. *Street in Pskov,* 1913
7. *Winter Landscape,* 1917
8. *Village Landscape,* undated

Goldblatt, Yakov Semyonovitch (1860–not earlier than 1914)

1. *Socrates in the Dungeon before His Death,* 1888 (For this picture Goldblatt was awarded in 1888 the gold medal first class and the title of classic artist first grade.)

Kishenevsky, Solomon Yakovlevitch (1863–1941?)

1. *Could Be a Man,* 1891
2. *Could Be a Man,* undated
3. *Man on the Sea Shore,* undated

Levitan, Isaak Ilyich (1860–1900)

1. *Shed, in the Woods,* late 1870s–early 1880s
2. *Ostankino,* early 1880s
3. *Wild Cherry Tree,* early 1880s
4. *Wheat-Sheaves and Trees beyond the River,* first half 1880s
5. *Small Hose with Willows,* first half 1880s
6. *Edge of the Forest,* first half 1880s

7. *Village. Peasant Huts,* first half 1880s
8. *Sea Shore. Crimea,* 1886
9. *Overgrown Pond,* 1887
10. *Golden Autumn. Small Village,* 1889
11. *Sea. Sunset,* 1880s
12. *Tree,* 1880s
13. *In a Birch Grove,* 1880s
14. *Trees and Bushes,* 1880s
15. *By the Sea Shore. Italy,* 1890
16. *Overcast Sky. Twilight,* undated
17. *Late Autumn,* 1894
18. *Spring. The Last Snow,* undated
19. *A Dull Day,* 1895
20. *Lake Como, Italy,* 1895
21. *By the Shore,* first half 1890s
22. *Pathway through a Leafy Wood with Ferns,* ca. 1895
23. *Moonlit Night in the Village,* 1897
24. *Meadow at the Edge of the Forest,* 1898
25. *Ravine,* 1898
26. *Quietness,* 1898
27. *Early Spring,* 1898
28. *The Brook,* 1899
29. *Dusk. The Moon,* undated
30. *Dusk. The Moon,* 1899
31. *Swamp,* second half 1890s
32. *Lake. Shed at the Edge of the Woods,* undated
33. *Lake,* 1899–1900
34. *Harvesting the Hay,* 1900
35. *River Valley. Autumn,* undated
36. *Autumn Landscape,* undated
37. *Autumn Landscape with Church,* undated
38. *Landscape with Buildings,* undated

Possibly by Levitan

1. *Winter's Day,* undated
2. *Village. Evening,* undated

Pasternak, Leonid Osipovitch (1862–1945)

1. *Lev Nikolayevitch Tolstoi with His Family at Yasnaya Polyana,* 1902
2. *Session of the Council of Artist-Teachers of the Moscow School of Painting, Sculpture and Architecture,* 1902
3. *Girl Student,* undated
4. *Alexander II Hunting,* undated
5. *Under the Green Lamp (Reading),* undated

Pevsner, Natan (Antoine) Abramovitch (1886–1962)

1. *Absinthe,* 1922 (1933?)

Segal, Ovsei Isaakovitch (1862–1946)

1. *Portrait of Sergei Alexandrovitch Olkhin (1845–1917),* 1905
2. *Portrait of Helena Petrovna Olkhina, née Becketova (1850–1912), Wife of S. A. Olkhin,* 1905

Falk, Robert Rafailovitch (1886–1958)

1. *Old Ruza,* 1913
2. *Old Man,* 1913
3. *Crimean Village,* 1915
4. *Crimea. Lombardy Poplar,* 1915
5. *Valley in the Crimea,* undated
6. *Portrait of an Unknown Man,* undated
7. *Still-life. Crockery and Fruit,* undated
8. *Hospital Courtyard,* 1943 exhibition

Chagall, Marc Zakharovitch (1887–1985)

1. *Father,* 1914
2. *Small Shop in Vitebsk,* 1914
3. *Mirror,* 1915
4. *Red Jew,* 1915
5. *Going for a Walk,* 1917

Shkolnik, Yosif Solomonovitch (1883–1926)

1. *Landscape,* undated
2. *Street,* undated
3. *Still-life with Vases,* undated
4. *Still-life with Yellow Tablecloth,* undated
5. *Provincial Scene,* undated
6. *Winter Landscape,* undated
7. *Pond with Boats and a Raft,* undated

Sternberg, David Petrovitch (1881–1948)

1. *Breakfast,* undated
2. *Landscape,* undated
3. *Cubist Still-Life,* undated
4. *Writing Desk,* undated

BIBLIOGRAPHY

ENCYCLOPEDIAS

1. *Bolshaya sovietskaya entsiklopedia,* 1st edition, Moscow, 1926–1947.
2. *Bolshaya sovietskaya entsiklopedia,* 3rd edition, Moscow, 1970–1978.
3. *Yevreiskaya entsiklopedia.* A collection of information about Judaism and its culture in the past and present. Vols. 1–16. St. Petersburg, 1906–1914.
4. *Kratkaya yevreiskaya entsiklopedia.* Vol. 1. Jerusalem, 1976.
5. *Entsiklopedichesky slovar* (Russian Encyclopedic Dictionary). Vols. 1–86. St. Petersburg, Brockhaus and Yefron, 1889–1907.

DIRECTORIES, GUIDEBOOKS, ADDRESS BOOKS

1. *Akademia Nauk SSSR* (Academy of Sciences of the USSR). Personal Staff List. Vols. 1–2. Moscow, Na'uka, 1974.
2. *Vyes Leningrad* (All Leningrad). Leningrad, 1925–1935.
3. *Vyes Peterburg.* Directory and Address Book. St. Petersburg. Publisher: A. S. Suvorin "Novoye vremya." St. Petersburg, 1892–1914.
4. *Vyes Petrograd* (All Petrograd) "Novoye vremya." Petrograd, 1915–1917 and 1922.

5. K. Gorbachev and E. Khablo. *Pochemu Tak Nazvany?* (Why Are They So Called?). Leningrad, Lenizdat, 1975.
6. *Yevreisky Yezhedodnik* (Jewish Year Book) for 1918–1919. Editor: B. A. Goldberg. Publisher: Kadima. Petrograd, 1918.
7. V. Mikhnevitch. *Peterburg Vyes Kak Na Ladoni* (All of St. Petersburg, Like the Palm of Your Hand). St. Petersburg, 1874.
8. K. M. Nistrem. "Address Calendar of St. Petersburg's Inhabitants." Vols. 1–3. St. Petersburg, 1844.
9. *St. Petersburg Necropolis.* Publisher: Grand Prince Nikolai. Mikhailovitch, St. Petersburg, 1912.
10. *Putyevodityel Po Peterburgu* (Guidebook around St. Petersburg). St. Petersburg, 1913.
11. *Putyevodityel Po Leningradu* (Guidebook around Leningrad). Leningrad, 1978.
12. *Sankt-Peterburgsky Kalendar na 1878* (St. Petersburg Calendar for 1878). St. Petersburg, 1877.
13. *Spravochnaya Kniga "Rassveta"* (The "Rassvet" Directory)—supplement to the newspaper *Rassvet.* St. Petersburg, 1910.
14. Tsylov. *Urban Indicator or Address Book for 1849.* St. Petersburg, 1848.

STATISTICAL SUMMARIES

1. Jews in the USSR. Report on Research by the Statistical-Economic Commission appointed by ORT. No. 4. Moscow, ORT, 1929.
2. The Jewish Population in the USSR in Tables and Diagrams. Issue No. 5. Publishers: L. G. Zinger and B. S. Engel. Editor: Z. L. Mindlin. Central Publication of the Peoples of the USSR. Moscow, Statistical-Economic Commission Publication House appointed by ORT, 1930.
3. The Jewish Population of the USSR. Report on Research, compiled by L. G. Zinger. Editor: Z. L. Mindlin. No. 1. Publisher: Central Committee of ORT. Moscow, 1927.
4. Report on the Saint-Petersburg Schools of OPE for 1901. St. Petersburg, 1902.
5. Report of the Saint-Petersburg Society for Relief for Poor Jews for the Year 1907. St. Petersburg, 1908.

BIBLIOGRAPHICAL COLLECTIONS

1. A. M. Lisovsky. *Bibliography of Russian Periodical Press,* 1703–1900. Petrograd, 1915.
2. *Russian Periodical Press, 1895–1917.* General Editors: A. G. Dementyeva and others. Moscow, 1957.
3. *Russian Periodical Press, 1702–1894.* General Editors: A. G. Dementyeva and others. Moscow, 1959.
4. *Sistematichesky Ukazatyel Literaturi O Yevreyakh Na Russkom Yazikye* (Systematic Guide to Literature about the Jews Written in Russian) (1708–December 1889). St. Petersburg, 1893.
5. I. V. Yashunsky. *Jewish Periodical Press in the Years 1917 and 1918.* Petrograd. Gosizdat, 1920.

PERIODICAL PUBLICATIONS

1. *Biblioteka Yevreiskoi Semyi I Shkoli* (Library for the Jewish Family and School). No. 10. Bar-Mitzvo. General Editor: M. I. Daiches. St. Petersburg, 1914.

2. *Budushchnost* (Newspaper). Editor: S. O. Grusenberg. St. Petersburg, 1900–1914.

3. *Vestnik Yevreiskogo Prosveshcheniya.* Nos. 47–48, 1916. Petrograd, organ of the OPE. Editors: M. G. Eisenstadt and others.

4. *Vestnik OPE.* Editor: Y. B. Eiger. St. Petersburg, 1910–1913.

5. *Voskhod,* 1883, Books V–VIII. Editor: A. E. Landau. St. Petersburg, 1881–1889.

6. *Voskhod,* 1884, Book II.

7. *Voskhod,* 1885, Books V–VII.

8. *Voskhod,* 1886, Books III–V.

9. *Voskhod,* 1887, Books V–VI.

10. *Voskhod,* 1894.

11. *Gakedem* (Hebrew "Ha-Kedem" — The East). St. Petersburg, 1907. Editors: I. Yu. Markon, A. Zaraovsky. I–IV.

12. *Yevreiskaya Zhizn.* Editors: M. D. Rivkin and others. St. Petersburg, 1904–1907.

13. *Yevreiskaya Mysl.* Vol. I. Editor: S. N. Ginzburg. Petrograd, 1922.

14. *Yevreiskaya Starina.* Editors: S. M. Dubnow and others. St. Petersburg/Leningrad, 1909–1930.

15. *Yevreisky Almanakh.* Petrograd, 1923.

16. *Yevreisky Vestnik.* Organ of OPE. Petrograd, 1922.

17. *Yevreisky Vestnik.* Leningrad, 1928.

18. *Literaturnoye Prilozheniye K Nivye* (Literary Supplement to "Niva"). St. Petersburg, 1913.

19. *Nash Put.* Petrograd, 1916.

20. *Noviy Put.* Moscow, 1916.

21. *Rassvet.* Editors: G. L. Zeitlin and others. St. Petersburg, 1907–1915.

22. Advertising pamphlet of the book publisher Vostok for 1913, St. Petersburg, 1913.

23 *Russky Arkhiv* (Russian Archives). St. Petersburg, 1870.

LITERATURE, JOURNALISM

1. I. E. Babel, *Izbrannoye* (Selected Works). Moscow, 1966.

2. V. I. Binstock and S. A. Novoselsky. "Yevrei v Leningradye (Petrogradye) 1900–1924" (Jews in Leningrad/Petrograd 1900–1924). A demographic survey in the collection: *Voprosy Biologii I Patologii Yevreyev* (Questions on the Biology and Pathology of the Jews). Leningrad, 1926.

3. M. Buber. *Put Cheloveka* (The Road for Man). Jerusalem, 1950.

4. N. A. Bukhbinder. *Istoriya Yevreiskogo Rabochego Dvizheniya V Rossii* (History of the Jewish workers' movement in Russia). Leningrad, 1925.

5. H. N. Bialik. *Songs and Poems.* Translated by V. Jabotinsky, Berlin, 1922.

6. "Curriculum of Tuition for the Courses of Oriental Studies." Nos. 1–4. *Hakedem,* 1907.

7. M. Weinstein. *Yevreiskaya Narodnaya Muzika* (Jewish Folk Music). Leningrad Conservatoire. Diploma Thesis. Leningrad, 1983.

8. T. B. Geilikman. *Istoriya Obshchestvennogo Dvizheniya Yevreyev V Polshe I Ros-*

sii (History of the Social Movement of the Jews in Poland and Russia). Moscow, Gosizdat, 1930.

9. Y. I. Gessen (Hessen). *Istoriya Yevreiskogo Naroda V Rossii* (History of the Jewish People in Russia). Vols. 1–2. Leningrad, 1925–1927.

10. Y. I. Gimpelson. *Zakony O Yevreyakh* (Laws Affecting the Jews). St. Petersburg, 1914.

11. I. Y. Guenzburg. *Iz Proshlogo* (Out of the Past). Leningrad, 1924.

12. L. O. Gordon. *K Istorii Poseleniya Yevreyev V Peterburgye* (On the History of the Settlement of the Jews in St. Petersburg). Voskhod. Books I–II. St. Petersburg, 1881.

13. L. O. Gordon. "Tyurma I Ssylka—Epizod Iz Moyei Zhizni" (Prison and Exile—An Episode in My Life). Posmertnye zapiski (Posthumous Notes). Perezhitoye. Vol. IV. St. Petersburg, 1913.

14. M. Gorev. *Protiv Antisemitov. Otcherki I Zarisovki* (Against the Anti-Semites. Sketches and Drawings). Moscow-Leningrad, Gosizdat, 1928.

15. S. G. Lozinsky. "Yevreisky Universitet." *Yevreisky Vestnik.* April 1922.

16. M. Gorky. "Yevreisky Vopros" (The Jewish Question). In the collection *Rannyaya Revolyutsionnaya Publitsistika* (Early Revolutionary Journalism). OGIZ, 1938.

17. L. Grossman. *Ispoved Odnogo Yevreya* (Confession of a Jew). Moscow-Leningrad, 1924.

18. S. O. Grusenberg. *Yevreiskoye Naseleniye Peterburga V Sotsialnom I Sanitarnom Otnoshenii* (The Jewish Population of St. Petersburg from a Social and Medical Point of View). Statistichesky otcherk (A Statistical Sketch). Voskhod, 1891. Books I–II, St. Petersburg, 1891.

19. Kh. D. Gurevitch. *Samopomoshch Remeslennikov* (Self-Help for Artisans) (Yiddish). Publisher: ORT, St. Petersburg, 1911.

20. F. M. Dostoyevsky. *Dnevnik Pisatelya* (A Writer's Diary). Collected Works, Leningrad, Na'uka, 1983.

21. S. M. Dubnow. *Ob Izuchenii Istorii Russkikh Yevreyev I Ob Utchrezhdenii Russko-Yevreiskogo Istoritcheskogo Obshchestva* (On the Study of the History of Russian Jews and on the Formation of the Russian-Jewish Historical Society). Voskhod. Books 4–9, 1891.

22. S. M. Dubnow. *Pisma O Starom I Novom Yevreistve* (Letters about Old and New Jewry), 1897–1907. St. Petersburg, 1907.

23. S. M. Dubnow. *Vsyeobshchaya Istoriya Yevreyev* (Universal History of the Jews). Vols. 1–5. St. Petersburg, 1905–1914.

24. S. M. Dubnow. *Yevrei V Rossii V Tsarstvovaniye Alexandra III,* Kniga I. "Yevrei V Rossii I Zapadnoi Yevropye V Epokhu Antisemitskoi Reaktsii" (The Jews in Russia during the Reign of Alexander III. Book I. The Jews in Russia and Western Europe during the Period of the Anti-Semitic Reaction). Publisher: A. D. Frenkel, Moscow and Leningrad, 1923.

25. S. M. Dubnow. *Kniga Zhizni* (Book of My Life.) "Recollections and Reflections." Volume 2, "Materials for the History of My Time." Riga, 1935.

26. D. S. Zak. *Formy Ekonomicheskoi Samopomoshchi V Oblasti Remeslennogo Truda* (Forms of Economic Self-help in the Field of Craft Labor). Publisher: ORT. St. Petersburg, 1911.

27. D. Zaslavsky. *Yevrei V Russkoi Literaturye* (Jews in Russian Literature). Yevreiskaya Letopis, Collection I. Petrograd, 1923.

28. *Yevreiskaya Antologiya—Sbornik Yevreiskoi Poezii* (A Jewish Anthology—

Collection of Jewish Poetry), Moscow, 1918 (or 1919). Editors: V. F. Khodasevitch, L. B. Yaffe. Publisher: "Saffrut." Shimonovitch's poem "The Sphinxes" was published here.

29. A. A. Ignatiev. *Pyatdesyat Let V Stroyu* (Fifty Years in Construction). Publisher: Krymizdat. Simferopol, 1953.

30. G. Kanovitch. *Svetchi Na Vetru* (Candles in the Wind). Moscow, Sovietsky Pisatyel, 1982.

31. V. O. Klutchevsky. *Sochineniya* (Works). Vols. 1–8. Moscow, 1958.

32. L. Klyachko. "Tainstvenny Kabinet" (The Secret Cabinet). Yevreiskaya Letopis No. 4, Moscow-Leningrad, 1926.

33. L. Klyachko. *Povesti Proshlogo* (Tales of the Past). Leningrad, 1930.

34. "K Obshchemu Sobraniyu Odesskogo Palestinskogo Komiteta" (For the General Assembly of the Odessa Palestine Committee). Rassvet, 1912, No. 1.

35. A. Gornfeld. "S. A. An-sky." *Yevreisky vestnik*. April 1922.

36. I. I. Krupnik. *Problemy Etnograficheskogo Izucheniya Yevreyev V SSSR* (Problems of the Ethnographic Study of the Jews in the USSR). Sovietish Heimland, Moscow, 1982.

37. M. I. Kulisher. *Velikaya Frantsuzskaya Revolutsiya I Yevreisky Vopros* (The Great French Revolution and the Jewish Question). Leningrad, OPE, 1927.

38. Doizber Levin. *Desyat Vagonov* (Ten Wagons). Moscow-Leningrad, 1931.

39. D. Krivitski. *Ikhio Ravrebbe*—Coll. Zvagil, 1962. Publication of the Association of Emigrants from Volhynia Province in the USA.

40. S. G. Lozinsky. *Sotsialniye Korni Antisemitizma V Sredniye Veka I V Novoye Vremya* (The Social Roots of Anti-Semitism in the Middle Ages and Later). Leningrad, OPE, 1929.

41. V. Lvov-Rogachevsky. "Russko-Yevreiskaya Literatura" (Russian-Jewish Literature). With an introduction by B. Gorev—*Russkaya Literatura I Yevrei* (Russian Literature and the Jews). Moscow, Gosizdat, 1922.

42. O. Liubomirsky. "Mikhoels." Moscow, *Iskusstvo,* 1938.

43. M. Maimon. "Istoriya Odnoi Kartiny" (The Story of a Certain Picture). Yevreiskaya Letopis, Collection I. Petrograd, 1923.

44. L. I. Mandelstam. *Perezhitoye* (Past Experience). St. Petersburg, Brockhaus and Yefron, 1910.

45. O. E. Mandelstam. *Shum Vremeni* (The Noise of Time). St. Petersburg, 1925.

46. Yu. I. Markon, article on Voznitzin in *Perezhitoye* (Past Experience). Vols. II–IV. St. Petersburg, Brockhaus and Yefron, 1910–1913.

47. S. Y. Marshak. *"Nad Mogiloi"* (Over the Grave). *Yevreiskaya Zhizn,* No. 8, St. Petersburg, 1904.

48. S. Y. Marshak. *O Sebye* (About Myself). Vol. 1. Moscow, 1968.

49. L. Nevakhovitch, *Vopl Dshcheri Iyudeiskoi* (The Wailing of the Daughter of Judaea). St. Petersburg, 1803.

50. I. G. Orshansky. *Russkoye Zakonodatyelstvo Ob Yevreyakh. Otcherki I Issledovaniya* (Russian Legislation Concerning the Jews. Essays and Research). St. Petersburg, 1877.

51. L. Y. Sternberg. *Pamyati* (Memoirs) (1861–1927). Publisher: Academy of Sciences of the USSR. Leningrad, 1930.

52. *Pamyati Professora E. E. Klionskogo. Nekrolog* (The Problems of Tuberculosis). No. 1. Moscow, Medgiz, 1962.

53. *Perezhitoye* (Past Experience). A collection devoted to the social and cultural history of the Jews in Russia. Contributors included S. An-sky, A. Braudo, and M. Vishnitzer. Vols. 1–4, St. Petersburg, 1909–1913.

54. L. S. Pinsker. *Auto-emancipation.* St. Petersburg, 1898.

55. Y. I. Ravrebbe. "Poeziya I Zhizn." *Yevreisky Vestnik,* No. 3. Petrograd, June 1922.

56. Y. I. Ravrebbe. "Svadba Makarovskogo Tzadika."—Yevreiskaya Letopis, Collection 4.

57. M. S. Rivesman. "Vospominaniya I Vstrechi" (Recollections and Meetings). Yevreiskaya Letopis, Vol. III. Leningrad and Moscow, 1924.

58. G. Rosenzweig. "Shtrikhi Proshlogo" (Shades of the Past). Yevreiskaya Letopis, collection IV. Leningrad, 1926.

59. Z. Rubashov. Yechiel Ravrebbe—Collection Zvagil, 1956, 1962. Publication of the Association of Emigrants from Volhynia Province in the USA.

60. *Russkoye Obshchestvo Dlya Izucheniya Yevreiskoi Zhizni (Ustav Obshchestva). Literaturno-muzikalny Vecher* (Russian Society for the Study of Jewish Life—Personnel of the Society). Literary-musical evening. Petrograd, March 23, 1916.

61. *Safrut.* Literary-scientific collection. Editor: L. Yaffe. Books 1 and 2. Moscow, 1918.

62 V. V. Stassov. *Po Povodu Postroiki Sinagogi V Peterburgye* (Regarding the Construction of the Synagogue in St. Petersburg). Yevreiskaya biblioteka, St. Petersburg, 1871.

63. V. V. Struve. *Izrail V Yegiptye* (Israel in Egypt). Leningrad, OPE, 1920.

64. A. S. Tager. *Tsarskaya Rossiya I Dyelo Beilisa* (Tsarist Russia and the Beilis Case). Sovietskoye Zakonodatyelstvo. Moscow, OGIZ, 1934.

65. S. L. Zinberg. "Pervye Sotsialisticheskiye Organy V Yevreiskoi Literaturye" (The First Socialist Organs in Jewish Literature). Perezhitoye, Vol. I. St. Petersburg, 1909.

66. S. L. Zinberg. *Istoriya Yevreiskoi Pechati V Rossii V Svyazi S Obshchestvennimi Techeniyami* (The History of the Jewish Press in Russia and its Connection with Public Trends). Petrograd, 1915.

67. *Chin I Obryad Osvyashcheniya Doma Otpevaniya Na Yevreiskom Preobrazhenskom Kladbishche V Sankt-Peterburgye 23 Sentyabrya 1912 Goda* (Order of Service for the Ceremony of the Consecration of the House of Funeral Prayers at the Preobrazhensky Jewish Cemetery in Saint Petersburg on September 23, 1912).

68. T. Shatilova. "Epizodi Iz Zhizni Yevreiskikh Studentov" (Incidents in the Lives of Jewish Students). Yevreiskaya Letopis, Vol. 2. Petrograd-Moscow, 1923.

69. *Shcheet* (The Shield). Literary anthology under the general editorship of L. Andreyev, M. Gorky, F. Sologub. Moscow, 1915.

70. M. B. Epstein. "K Istorii Yevreiskoi Kolonii V Peterburgye" (On the History of Jewish Settlement in St. Petersburg). Yevreiskaya Letopis, Vol. 2. Petrograd-Moscow, 1923.

71. N. V. Yukhnyeva. *Peterburg—Mnogonatsionalnaya Stolitsa* (St. Petersburg—Multi-national Capital). Collection: Stariy Peterburg. Leningrad, Na'uka, 1982.

72. N. V. Yukhnyeva. *Etnichesky Sostav I Etnosotsialnaya Struktura Naseleniya Peterburga* (The Ethnic Composition and the Ethnosocial Structure of the Population of St. Petersburg). Leningrad, Na'uka, 1984.

Bertha Ioffe	born 1902 in Suvalki — daughter of the St. Petersburg rabbi.
Neha Aaronovna	born 1895 in Vitebsk — wife of E. E. Klionsky.
L. P.	born 1907 in Proskurov — a self-educated, erudite person who was acquainted with Y. I. Ravrebbe.
P. S.	born 1914, brought up as a member of Ravrebbe's family.
S. M.	born 1907 in Vitebsk, artist, a friend of S. B. Yudovin.
A. B.	born 1910 in St. Petersburg — an elderly resident of Vassilevsky Ostrov.
D. N.	born 1912 in Vitebsk, artist, a friend of S. B. Yudovin.
A. O.	born 1911 in Polonnoye; taught in the Jewish school on Vassilevsky Ostrov in the early 1930s.

GAZETTEER

STREET NAMES USED IN THIS VOLUME WHERE THE NAMES HAVE CHANGED

Prerevolutionary name	*Postrevolutionary name*
Admiralteisky	Krushteina
Alexandrovskaya	Ostrovskogo
Angleeskaya Naberezhnaya	Krasnogo Flota
Angleesky	Macleana
Basseinaya	Nekrassova
Bolshaya Masterskaya	Lermontovsky
Bolshaya Monetnaya	Skorokhodova
Bolshaya Morskaya	Herzena
Bolshogo Teatra	Teatralnaya
Bolshoi (on Petrogradskaya Storona)	Karla Liebknekhta
Bolshoi Kazatchiy	Ilyicha
Dvortsovaya	Uritsky
Ertelev	Chekhova
Furshtadskaya	Petra Lavrova
Galernaya	Krasnaya
Gagarinskaya	Furmanova

Prerevolutionary name	Postrevolutionary name
Gorokhovaya	Dzherzhinskogo
Italianskaya	Rakova
Kalashnikovsky	Bakunina
Kamenno-Ostrovsky	Kirovsky
Kirochnaya	Saltykova-Shchedrina
Konnogvardeisky	Profsoyuzov
Leonov	Zamyatin
Leshtukov	Dzhamboula
Lesnoi Uchastok	Bolshaya Obyezdnaya
Liteiny	Volodarskogo
Malaya Konyushennaya	Sofia Perovskoi
Malaya Morskaya	Gogolya
Maly Prospekt	Shchorsa
Maly Tsarskoselsky	Malo Dyetskoselsky
Mikhailovskaya (ploshchad)	Lassala (later Iskusstv)
Mikhailovskaya (ulitsa)	Brodskogo
Millionaya	Khalturina
Nadezhdinskaya	Mayakovskogo
Nikolaevskaya	Marata
Nikolsky	Myasnikova
Nizhegorodskaya	Lebedeva
Nobelevskaya	Samoilovoi
Offitserskaya	Dekabristov (ulitsa)
Panteleimonovskaya	Pestelya
Peterhofskoye	Stachek
Politseisky	Narodny
Pryadilny	Labutina
Rizhsky	Ogorodnikova
Rozhdestvenskaya	Sovietskaya
Rumyantsevskaya	Shevchenko
Senatskaya	Dekabristov ploshchad
Sergievskogo	Tchaikovskogo
Shpalernaya	Voinova
Simeonovskaya	Belinskogo
Solovevsky	Repina
Spasskaya	Rileyeva
Tairov	Brinko
Torgovaya	Soyuza Petchatnikov
Troitskaya	Rubinshteina
Troitsky	Moskvina
Usatchev	Makarenko
Voskresensky	Chernyshevsky
Voznesenskogo	Mayorova
Yamskaya	Dostoyevskogo
Yekaterinensky (canal)	Griboyedova (canal)
Yekateringofsky	Rimskogo-Korsakova
Zabalkansky	Moskovsky
Zakharyevskaya	Kalyaeva
Znamenskaya	Vosstaniya

Postrevolutionary name	Prerevolutionary name
Bakunina	Kalashnikovsky
Belinskogo	Simeonovskaya
Bolshaya Obyezdnaya	Lesnoi Uchastok
Brinko	Tairov
Brodskogo	Mikhailovskaya
Chekhova	Ertelev
Chernyshevsky	Voskresensky
Dekabristov (ploshchad)	Senatskaya
Dekabristov (ulitsa)	Offitserskaya
Dostoyevskogo	Yamskaya
Dzhamboula	Leshtukov
Dzherzhinskogo	Gorokhovaya
Furmanova	Gagarinskaya
Gogolya	Malaya Morskaya
Griboyedova (canal)	Yekaterinensky (canal)
Herzena	Bolshaya Morskaya
Ilyicha	Bolshoi Kazatchiy
Iskusstv	Mikhailovskaya
Kalyaeva	Zakharyevskaya
Karla Liebknekhta	Bolshoi (on Petrogradskaya Storona)
Khalturina	Millionaya
Kirovsky	Kamenno-Ostrovsky
Krasnaya	Galernaya
Krasnogo Flota	Angleeskaya
Krushteina	Admiralteisky
Labutina	Pryadilny
Lassala	Mikhailovskaya
Lebedeva	Nizhegorodskaya
Lermontovsky	Bolshaya Masterskaya
Macleana	Angleesky
Makarenko	Usatchev
Malo Dyetskoselsky	Maly Tsarskoselsky
Maly	Shchorsa
Marata	Nikolaevskaya
Mayakovskogo	Nadezhdinskaya
Mayorova	Voznesenskogo
Moskovsky	Zabalkansky
Moskvina	Troitsky
Myasnikova	Nikolsky
Narodny	Politseisky
Nekrassova	Basseinaya
Ogorodnikova	Rizhsky
Ostrovskogo	Alexandrovskaya
Pestelya	Panteleimonovskaya
Petra Lavrova	Furshtadskaya
Profsoyuzov	Konnogvardeisky

Postrevolutionary name	Prerevolutionary name
Rakova	Italianskaya
Repina	Solovevsky
Rileyeva	Spasskaya
Rimskogo-Korsakova	Yekateringofsky
Rubinshteina	Troitskaya
Saltykova-Shchedrina	Kirochnaya
Shchorsa	Maly Prospekt
Shevchenko	Rumyantsevskaya
Skorokhodova	Bolshaya Monetnaya
Sofia Perovskoi	Malaya Konyushennaya
Sovietskaya	Rozhdestvenskaya
Soyuza Petchatnichov	Torgovaya
Stachek	Peterhofskoye
Tchaikovskogo	Sergievskogo
Teatralnaya	Bolshogo Teatra
Uritsky	Dvortsovaya
Voinova	Shpalernaya
Volodarskogo	Liteiny
Vosstaniya	Znamenskaya
Zamyatin	Leonov